IRENE E. HARVEY is Assistant Professor
of Philosophy at Pennsylvania State University and author of several articles on the
thought of Derrida, Nietzsche, and Hegel.

DERRIDA AND THE ECONOMY OF
DIFFÉRANCE

*Studies in Phenomenology and
Existential Philosophy*

DERRIDA AND THE ECONOMY
OF *DIFFÉRANCE*

IRENE E. HARVEY

INDIANA UNIVERSITY PRESS • BLOOMINGTON

Library of Congress Cataloging in Publication Data

Harvey, Irene E., 1953–
Derrida and the economy of différance.

(Studies in phenomenology and existential
philosophy)
Bibliography: p.
Includes Index.
1. Derrida, Jacques.   I. Title.   II. Series.
B2430.D484H37 1985   194   84-48249
ISBN 0-253-31685-5

For the genius of Jacques Derrida—
In admiration, respect and the
deepest gratitude.

Merci.

CONTENTS

THREE OPEN LETTERS

In place of a preface I wish to address three open letters: one to the literary critics who have embraced the work of Derrida, a second to the philosophic community who for the most part have rejected his work *a priori,* and a third, no less important, to Derrida himself as the inspiration for the text that follows. I hope in these letters to say more about what the text will not be about, will not presuppose, and will not aim to do than the reverse. I feel that textuality is a *response* and calls forth, or requests, a response—indeed many, varied, and conflicting responses. With this in mind, I invite response, not only from literary critics and philosophers, but perhaps most directly from them. Finally, I wish to propose the text that follows as a response to the current readings, treatments, and what we consider to be (for the most part) rather violent misunderstandings and misinterpretations of the *philosophic* significance of the work of Jacques Derrida.

Open Letter to Literary Critics

There is today a revolution occurring in literary criticism, particularly in the United States. One can no longer simply interpret texts more appropriately or less, adequately or not, nor simply address the tradition of criticism and the canonization, both of texts and interpretations, without *reflexively* considering methodology. This, as you well know, has generated the domain of inquiry, research, teaching, and most evidently more writing which is presently called *Literary Theory.* Although widely considered the most controversial new development in literary criticism, literary theory is recognized by all as something to be taken seriously and no longer possible to avoid. As you are also well aware, this move towards the reflexivity of criticism entails a variety of methods, among them the psychoanalytic, political, hermeneutic, and archaeological, and of course, the most controversial and perhaps the most powerful: *deconstruction.* Although originally developed by Derrida as a strategy of textual analysis, the adoption and interpretation of deconstruction in the United States have never been and perhaps never will be canonized. In short, there is no deconstructionist orthodoxy at present. Instead, we have of course, the "Yale School," more familiarly known by the names of its adherents: De Man, Hartman, Bloom and Miller. We also have left- and right-wing offshoots which are scattered across the United States and usually hold token positions as "the theorist" in most English departments.

Theory and, more particularly, the adopted "deconstructionist" type is considered by those against it to be destructive of proper criticism, destructive of meaning itself, and ultimately destructive of the practice of criticism. Traditional criticism, it is argued, will no longer be needed if deconstruction holds sway. The undermining of a discipline is precisely what they see to be at stake here. Those "for" deconstruction, on the other hand, see a powerful tool for the "critical" examination of the presuppositions of that discipline and a bringing to light of its "hidden agenda"; that is the revelation of its structures of analysis, the structures of textuality, and the preconditions of possibilities of interpretation as unbeknownst, most amazingly, to those who practice the business of criticism.

Our purpose in laying out this ground, indeed the battleground, that most of you are already so familiar with in your daily practices of criticism and life in English or Comparative Literature Departments, is to claim that the "Derrida" and indeed the "deconstruction" that you take to be all too familiar are not sufficient to provide a grasp of what it seems to me Derrida, the philosopher, is claiming, doing, and proposing. My aim, therefore, is to suggest a Derrida and a deconstruction that rely on his textual practice and his own claims concerning the "theory" behind it in a more rigorously *philosophic* way than hitherto. This is not an attempt to claim a privileged reading, nor to set up an orthodoxy (always the dangers), but rather to illuminate aspects of Derrida's work which I feel have for the most part been neglected. Of course, if one's "foreconceptions" according to the current interpretations of Derrida are fixed, the following text and its corrective (supplementary) effort will be of no import. However, I do insist that justice has not yet been done to the seriousness of Derrida's project, despite his popularity at Yale and elsewhere, despite his widespread influence—both positive and negative—and despite the controversy that is now raging over "the significance of deconstruction."

Open Letter to the Philosophic Community

The contemporary philosophic community, if one can appropriately use the term "community" for such a heterogeneous group, has for the most part, until recently and outside of France, ignored or openly rejected *in toto* the work of Derrida. The reasons for this outright rejection, prior to debate, and prior to his being read thoroughly, have never been clear to me except for the fact that evidently there has been a sense of "illegitimacy" attributed to Derrida with respect to his possible membership in this same community. This "sense of illegitimacy" and the general unwillingness to take his work seriously have been founded I believe more on his stylistic manner of exposition than the actual content of his work. In addition, the rapidity with which "deconstruction" has been embraced by the literary critical community— either as ally or foe—has certainly been a deterrent, or perhaps an excuse, for the philosophic community to avoid having to deal with Derrida.

This situation is, however, in the process of change, and a re-evaluation of the possibility that Derrida might indeed be a philosopher, and even perhaps the most significant of our time, is under way. This re-evaluation is most prominent within the philosophic circles involved in or having a legacy from phenomenology, and of those, specifically the philosophers concerned with Husserl and Heidegger. In short, Derrida is beginning to be recognized as having not only a "deconstructive strategy of textual interpretation" to offer, but also perhaps a contribution to be made concerning the relation of textuality to philosophy as a whole, as a tradition, and as a discourse. This "turn" in the reading of Derrida is at the moment only in its infancy, but nonetheless there is a growing awareness that we may yet have to deal with this Derrida, and worse, with the tradition he does represent.

This tradition, in which I aim here to situate Derrida's contribution to the philosophic enterprise, is that of Continental philosophy: from Kant, Hegel, and Nietzsche, through Husserl, Heidegger, and Levinas. Despite the tendency of some analytic philosophers to reject this as a philosophic tradition, there is a thorough response by Derrida to these analysts as represented—perhaps too narrowly, but nonetheless—by Searle and Austin.

My attempt here to respond to the "philosophic community in general" is an attempt to strengthen the philosophical legitimacy of Derrida's work, and thus to locate his problematics, assumptions, and the structure of his work within a tradition that we take to be familiar. Within this effort, I seek to expose the "conservative side" of Derrida's contribution; the lawbound, systematic, and rigorous (in every philosophic sense of that term) aspects which he himself relies on and openly claims to endorse.

I, of course, cannot claim and do not claim to have the essence of Derrida's work laid out here, or that this might ever be possible. Neither do I claim to judge his contribution to the history of philosophy once and for all—as if anyone could ever do that. But I do claim to have uncovered a new version, and a serious one, of the work that Derrida has done as philosophy, within philosophy, and as a response and perhaps a challenge to philosophy as a tradition, as a whole. I insist that his work is epoch-making and that he has gone "beyond Heidegger" in the sense of having achieved a more complete, more extended, more articulate elaboration of something for the most part left unthematized yet within the work of Heidegger. This, I feel, is the structure out of which a tradition grows.

Open Letter to Derrida: An Apology

As we both know, the processes of representation, commentary, and worst of all interpretation invoke an unavoidable violence which can never fully be taken into account or guarded against. This is no less true of the text that follows despite my attempts to "do justice" and be at least adequate to the task of re-articulating your work, which is in turn an articulation of certain aspects of it for the first time. Further, as we both realize, despite my having worked with you for three years in Paris, asking questions of clarification, attempting to realize textual play and ambiguities, and even despite your having read this text as it developed, there are no guarantees to claims of accuracy, appropriateness, or truth which can on those grounds be warranted.

The limits of the project have always been painfully clear to me, and my awareness of these limits has only increased as the text grew. Now that it is done, I wish only to recognize here publicly, in print, how indebted to you I am even in order to make the above apology and disclaimer of the work. Your influence on my thinking will doubtless continue for many years, but I do wish to state here, publicly again, that the debtor/indebted relation must also change. Violation, or perhaps betrayal, is the necessary structure; one which can only be deferred but not avoided *ad infinitum*. In the final prefacing phrase here I wish to acknowledge the germ of that "next step"—which is no doubt "present" within this project—of developing a philosophy of textuality. It is a project which I realize you have long since rejected, but which I feel is not only possible but necessary.

ACKNOWLEDGMENTS

I wish to acknowledge my profound indebtedness to two major thinkers of our time with whom I have worked and whose works have formed a foundation from which this text grew. It is significant to note that neither of these thinkers' names appear in the text that follows despite my reliance on them and their work. One could say that they have not herein been recognized or rather that they have not been objectified or thematized as such. It is always on this second, more profound, level that intertextuality plays its constitutive role, it seems to me. It is simply the case that their works were not the object of this text to analyse, but the reasons are more significant than this. The absence of objectification of one's ground, source, and resource is the crucial role that not only the lifeworld but also the horizons of possibility play in the framing or focusing of anything as an object, as Husserl and Heidegger have adequately shown. Nevertheless, my indebtedness to these two theorists involves more than the structure of figure/ground or contrast phenomena—as the place from which I come and from which I now distinguish myself. The latter is no doubt true but inadequate in its formulation of these relations. Any thematization of this supportive, contextual, fundamental role that these two people have played in my life and especially in my work in the past five years would necessarily portray this inadequacy.

With respect, friendship and sincerity I thank both, Paul Ricoeur and John O'Neill, for having played such constitutive roles in the development of my thinking, my work, and of course, this text.

DERRIDA AND THE ECONOMY OF
DIFFÉRANCE

INTRODUCTION
DERRIDA'S KANTIAN AFFILIATION
OR
PROLEGOMENA TO THE
DECONSTRUCTION
OF METAPHYSICS AND THE
RECOGNITION
OF DIFFÉRANCE

> The world is tired of metaphysical asser-
> tions; it wants to know the *possibility* of this
> science, the *sources* from which certainty
> therein can be derived, and certain criteria
> by which it may distinguish the dialectical il-
> lusion of pure reason from truth. To this the
> critic seems to possess a key, otherwise he
> would never have spoken out in such a high
> tone [my emphasis].[1]

> Immanuel Kant (1783)

In some respects this platform and program for Kant's project concerning "any future metaphysics" could well be seen as the basis for Derrida's work to date. There is no doubt that deconstruction is concerned
to show the "conditions of the possibility of metaphysics," its
"sources," its legitimate range of application, and thus the *limits* of
philosophy as such. Yet the need to "distinguish the dialectical illusion
from truth," to see the "critic as being in possession of a key," and the
need for "certain criteria," as the *telos* of the project are certainly not
compatible with Derrida's aims. Indeed for the latter, "truth," in the

I

philosophic tradition of the West, has always been determined by the *Logos* which is, as Hegel has adequately shown, "the dialectic of pure reason itself." The notion of anyone, least of all perhaps "the critic," as being in possession of a *key*—indeed the demand for such a center at all—is certainly also placed in question by Derrida. And finally, the *telos* of "certain criteria" have always been determined by Reason as such, according to Derrida, and thus is itself in need of deconstruction.

Nevertheless, the Kantian affiliations of Derrida's position(s) cannot be rejected so easily. Kant's notion of critique as his strategy for revealing the conditions of the possibility, the origins, and hence the limits of metaphysics is certainly, if not the model, a predecessor for Derrida's notion of deconstruction. The problems initiated by the "unbounded use of our Reason" are also a mutual concern for these two thinkers. The transformation of the given into a sign for the "not given" but presupposed is certainly a common strategy as well. Yet, despite the overlap of the notion that "from the moment that there is meaning we have nothing but *signs*"[2] for Derrida, and "representations" or "appearances" for Kant, we cannot conclude that this in fact means the same thing. To the contrary, while for Kant the thing in itself can "never be known"[3] yet must be assumed *a priori;* for Derrida, the thing in itself always escapes,[4] and indeed the fact that we have nothing but re-presentations does not require an originary presentation. The latter is a *result* of the former, not its origin. More precisely, the notion of "origin" itself must be realized as a result, and the non-origin of "origin" brought to light. For Kant, of course this makes no sense; for all that is meaningful requires an intuition, on the one hand, and, on the other, its synthesis with one of the pure concepts of the Understanding. For Derrida, the situation is quite the reverse, as he has shown in his analysis of Husserl. The possibility of the *lack* of intuition of the object is precisely the condition of the possibility of meaning itself. It is the absence of the object and *a fortiori* of the subject ("my death") which is the condition of the possibility of intelligibility or meaningfulness. At this juncture Kant and Derrida could not be further apart. Yet, Kant's ultimate question is: "How is nature itself possible?"[5] And certainly so is Derrida's, as his analyses of Husserl, Rousseau, Heidegger, and Hegel (among others) clearly indicate.

The labyrinth affiliation here must therefore be explicated not as "Derrida's legacy"—acknowledged or unacknowledged—from Kant, but rather as prolegomena to the deconstruction of metaphysics and to the recognition of *différance*. Instead of attempting to subsume Derrida's notion of deconstruction under that of critique, and *a fortiori* his notion of metaphysics and its origin under Kant's, we shall attempt here, by way of an introduction to *Derrida and the Economy of Différance,* to radically distinguish Derrida's project from Kant's. The apparent affiliation will be shown to be nothing less than a confusion based on certain metaphysical assumptions which themselves, Derrida will claim, are in need of deconstruction. However, the usefulness of such a comparison, we hope, will be to take the reader quite simply from the "known to the unknown," explicating the distinctions and differences so as to prevent the possible usurpation of the radicality of Derrida's unique position within the conservatism of the Kantian projection or *Weltanschauung.* It might be more appropriate to begin with such a differential analysis of Derrida and Heidegger or Derrida and Hegel, but these issues will be treated in the context of "the re-cognition of *différance*" as such much later in our project and necessarily at a more complex level than the nature of an introduction will allow.

I. Critique and Deconstruction

It is because it extends to solid structures, to "material" institutions, and not only to discourses or meaningful representations that *deconstruction* is always distinguishable from an analysis or a *critique* [my emphasis].[6]

Derrida

By *criticism,* however, a standard is given to our judgement whereby knowledge may be with certainty distinguished from pseudo-science and firmly founded, being brought into full operation in *metaphysics*—a mode of thought extending by degrees its beneficial influence over every other use of reason, at once infusing into it the true philosophic spirit [my emphasis].[7]

Kant

Not only can deconstruction, for Derrida, be distinguished from critique, for Kant, according to the differences in the range of its effects, but it can also be isolated from Kant's project according to more profound differential directions and projects for their respective aims. We shall thus begin with Kant's explication of his notion of critique as method in order then to distinguish in context the radically differing concerns embedded in what only seems to be a common interest, namely, the foundations and origins of metaphysics itself or, in short, its conditions of possibility.

Kant outlines the specific methodology of critique in the following way:

> And thus I conclude the analytic solution of the main question which I had proposed: "How is metaphysics in general possible?" by ascending from the data of actual use, as shown in its consequences, to the grounds of its possibility.[8]

"Critique" as method is thus concerned with a certain deduction from the "actual" (in this case the fact of the existence of pure mathematics and pure physics which depend upon and use "synthetic judgments *a priori*") to that which is necessarily *presupposed* therein and which makes the "actual" possible. The problem for Kant is that although the "actual" can be experienced (as a synthesis of intuition and pure concepts of the Understanding) the conditions of its possibility can never be or become an experience.

Deconstruction is also concerned with the conditions of the possibility of that which is taken to be *actual* and, in particular, with that which is taken to be *given* as self-sufficient. As with Kant, Derrida claims that the "actual" or "given" is a *result* or a product of that which, although not given as such, is signaled or represented therein. The parallel cannot be pursued further, however, since at this point Kant and Derrida begin to speak of radically different issues. As Kant pursues the conditions of the possibility of the given and, in turn, of metaphysics, he interposes *Nature* between the two in the following manner. The fact that "pure synthetic judgments *a priori*" are not only possible but required for metaphysics leads Kant to claim that: (i) the actuality of pure mathematics and pure physics indicates that we can and do make pure synthetic cognitions *a priori;* and (ii) the fact that we make these judgments reliably, therein constituting knowledge which is objectively valid, indicates a certain *closed system* of categories "which can be articulated fully" and which are inherent in the nature of the Understanding itself. 'Nature' is thus for Kant a result of our Understanding guided by the Ideas of Reason, which gives it its laws. Indeed, the pure concepts in this connection are shown by critique to be the law of the laws. Nature, for Derrida, is also a result; but it is hardly constituted by such inherent structures of the human mind or of human experience. In order to see the source of this divergence, let us return to the methodology which allows Kant to make such discoveries.

The aim of critique, Kant tells us, is to "*limit the pretensions* of Pure Reason" and to "guard its bounds with respect to its empirical use."[9] In addition, therefore, he is concerned with just "how far Reason is to be trusted, and why only so far and no further." In order to do this he claims a "final determination, on principles" is required. The results of such a determination, should it be possible (which Kant's First Critique has aimed to prove), would be the firm, secure, and legitimate grounds of metaphysics itself. Presupposed in this approach, however, is a certain notion of *origin* which becomes simultaneously (within metaphysics, for Derrida) the *telos* and *limit* of the *proper* use of metaphysics, for Kant. Indeed, it is the *concept* of metaphysics that Kant seems to be after (if we might rely on Hegel here for a moment). As Kant himself admits, the notion of the concept is a delimitation of the proper with respect to the thing in question. Indeed, it is the "proper" of metaphysics which critique is aiming to demarcate. In so doing Kant would make of metaphysics a "legitimate science." As he says:

> . . . to organize any knowledge as science, it will be necessary first to determine accurately those peculiar features which *no other science* has in common with it, constituting its peculiarity; otherwise the boundaries of all sciences become confused [my emphasis].[10]

But prior to the possibility of establishing metaphysics as science, Kant is concerned to show that his method of critique itself is already and necessarily a science too. The conditions for this possibility entail a certain *completeness*—indeed, a *closure* which we should recall is one of the "unavoidable" Ideas of Pure Reason—and *perfection*.[11] This completeness is thus in a certain way "necessarily assumed" by Kant according to his own principles, but this is not our concern for the moment.

In the process of critique, therefore, Kant asks how various given, actually existing "things" are possible. In asking such a question, in such a manner, he is concerned as he says with the "roots and peculiarity" of the thing in question. For metaphysics, in particular, he is concerned with the "occupation of Reason merely with itself."[12] We shall address this determination of metaphysics in comparison with Derrida's in our upcoming section, but for the moment we should return to Derrida's notion of deconstruction, as it might appear to overlap or intertwine with Kant's notion of critique as explicated above.

Despite appearances, the aims of deconstruction could not be further ultimately from those of critique. Rather than aiming towards the "proper role of metaphysics" and reason (interchangeable terms, for Derrida) deconstruction is concerned with the presupposition of *'propriety'* itself; how this notion is in fact possible. In addition, rather than aiming to constitute metaphysics as science, deconstruction is concerned with the scientificity of science itself as determined (by Kant also) by the presupposed metaphysical opposition of interior/exterior, as if radically dissociable. Deconstruction, in turn, is concerned with the conditions of the possibility of objectivity itself as produced by Reason but not as necessarily universally valid. It is this notion of universality itself, *a fortiori* as determined by a constituting consciousness or 'I think' as the centre and ultimate source for all knowing, that deconstruction is concerned to analyze. Deconstruction, albeit therefore in search of the conditions of the possibility, the circumscription of limits, the "origins" and sources of metaphysics and certain so-called *a priori* synthetic judgments, goes at least one step further than Kant in the following respect. That upon which Kant's analysis or critique *rests* (i.e., a certain notion of the proper, of the object, of scientificity, of completeness, totality, and closure, as the grounds of all grounds) forms precisely the *focus* for the work of deconstruction itself. Nevertheless, deconstruction is not aiming to deconstruct Kant only but rather the "entire tradition of metaphysics" (synonymous with philosophy, according to Derrida).

We might now understand Derrida's own claims for the recognition of the difference between deconstruction and critique in that the "material institutions" which deconstruction reaches and is concerned to analyze not only include universities and institutes of learning in general, but also the socio-historical and political conditions (under the name of philosophy essentially) upon which these institutions stand. One might therefore legitimately, at least for the moment, consider deconstruction as a critique of critique, therein not undermining critique as Kant has elaborated this process, but rather showing precisely *its* conditions of possibility which, as Kant would argue, lie necessarily *outside* that system.

4. Metaphysics—History, Nature and Desire

As we have shown, the focus of concern for both Kant's critique and Derrida's deconstruction is the ground, origin, or conditions of possi-

bility of that which they both name: metaphysics. The fact that they
mean radically different things by this same name does not however
eradicate the necessity of an examination of this difference, on the one
hand, and, as we shall see, certain profound aspects of similarity. With
this double explication in mind we shall approach the issue of metaphysics as such, for both thinkers, from three standpoints: (i) its history, or
historical foundations and manifestations; (ii) its nature, or fundamental, indeed essential characteristics; and (iii) the "desire" in the heart of
metaphysics, which in itself is not metaphysical. As in our preceding
analysis we shall elaborate Kant's position on these matters and inter-
pose Derrida's with specific reference to the former. We shall not therefore fully elaborate Derrida's position as such (as if that were a
possibility anyway), since we will focus exclusively on his position
with respect to metaphysics as such in Section II.

(a) History

Kant's concern with the history of metaphysics is a lament for the
evident multiplicity and variance over time of this "would-be" science.
The differences from one age to another in that which is "called"
metaphysics is testament, for him, that it has not yet been rigorously
founded. Hence the historical difference is invoked as evidence of the
need for his answer to the problem: critique itself. As he says, "critique
is to metaphysics as chemistry is to alchemy, or astronomy to astrol-
ogy."[13] This set of analogies is indicative, for Kant, of a certain legitimacy and profundity of his—the first—scientific ground for the
essentially required *science of metaphysics.* With this in mind, he
claims that

> . . . in all ages one metaphysics has contradicted another, either in its
> assertions or their proofs, and thus has itself destroyed its own claim to
> lasting assent.[14]

There is thus for Kant no underlying unity to this historical multiplicity.
Rather, we have a situation of confusion and illusion based on "the
unbounded use of our reason." The reasons for this will be shown in
detail shortly, and they concern the Desire which leads us to metaphysics to begin with, but first we should compare this claim for the historical diversity of metaphysics to Derrida's claim that a certain essential
unity persists beneath the evident and only apparent differences. Paradoxically, at this juncture we find Derrida to be more of a metaphysician (according to his own definition) than a deconstructor. We should

recall, however, that "borrowing the tools of metaphysics" is a prerequisite for the deconstructive activity itself.

Initially, Derrida asks the question of whether one can "legitimately" unite all differences in the history of metaphysics into one essential concept of the same:

> Can one consider philosophy as such (metaphysics as such, or onto-theology) without being forced to submit, with this pretension to unity and oneness, to an impregnable and imperial totality of an order? If there are margins is there still a philosophy as such?

His answer: "No answer. Perhaps no question either, in the final analysis."[15] We should notice several important aspects of this framing of the issue for Derrida. First, he poses the issue of the unity of metaphysics as a question; indeed, an open question. Since the form of questions determines possible responses, it must be surprising to find "no answer" as his answer and, in turn, no question either. The reason for this is that by using what Derrida will call metaphysics (based primarily on Plato) against itself in this way, the form of the question, although formally metaphysical, produces a situation where the response can no longer be restricted or constrained by that same form. In short, the impossibility of the answer shatters the form of the question, which is also the essence of metaphysics. Secondly, in the bracketed space of the question Derrida inserts "metaphysics as such" or "onto-theology" as if equivalent or exchangeable terms with 'philosophy as such' which is the announced, explicit subject or issue for the question. The slide therefore initiates a further unity, unaddressed as such but assumed by Derrida, which evidently entails philosophy, metaphysics, and onto-theology. Thus, despite the explicit open-endedness of the formation of the issue, Derrida in fact closes the question solidly with this unthematized but assumed concept of philosophy as such.

This closing of the question is no accident, since he goes on to claim explicitly not only that the history of metaphysics is Reason's "history of the Concept" and thus lacking all fundamental historicity as such in the sense of radically discontinuous differences, but also that the center of metaphysics (philosophy or onto-theology) can be located and articulated as such in the following respect:

> The history of (the only) metaphysics which has *in spite of all differences,* not only from Plato to Hegel (even including Leibniz) but also beyond these apparent limits, from the Pre-Socratics to Heidegger, al-

ways assigned the *origin of truth* in general to the *Logos* [my emphasis].[16]

Thus, in the one name metaphysics we have truth, *Logos*, Reason, onto-theology, and indeed philosophy as such. We also have all "modes of analysis, interpretation, and understanding in the Western world" and all languages of the West.[17] We shall shortly address the conditions of the possibility of this extensive *range* that Derrida assigns to metaphysics, but first let us return to Kant and his lament over the irreducibility of these historical differences and their significance concerning the pseudo-scientific state of all pre-critical metaphysics.

(b) Nature

. . . for *reason is ever present,* while laws of nature must usually be discovered with labour. So *metaphysics* floated to the surface, like foam, which dissolved the moment it was scooped off. But immediately there appeared a new supply on the surface. . . [my emphasis].[18]

For Kant, the *nature* of reason paradoxically produces in itself the continual resurgence, although in a continually inadequate form, of metaphysics. In order to understand this we need only recall that the realm of 'nature' for Kant is restricted to the pure concepts of the Understanding which in themselves "give the laws to nature"; and which, indeed, thereby constitute nature itself as law-bound. Hence, Reason is itself necessarily exempt from the "call of nature," and it is precisely this which has led to the problems in founding a scientific and thereby limited notion of metaphysics as such. We shall not pursue this double use of 'nature' in Kant but wish only to point out that, for him there is an "underlying harmony between Reason and the Understanding," although precisely what or what this is based on cannot be known. For Derrida, the notion of Nature is equivalent to metaphysics, Reason, and the *Logos*—in short, the Concept itself. We should bear in mind, therefore, that despite the apparently similar terminology of Kant and Derrida, each of these overlapping terms has a radically different meaning for them in their respective systems of thought.

The precise realm and peculiarity of metaphysics—that "favourite child of Reason"—for Kant can be defined as "that domain which necessarily *exceeds the bounds* of experience." Further, "metaphysics is *properly* concerned with synthetical propositions *a priori,* and these alone constitute its *end.*"[19] In addition, he says, "its very *concept* implies that they cannot be empirical. Its principle . . . must never be derived from experience."[20] Thus experience as it is—and especially its very *possibility* of being just as it is and not otherwise—is the field which opens out onto what Kant calls metaphysics. Not being an experience itself, metaphysics is nevertheless the necessary condition of the possibility of all experience and *a fortiori* of all *meaning*.

Kant's notion of 'experience' is worth recalling at this juncture since it too differs radically from that of Derrida and will aid us in disentangling the two thinkers. 'Experience', for Kant, involves a synthesis of sensible intuitions and pure concepts of the Understanding and in this respect can never entail pure unmediated intuition. Should we have such an unmediated 'experience', it can never become an object of knowledge (the truth of experience for Kant—its universality or objective validity for all), but rather must remain in the realm of illusion, fiction, and thus 'subjective confusion'. In addition, should we consider only the pure concepts of the Understanding apart from any intuition to 'fill' them, this could *never* be a *meaningful* object. Meaning is itself absolutely contingent upon intuition as it inhabits one of the pure concepts.

Comparing these notions with those of Derrida we have a world of difference opened up. Meaning and indeed its condition of possibility for Derrida, as for Husserl, is the very *absence* of intuition itself. The fact that both subject and object *can* be absent from a 'sign' is precisely the necessary prerequisite which constitutes the sign's meaningfulness for any subject and any object. Concerning the notion of *experience* as the *necessary result* of *metaphysics,* once again we find Derrida in disaccord. First, experience for Derrida is always mediated by the sign and is in turn itself a sign. One might argue that for Kant we have nothing but representations and appearances, and never the presentation of the thing itself. However, for Derrida, this indicates not that there must be a hidden origin from which experience is a result and a mere sign, but rather that "origin" is itself a sign and a result. There is no originary presence for Derrida—either in conceptuality or in experience as such. Contrary to Husserl, the moment of the "living presence," the moment of evidence, the foundation of all truth and objective knowledge is a result of a "more fundamental" absence— indeed the movement of *différance* itself as we shall see shortly.

For Kant, metaphysics extends beyond all possible experience, and is therein freed from a certain responsibility to truth. Kant's deduction of this conclusion concerning the necessary potential of fiction of metaphysics includes the following:

> *Metaphysics* has not only to do with concepts of Nature, which always find their application in experience, but also with pure rational concepts, which never can be given in any possible experience whatever. Consequently, it deals with concepts whose objective reality . . . and with assertions whose *truth or falsity* cannot be discovered or confirmed by experience [my emphasis].[21]

We see Husserl's reliance on Kant here by a certain inversion showing thereby their mutual concern with the "living present" moments of experience as the condition for the truth (and falsity) of judgments concerning the latter. Hegel, too, relies on this. But for Derrida metaphysics, on the one hand, *is* the realm of Reason, *Logos,* and truth simply, and yet on the other, entails an (albeit effaced) realm of metaphor and myth which is intrinsic to it. It is the effacement of this "non-metaphysical" ground which for Derrida constitutes metaphysics itself. Kant also partakes of this effacement as we shall see in his definition of this 'independance' of Reason and *a fortiori* "the child of metaphysics." But again a difference will emerge. The independence for Kant consists not only of the necessary transcendence of metaphysics from the realm of experience, but also of a certain play of Reason with itself. (We shall see shortly that this is the necessary *supplement* of Nature, for Derrida.) This play, although a finite, fixed, and complete structure, is essentially boundless, Kant claims. We will always have things to discover and can discover infinitely within the things which we have. The essential claim here for the essence of metaphysics itself entails the nature of Reason therefore, and this entails the following:

> . . . here is an advantage upon which, of all possible sciences, *metaphysics* alone can with certainty reckon: that it can be brought to such completion and fixity as to be in need of no further change or be subject to any augmentation by new discoveries; because here *reason has the sources of its knowledge in itself,* not in objects and their observation, by which its stock of knowledge could be further increased [my emphasis].[22]

This is what Derrida will call the "*logos* believing itself to be its own father." Not only is the sign, or writing in general, effaced in this structure of Kant's, but also the essential factuality which allows for such a deduction to occur. It is to *these* effacements therefore that Derrida will turn his attention rather than, as he might say, stopping short within the "closed circle" of Reason secure in itself, with itself, excluding and thereby controlling its other and indeed all otherness—empirical, conscious, unconscious, fictive, occult and essentially non-reasonable and non-metaphysical. Any essential relation between these is however denied and totally unaddressed in fact by Kant—in short, excluded. It is the latter, however, which is the condition of the possibility of that which in the end and from the beginning Kant will call Pure Reason, which ultimately for Derrida is synonymous with metaphysics. Before approaching further the question of "sources," "origins," or "non-origins" of metaphysics, let us take a brief detour through the realm of desire as the heart of metaphysics for *both* Derrida and Kant.

(c) Desire

For Kant metaphysics is a result of a "*natural* predisposition of our reason" and indeed it is "placed in us by nature itself."[23] In this respect, therefore, Kant returns to the necessity and unavoidability—indeed one might call it ontological, aspect of the condition of the possibility—of this metaphysical predisposition. As he says,

> . . . metaphysics in its fundamental features . . . is placed in us *by nature itself* and cannot be considered the production of arbitrary choice or a casual enlargement in the progress of experience from which it is quite disparate [my emphasis].[24]

Thus nature (or the product of the pure concepts of the Understanding) gives way to that which transcends itself. Yet in Kant's thought this transcendence from nature by nature is itself authorized by that same nature. We should recall that one of Kant's fundamental questions which orients his "critique" is the search for "how nature is possible." It now seems that nature engenders: (i) itself, purely and simply; yet also (ii) that which necessarily (naturally that is) transcends itself.

For Derrida, we do not have this self-transcendence, since the basis of 'nature' returns us to the 'essentiality' (and essential non-naturality) of the supplement as that "dangerous addition" to that which admits of no lack and no need of the supplement. Nature, for Derrida, is constituted as the effacement of the necessity of the supplement. The supplement is of course the level of representation, the sign, mimesis, culture, history, time, and space. Returning to Kant, we find that metaphysics as a natural product of nature itself also transcends the level of space and time but for different reasons. Space and time for Kant are pure intuitions of sensibility and thus form part of the conditions of the possibility of experience. Since metaphysics necessarily transcends experience, it in turn has no need of the space/time coordinates which inhabit sensibility and thus experience itself. We shall see that for Derrida metaphysics does not in fact and can never radically exceed the spacio-temporalization characteristic of the world, but for now let us return to the "desire of metaphysics" and its *assumed* naturality.

For Kant, there is a certain distance from 'presence', the origin, the ground which cannot be eradicated by any attempts of metaphysics or reason. Nevertheless, the *desire* to reach this level—that of things themselves—is implanted in our reason. Thus we have an impossible demand at the heart of Kant's system: a double bind in the form of the desire for that which can never be attained. As he says:

> In the knowledge of them (things in themselves) alone can reason hope to *satisfy its desire* for completeness proceeding from the conditioned to the unconditioned [my emphasis].[25]

For Derrida, as well, metaphysics is characterized by a necessarily thwarted desire which is in content as well as form not unlike Kant's notion. Derrida insists that the "desire for a transcendental signified"— pure meaning, pure signification without the material support of the sign or the empirical, total undivided, unabashed, transparent, nude, present, and identical to itself truth—inhabits metaphysics. Such is the desire at least, he says. But such is also the impossible demand which sets up the condition of the possibility of metaphysics itself and *a fortiori* the infinity of its lifespan. In short, the immortality of metaphysics, for Derrida, is its very impossibility. One might therefore call it an Idea in the Kantian sense. And indeed Kant installs the future of metaphysics in the same tragic yet asymptotic design:

> That the *human mind* will ever give up metaphysical researches is as little to be expected as that we, to avoid inhaling impure air, should prefer to give up breathing altogether. There will, therefore, *always* be a metaphysics in the world; nay, everyone, especially every reflective *man,* will have it, and for want of a recognized standard will shape it for himself after his own pattern [my emphasis].[26]

And with this we return to the initial historical demarcation of the "problem of metaphysics" for Kant—its multiplicity and therefore unsure, unscientific foundations. The limits of his own critique seem to be emerging here.

Returning to Derrida, whose intention with deconstruction was the "deconstruction of metaphysics," we find a parallel result./Far from destroying metaphysics or undoing its conditions of possibility, deconstruction instead is condemned to a certain participant-observational role in the following sense. It participates certainly in the history of metaphysics as the history of philosophy, just as Kant's critique has done despite the former's attempt to step outside and consider the "unacknowledged foundations of the same." Yet it remains an observer in the sense that, although illustrating the limits and conditions of the possibility of metaphysics—as a primarily Western post-Platonic phenomena—it does not prohibit in the slightest the continuation and indeed paradoxical affirmation of that same history. /

C. The Origins of Metaphysics

With the discovery of the Pure concepts of the Understanding, the Ideas of Pure Reason, and their constitutive and regulative roles respectively in the constitution of objectively valid knowledge, Kant concludes:

> And thus we have at last *something definite* upon which to depend in all metaphysical enterprises [my emphasis].[27]

And with the discovery of the movement of *différance* as the constitutive underpinning which in turn unravels and delegitimizes the metaphysics of presence, Derrida concludes:

> . . . the metaphysics of the logos, of presence and of consciousness must reflect upon *writing* as *its death* and *its resource*.[28]

Thus, despite the apparently similar intentions of 'critique' for Kant and of 'deconstruction' for Derrida, we have certainly not, in the search for the conditions of the possibility of metaphysics, arrived at the same end point. Indeed it will be shown that precisely where Kant's investigation ends, Derrida's begins. It is the finitude and closure of the system of the pure concepts and the autonomy and exclusivity of Reason as self-originating to which Derrida objects and indeed aims to deconstruct from the beginning. We shall therefore approach Kant's conclusions with respect to: (i) the autonomy of Reason and (ii) the limits of knowledge *a priori*, in order to reveal, if not the starting point or *'fil conducteur'* for Derrida's project as a whole, at least that which he includes within the "metaphysics of presence" which he takes to task. Once again we shall limit our analysis here more to Kant's proclamations than to Derrida's, since the latter is the subject of the main body of the present work. True to the method of prolegomena, however, the results of our analysis that follows will be introduced here in an analytic rather than deductive manner. Thus rather than proving Derrida's position, or deducing it logically, we shall simply state in this the context of his Kantian affiliation his claims as such concerning the "origins of metaphysics."

(a) The Autonomy of Reason

Kant insists that in order to have a *reliable* basis for metaphysics, a certain *completeness* is required concerning the principles for the use of the Understanding. These principles are the Ideas of Pure Reason whose function is to *guide* our use of the concepts but not to thereby constitute knowledge or experience. The principles regulate this very process; i.e., govern it, rule over it. The Ideas therefore set the *bounds* of legitimacy for "all possible experience." The *closure* which allows for this "total enumeration" of principles is on the one hand, the self-sufficiency ascribed to Reason; yet, on the other, this can never in fact be maintained absolutely. Indeed, although Kant does not explicitly state as much, the conditions of the possibility of the legitimate use of Reason are essentially themselves what one might call "Ideas in the Kantian sense." That is, closure as such is never possible because of the peculiar relation Reason bears to the Understanding. Indeed, it is the "natural tendency" of Reason to *"seduce"* the latter which must be guarded against, Kant tells us. Paradoxically, he says further that metaphysics is the "favourite child of Reason" and that metaphysics requires a certain connection of the Ideas of Pure Reason with the Pure Concepts of the Understanding. It is in this connection that Kant aims to demarcate the *proper* concepts of the Understanding from those that would masquerade as such. Kant explains the *seduction* of the Understanding by Reason in the following way:

> These then are the *transcendental Ideas,* which in accordance with the true but hidden ends of the natural destiny of our Reason, aim not at

extravagant concepts, but at the unbounded extension of their empirical use, yet *seduce the understanding* by an *unavoidable illusion* to a transcendent use, which though deceitful, *cannot be restrained* within the bounds of experience by any resolution, but only by scientific instruction and with much difficulty [my emphasis].[29]

We should perhaps not overlook the system of sexual metaphors Kant not only invokes here but seems to rely on rather heavily, although we will at this juncture, since our purpose here is more limited. The point is that Reason not only can but does at times "lose its head" and overextend itself by virtue of its "own nature." This nature of Reason is, as the origin of metaphysics (at least its Father evidently for Kant), precisely our concern here. As a nature it has laws; indeed, it gives itself laws, Kant claims, and further: "the law is reason's own production."[30] It is precisely this which allows us to comprehend the same, Kant insists.

Derrida's position on these matters differs radically from Kant's. First, we should recall that for Derrida (although he does not thematize it as such, but rather seems to assume it) Reason and metaphysics and nature are equivalent or at least interchangeable, substitutable terms. Hence, for Kant to claim that Reason and the pure concepts of the Understanding are the origins of metaphysics would make no sense from a Derridean point of view. These three terms do not relate in a hierarchical fashion or in a genealogical one for Derrida. Rather, Reason has always been considered the essence of "nature," "truth," the "Concept," and certainly *a fortiori* metaphysics. But for Kant one could argue that Reason is the Father of metaphysics, as we have shown—figuratively and literally—if we can still rely on such a distinction.

For Kant there is a certain transparency possible within the realm of Reason itself:

> Since all illusion consists in holding the subjective ground of our judgments to be objective, a *self-knowledge* of pure reason in its transcendent (presumptuous) use is the sole *preservative* from the *aberrations* into which Reason falls when it mistakes its calling and transcendently refers to the object that which concerns only its own subject and its guidance in all immanent use [my emphasis].[31]

This *self-knowledge* paradoxically transcends the bounds of that which Kant will allow for "legitimately objective knowledge," by definition. However, this transgression is not our present concern. The notion of a

Reason that is on the one hand *closed,* in terms of its operating principles, yet on the other, given to *transgressing* its own legitimate bounds *by nature* (therein seducing nature, we should recall, under the name of the pure concepts of the Understanding which "give the laws to nature") leads us necessarily to a profound contradiction within the heart of Reason itself. Kant admits as much and calls this "the antinomy of pure Reason." The escape from this is of course the constitution of the *abyss* between two realms: that of things in themselves and that of appearances. The abyss itself is of course neither.

Derrida's objections might well be raised at this point. This notion of "Reason's self-knowledge" as though unmediated by the sign, by absence, or *a fortiori* by writing—empirical or otherwise—is the focus of his analysis itself of the "metaphysics of presence." In short, the notion of a pure transparency in the heart of Reason is precisely that which is in need of deconstruction. In addition, he is concerned with the *abyss* which Kant's system inevitably constitutes and thus *a posteriori* bridges—bridges which it builds again and again across it by way of analogy.[32] The relation between the 'things in themselves' and their 'appearances' we should recall for Derrida is based on an underlying presupposed unity of the notion of representation. The presentation$_1$ (appearance on the one hand for Kant) is thus unmasked as essentially a representation yet, on the other hand, the presentation$_2$ (in the sense of the thing in itself—the origin of appearances and hence the essentially original presentation) is a *result,* a derivative presentation based on the presentation of appearance, and hence can be realized as essentially representation. One could exchange the terms of this closed, all-too binary system endlessly with opposing results each time. Such are the antinomies of Reason, as Kant explained before. The point, for Derrida, is that what has been effaced in Kant's system and in the entire history of metaphysics is its very condition of possibility—the sign itself as essential. The role of writing as the constitution of Being in the most profound sense. We shall return to this. But first let us examine the "essentially unknowable" which Kant does install, paradoxically to be sure, in the heart of Reason itself.

b. The Unknowable Center

Although "Reason contains in itself the *source of Ideas*" (by which Kant means "the *necessary* concepts whose object cannot be given in experience"[33]), there remains nonetheless an essential abyss in the heart of Reason itself which even it can never know *a priori*. We shall also explore here the center of the pure Concepts of the Understanding, which Kant also confessed remains confined to the darkened abyss of the *unknowable*. His final word on the sensibility, the Understanding, and indeed Reason as such is the term *constitution* itself, as we shall see, and it is here that his deduction and analysis rest. His justification for such a terminus is simply that constitution of the human mind as such beyond which or more deeply into which one cannot reasonably pursue. We shall see that this is precisely the realm of Derrida's concern. But first, the abyss of reason as Kant describes it.

For Kant, the unreachable limits of our proper use of Reason include

> . . . a property of the thing in itself, a property whose *possibility* we *cannot comprehend*. I mean we cannot comprehend *how* the ought should determine (even if it never has actually determined) its activity and could become thus the *cause* of actions whose effect is an appearance in the sensible world [my emphasis].[34]

The reasons for this impossibility of comprehension are given explicitly by Kant, and we shall not repeat them here. Suffice it to say that this is the *nature* of Reason for him. It is the *law* therefore of the abyss within, that which allows for knowledge as such.

In the heart of the Understanding we find perhaps not the same thing but at least the same short-circuiting of the investigation of the grounds, origins, and conditions of possibility of knowledge and *a fortiori* metaphysics as such. As he says concerning the pure concepts of the Understanding, "although *what* they are and precisely *how many* there are can be exactly determined, *why* they are just these and not others and from whence they come cannot be known." Thus he says we have "special concepts *originally begotten* [another sexual metaphor!] in the Understanding which make possible the objective validity of the judgment of experience."[35] A certain *immaculate conception* therefore seems to have occurred at this point, as Derrida would say.[36] The original "conception" of the concepts themselves is thus announced by Kant, yet denied as a legitimate focus of investigation in our search for knowledge. One might well wonder at the origin of this taboo in the search for origins. For Derrida, on the contrary, the "non-origin of origin" is precisely his focus. It is the place where the said oppositions of metaphysics (such as essence/appearance; inside/outside) are revealed to have their "secret copulating relationship"[37] which in turn gives birth (as Kant admits) to that which we, within metaphysics, name concepts as such. Indeed, *pure* concepts. The non-pure origin of purity and impurity—the distinction itself as an abyss—is also one of Derrida's primary concerns.

Finally, returning to Kant's *"coitus interruptus"* program of investigation here, we find that the reason we have "pure concepts of the Understanding" and "sensible intuitions" as we do—indeed the reason we have nature as such as lawbound according to the pure concepts of the Understanding guided by the necessarily *a priori* Ideas of Reason—is simply this:

> (i) The answer is: by means of the *constitution (Beschaffenheit)* of our sensibility [my emphasis].

and

> (ii) The answer must be: It (the totality of rules that we call nature) is only possible by means of the *constitution (Beschaffenheit)* of our understanding, according to which all the above representations of the sensibility are *necessarily* referred to *a consciousness* and by the *particular way* in which we think, namely by rules . . . [my emphasis].[38]

Thus we arrive at the essential *constitution (Beschaffenheit)* which for Kant is a given—*a priori*. Hence he not only pursues it no further, he insists that there can be necessarily no answer to such a question as the origin of this "constitution." In this way the closure is sustained for his system and its security installed *a fortiori*. Yet, such a constitution of our "nature" is not entirely without its problems, as Kant is the first to point out. The "transgressions" Reason is given to can only be explained as "aberrations," "illusions," fictive flights of fantasy, the "pure beings of the Understanding" which necessarily "arise"—unfounded in experience—which cannot therefore be proven to be either true or false; and, finally, the "necessary assumption" of the things in themselves are realms which Kant must have wished he had never discovered. They are the "troublesome" aspects which we must "struggle against by scientific instruction yet with much difficulty."

This tension within Kant's system as such, one might argue, is precisely the focus for Derrida's investigations. That which leads Kant to rely on the notion of *constitution (Beschaffenheit)* as such, which cannot be known further, since in the process we would always necessarily rely on that same "object of investigation," is that which Derrida aims to reveal the *conditions of the possibility of* and in turn, necessarily, the conditions of the—more rigorously speaking—impossibility of.

The limits of metaphysics, for Derrida, far from engulfing this analysis in a *reasoned circle,*[39] extend the opening or the abyss and reveal a certain "inessentiality" in the heart of essence, a certain irreducible absence in the heart of presence; and more than Kant would or perhaps could admit in fact, a certain Desire in the heart of Reason. This however, is not a center or a ground for Derrida but the ungrounded ground of ground, or that which allows for the constitution of the notion of ground itself and in turn for the notion of constitution itself—Kant's ultimate ground. This "more originary" origin, which is profoundly not an origin for Derrida, is called by him, *différance* and by us, in the text that follows, *The Economy of Différance.*

Section I
The Principles and the Practice
of Deconstruction

I

THE PRINCIPLES

Derrida defines deconstruction more by what it is not than what it is. A summary of this negative determination would include the following list as a minimal outline or sketch of the field we intend to analyze here: (Deconstruction is not) (a) metaphysics, as per the Western tradition; (b) "philosophizing with a hammer," as per Nietzsche; (c) "the destruction of metaphysics," as per Heidegger; (d) dialectics, as per Hegel; (e) semiology, as per Saussure; (f) structuralism, as per Lévi-Strauss; (g) archaeology, as per Foucault; (h) textual psychoanalysis, as per Freud; (i) literary criticism, as per the "New Critics"; (j) philosophy or epistemology, as per Plato and Socrates; (k) a theory/logic/science of textuality, as per Barthes; (l) hermeneutics, as per Gadamer; (m) "Un Coup des Dès," as per Mallarmé; (n) transcendental phenomenology, as per Husserl; (o) a critique of pure reason, as per Kant; (p) an empiricism, as per Locke and Condillac; (q) a "theatre of cruelty," as per Artaud; (r) a commentary, as per Hyppolite; (s) a translation, as per Benjamin; (t) a signature, as per Ponge; (u) a corrective reading, as per Lacan; (v) a book of questions, as per Jabès; (w) an infinity exceeding all totality, as per Levinas; (x) a painting, as per Adami; (y) a journey to the castle, as per Kafka; nor (z) the celebration of a Wake, as per Joyce.

We now seem to be no closer to understanding what deconstruction *is,* although we know what it is not. This is only true if we exclude *is not* from *is,* or not-Being from Being, absence from presence; in short, if we think in terms of classical Western metaphysics. The question of what is proper to deconstruction, formulated in this way, excludes the other, negative, reversed side. The interdependence of these oppositions is therein denied. To ask "what is . . ." anything, therefore, is to install the response, indeed the possibility of a response, within metaphysics. It is precisely this formulation, as organized by and organizing (therein sustaining) metaphysics, that Derrida wishes to draw to our attention. It is not surprising therefore that when asked what deconstruction *is,* he responds with a neither this nor that *(ni/ni)* formulation. From within metaphysics one is denied meaning by this. The organization of thought by metaphysics is such that one asks: "which one?" to each pair of binary oppositions. The structure is either/or, not both/and, and thus to say neither seems to invoke an abdication of responsibility and an unwillingness to be committed to a position. This leads to the false conclusion that deconstruction must therefore claim a neutrality and a certain non-allegiance to anything (except perhaps itself). This criticism has been thrust at Derrida, and his response is the following: "I insist that deconstruction is not neutral. It intervenes."[1] Once again we have a negative determination of the issue and seem to be no better off. We propose the following explanation of the problem. To claim either one side or the other of metaphysical oppositions is incorrect for Derrida because of the radical exteriority this presupposes and sustains between one "side" and the "other." In saying that deconstruction is not neutral, he seems to us to be saying that it is not in the middle "between" this pair of oppositions but neither is it outside or inside metaphysics absolutely. The key is "absolutely" here. In some respects deconstruction *is* what he claims it is not, but not totally. Thus it is not metaphysics, for example, although it depends on and borrows its tools from metaphysics. Indeed it *copies* metaphysics. More of this specific method later. For now we wish only to *suspend* the question of *le propre* of deconstruction by showing its illegitimacy here. The paradox of course is the following: If deconstruction both is and is not metaphysics, or is both inside and outside it (which is the same thing), then there must indeed be a level or aspect or stage of deconstruction that can be described within metaphysical determinations; i.e., answer to the question "what is?" This is in fact the case, and we shall be addressing precisely this level; but we insist that: (a) this is not the *essence* of deconstruction; (b) it is an incomplete determination; and yet (c) these aspects we propose to explicate here are essential as components of deconstruction. What is missing here or exceeds this formulation are the relations of deconstruction to metaphysics and to *différance.* These are questions of economy, however, and will be treated there.

(a) "Le Fil Conducteur"

We must begin wherever we are and the thought of the trace, which cannot not take the scent into account, has already taught us that it was impossible to justify a point of departure absolutely.[2]

"*Le fil conducteur*" is always Derrida's point of departure for his deconstructive projects. It should be translated into English in at least the following diverse manners: (a) guiding line; (b) transmitting wire; (c) main stream; and (d) leading thread. These four systems of metaphors should not be forgotten as we proceed here since they will become the key to hidden presuppositions about the nature of textuality for Derrida. But we must begin at the beginning: that is, the opening of deconstruction.

As deconstruction moves towards the text of its choice, it approaches armed with certain goals or intentions. Derrida himself makes these explicit in the following manners: (a) as the deconstruction of metaphysics; (b) to "produce the law of the relationship between metaphysics and non-metaphysics"; (c) "to reveal the economy of a written text"; (d) to undo onto-theology"; (e) "to leave a track in the text it analyses"; and (f) "to aim at a certain relationship, unperceived by the writer, between what he commands and what he does not command of the patterns of language that he uses."[3]

Our first question must be: Are these all the same thing essentially or do they form a multitude of projects and hence directions for deconstruction? Our second question concerns the possibility of fulfillment; that is, as intentions are they to be considered as Ideas in the Kantian sense and therefore infinite and unreachable goals or as intentions as Husserl uses the term such that their fulfillment is intrinsically possible, especially as concerns the project of the *epistème,* science, or truth? This initiates the problem of the relation of deconstruction to truth. Is it submitted and thus committed to a project of truth? Or does this question make any sense? That is, are we already outside of the opposition of truth and falsity? Are we approaching an ontology? or is deconstruction a sort of *play* with its object that changes nothing? This would involve the distinction between work and play as utilized by Hegel. If deconstruction is aiming to alter metaphysics or if this is what "intervene" means for Derrida, then it must be considered work and not play. Its "presence" will therefore be expected to make a difference. Indeed Derrida substitutes the term "*le travail textuel*" for deconstruction throughout his discussion of the same in *Positions.* We suspend any final judgment on this for the present, however.

Let us begin by presupposing a certain identity of deconstruction as a project that is unified, systematic, identifiable, and hence also repeatable. This would mean that the seemingly disparate claims listed above that Derrida makes regarding the aims of deconstruction should be unifiable or capable of synthesis into a systematic totality. The first two claims involve: (a) the deconstruction of metaphysics and (b) the production of the law of the relationship between metaphysics and non-metaphysics. This means, when united, that in deconstructing metaphysics two other phenomena must appear: a law and non-metaphysics. Since deconstruction claims to *produce* this law, one might imagine that it did not exist prior to the action of deconstruction. Derrida insists, however, that the active-productive relation here must be tempered with a passive-revelatory one such that deconstruction participates in this production but is in a certain sense not totally responsible for it. Specific historical conditions have allowed for the possibility of deconstruction and thus for this shift that it seems to inaugurate in the infinite dominance of metaphysics. We will examine this later in terms of the presuppositions of deconstruction as exposed by Derrida and also beyond this. For now we wish to point out that in the deconstruction of metaphysics it seems that non-metaphysics emerges and does so in a particular fixed relation to metaphysics. This relation will be described by deconstruction.

The third aspect, "to reveal the economy of a written text," will shed some light on the structure we are building. The written text is presumably the locus of this deconstructive activity (in this context) wherein deconstruction finds metaphysics, non-metaphysics, and the law of their relation. This law is explained here as an economy. We now know, or at least can anticipate, the relation of metaphysics to non-metaphysics: an economy. This entails an exchange, but what is exchanged? Power also seems implied here and perhaps signs, but more than this we cannot yet foresee.

Deconstruction also promises us the "undoing of onto-theology." Is this reducible or identifiable with metaphysics? Derrida says yes and also that this is "the age of the sign." We now have the problem of presence emerging as the "guiding line" of metaphysics and hence as the "archenemy" of deconstruction. Onto-theology maintains a God of presence; indeed the presence of God is just this and suspends death infinitely. In addition, history and life and man become "mere signs," and indeed the sign becomes "mere" in this system. Thus deconstruction seems to be after the death of God and the life of man, but nothing could be further from its intent. In fact it intends to *limit* metaphysics, not kill it, to limit "God" and therein liberate the notion of the sacred (decenter it), and further to recognize death as essential, and man as not inessential but not the center of the world. Indeed to substitute a world without a center. We are already ahead of ourselves and beyond deconstruction. We must return to its intentions and deal with its accomplishments and abortions later.

Deconstruction claims in its process, or the wake of its movement, to leave a track in the text. Is this what is meant by "deconstructing metaphysics"? Presumably so. What sort of track must this be, and what effect must this have on the text and hence on metaphysics? The track is a memory in a certain sense; a difference that is inserted in the heart of presence. Yet Derrida would deny such a formulation. His wording might be instead that the track has always already been there but is only revealed by deconstruction. He emphasizes the passive yet also denies the eidetic sphere. We must include portions of both, therefore, in order to understand this. The results of this track seem to have an effect all their own, as if deconstruction is a preliminary tracking procedure (more like trapping) which after its activity produces an effect in philosophy. This seems consistent with the schema for the new series of texts entitled "Philosophie en Effet," for which Derrida is a founding member. Thus deconstruction itself seems to be a preparation for something else. It indeed is this—both for an explosion in philosophy and the opening which will found Grammatology (although perhaps under a different name). This is perhaps the "crevice" that Derrida speaks of through which one can only "catch a glimpse of the as yet unnameable."

The final aspect of our synthesis involves the "aiming towards a certain relationship, unperceived by the writer, between what he commands and what he does not command of the patterns of language that he uses." It would be too simple to suppose that "what he commands" is metaphysics and "what he does not command" is not metaphysics. Deconstruction is much more subtle, since what the writer seems to command is only one level of that which he does not. Thus metaphysical control of textuality is an implicit process and not generally one wielded by a writer. It is this controlling system that deconstruction attempts to reveal initially and secondly to deconstruct (assuming that revelation is distinct from this). We seem to have a level of unconscious textual production in occurrence here and one that deconstruction aims to reveal. Indeed deconstruction searches for "symptoms" of this underlying level in order to locate and track it. The track does not wander aimlessly through the textual world, however. Once again we find a delimitation of the relation of the known to the unknown, or a law, as Derrida announced earlier, and one which takes us from one level to the other. On the one hand, this law is "available" to us *after* the revelation and recognition of what was formerly invisible. Thus the problem emerges as to how one moves from the known to the unknown in order to initiate the process of deconstruction. Since this law is available only after, from whence does the "fil conducteur" originate? Although Derrida confesses to no absolute justification for this beginning, we wish to illustrate the process by which deconstruction intends to achieve these goals. But first several issues remain to be clarified.

The synthesis of the various descriptions given by Derrida seems, given the above explication, to be not only plausible but also consistent with Derrida's "intentions" as a whole. But are these goals or Ideas in the Kantian sense? That is, is it possible to actually deconstruct metaphysics? Not once and for all, Derrida will answer. Metaphysics, as we have shown, is not to be killed but only limited. Indeed it is already limited, more precisely speaking, but this is not yet recognized. In addition to this limitation however, metaphysics seems to have a tendency to resurge and to return with its infinitizing project. Thus the work of deconstruction is never to be accomplished as such. This relation, as an economy, will be treated in greater detail later but we wish here to at least pose the issue as a limit. This seems to answer our second query regarding the fulfillment of these intentions of deconstruction. But if they are intrinsically nonfulfillable, then the issue of truth, science and the *epistème* must be faced. What is the relationship of deconstruction to truth? Derrida aims to free the notions of science and truth from the logocentrism of metaphysics and to establish them elsewhere, or at least *also* elsewhere. Thus it seems that deconstruction hopes to found a new possibility for truth and the meaning of science, indeed to extend the limits of meaningfulness itself. If this is so, as it seems to us, it is impossible to ask whether deconstruction is true or not, since it does not and cannot respond to such a question. It intends to inaugurate a new meaning for truth and thus exceeds the question. This excess is not however an ontology despite the seemingly infinite distance deconstruction may appear from its goal. The act of deconstruction, once the track is made, can never be undone and makes a difference that remains unforgettable within metaphysics. This procedure as such must now be examined.

(b) Castration and Mimesis

. . . the most general title of the problem would be: castration and mimesis.[4]

This "problem" is the actual work of deconstruction. We already know that this work is empirical in a certain sense. That is, it is a textual practice more than a theory, although it presupposes and aims towards the latter. But what is castrated and what is mimed? Is this the same thing? Are these actions directed towards the same thing? Do they have a temporal order or relation—simultaneous or sequential? And finally, why castration *and* mimesis? Does not one undo the possibility of the other? Is this double movement coherent with itself? How can these opposing propositions be united within the term 'deconstruction'? We shall attempt first to answer these questions according to Derrida and secondly to point out some areas of insoluable enigmas that seem to be lurking within this "method." It is again worthy of note that for Derrida the question of method is in itself an 'exorbitant' one. This means it extends outside of the 'orbit' of classical metaphysics of the *Logos*. In short, there can be no adequate reasons given, if one determines adequacy by Reason itself. However, this "exorbitancy" extends only to the *"fil conducteur,"* to the opening line, and although leaving a trace throughout the textual work of deconstruction, it does so only as an uneasy horizon, not in each detail. What this means is that deconstruction, as a process that is repeatable and not totally idiomatic or determined by the text it aims to analyze, resists the self-effacement that is so characteristic of the treatment of the sign in classical metaphysics. It is this residue that we must examine presently.

In general terms "castration and mimesis" describes the double register or double reading that deconstruction conducts simultaneously. On the one hand, the text analyzed is to be borrowed from, to be reproduced as if deconstruction were merely a doubling commentary. But on the other hand, in this process certain spaces are made in the text, certain questions are asked, certain re-marks are produced, a certain "track" is left in the "original" text which leaves it not dissimilar from its state prior to deconstruction, but nonetheless, not the same. These re-marks are cuts in the text, Derrida does not hesitate to point out, and as such perform the work of castration. In a certain sense then it is *Logos* itself, as phallocentric, that is being clipped as deconstruction works its way through the text. But these generalities leave one wondering nevertheless about the "actual" method of deconstruction. Where does one cut? What is borrowed? What is copied and what is cut? Where does the doubling stop and the re-mark over and above this begin?

As to the question of borrowing, Derrida claims, although we disagree, that deconstruction borrows *all* its resources from the text it analyzes:

> The movements of deconstruction do not destroy structures from the outside. They are not possible nor can they take accurate aim except by *inhabiting* those structures. Inhabiting them in a certain way . . . operating necessarily from the inside, *borrowing all* the strategic and economic resources of subversion from the old structure, borrowing them structurally that is to say without being able to isolate their elements and atoms, the enterprise of deconstruction always in a certain way falls prey to its own work [my emphasis].[5]

He qualifies the borrowing as structural however and not atomistic. What this entails is a general strategy, a general style with general principles that cross-cut particular places and times in a text and link, at a certain level, one region to another. We insist that the borrowing is not total, however, for the following reasons: (a) there are qualities that are proper to deconstruction alone and distinguish it irreducibly from the text it analyzes, in each case and in general; (b) the act of borrowing is itself not borrowed from the structure under analysis; and (c) without something proper to deconstruction it could leave no trace in the text, and would therefore be invisible after its work was completed, in a particular case, therein not making even the slightest difference.

But what does it mean to *inhabit* those structures? To work from the *inside* of a text without attacking it externally? Derrida's usage of biological metaphors here must be noted since later he claims the work of deconstruction is "parasitic"—not symbiotic, but parasitic. The metaphors of living organisms are significant since there is a certain life and thus death, a certain finitude introduced here. What this entails is not properly the domain of methodology and will be treated later in terms of the presuppositions of deconstruction when we arrive there. For the present it is worthy of note that there is something lurking behind Derrida's explicit claims, something that orients the style of deconstruction itself. In addition the self-effacing claim that *all* the resources are borrowed will reappear in terms of Derrida's portrayal of metaphysics itself, also deconstruction's target we should recall.

The first step in deconstruction, once the borrowing is done, although this is never an accomplished, completed task, is "to exhaust the resources of the concept [borrowed] . . . before attaining and in order to obtain by deconstruction, its ultimate foundation." To "exhaust the resources of a concept" must mean to use it and indeed to use it up. However, the nature of the concept is such that it claims an infinite range—indeed one that can go on forever. It is not a "material" that has the quality, weakness or potential of being exhausted. It has intrinsically an infinite capacity or is infinitely inexhaustible. However, Derrida insists that this is not the case. It s difficult to say whether he presupposes conceptual exhaustiveness or actually finds it and then draws his conclusion from the findings, scientifically, as it were. But what is the sign for this exhaustion? Indeed, what is the *limit* of the concept? It is meaningfulness. It is the very possibility of meaning. When the concept no longer makes any sense its resources have been exhausted. More precisely we will have reached the *limits* of its usefulness. It is this limit that Derrida wishes to approach and point out, therein transgressing it at the same instant. It is the usage of the concept within and until its limits present themselves (as it were) that entails mimesis or repetition (without representation), and it is the crossing of the boundary, asking the nonsensical, meaningless question, according to the rules of questionability, that entails a certain castration. It is precisely this boundary crossing that illumines the limits of logocentric metaphysics. The "backward glance" is also a forward thrust, and what it reveals are limits which have no "legitimate right" to be there. That is, as we mentioned above, the concept is defined in its essence as infinite, yet we reach a space where its "infinite range" does not apply. These are the places that Derrida will mark in his "textual work" or deconstruction. These are the places where the trace of the work makes itself felt in metaphysics itself. This contradiction will need to be integrated, to itself be overcome within metaphysics itself since it is based on non-contradiction. The struggle is only in its infancy here however.

It is still unclear *how* deconstruction borrows and what it borrows from the old structure. How is the selection made and indeed what is selected? Derrida claims that certain terms in a text, or certain structures, more precisely, must be treated as symptoms or signs which if followed throughout the text will reveal an underlying system of constraints operating in the text and indeed that this almost totally invisible structure is that which governs, commands, and organizes the textual production itself. What we read is a result, an effect, and what we must seek is how the text as such, as given, came and comes to be constituted as such. The presuppositions here that allow for deconstruction's work will be examined shortly, but first the symptoms:

> . . . as the primordial and indispensable phase, in fact and in principle, of
> the development of this problematic, consists in questioning the internal
> structure of these texts as *symptoms;* as that is the only condition for
> determining these symptoms themselves in the totality of their meta-
> physical appurtenance. I draw my argument from them in order to iso-
> late, in Rousseau [for example] and in Rousseauism the theory of
> writing [my emphasis].[6]

At present we are not concerned with the results and the implications
of deconstruction but rather with how it is that those results are ob-
tained, be they productions or revelations or both, as Derrida claims.
Now we are instructed to question the internal structure as a symptom.
This can only mean to treat it as a sign—indeed a sign in the classical
sense—for something else. It is now a signifying structure but not in
the sense of having a referent elsewhere. Thus we remain *within* the
text itself in deconstruction, albeit treating the same as a sign. There is
no proper place for that which deconstruction finds in a sense, since if
there were it would be in the text explicitly. Instead what Derrida seeks
is that which allows for the text to be produced as such: "the law of the
relation between what the writer commands and what he does not
command of the patterns of language that he uses." Thus the relation of
the given text to its "other side" must have a certain consistency. It is
this that deconstruction hopes to uncover and indeed requires in order
to work at all. The "symptom," to use Derrida's system of metaphors,
must point us towards a disease but must therefore be a system or
collection of symptoms. One is never enough to define a disease.
Rather the interrelation of various ones together is essential. Assuming
for a moment that this medical terminology underlies Derrida's "treatment" of textuality in the form of deconstruction, we can now understand better how deconstruction manifests itself. More specifically, one
could show that Derrida tends to select for the *"fil conducteur"* a term
or a system of terms which are linked either directly or indirectly to
that "other side" of classical metaphysical oppositions which have
been excluded from the realm of the Good, the True, and the Reasonable; in short, the meaningful. These terms are not difficult to spot.
For instance we have the supplement, metaphor, women, poesis,
mimesis, writing, the sign, the empirical, history, finitude, limit, impurity, non-simplicity. The list, although not infinite, seems to go on
forever. We will examine in detail the actual work of deconstruction in
practice with respect to the works of Husserl and Saussure in the
second section of this work, where the meaning of the method here

expounded necessarily more as a theory than a practice will become more clear. At present we are attempting only to lay out general propositions of style in order that an outline as a whole of "the textual work" can be glimpsed in the distance, albeit within the crevice, albeit still essentially unnameable.

Before leaving the interweaving of castration and mimesis we wish to add a few remarks on the trace. In following the thread or symptom in a text, what one finds is a certain pattern that emerges. This is indicative of a rupture within metaphysics itself, for Derrida, and thus the "places of rupture" must be localized. Deconstruction thus remarks or points out these places found *in* the text yet in some respects made almost invisible there. The negligible, or the footnote, or that which is held suspended in brackets tends also to be a good bet for the locus of a symptom. This irruption or blemish on the face of metaphysics is paradoxically what allows deconstruction to: (a) displace the seeming coherence of the text; (b) juxtapose the incoherencies one against the other—face to face, as it were; and (c) to do nothing. Metaphysics itself will take care of the rest. The active passivity or passive activity, although reproductive, respectful, and faithful to its borrowed text, nonetheless undermines it by virtue of its own principles. The results are described by Derrida in terms of a law, a logic, a play, and a primordiality which only metaphysics itself can authorize. It is precisely this authorization as absolute and limitless that deconstruction focuses on and aims to deconstruct. That is, to reveal its foundation as non-metaphysical. This is only contradictory if one absolutizes: (a) the terms of the opposition and (b) the opposition itself. Deconstruction presupposes that this is not done in order to grasp even a trace of its "textual work." Thus the risks of its operation begin to be felt.

(c) " . . . ne veut rien dire."[7]

The most obvious risks of deconstruction are twofold: (i) that it merely mimics, imitates or reproduces its "parent text" and leaves no trace of its work, and (ii) that it becomes its own enemy; that is, reified and absolutized into a sort of strategic metaphysics of detextualization. The first danger is perhaps more serious. Derrida has himself stated that deconstruction *"ne veut rien dire,"* and indeed this claim has returned to haunt him, notably in the interviews of *Positions*. To understand what he means by this, one must understand the theory of intentionality proposed by Husserl and how this forms the culmination of the history of philosophy with respect to the metaphysics of presence. We will not propose to short-circuit that essential work. However, we wish to point out that the *"vouloir-dire"* of Husserl, indeed of metaphysics in general (the presupposition of Husserl's phenomenology being within the latter will be taken up later in greater detail) has always, according to Derrida, been the determination and circumscription, indeed the condition of the possibility of meaning in general. It is not without consequence that meaning and intention are linked here and that they are constituted *only* in relation to an *object*. The point is that for Derrida to claim that deconstruction does not want to say anything, or more precisely has nothing to say—to speak of the nothing—is to say that he intends to exceed this preformulation that prescribes meaning according to metaphysics. He is well aware of the danger of such playfulness, given the continued predominance of metaphysical presuppositions in language and thought today. Thus he subjects his work to radical misinterpretation by this refusal to explicate *again* the meaning of meaning, and how metaphysical predeterminations of the same can be overcome. This is his project, as a whole, in a certain sense, and when asked what deconstruction means—he must say "nothing." We do not defend or attack this position he has taken but wish here only to explicate: (a) the possibilities of misunderstanding and nonrecognition; (b) why these are intrinsic and meaningful; and (c) why Derrida's claims are to be taken seriously, in a certain sense, as a rigorous attempt to understand the foundations of scientificity and the formation of form itself, and thus why the notion of "serious" as metaphysically engendered must be discarded. This means, as Derrida has responded to Searle—"Let's be serious!" In order to understand this danger of deconstruction falling back into metaphysics as merely a "copy," indeed as a "bad" copy at that, we must suspend or bracket out metaphysical determinations of meaning at the very instant that they appear and seem to make everything "perfectly clear." It is this clarity itself as a univocalization of the world that must be suspected. As Derrida says, regarding his project as a whole: (his intention *(vouloir dire)*)

> To make enigmatic what one thinks one understands by the words 'proximity', 'immediacy', 'presence' (the immediate (proche)) the own (propre) and the pre- of presence is my final intention of this work *(Of Grammatology)*. This deconstruction of presence accomplishes itself through the deconstruction of consciousness, and therefore through the

irreducible notion of the trace (spur), as it appears in both Nietzschean and Freudian discourse.[8]

To make enigmatic is to make resound, to make something oscillate, or vibrate, or ring between two poles of opposition. What this means is that a certain irreducible duplicity must appear, indeed is already latent or immanent within classical metaphysics itself, but is as yet unheard within most of the tradition. In a certain sense, if one is not listening for it, it will not be heard. Thus a preparation for this resounding *"Glas!"* is essential; a certain readiness or a certain distrust of the infinity that metaphysics promises us. The clarity and distinctness, and the readiness-to-hand of immediate understanding in its full presence will become problematized for and by deconstruction. What is found by this will be described later, since it exceeds the bounds of the principles of deconstruction.

This intention of Derrida's, however, as an intention, is also a unified project, albeit divided from within as we have tried to illustrate. In falling short of recognition as such, what seems to occur is a blinding attempt to synthesize these two poles, to unite the double register that is essential to the movement of deconstruction. To tie the two shoes together instead of lacing each one individually, albeit in a parallel fashion. As Derrida says, "one cannot walk in such a manner." Instead one will only trip and fall at the first attempt. We therefore propose that there be a double sense sustained in the understanding of Derrida, such that his terms, phrases, and texts be considered, on the one hand, *inside* metaphysics and, on the other, *outside* of metaphysics. In doing this the reading becomes a parody. It becomes the acting out of the castration and mimesis with each concept, as one moves at one moment with one foot, then with the other; each step of the way leading back again to the other side. Deconstruction, as we have seen, is this very oscillating movement that is not, as some have claimed, a simple shifting from one side (foot) to the other. Instead, deconstruction, if properly understood, walks through the text and, if improperly understood, leaves its tracks behind it. We will examine them shortly.

The second way of reducing Derrida's deconstruction is to grasp it as a theory in itself, as such, as it were, that contains a certain *eidos* or essentiality within its own proper bounds. This would be a machine-like robot that walks, indeed marches, over textuality, destroying the ground as a whole in its wake. What this entails is the making of deconstruction into a metaphysical concept. The idea of asking Derrida about his "thought" in general would entail such a maneuver. More specifically, this reification would deny the essentiality of the other that is *not* deconstruction for deconstruction's process itself. This other as other is metaphysics. To reduce deconstruction to metaphysics is to misunderstand both at the same time. The very difference that sustains the work of deconstruction would be lost in the collapse and metaphysics as such would sustain its infinitizing process. This is clearly an inexcusable violence and violation of the work of Derrida and misunderstands him totally. The sustenance of deconstruction is drawn from its relation to metaphysics, it is true, and indeed its tools of operation are borrowed from the same; but within this process the work of castration, of cutting into the text, of uncovering hidden laws, and of revealing a fracture within metaphysics that allows for its operation is a secondary yet essential aspect. The very secondariness is another problem of understanding that Derrida aims to deconstruct. Temporality itself is under fire here, as linear and as an effervescent Now that has always known its own past and forgets nothing. We shall treat the Now X with respect to the findings of deconstruction and will not pursue this further at present. The point here is simply that deconstruction: (a) is not nothing and (b) is not metaphysical, yet (c) it is not something and (d) is somewhat metaphysical. From a metaphysical standpoint, in claiming "A" and "-A" as coexistant properties of the same thing, one arrives at zero and knows nothing more of that object. From a deconstructive standpoint, if we can balance here for a moment, one must consider that in some respects, on some levels, in some styles, and at particular times "A" is the case, whereas at others, "-A" is the case. The unity of the object is thus sustained and yet shattered at the same time. The problem is certainly the localization of meaning *inside* the closure of the "object" whatever sort of "thing" that might be. In order, therefore, to catch the drift or scent of deconstruction more fully, we propose an examination beyond these limits (although a proper explanation was required and its resources exhausted as a preliminary phase of operation) and into a realm of relations that can only be described within the framework of an economy.

II

DECONSTRUCTIVE GESTURES

(a) Introduction

To avoid subsuming "deconstruction" within the metaphysical dichotomy and predetermined opposition of theory and practice, form and content, ideal and real, and thus purity and impurity or inside and outside, we shall propose here to examine what we shall tentatively name: deconstructive gestures. Rather than taking one "privileged example" of Derrida's analysis, we shall instead attempt to trace a certain parallelism between two particular deconstructive practices. The usage of a "privileged example" shall be avoided here due to the implicit metaphysical determination of "exemplarity" within the notions of sign, origin, presence, absence, and ultimately the representation of the general (law) within the particular (facticity). Since these determinations are issues and structures to be placed in question, indeed deconstructed, by Derrida, we suggest that the tautological formulation of using that which we hope to clarify in the act of clarification should be avoided here. Therefore we shall also attempt to avoid a mimetic procedure concerning the relation of our work to Derrida's. With this last limitation in mind, we propose therefore to avoid the deconstruction of deconstruction here. This is not our task at present, although it may indeed emerge as not only an unavoidable, essential, necessary, and perhaps timely project but also the most precise clarification of the structure, functioning, and aims of deconstruction itself.

Instead and for the moment, therefore, we propose a more modest approach here. We shall use Derrida's deconstructions of Husserl and Saussure as our "case studies" and shall attempt to track, by using the notion of parallelism or perhaps parallelogram, a certain process common to both particular studies. Finally, we shall leave the question open as to whether these repeated, repeating, and therefore repeatable (ideal?) gestures do indeed form that which could, within metaphysics, be called the concept of deconstruction; or more precisely, a theory of the practice of deconstructive gestures. We shall perhaps, however, point towards such a necessity.

(b) Announcing the Limits

In Derrida's analysis of Saussure he states his intention of the deconstruction in the following way:

> I hope my intention is clear. I think Saussure's reasons are good. I do not question, on the level on which he says it, the truth of what Saussure says in such a tone. . . . I would rather *announce the limits* and the *presuppositions* of what seems here to be self-evident and what seems to me to retain the character and validity of evidence [*General Linguistics*, my emphasis].[1]

It is clear, therefore, at least on the level of Derrida's intentions, that he is not attempting a critique of Saussure, nor is he attempting to overcome or denounce the Saussurian project of the *Course*. Instead he is concerned with the demarcation—by Saussure and by the project of founding a general science of linguistics—of the *limits* of that project itself. The *limits,* for Derrida, invoke certain presuppositions which remain active but latent or hidden within that which is thereby limited or framed. Indeed the notion of "limit," for Derrida, is precisely that which is "in need" of deconstruction, as we shall see. The limit of a project is a demarcation of its range or field or relevance or applicability. It is the circumscription of the inside and outside of the object of that science. It is the scientificity of science itself, Derrida insists. As he says,

> Saussure thus begins by positing that writing is "unrelated to [the] . . . inner system" of language. External/internal, image/reality, representation/presence, such is *the old grid to which is given the task of outlining the domain of a science* [my emphasis].[2]

Thus the significance of the "limits" is delimited by Derrida. We might recall that his analysis of Saussure's *Course* here is concerned with the possibility of founding a science called Grammatology within which such a "general science of linguistics" as Saussure's might legitimately be situated. We shall see, however, that Grammatology for Derrida remains an Idea in the Kantian sense. Precisely why this is the case is what will interest us here. But first we must explore Derrida's demarcation of the "limits" of deconstruction with respect to Husserl.

Derrida's initial gesture in his deconstruction of Husserl is concerned with the question of whether the *"découpage"* or demarcation of the limits, indeed the reduction of metaphysics itself, is not already a sign for the very presence of metaphysics which Husserl posits explicitly as absent or exterior to his project. As Derrida says, Husserl

> . . . places all constituted knowledge *out of circulation* [*hors circuit*], he insists on the necessary absence of presuppositions . . . whether they be from metaphysics, psychology, or the natural sciences [my emphasis].[3]

Derrida's own intention here is therefore brought to light, since he once again focuses on the gesture of "exclusion" which is used to initiate a project—indeed to found a new "science." In order to pursue the meaning of this gesture of exclusion, Derrida considers it to be a sign for something not presented as such. This transformation of the given, explicit, *"vouloir-dire"* into a signifying function shall be the focus of the following section concerning Derrida's *use* ("borrowing") of metaphysical structures, but for now we wish to point towards the reason for Derrida's openings and explicit (stated) intentions in his deconstructions of both Husserl and Saussure. We must pursue this limitation of limits a little further therefore.

Each time Husserl makes a *distinction* with respect to the sign, language, and signification in general, in particular, Derrida seems to take very careful notice. In fact these are the passages he selects in accordance with his concern for the double significance of exclusion as a more profound but hidden (illegitimate) act of inclusion. For example:

> We *should* consider here the last *exclusion*—or reduction—to which Husserl has invited us in order to isolate the purity specific to expression [my emphasis].[4]

Further:

> Without such *distinctions* no *pure* logical grammar would be possible. We know in effect that pure logical grammar depends entirely on the *distinction* between *Widersinnigkeit* and *Sinnlosigkeit* [my emphasis].[5]

We shall not trace here the intricacies and complexities of the contexts of Husserl's phenomenology that Derrida aims to place in question in the demarcation of its limits, as they in turn represent yet larger and therefore a more narrow demarcation of the field itself. We wish however to show that: (i) Derrida's concern with the "limits" is a concern with that which they "represent"; (ii) he limits himself in the opening gestures of deconstruction to a focus on the explicit *intent* of the project at hand and how its field of relevance, indeed the "object" of its discourse, is framed or marked using the distinction of inside/outside in accordance with the metaphysical presuppositions therein entailed.

Returning to Saussure we find the "same" intense concern for his limitations or more precisely for his representative gestures of exclusion and inclusion, for Derrida. For instance:

> The *limits* have already begun to appear: *why* does a project of general linguistics concerning the internal system in general of language in general, *outline the limits of its field* by *excluding,* as exteriority in general, a particular system of writing, however important it might be, even were it to be in fact universal? A particular system has precisely for its *principle* or at least for its declared project to be *exterior* to the spoken language [my emphasis].[6]

Not only does this concern parallel Derrida's concern with Husserl, it seems to mirror his approach there almost exactly. The *reason* for the "limits" being set precisely *where* they are and therein excluding or including precisely what they do is clearly the concern for deconstruction. It is the opening deconstructive gesture itself one could argue. We shall not explore why this limit is set upon deconstruction itself, yet but wish at least here to mark, indeed to re-mark, that it exists and that it repeats from one deconstruction to another. This repetition is already significant, as we shall explore presently.

A final word on the limits, however, seems necessary here. Derrida's exploration of the gestures of exclusion (inclusion) also focuses on the "questions left unasked" by the "author/text" under analysis. These questions are absolutely context-specific and must be approached as such by us as well. However, they do once again signify a certain level of "law" within the text, which Derrida will claim is not only unexamined by the author and *a fortiori* his/her intentions but in fact *governs* the same. Indeed this duplicity of implicit textual laws and explicit authorial intent will become of increasing significance for us and for Derrida in this examination of deconstructive gestures. But first, the notion of the unasked questions.

For Derrida, as for Heidegger, the form of the question always already prescribes the form and *a fortiori* the content of the response. The question's form is precisely the condition of the possibility or impossibility of the response. Thus it may seem perhaps somewhat strange for Derrida to be asking questions which he claims the writers do not ask. On what basis are these questions "ask-able" and why and where do they arise?

In Saussure, Derrida suggests the following implicit contract with metaphysics, based on a certain form of Saussure's questioning:

> . . . as long as one *poses the question* of the relationships between speech and writing in the light of the indivisible units of 'thought-sound', there will *always* be the *ready response.* Writing will be 'phonetic', it will be the *outside,* the *exterior* representation of language and of 'thought-sound' [my emphasis].[7]

The question Saussure does not ask himself here is precisely that which Derrida is concerned with. Why and how is it that this contract presupposes a certain metaphysical determination of writing and *a fortiori* of the sign? It is the *ground* of the question that concerns Derrida therefore, at least in this context. With Husserl he is concerned more directly with that which is *never* placed in question:

> The themes presented here are *never placed in question* by Husserl. They are left, on the contrary, to be confirmed repeatedly [my emphasis].[8]

And again:

> On the one hand, Husserl seems to repress with dogmatic haste a question concerning the structure of the sign in general . . . *he does not ask himself what the sign is in general.* The sign in general, which he certainly requires in the beginning and which he certainly recognizes as a centre of meaning, can only obtain its unity from an essence, it must necessarily be governed by that [my emphasis].[9]

Therefore, in the process of asking or even revealing the "unasked questions" for both Husserl and Saussure, Derrida seems to be concerned with that which remains hidden from view for both Husserl and Saussure but which therein sustains its hold on the form of their discourses and indeed the very projects of their work. In fact, Derrida explicitly claims to be concerned with "the relation between that which a writer commands and does not command of the patterns of language that he or she uses." This difference will appear in the process of deconstruction initially as a *contradiction* (within a metaphysical vision) but later, as we shall see, as the movement of *différance* itself.

The deconstructive gesture thus turns towards this duplicity which it will claim is: (i) irreducible, and thus (ii) constitutive of textuality in general. We are still however at the stage of the initial limitations and circumscriptions of deconstruction itself, we should recall.

The duplicity in Husserl's project appears for Derrida in the following manner:

> And in fact along the entire itinerary which ends with the *Origin of Geometry,* Husserl accords increasing attention to that which, in signification, in language, and in inscription, consigns ideal objectivity, produces truth or ideality rather than simply recording it. *But this latter movement is not simple. This is our problem here* and we should return to it [my emphasis].[10]

Derrida continues here to explain a certain double structure within phenomenology which entails on the one hand, the reduction of "naive ontology" and yet "another necessity also confirms the classical metaphysics of presence and marks the adherence of phenomenology to classical ontology."[11] Further: "it is this *adherence* that we have chosen to examine further." Indeed, the interest of deconstruction is here at stake and stated explicitly. It would seem to be none other than the following twofold demonstration: (i) that the duplicity exists; and (ii) that it is essential. With Saussure, we find the same issue therefore rising to the surface, for Derrida, as the intention and thus (perhaps) telos of deconstruction. For example:

> Yet the *intention* that institutes general linguistics as a *science* remains in this respect within a *contradiction.* Its *declared purpose* indeed confirms, saying what goes without saying, the subordination of grammatology, the historico-metaphysical reduction of writing to the rank of an instrument enslaved to full and ordinary spoken language. But *another gesture* (not another statement of purpose, for here what does not go without saying is done without being said, written without being uttered) liberates the future of a general grammatology of which linguistics-phonology would only be a dependent and *circumscribed* area [my emphasis].

And further:

> Let us follow this tension between gesture and statement in Saussure.[12]

We now have the limits and intentions of the deconstructive gestures clearly stated, or so it would seem. The textual contradictions form a certain center, a certain recurring form or basis for the tracking procedure of deconstruction. We should recall that the principles claim to "leave a track in the text it analyses." Presumably this track or mark, which remains as the result or product of the deconstructive gesture, is the trace of the trace itself. Presumably this track is therefore: (i) already there in the text; yet (ii) not presented as such but paradoxically (iii) "presented," to the deconstructive eye at least, as a certain circumscribed, indeed representative and represented absence *within* the text itself. It is to this constitution of the "track" by the gesture of deconstruction that we shall now turn our attention. The conditions of the possibility of the trace of the trace shall become, if not self-evident or present, at least signified or marked by this our procedure here, we hope.

(c) Borrowed Structures and Inhabiting Texts

Derrida openly claims to "borrow his tools for deconstruction from metaphysics itself" and "to inhabit the text under analysis in a certain way" such that the results of deconstruction and the deconstructive project itself "always and in a certain way falls victim to its own work."[13] It is this "adherence that we have chosen to be interested in." Indeed this borrowing procedure forms the very procedure of deconstruction itself in its "empirical," contextual manifestations, we suggest. One might consider first that the notion of borrowing from metaphysics involves a certain *usage* of metaphysics, quite simply. And perhaps a certain *misuse* since borrowing implies a certain *impropriety,* a certain "misfitting" of the borrowed and the borrower. However, it is significant to notice that Derrida does not claim to steal, hide, or threaten the "tools of metaphysics" but rather first to borrow them and secondly, to deconstruct them. Indeed the latter is the precondition and telos of the former. Thus we can already see a certain intimacy within the relation of deconstruction to metaphysics; perhaps a certain impropriety but above all a certain *contract.* In fact an economy is beginning to take shape here. Before exploring these general relations further, we must return to the specific gestures of deconstruction with respect to this "borrowing," "inhabiting," and "falling victim to" the tools and structures of metaphysics as exemplified in his analyses of Saussure and Husserl. (We too shall begin to borrow more heavily from metaphysics at this juncture, since it seems in keeping with the tracing or following of the subject matter at hand.)

Derrida's analyses of Husserl and Saussure use no less than nine major principles or "tools" of classical, traditional, Western metaphysics. These include: (i) the Concept in general; (ii) the transformation of chance into necessity; (iii) metaphysical forms of questions; (iv) the search for "conditions of possibility"; (v) the syllogism; premise/consequence relations of necessity; (vi) criteria of essence or necessity for judgment; (vii) the principle of non-contradiction; (viii) essence/appearance distinctions; and (ix) the metaphysical determination of the sign.

We shall attempt to show precisely where and how Derrida uses metaphysics in specific contexts with respect to these two deconstructions. Finally, we shall propose some possible reasons for Derrida's heavy reliance on this same structure which, we should not forget, he aims to deconstruct. It is not simply a contradiction, in the classical metaphysical sense, that Derrida will be found engaged in here although it may appear as such initially. Neither is deconstruction, in our case studies, simply: (i) redeemable by metaphysics; (ii) condemned to it; or (iii) detachable from it. As Derrida himself has claimed, it is not the *attachment* or complicity with metaphysics that he denounces or is concerned with but rather the *necessity* of this attachment.[14] Despite his attempt to "slowly detach his project from the concepts of metaphysics," it will be argued here that this is simply (a) not possible and (b) not conceivable except as an Idea in the Kantian sense. Indeed to radically "escape" from metaphysics would mean the end of all communication and all conditions of the possibility of the same. It is this paradoxical conclusion within Derrida's deconstructive gestures, in particular as he uses/borrows the tools of metaphysics, that we shall attempt to trace here.

(i) The Concept in General

Once Derrida has circumscribed the limits of his concerns with Husserl, with the First Investigation and within the first major distinction between one type of sign and another, he begins to analyze the conditions of the possibility of this "act of exclusion." If "indication and expression," the *two* types of signs, are indeed two *types of signs,* then Derrida suggests, they necessarily entail the *concept* of the sign in general. In drawing such a conclusion, the use of the metaphysical structure of genus and species is clearly invoked as well. Derrida explains his conclusion in the following way:

> . . . concerning the meaning of *Zeigen in general* which . . . can in turn be modified as *Hinzeigen* or as *Anzeigen,* not a single original question is asked.[15]

Not only is this "hidden conceptual ground" revealed by Derrida here, or perhaps simply invoked as a *necessary* presupposition, he goes on to suggest that the very *need* for such a concept, on the one hand, and yet the *absence* of Husserl's recognition of this or questioning of it indicates something more. We should recall that Husserl aimed to reduce all pre-constituted knowledge and to avoid the use of metaphysics in his phenomenology. Derrida suggests however that: "This absence of the question concerning the point of departure and the preunderstanding of the traditional operational *concept* is necessarily a dogmatism."[16] And further: "This would be a classical procedure." In response to his own apparent objections here Derrida seems to save Husserl, however, by showing that perhaps the latter does not *in fact* presuppose a conceptual unity for the sign and indeed does not require a concept of the sign in general for his distinction. However, Derrida's "metaphysical *démarche*" returns again and again to install Husserl solidly and squarely within the tradition of metaphysics on this same basis. Concerning the use of the term "life" to describe both the empirical and the transcendental realm, Husserl seems again to invoke a more general *concept* of life in general which would both precede and transcend the distinction produced by the reduction. On this point Derrida does not make an alternative suggestion concerning the other possible reasons for such a "common root" but rather "condemns" Husserl outright for presupposing and indeed requiring a metaphysical ground for his phenomenology. Derrida's line of argument is worthy of repeating here.

> The *unity of living,* the focus of *Lebendigkeit* which diffracts its light in all the fundamental concepts of phenomenology . . . escapes the tran-.cendental reduction and as unity of worldly life and transcendental life, even opens up the way for it. When *empirical life* or even the pure psychic region are placed in parenthesis, it is again a *transcendental life* . . . that Husserl discovers. And thus he thematizes this *unity of the concept of life* without however posing it as a question.

And finally:

> The common root which allows for all these metaphors seems to us again to be the *concept of life* [my emphasis].[17]

Thus in finding two uses of the "same" name, or the same term, albeit in different circumstances and in different contexts, Derrida insists in this case in particular at least that a metaphysical concept which unites the two instances is necessarily at work. Indeed the "concept" in general is the condition of the possibility of each individual case for Derrida as for Plato, as we shall see.

Another instance of Derrida's invocation of the concept in his analysis of Husserl seems particularly relevant here. Husserl distinguishes in an analogous fashion, Derrida tells us, between *Hinweiss* and *Beweiss,* or indication and demonstration, just after his initial (and problematic, according to Derrida) distinction between the "two types of signs." Once again the fact that *Hinweiss* and *Beweiss* seem to be sharing the notion of "showing in general" as their ground prior to their distinction leads Derrida to suggest that the distinction *presupposes* a hidden identity. As he says:

> What is *showing in general* prior to its division into indication by pointing with a finger *(Hinweiss)* to the unseen and into demonstration *(Beweiss)* as bringing into view with the evidence of a proof?[18]

The ultimate conclusions for Husserl's phenomenology, if Derrida is correct here, are not however our present concern. We do wish to show simply that Derrida's use of the *concept* of the concept is in this analysis of Husserl a key gesture within deconstruction itself.

(ii) From Chance to Necessity

In Derrida's analysis of Saussure he is concerned once again with that which is "hidden" below the surface, as it were, of Saussure's discourse itself. In Saussure's examination of the relation of speech to writing, he considers the following characteristics as essential: (i) that speech is more originary than writing; (ii) that writing is thus "exterior" to speech but used to supplement, imitate or copy it; (iii) that the model of writing is based on "phonetic" writing, since this is evidently close to the *phonè* of speech itself. Derrida considers these preconditions of Saussure's science of linguistics to be: (i) not arbitrary, yet (ii) not essential either. Paradoxically, Saussure considered them to be "natural" and therefore essential. The difference here is the difference between that which is "not capricious," yet that which can no longer be considered restrained or captured by the concept of nature.

In detail, Derrida's analysis takes the following form. He suggests that: "It is *not by chance* that the exclusive consideration of phonetic writing permits a response to the exigencies of the 'internal system'. The basic functional principle of phonetic writing is precisely to respect and protect the integrity of the 'internal system' of the language, even if in fact, it does not succeed in doing so." Further, "the Saussurian *limit does not respond by a mere happy coincidence* to the scientific exigency of the 'internal system'. That exigency is itself constituted as the epistemological exigency in general, by the very possibility of phonetic writing and by the exteriority of the 'notation' to internal logic."[19] We shall explore further Derrida's use of the metaphysical notion of the sign at a later stage, but here we should remark that Derrida is concerned to show the *necessity*—not metaphysical, yet also and necessarily metaphysical—which resides within and behind (indeed controls) a certain distinction and formulation in Saussure's project.

Saussure also considers writing as a problem and a threat to the interiority of speech and the *phonè*. This formulation also has a long tradition, Derrida reminds us, as he returns the frame to the text of Plato's *Phaedrus*. However, Saussure continues on to expose the problem of writing's possible "usurpation" of speech—as its replacement, representative, and finally its violent substitute. This moment is *no accident* either, Derrida insists. The fact that this is *possible* on the one hand, and indeed a constant threat, indicates a certain necessity also in this chance or apparently accidental, incidental situation. Derrida thus claims:

> . . . the "usurpation" of which Saussure speaks, the violence by which writing would substitute itself for its own origin, for that which ought not to have engendered it but to have been engendered from itself—such a reversal of power *cannot be an accidental aberration.* Usurpation *necessarily* refers us to a profound *possibility* of *essence.* This is without a doubt *inscribed* within speech and he *should have* questioned it; perhaps even started from it [my emphasis].[20]

We shall leave aside the injunction of "ought" here, but we cannot avoid remarking the invocation of the metaphysical injunction of "cannot be an accidental aberration" and the *necessity* to which this necessarily (it would seem) refers us. This ultimate necessity is, for Derrida, as he says, "a profound possibility of essence." Paradoxical conclusions to be sure, since it would seem that it is this "essential" structure that deconstruction aims to place in question. Derrida's reliance on the "structures of metaphysics" must not, however, suggest that he is a metaphysician plain and simple. Instead, or as well, his reliance is a certain *infidelity* and indeed an infidelity that he seems to be in search of with his "deconstructive gestures" as intrinsic, necessary, and essential to textuality or perhaps to the "act of writing" itself. As he says, he is concerned to reveal *laws,* economic relations, and certain *necessities* by deconstruction and therefore, in the process, "respects" and "uses" metaphysics itself. As a reminder of his notion of *différance* as it relates to metaphysics we suggest the following distinction: "The instituted trace is 'unmotivated' but not capricious. For us, the rupture of that 'natural attachment' places in question the idea of *naturalness* rather than that of *attachment*."[21] If we were to apply Derrida to Derrida here we might suggest a certain common ground between "natural" and "attachment" and indeed the revindication of "attachment" as *necessary* certainly presupposes a very particular structure and a very particular tradition. But we must return first to Derrida's other manners of usage or borrowing of the "tools of metaphysics."

(iii) The Form of the Question

The process of deconstruction of both Husserl and Saussure seems particularly concerned with the presentation of ideas or possibilities of interpretation in the form of questions. Indeed Derrida, as we have already shown, tends to focus on what he calls the "unasked questions," which seem to necessarily arise in the arguments he analyzes but which seem to have been "hidden from the view" of their respective authors. The significance of the "unasked questions" is always revealing for Derrida. But his own usage of the question explicitly seems a clear investment in the tools of metaphysics since the form of his questions almost always situates the responses within metaphysics itself. For example, the question "what is . . . ?" necessarily, Derrida himself tells us, situates the response within a metaphysical form so that one therein constitutes an "object" with an inside/outside, the possibility of presence and absence, a subject in relation to it, etc. "What is . . . ?" is thus the paradigm *par excellence* of the metaphysically structured question. The second most powerful metaphysical question must be that of "why?" or *"pourquoi?"* As Derrida once again tells us, this formulation depends on the metaphysical notions of sign, representation, teleology, a certain historicity, presence/absence, etc. Yet we shall find that Derrida himself in his analyses of Husserl and Saussure not only uses these forms but situates his arguments between one set of questions and another continually. The implications of such a framework seem perhaps self-evidently metaphysical, yet once again we should be cautious with such a readily available "usurpation" of Derrida here. The results of his use of metaphysics, even of the asking of these necessarily metaphysically framed questions, do not simply provide a *confirmation* of that same tradition. We shall see why presently, as the tenets of metaphysics begin to be revealed as in contradition (perhaps necessarily) with themselves. But first, the questions Derrida asks of Husserl and Saussure.

His questions for Husserl, predictably enough according to a certain homology of concern between Derrida and Husserl, focus very often on the issue of origin. Hence he asks: "From whence comes . . . ?" and "From whence . . . ?" In addition, he asks (concerning the authority which allows Husserl to do what he does): "How can one justify . . . ?" and "What gives its authority . . . ?"[22] Are these not metaphysically formulated questions? Do they not presuppose and therein preformulate and precondition their possible responses as necessarily metaphysical as well? As Derrida asks "From whence comes . . . ?" or "How can one justify . . . ?" he seems therefore to be presupposing something not presented as such yet: (i) more originary; and (ii) the basis of a certain authority, a certain power, or a certain governing. These assumptions are no accident, as we shall see later.

In his analysis of Saussure, Derrida typically asks the following sorts of questions: (i) "what has been invested . . . ?"; (ii) "what prohibition . . . ?"; (iii) "why determine . . . ?"; (iv) "why should the mother tongue . . . ?"; (v) "why should . . . ?"; and (vi) "why wish . . . ?"[23] *Why* indeed is the issue here once again. As Derrida tells us, "why" insists upon a hidden or presupposed *reason* for that which is given, and this reason is thus in a certain sense necessarily: (i) more originary, and (ii) a certain authority, power or controlling force behind that which appears. The parallel structure of the deconstructive gestures for Husserl's texts are striking and unavoidable here.

It is clear that Derrida is ultimately asking: What do these limits and presuppositions signify? And it is equally clear that his answer is both: (i) metaphysics and (ii) non-metaphysics. The "origin" of the origin is not an origin, we should recall, but rather it is *différance*. Further, it is clear that Derrida is concerned with a twofold revelatory procedure here. Initially he is concerned with the revelation of metaphysical determinations within a text, behind the back or hidden within that which a "writer controls" in his/her text. Secondly (and no less primarily), he is concerned with the origin and presuppositions or limits of that same metaphysics. Clearly then the asking of metaphysically formed questions sets up the possibility of the extension of our analysis and of looking beyond or beneath that same metaphysics. This will become increasingly clear as we proceed, we expect.

(iv) Conditions of Possibility

Derrida's questions are but one gesture in his search for the *conditions of the possibility* of the given text, argument, or stated intention of the author and in turn for the conditions of the possibility of those *same* conditions. However, this structure itself is not placed in question by Derrida, explicitly at least, as we shall see. Instead he seems to use it to its limits of possibility; indeed to "exhaust" it, as he says, and therein show its range of relevance in the revelation of the moment of irrelevance. We shall therefore attempt here to trace Derrida's invocation of this formulation (as evidently borrowed from Kant) and to show how this functions within what is becoming apparently a system of "deconstructive gestures."

As we have already shown by implication (though we have not thematized it as such), Derrida's approach to the text presupposes a certain duplicity of layers or levels within that same text. One level is the "given," and the second we might call its "conditions of possibility." The first three borrowed metaphysical structures analyzed here all lead to this level and open out onto its possibility or presupposition as such. Rather than analyze precisely what these conditions of possibility are (indeed this will be shown to be *différance* for Derrida, later in this project), we shall here attempt to expose the gesture of distinction introduced in Derrida's analyses which sets up or reveals a relation of dependence between the given (presented) level and the non-given (non-presented) but nonetheless essential second level.

In the deconstruction of Husserl, we find this gesture in search of the conditions of the possibility at work in the following ways. Derrida asks:

> *In view of what* is the structure of inner life here "simplified" and *for what* is the choice of examples *revealing* in Husserl's project [my emphasis]?[24]

Not only is the given textual structure considered a sign here, for Derrida, it is considered within a *teleological* system. The reasons for, as telos and origin, the way Husserl does what he does are clearly the concern of deconstruction in this instance. These reasons and this metaphysical organization of what might be termed the entelechy of the text under analysis are nothing less or other than its conditions of possibility.

Another indicative gesture in the search for "underlying conditions" is the *establishment* of a relation of *dependence.* For example, Derrida insists that the juridical value of the essential distinction in Husserl's phenomenology of *'le fait'* and *'le droit'* *"depends entirely* on language and within this, on the validity of the radical distinction between index and expression."[25] As we know, this "radical distinction" cannot be sustained, according to Derrida, and therefore since this distinction is the condition of the possibility of yet another distinction this latter can no longer be rigorously sustained either. Such is the apparent conclusion in this drama. It hinges upon the invocation of a hierarchical system of dependence, indeed of genealogy, one might call it, which once shown to be in a certain sense illegitimate can no longer serve to legitimate other terms or functions which *necessarily* depend on the same. Two movements of dependence are thus invoked at the same instant in this gesture. On the one hand, the necessity of the bond is invoked with *"dépend tout entière"* but, on the other hand, another distinction is therein eroded away. Thus it is clear that by invoking the structural necessity of "conditions of possibility" the deconstructive gesture *inverts* this same structure to illustrate precisely the "conditions of *im*possibility." The hinge for this demonstration, of course, is the issue of *legitimacy* or *validity,* as Derrida calls it. The presupposed metaphysical determination of "validity" clearly invoked here is not placed in question by Derrida except insofar as he is concerned with its "conditions of possibility" as well. This, as we shall see, is a much larger issue and indeed orients the entire movement of deconstruction itself. Yet another example of the invocation of the conditions of possibility in the deconstruction of Husserl reveals another "form" of positioning this question. As is well known, Husserl considers the possibility of the "absence of intuition" in the usage of discourse as not destructive or harmful to the meaning of that same discourse. In short, he invokes this possibility as a *possibility* and as a certain allowable situation. For Derrida, however, this opening is not simply one possibility among others but instead a sign of the conditions of the possibility of signification in general. Not only is the absence of the intuition of the object "spoken about" or referred to a structural condition for meaningful discourse, but also the absence of the subject—indeed "my death," as he says—is *structurally required.* In the shift from one characteristic among others to the level of essential preconditions, the deconstructive gesture is as follows:

> The absence of intuition—and hence of the subject of intuition—is not only tolerated by the discourse, it is *required* by the structure of signification in general [my emphasis].[26]

We should recall that Husserl "never asks the question" or even considers the possibility of the notion of "signification in general." Indeed Derrida points this out as revealing a certain absence of the questioning of Husserl's presuppositions which are thereby metaphysical ones. In this second gesture, built on the first, Derrida invokes metaphysics—signification *in general*—in order to show that Husserl does not extend or realize a certain shift in levels from message to code when he speaks of this absence. In addition, Derrida will continue to extend this issue, or circle back, to find absence at the heart of presence. We must not however follow that procedure at this juncture. Suffice it to say that in the end Derrida concludes: "This alterity itself is the condition of presence. . . ."[27]

With respect to Saussure we find the same Kantian structure at work in the deconstructive effort to separate, in a hierarchical fashion, elements which only apparently seem to be on the same level or logical type. For instance:

> I would wish rather to suggest that the *alleged derivativeness* of writing, however real and massive, *was possible only on one condition,* that the "original," "natural," etc., language had never existed, never been intact and untouched by writing, that it had itself always been a writing [my emphasis].[2]

The overlapping concern for absence in the heart of presence or full speech shall not be our primary focus here in relating this gesture to those in the deconstruction of Husserl. However, it is worthy of notice. As we have shown, Derrida is concerned with the "ethnocentric" gesture of including speech within the interiority of the *Logos* and Reason and indeed science and evidence, and simultaneously the exclusion of writing from the same. This gesture, in Saussure, of exclusion/inclusion has "conditions of possibility" Derrida insists, and once again these conditions of possibility reveal precisely the inverse of their apparently stabilizing claim—the conditions of the *im*possibility of that same distinction. Within this gesture, of course, we shall find a certain essence/appearance distinction being invoked, but we shall return to that shortly. For now, we wish to suggest the *paradox* within the deconstructive search for the conditions of possibility. The inverse of this form (once it is invoked) is no accident, as we shall see.

A final example of this structure will perhaps help to clarify this essentiality. Derrida, with reference to Saussure's fears concerning the threats and dangers of writing has claimed earlier that this *possibility* is no accident but rather the very fact of its possibility indicates something more. Once again possibility is changed or revealed to be essentiality and necessity.

> The scandal of "usurpation" invites us expressly and intrinsically to do that [problematize the relation of speech and writing]. *How was that trap and usurpation possible?* Saussure never replies to this question beyond a psychology of the passions or the imagination.

Further:

> What Saussure does not question here is the *essential possibility* of nonintuition [my emphasis].[29]

Thus the deconstructive gesture in this situation transforms what Saussure declares or states into a *result* or a product of something that he "does not question" and yet does indeed *thereby* describe. This duplicity will also provide us with *evidence* at a later stage concerning the role of contradiction and the laws of non-contradiction for textuality, for deconstruction. Suffice it to say that the invocation of conditions of possibility invokes thereby a certain *necessity* to the possibility and thus an essentiality to the conditions. Indeed how this "trap" is possible shall increasingly be the subject of our concern here.

(v) *The Syllogism*

The syllogism, in the tradition of Western thought, operates within a twofold possibility. One results in the *deductive* argument and the other in the *inductive*. Regardless of whether one proceeds from the general law to the particular example of it (deductively) or the reverse (inductively), one is locked, in this system, into a logic of premise and conclusion; a logic of necessity and ultimately of evidence and truth. Deconstruction is, of course, concerned to deconstruct this same tradition and to place in question the legitimacy or validity of this structure of argumentation. Not a vicious circle, to be sure, but a difficult one to trace. Our concern here, however, is to trace the appearance of this formulation within deconstruction itself. It will be shown indeed to be *borrowed,* as Derrida says, and yet once again to promote paradoxical conclusions with respect—predictably—to the legitimacy and validity (or truth) or deconstruction's results as such.

In a certain sense the style of deconstruction is consistently within this syllogistic structure as outlined above. It rarely deviates from this style of "argumentation" characteristic of metaphysics, and this in turn *allows* for a certain legitimacy of deconstruction in general within the tradition. However, this is not our concern here. Instead we propose to examine where deconstruction exposes the *need* for certain conclusions or consequences, according to the premises as given, but where such conclusions are not drawn. This absence is seen to be a certain *resistance* (by Husserl, for instance) and in turn a response to a certain *desire,* which once again is not by chance and therefore not reducible to the particularity of Husserl's desire. Specifically, Derrida suggests:

> The maintaining of this difference—in the history of metaphysics and also in Husserl—does it not respond to an *obstinate desire* to save presence and to reduce or derive the sign [my emphasis]?[30]

If this can be shown to be the case, that is, if Husserl's premises *should* lead us to another conclusion logically, then according to the principles and conditions of legitimacy, Husserl's argument must be revealed as "illegitimate." If it responds instead to a desire rather than to Reason, can we accept (in truth as truth) his conclusions? Yet, if these are to be our conclusions here, in accordance with Derrida, we find yet another paradox. All Reason is governed by Desire, for Derrida, and thus the illegitimacy, as the non-essential, non-necessity of Husserl's position is revealed as its inverse—essential and necessary but only, strictly that is, in accordance with the tenets of Reason. Derrida asks again,

> Why, from the same premises, does Husserl refuse to draw these consequences?

And he answers:

> It is because the motif of full presence, the intuitionist imperative and the project of knowledge continue to command—at a distance, let us say—the totality of the description. In one and the same movement Husserl describes and effaces the emancipation of the discourse as non-knowledge.[31]

Therefore Derrida will argue that the metaphysical demands are therein found to be not only operative but controlling Husserl's argumentation. Paradoxically, once again, we find that rather than thereby constituting a certain consistency (i.e., in accordance with the metaphysical demands of the syllogistic form of argumentation itself) this metaphysical governing (from within, as it were) is precisely that which sets Husserl off the track of metaphysics itself. The total control by metaphysics is never total, it would seem.

The deconstructive gestures of concern with the structure of argumentation appear perhaps more clearly with respect to the analysis of Saussure. We should recall that the process of using an example from which one generates a more general, indeed perhaps universal law or rule is known in traditional metaphysics as induction. In Derrida's choice of Saussure as a "telling example," therefore, he is forced to expose the reliance of deconstruction on this same structure.

> I obviously treat the Saussurian text at the moment only as *a telling example* within a given situation, without professing to use the concepts required by the functioning of which I have just spoken. [beyond metaphysics] My justification would be as follows . . . [my emphasis].[32]

And he continues to demarcate the reasons and range of deconstruction in general. The important point here is that the structure of "exemplarity" is invoked by deconstruction itself in order to show something within Saussure which extends beyond Saussure and indeed is indicative of "a general treatment of writing." Yet within Saussure's argument, deconstruction is concerned with the limitations of exemplarity itself as it necessarily moves from the specific particular case to the general, even universal law governing or ordering that same particular. With respect to Saussure's claims to found a *general* science of linguistics, therefore, deconstruction takes issue with the *basis* of this same generality. Phonetic writing is the *particular case* for Saussure, which is in turn, via the structure of exemplarity, transformed into the model for writing in general. It is no accident that this type of writing—phonetic—is the dominant mode in the western world, however. That this particular type of writing is used as the basis for a "general science of linguistics" in its concern with the relations of speech to writing in general is indicative for deconstruction that an *illegitimate,* dogmatic prejudice is at work. Thus, on the one hand, Derrida says,

> [the factor of phonetic writing] does not respond to any necessity of an absolute and universal essence. Using this as a point of departure, Saussure defines the project and object of *general* linguistics.[33]

But, on the other, he is concerned to show that this "dogmatism" (non-metaphysics) is not peculiar to Saussure. It is instead *exemplary:*

> This representative determination does not translate a choice or an evaluation, does not betray a psychological or metaphysical presupposition peculiar to Saussure; it describes or rather reflects the structure of a certain type of writing: phonetic writing, which we use and within

whose element the *epistème in general* (science and philosophy) and linguistics in particular *could* be founded.[34]

Thus the paradox of this deconstructive gesture is revealed. Derrida is concerned to show: (a) that the general science of linguistics is based on an example or model which is in no sense general; yet (b) that this situation itself—or using an illegitimate example as not in fact general but Western—is in fact general. It constitutes that which we call *generality* itself. The military form here is not by chance either. Thus the syllogism is used by deconstruction, it would seem, to show the illegitimacy of its own claims. This pattern will recur again shortly as we shall see.

(vi) The Criteria

Along with the deconstructive use of metaphysical forms of argumentation, the placing in question of exemplarity itself and the transformation of "chance" into necessity, deconstruction seems to invoke metaphysical *criteria;* that is, necessity as criteria as one of its tools. More specific than simply "conditions of possibility," the injunction of criteria seems to be a search for particular *rules* in operation within the text that allow for its development or functioning as such. We should recall that it is metaphysics that demands criteria for a system of argumentation and especially for conclusions drawn therefrom. Thus deconstruction's focus on this level seems to be the search for criteria which does not have the criteria of being legitimate or valid criteria, by definition. The criteria for deconstruction's usage here is of course, as stated initially, in a certain sense illegitimate (since it is a borrowed tool), yet in another sense the most rigorous and legitimate possible— indeed almost indistinguishable from metaphysics itself at this juncture.

Derrida not only uses the metaphysical notion of criteria, he is also in search of the same in his analyses of Husserl and Saussure. The criteria, or that which necessitates the "logic" of their argumentation will be shown to be, on the one hand, metaphysics itself, yet also, paradoxically, non-metaphysics as well. We might recall that one of the guiding threads or intentions of deconstruction itself is to "reveal the law of the relation between metaphysics and non-metaphysics." It is thus at this point in our analysis that this duplicity itself will begin to take on the form of a law, or at least it *should* if Derrida's "practice" here remains within the scope of his principles as outlined above.

In his analysis of Husserl we find certain indicative gestures which at the same time *demand* criteria that apparently are not legitimately (according to metaphysics) present and yet also rely on those same criteria to make the demands. For example, once Derrida has invoked the concept of the "sign in general" as lurking behind Husserl's distinction of "two types of signs" (indication and expression), he insists that the following conclusion must be drawn:

> Now *if* one admits, as we have attempted to show, that every sign in general has an originarily repetitive structure, the distinction between fictive and effective usage of the sign is threatened. The sign is originally wrought by fiction. From this point on, whether with respect to indicative communication or expression, there is *no sure criteria to distinguish* between *internal language* and *external language* [my emphasis].

Yet

> Such a distinction is however indispensable to Husserl.[35]

We should notice several metaphysical features of Derrida's line of argument here: First, the "if/then" structure as relying on 'premise/conclusion' or indeed a certain syllogistic formulation; second, the concept of the sign in general, as already mentioned; third, the usage of *"originairement"* is, it would seem, a euphemism in this context for the metaphysical term *essence* or even ontology; and fourth, the *telos* and origin of the argument itself entail a metaphysical or epistemological necessity; that is, the question of the certainty of criteria. Further, without such *grounds* or foundation Derrida insists: "In declaring the *illegitimacy* of this distinction one therein prescribes a chain of serious consequences for phenomenology."[36] The reliance on metaphysics at this point should also be transparent. The issue of criteria or necessity as necessarily linked with a certain *legitimacy,* indeed a *proper* relation, certainly seems paradoxical in the hands of Derrida. Finally, the (necessary) chain of consequences that would follow for phenomenology is certainly only in accordance with metaphysical claims of necessary logical structures. Yet all of this is precisely the *consistent* gesture of deconstruction itself, as we shall see shortly. The usage of metaphysics against itself, in this case Husserl against himself, will increasingly become our main concern. This structure, too, tends to repeat from one deconstruction to another.

Returning to Husserl for the moment, we find deconstruction again drawing the conclusions of a certain illegitimacy, indeed insecurity, in the heart of the foundations of phenomenology once another underlying metaphysical concept has been realized. In this case, it is the concept of 'life' which, as we have shown earlier, underlies the distinction of 'empirical life' and 'transcendental life', and which it seems to Derrida that Husserl overlooked. The consequences of this omission are threatening to the "rigor" and indeed very possibility of phenomenology, Derrida insists.

> In determining the "living" we begin to name therefore the *insecure resource* of discourse the precise point where it can *no longer be assured* of its possibility or its rigor within the nuance [my emphasis].[37]

Thus the issue of criteria becomes the issue of foundations in the deconstructive gesture here and in turn threatens the *criteria* for the same. If the ground of the ground can no longer be established as certain, rigorous, and within the bounds of metaphysics, on the one hand, yet these grounds are precisely within metaphysics, and it is this that menaces the Husserlian project, then, paradoxically, Derrida claims, the *basis* of the system must be realized as necessarily *illegitimate* according to its own principle and *a fortiori* according to the principles of metaphysical grounds and criteria in general. The meeting and the non-meeting of these criteria take place, however, on different levels as we shall see presently.

The question of "rights," as determined by metaphysics, also enters into the deconstructive gesture at this stage. Using metaphysics again Derrida insists that there is a "common root" (indeed a common origin or concept) which "retention" and "representation" share in Husserl's analysis, but it is one that the latter fails to expose or thematize as such. The lack of this exposure and yet the dependence thereon is of course significant for Derrida. Absence is always a sign for him, as we have shown. But in this particular case he continues further to draw what seem to be necessary conclusions according to a certain invocation of *rights*. The rights or criteria here are once again none other than those of metaphysics; in particular its determination of the structure of argumentation. The following statement reveals the open usage not only of this structure by Derrida but also of the terminology by which he formulates *his* chain of argument here:

> . . . one *should* be able to say *a priori* that their *common root*, the *possibility* of re-petition in the *most general form*, the trace of the most *universal* meaning is a possibility which ought to not only inhabit the pure actuality of the now, but *constitutes* it by the movement of difference itself which introduces it thereby [my emphasis].[38]

The "introduction" of *différance* at this moment shall occupy us shortly. At this point we wish only to show that the criteria for this deconstructive gesture here are; (i) metaphysical yet (ii) lead to the realm where these criteria not only no longer apply but which Derrida claims is their locus of origin or condition of possibility itself. One might consider the criteria of criteria here as the condition of the possibility and impossibility of criteria in general, therefore. One might also consider the conditions of the possibility of deconstruction here to be a certain *overdetermination* of the structure of metaphysics itself such that, when its own rules or principles are applied to its practice, the inconsistency between the two levels is therein revealed. And this inconsistency is not a simple contradiction (although it will appear initially as such) but rather an *economy;* a law-bound formulation or movement which, Derrida will claim, is the "becoming-form of form" or in Saussure's terms, the "becoming-sign of the symbol." The *process of detachment,* separation, exclusion, which (as will become increasingly evident) is never completely possible but necessarily (metaphysically, that is) presupposed. Let us return to Saussure for the moment and trace the path of these "criteria" for criteria which are essentially not criteria at all yet the only criteria possible, as this pattern parallels the same in Husserl.

The illegitimacy in Saussure's argumentation revolves around the "factor of phonetic writing," as announced earlier. For Derrida, this "does not correspond to any necessity of an absolute and universal essence."[39] Yet Saussure founds his *general* science of linguistics by using phonetic writing as his model for all writing in general. The usage, by Saussure in this case of the metaphysical structure of *induction* based upon an inadequate example is considered to be unfounded, illegitimate, and essentially non-essential but masquerading as essential, by Derrida. However, rather than objecting to the masquerade as such Derrida suggests that

> it is *right* to consider this teleology (of speech degenerating to writing) to be a Western ethnocentrism, a premathematical primitivism, and a preformalist intuitionism [my emphasis].[40]

It is *right,* he says. Right according to what? According necessarily to the criterion of judgment of metaphysics. Right in the sense of necessity. Derrida continues to show that the homology of phonetic writing and the scientific reliance on the *phonè* in relation to evidence is no accident, but rather responds to something essential within the determination of "scientificity" itself. But this essentiality is only essential within certain limits and boundaries. The infinity of the structure of essentiality is thereby placed in question here in the very recognition of the essential and necessary character of something that is neither essential nor necessary essentially and necessarily. As Derrida says,

> Even if this teleology responds to some absolute necessity, it should be problematized as such. The scandal of "usurpation" invites us expressly and intrinsically to do that.[41]

The value judgment invoked by the "scandal" in this gesture will be left in the margins for the moment but must be nonetheless noted as such. It does indeed lead to the non-metaphysical and perhaps non-borrowed grounds of deconstruction itself—its origin/*telos*/conditions of possibility (and impossibility, of course, at the same instant); in short, its illegitimacy according to the criteria set out by metaphysics of legitimacy. The "scandal of usurpation" will thus lead us to the conditions of the possibility of deconstruction itself, but we must remain with Saussure and his criteria for the moment here.

As with his analysis of Husserl, Derrida finds in Saussure the means of "opposing Saussure to himself" via the revealing of a hidden "common root" as the unacknowledged basis for a crucial distinction. Based on this "revelation," Derrida goes on to argue that a certain *necessary* consequence is therein realized:

> *If* one considers the now recognized fragility of the notions of pictogram, ideogram, etc., and the *uncertainty of the frontiers* between the so-called pictographic, ideographic and phonetic scripts, one realizes not only the *unwiseness of the Saussurian limitation* but the *need* for a general linguistics to abandon an entire family of concepts inherited from metaphysics . . . and clustering around the concept of arbitrariness [my emphasis].[42]

The *need* invoked here is clearly a result not only of the "recognition" Derrida points out, but also of certain metaphysical criteria invoked at once as the *basis* of Derrida's judgment here, and yet also, on another level, as the scandalizing force that is the cause of the illegitimacy of foundations herein revealed. Another paradoxical formulation and another paradoxical conclusion. The *need* here is double and divided, indeed perhaps even contradictory in its essence, as we shall see shortly. In fact if this is a *need* based on the criteria of necessity as determined by metaphysics, then a certain curious relation of *need* to *logic* seems to emerge here. The need for logic is perhaps the logic of need, just as Derrida will later claim the Desire in Reason is the Reason of Desire, and the hinge between superstition and science is what he calls the "hermeneutic compulsion."[43]

A final example of the illegitimate criteria of criteria in Saussure for the deconstructive desire involves the significance of the *tone* of argumentation, for Derrida. It is, at one point not so much *what* is being said as the *way* it is being said which is crucial for him. The *tone* of Saussure's "vehement argumentation" thus represents for Derrida a certain adherence to a traditional fear, a traditional tone, and indeed a metaphysically informed and organized tonality as such. Derrida begins:

> Thus incensed, Saussure's vehement argumentation aims at more than a theoretical error, more than a moral fault: at a sort of stain and primarily at a sin.[44]

The indication provided by Saussure's tone here is none other than the metaphysical denunciation of the body and a heightened concern with the purity of the mind and the sphere of the spiritual. Analogous to this, Derrida claims, is the determination of the speech/writing relation such that speech is allotted a privileged, prior, interior position, yet is thereby threatened with contamination from the body proper of writing and the sign as such. The tone counts, therefore, for the deconstructive gesture here of unravelling, *by analogy,* the hidden criteria, which are essentially, Derrida will show, not criteria at all (in the logical sense) but responses to desires, fear, etc. As he says:

> The contamination by writing, the fact or the threat of it, are denounced in the accents of a moralist or a preacher by the linguist from Geneva. *The tone counts;* it is as if at the moment when the modern science of the logos would come into its autonomy and its scientificity, it became *necessary* again to attack a heresy [my emphasis].[45]

We find the *same tone* concerning the "threat of writing" to "pure speech" as far back as Plato's *Phaedrus,* Derrida insists, and it is thus this same tradition that Saussure is bound to here and in fact is representing by the *tone* of his "vehement argumentation." We shall not pursue the tone of the deconstructive gesture here but suggest that this too is not irrelevant or insignificant in this context. That line of argument would lead us to a deconstruction of deconstruction—borrowing its tools which, as we are trying to show here, are already borrowed from metaphysics itself—and this is not our present concern.

It is clear at this point that the *criteria of necessity,* in accordance with metaphysics, are at once invoked by deconstruction with respect to Saussure and Husserl and used to reveal that it is precisely these criteria as the foundation for argumentation which neither Saussure nor Husserl fully adhere to. Their projects instead seem to rely on other, unacknowledged metaphysical foundations which, due to this hidden side, therein become illegitimate and undermine the logicity of the arguments as presented. This twofold layering of the textual contradiction, which seems to be the *focus* or center for deconstructive gestures in general, will now be our focus of concern here. Once again we should recall the principle of deconstruction which aims to reveal "that which a writer controls and that which he or she does not control of the patterns of language that he or she uses" and to show that this relation is not accidental, capricious, or random. Instead it will be precisely the *"economy of différance"* itself, as we shall attempt to prove as we follow the track of deconstruction itself.

(vii) Principles of Non-contradiction

> And if it is impossible for contradictories to be at the same time true of a given thing, it is evident that contraries too, cannot at the same time be true of it.
>
> Hence, either what is is affirmed or denied, or else what is not is affirmed or denied. (There can be no middle ground.)
>
> Aristotle[46]

Despite appearances, perhaps, the gestures of deconstruction concerning the approach to contradiction remain strictly within and true to this initial proclamation of the "principle of non-contradiction" by Aristotle. As we shall see, Derrida uses this principle in order to reveal: (i) a certain necessity of contradiction within textuality; (ii) a certain hierarchy in the relation of the two opponents; and (iii) the basis for the deconstructive gesture of aiming to "oppose the author to himself." The premise for this gesture might be considered the following claim made by Derrida himself: "No practice is ever totally faithful to its principle."[47] As we already know, it is the relation of fidelity to infidelity that concerns Derrida with respect to the tradition of metaphysics itself. With this in mind, his approach to both Husserl and Saussure invokes the principle of non-contradiction in order to legitimate or validate one of the contraries and in turn to invalidate or overturn the legitimacy of the other. Nevertheless, deconstruction intends, as we shall demonstrate, to sustain *both* aspects, both the legitimate and illegitimate claims made "by the text" in order to provoke the appearance of the *tension* that is the "play of différance" itself. This tension is increased in the deconstructive gesture at this point so as to draw "inverse" conclusions from the same given premises in each text, respectively. The inversion will in turn be shown to be a *sign* for something else which in itself is *not contradictory* and which in fact reveals the truth of the "only apparent" (in some ways) contradiction initially revealed. We shall attempt to follow this twofold process specifically in our two deconstructive examples and shall therein expose the logic of the logic of non-contradiction, at least according to Derrida. A final note of caution seems warranted here, however. To show the reliance of deconstruction on the principle of non-contradiction reveals its adherence, indeed its membership, within the tradition of metaphysics, properly speaking. But once again this is to be considered a means to an end, for Derrida, and not an end in itself, as we shall attempt to demonstrate in the following.

In the treatment of Saussure deconstruction claims to expose the following contradiction and its necessity:

> What Saussure saw without seeing, knew without being able to take into account, following in that entire metaphysical tradition, is that a certain model of writing was necessarily but provisionally imposed . . . as instrument and technique of representation of a system of language.[48]

In effect, therefore, deconstruction here is aiming towards that which Saussure "described and effaced at the same instant." That which he "sees without seeing" is that which his discourse writes, or is "written in the text," but which contradicts and indeed thereby undercuts his explicit, declared intentions. In short, the limits are beginning to show here for deconstruction. What this means is that two levels of textuality are beginning to appear and that these levels are in opposition to each other in more than one respect, such as: (a) conscious/ unconscious and (b) the level of theoretical claims as such and their manner of appearance or, if one prefers, a form/content distinction. The initial concern of deconstruction was the "stated intentions" of Saussure, we should recall, and what these intentions or statements of purpose and hence limits of the project indicated, presupposed, or necessitated. Now we have an apparent inversion within the text itself ("there is nothing outside of the text") of this intention which leads deconstruction towards the "contradiction." As Derrida says,

> But conversely . . . it is when he is not expressly dealing with writing, when he feels he has *closed* the parenthesis on that subject, that Saussure *opens* the field of a general grammatology [my emphasis].[49]

Thus it is what happens "behind the back" of the author here that seems to be of great importance for deconstruction. Indeed Saussure is credited with having "opened the field of a general grammatology," albeit without having "known what he was doing" and indeed having *intended* precisely the *reverse,* (at least according to reversed premises with respect to the priority of speech over writing, etc.). As we know it is the *closing* that *opens* which is always significant for deconstruction. The gesture here which seems contradictory is thus *embraced,* on the one hand, yet overcome, on the other, since evidently a "general science of linguistics," as explicated and intended by Saussure, cannot be simultaneously sustained with a general grammatology. Or at least not on the face of things. We shall see in the next section precisely how deconstruction does indeed *intend* to do this by a very specific act of "usurpation." But for the present, we must remark upon the double usage or use and abuse apparently of the "principle of non-contradiction." It seems to be abused (closing = opening) in the service of its ultimate sustenance, as we shall see again and again in this demonstration. For instance, concerning Saussure's problematic exclusions of the usurpation of speech by writing, Derrida says,

> . . . this explanation *excludes* all possibility of some natural relationship between speech and writing *at the moment* that it *affirms* it. Instead of deliberately dismissing the notions of nature and institution that it constantly uses, which ought to be done first, it confuses the two [my emphasis].[50]

Thus Saussure is seen here to violate his own exclusion and to violate the principal characteristic of metaphysics, which necessitates a certain distinction between nature and culture (or institution) which Saussure nevertheless depends upon. This "confusion," deconstruction will claim, is not without Reason or law. The coincidence of affirming and denying or including and excluding is the link to the principle of non-contradiction upon which deconstruction is based at this point. The raising of this issue *as* a *contradiction* thus becomes an *objection* at the same instant, according to the tradition of metaphysics or of legitimate argumentation, in particular with respect to the founding of a "new science." Thus Saussure seems to violate the conditions of the possibility of scientificity of his project itself. This violation is the strength of his text, for deconstruction, and not the reverse as we shall see.

The key principle or premise which allows deconstruction to show the "inverse" conclusions necessarily in Saussure is the notion of the "arbitrariness of the sign." If there is no natural bond between the sign and the thing signified, then the former cannot be considered an "image" or re-presentation of the latter. However Saussure seems to want to have it both ways in the following sense: He argues for the distance or arbitrary relation of the sign to that which it signifies, on the one hand, yet insists: (i) that writing remains a constant threat to speech; (ii) that writing is a sign for speech (consistant with the tradition of metaphysics); and (iii) that the threat posed by writing is necessarily accidental, since the two systems are not tied by any natural, that is necessary, bond. To be sure this might remind us of the "logic of the dream," as Freud has illustrated, in the sense of its apparent double-binds concerning the necessary and arbitrary characteristics of the sign and in particular the *relation* of speech to writing. In response to this "contradiction," Derrida says:

> One might therefore *challenge* in the very name of the arbitrariness of the sign, the Saussurian distinction of writing as 'image'—hence as natural symbol—of language [my emphasis].[51]

In addition, for Derrida, we never have neither a pure sign nor a pure symbol, but a continual process of the "becoming-sign of the symbol." This, as we shall see, is the paradoxical work of *différance*. At this point, however, the deconstructive gesture consists of recording the double invocation of nature or necessity and "the arbitrary" or accidental concerning the *same* relation at the same instant. Quite simply, this situation is a contradiction in terms. But what it means, for deconstruction, is that "what Saussure saw without seeing" was a certain *necessary* attachment (neither natural nor arbitrary) of the sign to the symbol, of writing to speech, and of presentation to representation. This conclusion *unites* the apparent contraries in a broader, wider context or field which, as we shall see shortly, "opens the field of grammatology." It is no accident that Derrida, with respect to this context in particular, argues for the *necessity* of usurpation once it has been shown to be *a priori possible.* The transformation of possibility into necessity will be gradually revealed as the inner coherence and consistency of an apparent initial contradiction. Nonetheless, it is clear that the logic of non-contradiction is here used to *show* a certain *illegitimacy,* according to metaphysics, in Saussure's argumentation.

Returning to the deconstruction of Husserl, we find the "same" process of the double usage of the principle of noncontradiction within Husserl's text and in the deconstructive gesture applied to it. Once again we initially find a discrepancy between Husserl's explicitly stated intentions and the conclusions one could necessarily draw from his own premises. More specifically, concerning the issue of the "absence of intuitions" and the meaingfulness of the sign, Husserl allows for the former within the realm of the latter. Yet this seems to be in *contradiction* with his own premises concerning the nature of the sign and its relation to ideality. The issue for Derrida here is precisely the conditions of the possibility of *repeatability,* and it is this that Husserl at once provides us with and yet later seems to violate. For instance:

> *Does Husserl not contradict* that which he had established concerning the difference between *Gegenstandlosigkeit* and *Bedeutungslosigkeit* when he writes: "the word 'I' names according to the situation, a different person each time and it does this by means of a continually new *Bedeutung*"?

Further:

> Does Husserl not contradict that which he affirms concerning the independence of the intention and the fulfilling intuition in writing: "That which each time constitutes its [the word 'I's] *Bedeutung* can only be living discourse and the intuitive givens one partakes of"?

And finally:

> Husserl's premises should have authorized us to say exactly the *opposite* [my emphasis].[52]

And exactly the opposite here (which would be legitimate) would be to recognize that the very *possibility* of non-intuition is the condition of the possibility of *Bedeutung* and not its abnormal, unusual, barely acceptable accidental situation. The very fact that we do understand the word "I" in the situation of the person's absence, fictionality, or death is testament to the fact, Derrida insists. Indeed that *death* characterizes the condition of the possibility of the sign is more precisely the absence that Husserl leads us toward yet which he then covers up again by drawing illegitimate, non-logical conclusions. The deconstructive gesture here is revealed once again in its use of the principle of non-contradiction against Husserl initially, but then to reveal a deeper, more profound consistency. The contradiction in the deconstructive gesture here, however, seems to be the following: (i) it condemns Husserl for not being faithful to his premises, that is, for violating the tenets of metaphysics; yet (ii) it condemns Husserl for being all too true to the presuppositions and preconditions of metaphysics itself. Indeed it finds metaphysics and non-metaphysics at the heart of Husserl's attempt to avoid the same and to establish a phenomenology prior to those same principles. Deconstruction here seems to be caught in a double-bind, until one realizes or recalls that it aims to reveal precisely this relation between "metaphysics and non-metaphysics" which is at one level a contradiction and yet at another not a contradiction at all. The relation of these levels is one of "mutual exclusion" within metaphysics and of mutual inclusion "beyond metaphysics." This too might be considered a contradiction, except that we shall see it more precisely described as an *economy*—as a play of presence and absence that, paradoxically to be sure, takes on a very definite, unified, consistent, and indeed *repeating* and repeatable *form*. This *parallel* to the structure of metaphysics itself is no accident.

The overturning of the intentions of the author in this context is not a simple rejection however, and this will be shown more explicitly in the next section. At the moment we should consider the image of *inversion* in the constitution of the contradiction that deconstruction seems to reveal at this juncture. Derrida's claims to draw *inverse conclusions* from the same premises stated by Husserl must be examined more closely. He says the following:

> One proceeds thus—contrary to the explicit intention of Husserl—to make the *Vorstellung* itself as such depend upon the possibility of repetition and the most simple *Vorstellung*—presentation—depend on the possibility of repetition and not the inverse. One derives the presence-of-the-present from repetition and not the inverse.[53]

Paradoxically by claiming "and not the inverse," the deconstructive gesture here is precisely to do what it seems to claim not to do—to invert. The style is significant here, since what appears as an explicit negation is in fact an affirmation. Granted the one side of the coin is attributed to Husserl and the other to deconstruction, but this process itself seems to link deconstruction to Husserl in a profound and perhaps unacknowledged respect. We might well ask: How is this inversion possible? On what grounds can deconstruction claim to invert a condition of dependence, indeed a hierarchical relation, so that the necessary conclusions to be drawn from Husserl's premises are the *inverse* of the latter's conclusions? On what grounds or by what criteria, therefore, *can* deconstruction operate in such a manner on the text of its choice? The paradoxical answer is certainly in accordance with the tenets of metaphysics, as we maintained from the outset. Deconstruction does not claim to violate metaphysics from without but to "faithfully repeat it in its totality" and to "make it insecure in its most secured self-evidences." Thus in applying the principle of non-contradiction to an apparent contradiction, two levels of legitimacy seem to be placed in question which include: (i) the legitimacy of explicit conclusions as drawn by the author; and (ii) the legitimacy of the principle of non-contradiction itself, as a principle, since it seems to be revealed as self-contradictory at this point. The inner contradiction of "non-contradiction" is that the shift to a vision of *levels* or logical types breaks the double bind and only apparently opposing forces. The "other" discreetly shifts to the background as the "same" moves into the field of vision. This play of contradiction and inversion will be shown itself to be irreducible for Derrida, *différance* and *a fortiori* deconstruction. Thus in turn and all the more paradoxically, it seems that the principle of non-contradiction, despite or perhaps because of *its* contradictory nature (as characteristic), is vindicated as essential after all. This contradiction may be the principal hinge which allows for or is the condition of the possibility and hence impossibility of deconstruction itself. It is still, however, too early to tell.

(VIII) Essence and Appearance

The founding opposition of the tradition of metaphysics, for Derrida, is that of form and content or form and matter, an opposition which is henceforth transformed into mind/body, presentation/representation, and ultimately essence and appearance. We should not necessarily, therefore, find it ironic that this opposition, too, shall be borrowed within the work of deconstruction itself. It could only be consistent to find this pattern as one of the animating structures of the very project which aims to undo this same structure by its very usage and "exhaustion." The deconstructive usage is however distinguishable, on the one hand, from the metaphysical usage in that, as one might expect, the *priority* of form is reversed or inverted in favor of that which appears at least to be a certain priority of content, or a priority of appearance over that of essence. We shall see that this is not in fact the case, but that this is necessarily the initial appearance of any attempt to overcome that same opposition. The appearance of reversal is, in addition, as we shall attempt to explain more fully later, the unavoidable legacy of the metaphysical predetermination and predestination of our mode of understanding and usage of discourse in the Western world.

In order to reveal this pre-established system of presuppositions as (i) one system among others, and hence (ii) not the only possible or essential mode of understanding or analysis, deconstruction in this context proposes another twofold process. Initially, that which will appear as the essence of the given text or its underlying law or necessity, its system of presuppositions as metaphysically determined, will be made apparent. Secondly the conditions of these conditions or "essence" of this essence will then be addressed, and, in so doing, the deconstructive gesture exposes the limits of the metaphysical system itself as it begins to contradict its own premises and its own laws of functioning. The Hegelian claim that "the essence of essence is appearance and thus the appearance of essence is essence" will not be the principle behind this deconstructive gesture, however, despite appearances. Instead, the very economy of essence/appearance will itself be placed in question or suspended in the same moment that deconstruction itself depends entirely on that system or economy. This duplicity should come as no surprise at this juncture.

In order to reveal this deconstructive gesture as such, we propose to examine: (i) the instances of its explicit occurrence in the analyses of Husserl and Saussure, and (ii) the instances of its necessary presupposition in the deconstructive gestures analyzed above. It is, in fact, a rare occurrence when Derrida explicitly uses the terminology of "essence" and "appearance" or "form" and "content" in his analyses, but this, of course, makes his reliance on this structure nonetheless pertinent and perhaps even more so.

In the deconstruction of Husserl, Derrida draws the following conclusion:

> The dominance of the now not only forms a system with the founding opposition of metaphysics, that is, of *form* and *content*. . . . It assures the tradition which sustains metaphysics.[54]

Thus we have the paradox revealed in Husserl's phenomenology that, despite his attempt to "bracket out" or reduce all metaphysical presuppositions in order to reach unmediated knowledge, Husserl's project and its presuppositions, in fact, confirm and assure the tradition of metaphysics itself. We should recall that Derrida makes no such claim of exclusion or purity for deconstruction but, in fact, proclaims precisely the reverse, although with an eye to the movement toward a "detachment" from the metaphysical concepts on which it depends. Therefore, the following usage of the form/content system of analysis against Husserl should come to us as no surprise:

> In spite of the motif of the punctual now as the arche-form of consciousness, the contents of the description in the *Lessons* and elsewhere, prohibit one to speak of a simple presence identical to itself.[55]

Within this deconstructive gesture we find not only the form/content (in the name of *"motif/contenu"*) distinction applied, but also a certain *valorization* of the latter as against the former. The *contents* seem to overturn the form in this instance, since they *prohibit* or in fact delegitimize a formulation that Husserl professed earlier in his work concerning the presence of consciousness to itself in the instant of absolute evidence or truth. The "legitimacy" or the conditions for this valorization, or, in fact, *inversion* of a given valorization by Husserl, are not however addressed by Derrida here. This issue will surface again in the context of his presuppositions which ground the former seven deconstructive gestures.

In the analysis of Saussure we find the phrase "reason of essence" invoked as a ground for the findings of deconstruction. As we have shown, Derrida is concerned here with the limits of the model and the presuppositions therein of phonetic writing for the "general science of linguistics" that Saussure proposes. As we have also shown, Derrida explains that this model does not respond to any necessity and by implication carries with it a certain dogmatism and indeed essentially a certain ethnocentrism. In addition, deconstruction claims: "that this model is an ideal explicitly directing a functioning which in fact is never completely phonetic. *In fact,* but also for *reasons of essence* to which I shall frequently return."[56] Indeed. The deconstructive gesture here seems to *equate* "fact" or appearance and "essence," or at least to find them coincident. The paradox of this equation or apparent leveling of what is (by metaphysics' definition) a hierarchical formulation is that

Derrida will insist that the *essentiality* in Saussure's project is one of historically situated contiguity, in fact, and that this has been defined as essentiality itself. Hence the neutrality or the universality of "essentiality" is itself placed in question, since it can no longer be used, according to Derrida, as an unlimited, indeed universal, atemporal, aspatial, radically decontextualized, or decontextualizing notion. In fact it is precisely the reverse, as we have shown.

The deconstructive gestures above, although not explicitly invoking the terminology of essence and appearance do, in fact, necessarily rely on this framework for the following reasons: the above gestures are all structures borrowed from metaphysics and since the form/content opposition is (according to Derrida) the founding one of that same structure, then by definition this particular opposition forms the ground, conditions of possibility, necessity, law, criteria, form of the form of the questions, the basis of the syllogism and certainly that of the "concept in general." Indeed the metaphysics of metaphysics might most appropriately name the conditions of the possibility or "essence" of deconstructive gestures themselves. What concerns us here however is not simply the coherence of the system of metaphysics itself, as borrowed *in toto* by deconstruction, but rather how and why in effect this "borrowing" procedure *inverts* that same structure and hence promotes results which do indeed "deconstruct the tradition of metaphysics" yet remains true to its principles in the most faithful, repetitive manner.

The gestures of the constitution of a "concept in general," the movement from "chance" to "necessity," the search for the "conditions of possibility" and for "criteria" all invoke a necessary duplicity of the text under analysis such that one *level* is inconsistent with or *differs* from the other. In addition, one level is considered the appearance, for deconstruction, and the other, that which it finds hidden "within what is written," is considered the essence, in a certain sense. This second level, the product or result of the work of deconstruction, is not an essence in the sense of being the law of the text, but rather is the condition of the possibility of revealing the "true" law of the text—the *relation* between the two levels or what we shall call the *economy of différance.*

Thus revealing the conditions of possibility or essence at one level or initially is only the first of a two-step process once again. In the second "step back" or questioning of the grounds therein revealed, the deconstructive gesture transforms the "revealed essence" into a "revealed but *mere* appearance" and turns instead towards yet another hidden level—the *true* essence. It seems evident therefore that in this process the following double relation of metaphysics to deconstruction can be revealed: (i) the *repetition* of the metaphysical gesture of the transformation of appearance into essence in fact seems to *invert* this same structure; yet (ii) the essence, to the second power, (as it were) can no longer be called an essence properly (that is metaphysically) speaking; hence (iii) the essence/appearance structure is vindicated with respect to the first "deconstructive" gesture here and, in turn, overcome with respect to its claims to universality as identical to essentiality. In short, the limits of that which is defined by metaphysics as limitless begin to appear in this process. Indeed deconstruction's second step in this process takes us out, down or up to a realm which metaphysics does not and indeed cannot define. It is from this "realm," which it is the telos of the work of deconstruction to reveal, that Derrida will insist requires not a "new set of concepts," but a new way of using the old ones—a new posture, a new position which will no longer be simple, present, or originary, but which *grounds* all of these in their innermost possibilities. We shall return to this "usurpation" of metaphysics in the process of revealing its limits in our next section.

The usage of the essence/appearance distinction also appears with respect to the borrowing of the principle of non-contradiction and of the syllogism for perhaps the most obvious of reasons. The syllogism, as we have shown, depends upon, if not the concept as such, at least its possibility. Indeed it presupposes and constitutes the concept as such in its establishment of a necessary relation between the particular and the universal. In turn, therefore, the deconstructive gesture of using the syllogism and of analyzing, for instance, a "telling example" shows the limits of *generalizability*—or syllogisticity—in the very act of Derrida's own generalization from that same example. This of course has already arisen in our analysis of Saussure.

The principle of non-contradition also relies on the essence/appearance distinction, not only to reveal the contradiction as such, but also to establish a resultant valorization of one "side" over the other—one is essential and the other mere appearance. But again this is only the first of a two-step process for deconstruction. The valorization of the "practice" as being "untrue" to its principles, or of the unwittingly described aspect of a text as contrary to its explicitly declared intentions leads not to the overcoming of the opposition or a simple *Aufhebung* or capture of one side by the other as the *law* of its possibility. Indeed this occurs, but in addition the "other side" is revealed as no less essential—indeed neither is the essence—but what is ultimately and necessarily revealed here will be shown to be the "origin" and "ground" of this duplicity itself. Predictably enough, this will be called *différance.* It is significant here, however, to realize that the *double gesture* of deconstruction is again realized. This is not only a repetition, therefore, of the "structure of metaphysics," but a repetition of a repetition; and it is this second-order repetition that creates the *inversion,* we suggest. The criterion for repetition, however, as we know from Derrida and *a fortiori* from Husserl, is a certain *ideality.* The condition of the possibility of repeatability is thus a certain metaphysical structure. At this juncture one might wonder whether deconstruction's "open admission" that it intends to 'borrow the structures of metaphysics' and to 'repeat' them 'faithfully' indeed takes this *second order* borrowing into account. If so, then what must be recognized *a priori* and from within is the very impossibility of the deconstructive project ever being realized as such. That is, the detachment from metaphysics is not only slow but is, in fact, an infinite task. It is an Idea in the Kantian sense, therefore, and indeed thereby, no more possible than impossible on the level of factuality or appearance and *a fortiori* on the level of essence or principles. With this second order *attachment* to metaphysics by deconstruction, we shall approach the final, for the moment, borrowed structure, which inhabits deconstruction as much as deconstruction inhabits it, we suggest. This structure is predictably the ultimate target for the deconstructive project itself—the metaphysical determination of the notion of the *sign.*

(ix) The Sign of Metaphysics

> It is thus the *idea of the sign* that must be *deconstructed* through a meditation upon writing which would merge, as it must, with the undoing of onto-theology, *faithfully repeating* it in its totality and making it insecure in its most assured evidences [my emphasis].[57]

For Derrida, the idea of the sign, according to metaphysics, involves the following characterizations: (i) a certain derivativeness or secondariness; (ii) a lack or absence; (iii) a duplication of something else, but inadequately done; (iv) a representation of a more originary presentation; and hence, (v) a certain inessentiality in its relation to that which it "re-presents." It is the sign, metaphysics insists, which is the origin of the contamination of purity—in all its forms—and especially with respect to that founding opposition we have just addressed, namely, form and content or essence and appearance. In turn the notion of writing, as a sign for full speech and that interiority wherein truth, evidence, and first principles are to be found and situated, has always been relegated to this secondary and inessential position. Thus Derrida insists that with the deconstruction of "writing," as the sign for the sign *par excellence,* the restitution of the essential place of the sign (indeed paradoxically as essential and irreducible) will be possible. Of course this opposition too must be overcome for Derrida, but we should recall that the apparent *reversal* of the metaphysical hierarchy is always the first stage of the deconstructive process. What we aim to demonstrate here, however, includes the following: (i) that deconstruction itself "borrows" this same notion of the sign which it aims to deconstruct and considers inappropriate in its very appropriation by metaphysics; and (ii) that the deconstructed notion of the sign and *a fortiori* of writing does indeed entail a radical shift from this earlier metaphysical position. The results of the deconstructive practices here will thus be shown to undermine (in a certain sense) the apparent conditions of the possibility of deconstruction itself. It is perhaps not a process whose results allow for its own repetition; yet, as we have demonstrated, the deconstructive gestures, to this point at least, do indeed show signs of repetition and therefore repeatability and, in turn, necessarily of a certain (although perhaps limited) *ideality.* If indeed this ideality in the heart of deconstruction can be demonstrated, as we are here attempting, then a certain profound *attachment* to metaphysics itself will therein be revealed as unavoidable on the one hand and necessarily essential on the other: an *essential contamination* which would therein confirm the initial claims and principles stated by Derrida in the process of deconstruction itself.

That deconstruction "borrows" or uses the metaphysical notion of the sign should perhaps by now be rather obvious. Each of the above "metaphysical structures" analyzed as being relied upon by deconstructive gestures can be shown to depend on this same metaphysical idea of the sign. The basic structure of the sign is a twofold one that thereby entails a certain division which is of a hierarchical and temporal nature. The hierarchy involves a certain primordial character given to that "for which" the sign stands—its origin and telos. The temporality of this relation involves the temporal *ordering* of the hierarchy such that the *non-sign* is always and necessarily the origin, as if by genealogy or filiation, of the *sign*. In short, the non-sign is the father and the child of the sign. Explicitly (within metaphysics as such) we have only the recognition of paternity and dependence here, not the reversal or extension of the relation entailed by the recognition of the double nature of the sign. Thus the non-sign as child is left suspended or bracketed out at this juncture but will be revealed by the deconstruction of the same.

The sign, for metaphysics, is, however, not a passive or neutral entity despite (and indeed because of) its "dependence" and secondariness. The inadequacy that characterizes the "sign" inscribes a certain bastardization, a certain illegitimacy and thus perversion or distortion of that which it signifies or represents. Indeed, it is the paradoxical role of the *copy* that the sign is made to play here. As we know from Plato, the good copy is a bad copy and necessarily vice versa. Thus it would seem that a double bind of adequacy and inadequacy characterizes the sign as well. Its proper function is necessarily that of *impropriety,* since it is not and can never be its own origin. Derrida's analysis of Reason for Hegel reveals the paradox of the "*Logos* believing itself to be its own father,"[58] but we must leave this issue aside for the moment. It will appear in greater detail within the realm of *différance.*

As we have shown, the sign for metaphysics is neither passive nor weak but rather provides a "supplement" to the origin which is, on the one hand, a positive addition *complementing* the former; but also and at the same time, Derrida will insist, its very supplementary function therein *threatens* that same origin it came along to assist. The representation can be and indeed is very often mistaken for the thing itself— in fact substitutes itself for it, represents it and thereby becomes "a force of its own." Before turning to the "deconstructed notion of the sign," which is already emerging here, we must consider the former deconstructive gestures in the light of this initial characterization of the sign.

Does Derrida not approach the text to be analyzed, its explicit intentions, its delimitation of its problematic, its asked and unasked questions as *signs* for something else which would be: (i) more *originary;* (ii) hidden yet signaled by the given; (iii) the origin and *telos* by way of presuppositions and assumptions of the given text; (iv) that which is threatened by that same system of signs as given which is known as the text? This latter characteristic shall be shown to *invert* the deconstructive claims, on the one hand, and also thereby to sustain and indeed legitimize them at the same time, as we shall proceed to explain.

It has already been shown that the deconstructive gestures above initiate a twofold process which is in search of a second but radically first level of the given text and that this radically first level is the prescription for the apparently first. It is, in short, the origin. If this were *simply* the case, however, we would find no difference between the deconstructive gestures and those of metaphysics, but in fact this is not the final word in our analysis. Instead, by the usage of this "sign" structure, deconstruction shows, contrary to metaphysics, that: (i) the sign is irreducible; (ii) there is a *necessary* relation between the "sign" and the "thing signified"; (iii) the thing signified is *also* a sign essentially and thus (iv) the relation between the representer and represented is not only one of *sign to sign* (the basis of meaning itself) but also forms an economy whose laws can be revealed and charted, indeed marked, by the work of deconstruction as such.

This deconstructed notion of the sign is thus not simply the return to an origin or to the thing-in-itself. Instead it reveals the constitution of the "origin plain and simple" as a *result* of the sign function, which in turn *effaces* that same signification infrastructure. Thus in appearance we have the thing-in-itself, for Derrida. But in appearance, to the second power, that is, on closer inspection or when we look *again:* "The thing in itself always escapes," he insists.[59]

In order to analyze more closely the results of these deconstructive gestures, we must consider the act of *usurpation* (another ultimately metaphysical gesture, we might add) as it relates to the revelation of *différance* at the heart of presence and *a fortiori* of *différance* itself as that which is necessarily "plus 'originaire' que l'originarité."[60] This usurpation of metaphysics within the economy of *différance* will appear, at first glance, not unlike the *Aufhebung* in Hegel's dialectical system. Indeed the usage by deconstruction of the "principle of non-contradiction" in its search for textual contradictions between "declarations" and "descriptions" will confirm such an analogy with Hegel. However, this interpretation of the economy herein realized should be suspended for the moment at least lest we "usurp" all too rapidly the *différance* aimed at by deconstruction within traditional metaphysics. We should recall that in the analysis of Saussure, Derrida insists that the usurpation (of speech by writing) that frightens the former should not be considered an "unhappy accident." Instead its essentiality must be realized. Indeed, in this analysis of the deconstructive gestures as they *necessarily* relate and are hinged upon (for better or for worse) the structures of metaphysics, we are proposing the same thing in reverse: not that the usurpation of metaphysics by *différance* is necessary and unavoidable, but rather that the *necessity of the attachment* that allows for both metaphysics and *différance* must be realized. It is this attachment which we shall henceforth refer to as the *economy of différance.*

(d) Reaffirming the Deconstructed: Usurpation Revealed

The final gesture of deconstruction seems to return us to our point of departure, but at a different level or at a different vantage point. In the conclusions of his analyses of both Husserl and Saussure, Derrida insists on the *value, truth,* and *significance* of the same systems of thought he has just deconstructed. But the conditions of this seemingly paradoxical affirmation appear to invert such claims. These conditions involve: (i) the acceptance of the revealed contradictions between levels of explicit and implicit argumentation; (ii) the demarcation of the limits of applicability of the "acceptable" truth, evidence, or significance; and finally, therefore, (iii) the recognition of the necessity of a context, indeed a "vast field," in which the given system of thought must be situated, therein establishing a more general, more universal "system," a more originary origin which, as we know, will be the economy of *différance.* We shall here attempt to trace this threefold shift, which, as we have announced, initially appears remarkably similar, in structure at least, to Hegel's notion of the *Aufhebung.* That which is overturned is ultimately sustained but nonetheless situated in a "wider," more all-encompassing context wherein the limits of the former become explicit. The deconstructive gesture at this point, which completes his analyses, entails in addition, however, the outline of the relation or movement which nonetheless continues within this "more general economy" as it relates to and sustains "the restricted one."[61] The notion of *différance* is thus at the same instant the "third term" in this "system" and also the movement itself which establishes the conditions of the possibility of deconstruction and metaphysics at the same instant. We must not therefore confuse "usurpation" as per the *Aufhebung* and its violence with the "usurpation" by *différance* within, beyond, and prior to the establishment of the classical Western system of thought known as metaphysics. This shall become increasingly evident as we proceed, we hope.

(i) Accepting Contradictions

At the same instant that Derrida reveals the contradictions between the "declared and the described" aspects of both Husserl's and Saussure's projects respectively, he insists that these contradictions are irreducible and therefore a necessity. Indeed it is towards the conditions of this necessity that he turns with his deconstructive project.

With respect to his analysis of Husserl, Derrida addresses this duplicity initially with a *reaffirmation* of the intentional level of Husserl's claims. For instance:

> This does not place in question the apodicticity of the phenomenological-transcendental description, and does not disrupt the founding value of presence. . . .[62]

Further:

> Contrary to the explicit intention of Husserl, but *not without taking it into account* [my emphasis]. . . .[63]

And finally:

> . . . a thought of the trace [différance] can no more break with a transcendental phenomenology than be reduced to it. In the deconstruction of the archè one does not make a choice.[64]

With an eye to the necessity of Husserl's system, according to his assumptions and presuppositions, deconstruction thus admits in addition its own *necessary* attachment to that same system. This attachment takes the form, as we have shown, of the borrowing of the structures of metaphysics in order to reveal the foundation of phenomenology as metaphysics itself. Nevertheless, Derrida *insists* that this process does not threaten Husserl's system in the least. Yet, he also *shows* the reverse. The very fact that Husserl aims to exclude these metaphysical assumptions and presuppositions and in turn relies on them clandestinely, as it were, does indeed threaten a certain level of veracity of his conclusions. It is significant, therefore, to keep this notion of *levels* of the text and hence of discourse in mind with respect to the "revealed contradictions" which deconstruction aims to "legitimate." The threat, therefore, posed by deconstruction is expressed by Derrida in the following manner:

> But if Husserl had to recognize the necessity of these "incarnations," even as beneficial threats, it is because an *underlying motif* was disturb-

ing the security of these traditional distinctions from within . . . [my emphasis.][65]

We should remark here that what deconstruction claims to have found it situates within the text, indeed within the formulation of the problem by Husserl himself. It does not claim, therefore, to *authorize* or produce anything, but rather, it would seem, to reveal something *already* there. This will become increasingly significant as we approach this *"motif profond."* But first we must address the threats posed by deconstruction, according to deconstruction, for phenomenology:

> If the punctuality of the instant is a myth, a spatial or mechanical metaphor, an inherited metaphysical concept or all of this at the same time, if the present of presence to oneself is not simple, if it is constituted in an imaginary and irreducible synthesis, then the whole of Husserl's argument is threatened in its principle.[66]

No greater threat could be suggested, and indeed, since deconstruction in fact does claim to show that which it treats as the premises of this threat, the conclusions seem obvious. Yet we should not be too quick to draw syllogistic conclusions at this point. A final example of the contradiction Derrida aims to reveal will demonstrate the limit of this threat for us. Derrida has just invoked the possibility of the presupposition of the general concept of sign as the ground for Husserl's distinction between indication and expression, as we have analyzed earlier. His conclusions, in accordance with such findings, are thus:

> If we could reply in the affirmative we would have to conclude, contrary to the express intention of Husserl, that even before becoming a method the "reduction" would already be at work in the most spontaneous act of spoken discourse, the simple practice of the spoken word, the power of expression. . . . This conclusion . . . would contradict at a certain level the explicit intention of Husserl.[67]

Thus it is clear that deconstruction, at this point, seems to overturn, at a certain level, the intentions and indeed the phenomenology of Husserl. But Derrida has also shown that this same phenomenology and those same intentions are not simply reducible to a mistaken identity or to "false" premises or promises. Instead it seems that deconstruction itself sustains a double relation to this same phenomenology. On the one hand, it relies upon it necessarily; on the other, it undermines it— equally necessarily. With this contradiction in mind, we must consider the "contradiction" deconstruction claims to find in Husserl's text itself. To clarify our issue here, let us return to the deconstructive treatment of Saussure as it applies to this double relation of deconstruction to phenomenology. The contradiction worthy of notice in Saussure's argument concerns the role of writing as it relates to speech, and the metaphysical presuppositions therein invoked, as we have shown. The conclusions Derrida draws entail the following:

> Once again, we *do not doubt the value* of these phonological arguments, the presuppositions behind which I have attempted to expose above. Once one assumes these presuppositions, it would be absurd to reintroduce confusedly a derivative writing in the area of oral language and within the system of this derivation. Not only would *ethnocentrism* not be avoided, but all the frontiers within the sphere of its legitimacy would be confused [my emphasis].[68]

Further, we should recall, his initial recognition of the truth of "what Saussure says" on a certain level, at least: "I hope my intention is clear. I think that Saussure's reasons are good. *I do not question,* on the level on which he says it, *the truth* of what Saussure says in such a tone."[69] And finally, with respect to temporality as it is used by and uses Saussure, Derrida says: "What is in question is not Saussure's affirmation of the temporal essence of discourse but the concept of time that *guides* this affirmation and analysis."[70] We should thus recall that deconstruction's initial gesture was concerned with the revelation of the *limits* in the form of inclusions, exclusions, unacknowledged assumptions, and presuppositions. In turn, therefore, its conclusions seem to be concerned with a certain stabilization of the only apparently threatened system under analysis. The search for the conditions of possibility of 'X' should not destroy 'X', Derrida seems to insist, but rather show how this became *necessary.* Such is the deconstructive allegiance to philosophy as such, we might add. Thus he safeguards that which he deconstructs, in a certain sense, but at the same time seems to threaten it by virtue of a certain *circumscription* of applicability, relevance, or significance proclaimed by that same system under analysis. This circumscription is announced in the form of an inner contradiction—within the text at hand—and, in addition, within deconstruction as such, at least in these two cases with which we are concerned at the moment. The double relation of acceptance and rejection of the deconstructed text will be shown to be precisely this movement towards the explicit demarcation of limits: its unacknowledged borders or frontiers, beyond which the system at hand cannot legitimately (according to its own and indeed deconstruction's adherence to metaphysics itself) extend. In the process, of course, deconstruction itself does extend beyond such limits. But first the outline of the outline must be brought in here.

(ii) Outlining the Limits

> I would rather *announce the limits* and the presuppositions of what seems here [in Saussure's discourse] to be self-evident and what seems to me to *retain the character and validity of evidence* [my emphasis].[71]

We suggest a return to this initial intention of deconstruction in its analysis of Saussure, since at this point the second level of this claim should become "self-evident" or visible. The double structure of announcing the limits of legitimacy and illegitimacy should thus be transparent. The closure, on the one hand, is an opening on the other at the same time, yet also by virtue of temporality itself, as we shall see. It is in short, as Derrida says, what "Saussure saw without seeing, knew without being able to take into account . . ." and it is this which will lead us to the conditions of the possibility and impossibility of grammatology, as we have already announced.

The revelation of the limits of Saussure's claims are thus in turn, for us, the revelation of the limits of deconstruction and its "object," *différance* itself. We suggested earlier that "Grammatology" might well be considered an Idea in the Kantian sense, according to Derrida's own description, and it is this notion that we must now address in more detail. With respect to the closure or limits of Saussure's linguistics, Derrida claims: "the *proper* space of a grammatology is at the same time opened and closed by the *Course*. . . ."[72] We shall see shortly that this is also the case with Husserl's phenomenology, for Derrida. The opening that is simultaneously a closure in Saussure, according to deconstruction, is, however, twofold once again. Initially we have the "declared" opening of a *general* science of linguistics, which via deconstruction we realize to be instead the closure of a general science of linguistics. It is, more precisely, a very specific, socio-politico-historically grounded notion, upon which the extrapolation (thus illegitimately) is performed to a certain universality. But Derrida also claims that there is indeed a certain legitimacy to this system, once its *limits* are drawn and it is situated in a "larger" more extensive, more general, or indeed truly general science of writing. In short, Saussure's linguistics retains its value for Derrida only within the context of a general grammatology. In this way the former project announces the latter in the very instant of not announcing it. That is, the unraveling of the truly limited in the apparently general reveals the truly general, which had hitherto been considered a subset or the "truly limited," originary ground. In short, the conditions of the possibility of the science of writing are announced here. But in turn, Derrida insists that this same *science* is aborted as such before it could ever be established since "this arche-writing . . . cannot and can *never* be recognized as the object of a science."[73] The issue here is again that with which we began concerning the conditions of the possibility of the scientificity of science, or the constitution of its object as such. If writing, or more precisely arche-writing (which we shall analyze at length in a later chapter) is the condition of the possibility of the constitution of objectivity yet also that which opens this same objectivity to the problematic demarcation of inside and outside (an opposition which we now know can no longer be sustained), then grammatology, as this science of science, can never begin, as Derrida says. Instead, and paradoxically, it has always already begun:

> . . . there has always been a writing. An arche-writing whose *necessity* and new concept I wish to indicate and outline here; and which I continue to call writing only because it *essentially* communicates with the vulgar concept of writing [my emphasis].[74]

Ths "essential communication" is precisely what interests us here. It is the condition of the possibility of deconstruction itself and of the irreducibility of: (i) the legitimacy of the deconstructed; and of (ii) the paradoxical results of deconstruction itself, which can never lead to "an object" of study. Derrida is not unaware of this plight, since, despite the goal of a certain detachment of the "new concepts" from the old, he says: "Therefore I admit the *necessity* of going through the *concept* of the arche-trace."[75] The key here is the common root of the concept, of course, which we shall see is ultimately irreducible for deconstruction itself. But first the economy of the relation of inside to outside as it appears in the results of the deconstruction of Saussure.

As we have shown, the notion of the "usurpation" of speech by writing is considered by Derrida to be "no accident," but rather essential, and therefore an unavoidable, prescribed necessity. The significance of the limits expressed by Saussure were then shown to be precisely their signifying function of an unacknowledged and unstated (yet written) complicity between the inside and outside. The "excluded" (writing) returns in the deconstructive analysis behind the scenes as the unacknowledged origin of that which itself claims to be the origin (speech). As Derrida says:

> . . . it is when he is not expressly dealing with writing, when he feels he has closed the parentheses on that subject that Saussure opens the field of a general grammatology.
>
> Then one realizes that what was chased off limits . . . writes itself within Saussure's discourse. Then we glimpse the germ of a profound but indirect explanation of the *usurpation* and the traps condemned in Chapter IV [my emphasis].[76]

We shall return to the parallel opening and closing gesture in the deconstruction of Husserl in a moment. At this point, however, the essentiality of "usurpation" must be expanded somewhat. The issue here, it seems to us, is that which has been *excluded* becomes in turn the *key* to the conditions of the possibility of that same originally demarcated system. If we consider this relation in terms of deconstruction and metaphysics, and the resultant *différance,* which is always already operative but excluded, we find a strikingly parallel operation. The initial act of deconstruction is one of the demarcation of the demarcation of limits expressly operative in the given text under analysis. In turn this demarcation by deconstruction reveals something officially exterior to these limits, which is in fact interior. That which is "exterior" to deconstruction is apparently metaphysics itself; yet, as we have shown, this in turn constitutes the very framework of the deconstructive gestures. Derrida acknowledges the same. That which is expressly excluded from metaphysics however must be *différance* as revealed by deconstruction. And in turn that which is expressly exterior to *"différance"* must be metaphysics. Yet, as we know from the results of deconstruction, the essentiality of the relations between deconstruction, metaphysics, and *différance* cannot be reduced. The very *complicity* of these "systems" is what allows, on the contrary, for the usurpation of metaphysics by *différance,* we suggest. It is thus not only possible but necessary for Derrida to claim that the limits of Saussure's project, once exposed, reveal simultaneously the conditions of the possibility and impossibility of grammatology. As he says,

> Or rather, since writing no longer relates to language as an extension or frontier, let us ask how language is a possibility founded on the general

possibility of writing. Demonstrating this, one could give at the same time an account of that alleged 'usurpation' which could not be an unhappy accident. It supposes on the contrary *a common root* and thus excludes the resemblance of the 'image', derivative or representative reflexion [my emphasis].[77]

We shall find not only a parallel formulation in the conclusions concerning Husserl but also a more precise (albeit unacknowledged by Derrida) explanation of the simultaneous conditions of possibility and impossibility of grammatology itself and *a fortiori* the "object" of *différance.*

Concerning the findings within the deconstruction of Husserl, Derrida initially concludes that the latter's "discourse is captured within a certain system or economy that it too does not comprehend or recognize."[78] Thus the deconstructive gesture appears here to perform a sort of double reverse reduction or a double opening which, as with Saussure, reveals the limits of one system as they open out onto another. As Derrida says,

> It is only a question of making the *original non-empirical space* of the foundation on the irreducible void appear from which is decided and arises the security of presence in the metaphysical form of ideality. It is *within this horizon* that we are here interrogating the phenomenological concept of the sign [my emphasis].[79]

As we know, "this horizon" is itself already beyond that which Husserl recognized as being within phenomenology proper. It is the horizon of metaphysics, or of the concept of the sign in general, as we have shown. But this horizon too opens out onto the "larger" one of *différance,* Derrida insists.

> That which we would finally wish to suggest is that the *'pour soi'* of the *'présence à soi'* . . . arises *in the movement of supplementarity* as original substitution, in the form of the 'in the place of'; that is to say, . . . in the operation itself of signification in general [my emphasis].[80]

We should remark here upon the usage (borrowed from metaphysics) of the terms *"originaire"* and "original" in the preceding citations. It is thus this "more originary" space that deconstruction is aiming to expose—indeed more originary than originarity itself, Derrida insists. What this means is that, on the one hand, deconstruction aims to replace, or indeed substitute for or represent, the origin of the origin to the second power. In short, this gesture seems to be a certain usurpation of the "notion of origin itself" yet, at the same time, installs a new one in its place. The difference between the first origin and the second, which is essentially not an origin, is simply that the second origin is not reducible to a unitary or simple structure. It is not singular, not an object, not a locus, and *a fortiori* not a subject as such. It is the realm of *différance.* Several paradoxes emerge however at this juncture. Initially, it seems that non-simplicity of the "more originary origin" is safeguarded precisely due to the necessity of the relation or the economy between *différance* and metaphysics itself. It is this relation which allows for the repetition (which is more precisely not repetition, as we shall explore in more detail later) and which produces or is the condition of the possibility of *ideality* itself. Indeed repeatability and ideality are interchangeable terms at this level. But the possibility of repetition is not a function of metaphysics or *différance* simply, but only and necessarily, we argue, of this interrelation. The structure of this relation is one of essentiality, in addition, and thus returns us to the realm of metaphysics, on the one hand, yet, due to a certain impropriety, keeps open the possibility of the revelation of *différance* at the heart of metaphysics. The revelation of this essentiality is betrayed via the notion of the "sign" itself, we suggest. The "common root" here is precisely this formulation in exactly the same manner as "usurpation" was revealed to be not merely possible but essential in our prior analysis of the deconstruction of Saussure. In this case we find an additional homology, however, between the aims of deconstruction and the structure of Husserl's phenomenology.

The final thrust of the deconstruction of Husserl involves a certain recognition by Derrida of that which he admits Husserl recognized. In short, the relation between ideality and non-ideality between *"en droit"* and *"en fait"* is realized as one of *"infinite deferment."* The former "principles" are thus established as Ideas in the Kantian sense, so that the latter non-ideality, reality, or practice forms a level intrinsically, abysmally separate from the first, yet guided by it nonetheless. Along these lines the deconstruction of Husserl becomes the realization of the *use of différance* within the very possibility of phenomenology's twofold structure itself. Far from "undoing" the Husserlian system, therefore, it seems that, in the end, deconstruction in fact borrows its very *telos,* and in turn its origin, from that same phenomenology. Let us examine Derrida's explicit claims on this matter:

> In its ideal value, the whole system of "essential distinctions" is thus a purely teleological structure.

> From this point on, these "essential distinctions" are caught in the following aporia: in fact, in reality they are never respected and Husserl recognizes this. By rights and ideally, they efface themselves as distinctions since they do not exist as distinctions except within the difference between right and fact, ideality and reality. Their possibility is their impossibility.[81]

As we have shown, this enigmatic conclusion is equally applicable to the "new science of grammatology." It is, in short, an Idea in the Kantian sense. In his final deconstructive gesture, however, Derrida seems not only to reinstall the legitimacy of Husserl's phenomenology within a "larger economy" and in turn situate this within the yet larger one of *différance,* but also to find *différance,* as the difference between *"le droit et le fait"* that "makes the world move," to be explicated as such by Husserl. This is not simply the economy of the contradiction, therefore, between that which Husserl "declares and that which describes," but rather the very condition of the possibility of the entire edifice of phenomenology and *"Husserl le reconnait."* A paradoxical relation to be sure. We should not be surprised however to find that the deconstruction of Husserl seems, on the one hand, to undo its own initial claims concerning this very significant contradiction in Husserl; and yet, on the other, deconstruction sustains itself as irreversible in the very revelation or indeed affirmation of that same "condition of the possibility of phenomenology itself." It is the recognition of the latter as such which is in turn re-applied to the "whole" of phenomenology, and it is in this return that the law is violated, as it were. Once again we find that the condition of its possibility is also and at the same instant the condition of its impossibility. In short, as Derrida says concerning the "explicit" principle of principles of phenomenology,

> The living present is in fact, really, effectively, etc. . . . . *deferred to infinity.* This *différance* is the difference between ideality and non-ideality.[82]

It should now be possible to understand more fully Derrida's principle of principles for deconstruction: that "no practice is ever totally faithful to its principles." It is precisely this difference that will in turn reveal the "play of *différance*" for the work/play, or perhaps we might now call it practice of deconstruction. It is now time to situate the limits of this "more general economy" itself, at least as outlined by Derrida initially and, in turn, as they necessarily "usurp" and perhaps invert that same "declared" outline or demarcation.

(iii) The Context of a General Economy

If we consider the most general *telos* of deconstruction at this juncture, it should lead us to the revelation of the limits and range of that
which Derrida has called *différance*. The system implied here, therefore, will be that of the threefold economy of deconstruction-
metaphysics-*différance* such that the former and the latter relate to
each other as origin and *telos* in a twofold manner. The origin of deconstruction is *différance,* yet the reverse is also true, as we have shown.
The difference, however, is that according to Derrida, *différance* can
no longer be considered an origin, pure and simple; and beyond Derrida, we suggest, the structure of deconstruction as the *origin* of *différance* and as the *telos* of deconstruction (with metaphysics playing the
role of mediator, in the Hegelian sense, here) entails a "subjective"
process of discovery or revelation. The reversal of this relation
whereby *différance* is considered the "origin," etc. entails a certain
"objective" state of affairs or reality. We shall not pursue this pre-
Heideggerian formulation of things at this point, but wish only to suggest: (i) a certain reversibility of the relation here; (ii) a certain
threefold economy; and (iii) a certain duplicity in that same reversibility which cannot be accounted for within the system of the economy of
différance itself. This problem will resurge within our analysis of *différance* as such and must be suspended therefore at this point. We wish
instead to consider the specific claims made for deconstruction's *telos,*
by Derrida, in its practices within his analyses of Husserl and Saussure.

Concerning Saussure, deconstruction aims toward the "deconstruction of the *greatest totality*—the concept of the *epistème* and logocentric metaphysics—within which are produced, without ever posing the
radical question of writing, *all* the Western methods of analysis, explication, reading or interpretation."[83] Such is the range (and hence limit)
of the *telos* of deconstruction, as *declared* by Derrida. Its extension, its
object is none other than "all the Western methods of analysis . . . ,"
etc., which conveniently enough *all* hinge upon "the concept of the
epistème and logocentric metaphysics." The unity of the latter concept
shall be addressed in detail in the following chapter but here we wish to
illustrate simply the *unifying structure* that deconstruction seems to
impose in the process of the formation of its "object" of analysis or
attack. In short, the demarcation of its limits entails, as Derrida himself
has shown, a certain gesture of *inclusion and exclusion* so as to establish an "object" of inquiry to begin with. The limits here are thus

claimed to be the "Western world" and its "methods of analysis, inter-pretation, etc." It might be significant for a deconstruction of decon-struction to consider precisely that which is *excluded* thereby and thus, if Derrida is correct concerning the "logic of the supplement" and the role of the "excluded" in the constitution of the "included," how this exclusion determines its "object" as such. The presupposition for such an analysis, of course, would be the very scientificity and epistemolog-ical value, indeed the adherence to a logocentric metaphysics, of de-construction itself. We have already shown that this would not exceed the demarcation of the project of deconstruction itself, according to Derrida. But for the moment, let us return to the *explicit limits* to which deconstruction is said to adhere.

The demarcation of limits, as we know, entails a certain closure as well as a certain measure or range of extension. With this latter aspect in mind let us consider Derrida's demarcation of these limits in relation to his analysis of Saussure:

> Now we must think that writing is at the same time *more exterior* to
> speech, not being its 'image' or symbol, and *more interior* to speech,
> which is already in itself a writing [my emphasis].[84]

One should notice initially that there is an explicit contradiction in-volved here which in turn will demarcate the "object" of writing. We should no longer be troubled by such a paradox since, as we know, writing will never become an "object." The second aspect of this claim worthy of notice here is the usage of "more" to extend that which Saussure has already outlined. The paradox here is that it was decon-struction itself which aimed to *limit* Saussure's project, therein: (i) showing its range of proper relevance; and (ii) showing the "more general economy" in which the project is necessarily situated. Yet now we find the results of deconstruction concerned to *extend* the range of precisely that which Saussure discovered. The difference is that this extension bridges the gap between linguistics and grammatology so as to reveal the "usurpation" we announced earlier as being the necessary result of the revelation of *différance* by deconstruction. Indeed this usurpation is described by Derrida again, with respect to Saussure, in its very relation to the "deconstruction of this tradition":

> *Deconstructing this tradition* will not therefore consist of reversing it, of
> making writing innocent. Rather of showing why the violence of writing
> does not befall an innocent language. There is an *originary* violence of

> writing because language is first, in a sense I shall gradually reveal,
> writing. *"Usurpation" has always already begun.* The sense of the right
> side appears in a mythological effect of return [my emphasis].⁵⁸

We might well ask *which* usurpation is at stake here, since we could
suggest at least three which "have always already begun." These include: (i) the usurpation of *différance* by metaphysics itself, since this
is the condition of the latter's possibility; (ii) the usurpation of the sign
by the metaphysics of presence; and (iii) the usurpation of metaphysics
by *différance* in the work of deconstruction. The unique historical
emergence of deconstruction as such remains strictly a Derridaean
idea, we insist, despite the fact that the attempt to dismantle the "tradition of metaphysics" has indeed perhaps always already begun necessarily with the very constitution of that same tradition. But this is
another story and another history, which we shall leave aside for the
moment here. Our present concern is with the structure of the *telos* of
deconstruction so as to reveal (or attempt to reveal) that which has
"*always* already begun." In short, does this formulation itself not necessarily *essentialize différance* itself? The "always" in this formulation
certainly removes the phenomenon of *différance* from the historico-
factual-reality which Derrida earlier, in agreement with Husserl, opposed (in a relation of *différance* certainly) to the level of principles,
ideality, and, in short, to the level of the concept in general, and
metaphysics in particular. We have thus almost returned, at this point,
to *differance* as an Idea in the Kantian sense as well, except that we
know *différance* is considered, for Derrida at least, to be the structure
of the relation which *allows for* the Idea in the Kantian sense to be
constituted *as* a *telos* and, *a fortiori,* we might add, as an origin. It is
clear that we must address in detail the concept of metaphysics for
Derrida in order to further clarify these relations, and we shall do
precisely that in the following chapter. For the moment we wish to add
a final remark concerning the *telos* of deconstruction with respect to
the analysis of Husserl.

We began by considering deconstruction's aim as an attempt to reduce the reduction itself so as to show its "conditions of possibility." It
is now time to reveal the findings of this double reduction which seems
to invert the first and therein the legitimacy of the process itself. Far
from being the result of a transcendental ego, Derrida insists, this
movement of *différance* provides the very condition of its possibility.
As he says:

This movement of *différance* does not arise from a transcendental subject. It *produces* that subject [my emphasis].[86]

No less than the transcendental subject, *différance* produces the empirical subject as well, as we have shown. In addition it produces the conditions of the possibility of their relation, which in turn is the ground of phenomenology as such for Husserl. We thus have the movement of usurpation by *différance* and for *différance* revealed at this stage. By being the *context* in which Husserl's system functions, it thereby usurps the role of the "control which implicitly governs" that system. Analogous indeed to the implicit but controlling role of metaphysics within phenomenology that Derrida claims to reveal.

The meaning of this parallel and indeed the others we have revealed in this analysis must be suspended from any definite closure at this juncture. It is not yet possible to say, we suggest, that the difference between metaphysics and *différance* is one that is governed by or organized by *either* metaphysics *or différance*. If we could, we would be within a neat Hegelian system with its third term usurping the other two—sustaining their "apparent contradiction," but overwhelming their limits and situating them in a larger system. The problem instead in this (our) context seems to be that *both différance* and metaphysics seem to *equally* govern this economy that unites and differentiates them. The role of deconstruction in this system seems to a certain degree to be self-sacrificial yet paradoxically also the origin and *telos* of *différance* itself. It is thus necessary to explore in greater detail the apparent contradictions between *différance* and metaphysics in order to reveal more clearly this perhaps not so general "economy of *différance*" as such.

Section II
Derrida and the Concept of Metaphysics

III

THE OBJECT
OF DECONSTRUCTION

> I am attempting to stay at the *limit* of
> philosophic discourse. I say limit and not
> death because I do not believe at all in what
> is currently called the death of philosophy
> (nor in whatever that would be, the book,
> man or God); especially since, as each of us
> knows, death entails a very specific effect.
>
> Jacques Derrida
> May 1972[1]

(a) Prelude: A Question for Socrates

PARMENIDES: Suppose for instance, one of us is master or slave of another; he is not of course, the slave of master itself, the essential master, nor, if he is master, is he master of slave itself, the essential slave, but being a man, is master of another man, whereas mastery itself is what it is (mastership) of slavery itself, and slavery itself is slavery to mastery itself. The significance of things in our world is not with reference to things in that other world, nor have these their significance with reference to us, but as I say, the things in that world are what they are with reference to one another, and so likewise are the things in our world. You see what I mean?

SOCRATES: Certainly I do.

PARMENIDES: Only a man of exceptional gifts will be able to see that a form, or essence, just by itself, does exist in each case, and it will require someone still more remarkable to discover it and to instruct another who has thoroughly examined all these difficulties.

SOCRATES: I admit that, Parmenides. I quite agree with what you are saying.

PARMENIDES: But on the other hand . . . if in view of all these difficulties and others like them, a man refuses to admit that forms of things exist or to distinguish a definite form in every case, he will have nothing on which to fix his thought, so long as he will not allow that each thing has a character which is always the same, and in so doing he will completely destroy the significance of all discourse. But of that consequence I think you are only too well aware.

SOCRATES: True.

PARMENIDES: What are you going to do about *philosophy* then? Where will you turn while the answers to these questions remain unknown?

SOCRATES: I can see no way out at the present moment.[2]

(b) Introduction: Derrida and the Question of Metaphysics

Edmond Jabès has recently claimed that, "To give priority to the question is to submit the response to an endless interrogation; it is to overthrow the power, to preserve the opening." ("Privilégier la question, c'est soumettre la réponse à une interrogation sans fin; c'est *faire basculer le pouvoir,* préserver l'ouverture.")[3] It is precisely this that Derrida does with metaphysics and which we propose to do with Derrida. The question of metaphysics for Derrida can thus be posed in the following manner: "Is philosophic discourse ruled?" ("Le discours philosophique est-il réglé?")[4]

In order to understand this question we must first interrogate it. Our subject here is clearly *"le discours philosophique,"* but what is this? Is there only one, as the article *"le"* seems to suggest? Is there a philosophical discourse as such? Is there such a thing as philosophy as such or in general? Further, what is the relation of philosophy to discourse in general? Are they distinguishable? Is philosophy dependent on discourse, as the adjective here is dependent on the noun to give it an identity or a form? Is discourse a thing to which philosophy could add itself as a property of the former? Is this relation reversible? Is there a discursive philosophy? Is philosophy necessarily discursive? or could it be otherwise? The object of our question is also clearly demarcated in the one term *'réglé'.* In English this term can be translated in the following divergent manners: (i) ruled, as with paper; lined; (ii) regular, steady, methodical (as habit); (iii) set, stated, fixed; and (iv) lawabiding (bound). Should we ask which one of these terms applies, or must we accept all four? Can we accept all four? Does this not divide our object, or more precisely, provide us with a multiplicity of objects which do not have a common essential ground? Do we then have an object? Is not the definition of object itself violated here? Yet we have a single term, albeit in French, which stands for all of these objects together. What then is the relation between signifier and signified here? How can we distinguish a particular signified if only one signifier stands for all of them? Which do we choose? Do we need to choose?

Our verb is the present indicative form of *"être"*—to be. Thus the question divides into two forms immediately: (i) as an issue of the here and now; the present, as not past and/or not future, and (ii) an issue of universality, eternity and thus a question which concerns a relation in general. Once again we are presented with a choice and/or a duplicity of the problem. If we assume it is a philosophical question, one must assume the issue is one of universality and is to be situated at the ontological level. If we assume a present which is not the past and/or not the future, we step into a historical relation which therein presupposes change and, in particular, a change in the relation we are herein examining.

We should perhaps also ask: What is the question here? What is the essence of the issue? What does this question mean? What does it intend to say? Does it have an intention? Must it have an intention or many or any at all? What does this presuppose? But why ask this question? What does the question itself, as a whole, presuppose? Are those presuppositions justifiable? Why? Why not? What is the question a sign for? Is it a symptom of something else? Does it only appear to be a question but is not one really? If it is really a question, then what is the answer to it? Is there only one answer? Only one question? Is there an answer at all?

Contrasting questions must also be posed. In asking about the philosophical discourse, is this as opposed to non-philosophical discourses? such as? Or is it opposed to non-discursive philosophy, as mentioned earlier? Or is such a thing possible? In asking if it is *"réglé,"* is this as opposed to *"pas réglé,"* in the past or future?

But what are the implications of this question? If it is *réglé,* then what does this mean? For the notion of *réglé* and for philosophy, and for discourse, for history, and for eternity? If it is not, likewise the above questions must be asked.

And finally, for the moment, what are the conditions of the possibility of the question? What must there be in order that it can be posed as such? Is this a historically conditioned question or a logically necessary one? or has it already been asked? Could it have been asked before? Can it ever be asked again?

The essential pivotal point from which all of these questions issue and which necessitates their logic and meaningfulness goes by the name of metaphysics, for Derrida. This structure of questionability, of interrogation, of seeking for answers, for understanding, for conceivability, for meaning itself is precisely the focus for Derrida's analysis. He will insist first upon a certain unity in all metaphysics, a metaphysics as such; upon a twofold structure within this essential metaphysics; and further upon the essence of this essence—the heart of metaphysics, its foundation and ultimate presupposition—as non-metaphysical. An essential violation. An essential infidelity. It is this analysis of metaphysics according to Derrida that we propose to explicate here. Since metaphysics simultaneously plays a *mediating* role between deconstruction and the revelation of *différance,* and also an *intermediary* position from the *arché* of deconstruction to the *telos* of *différance,* it is of essential importance in the understanding of Derrida's work as a whole. It should of course be remembered that Derrida's investigations have already made questionable the notions of "understanding" "his" "work" as a "whole." However, at present we too will and must rely on "the old names."

(c) Unity: Simple and Complex

[Derrida asks:] . . . can one consider philosophy as such (metaphysics as such, or onto-theology) without being forced to submit, with this pretention to unity and oneness, to an impregnable and imperial totality of an order? If there are margin*s*, is there still *a* philosophy, philosophy as such?
No answer. Perhaps no question either, in the final analysis.
The copulating correspondence, the opposition question/response is already situated within a structure, enveloped in the hollow of an ear that we wish to go and see.[5]

One of the most serious objections to Derrida's work of deconstruction has been concerned with his "presupposition" of the unity of philosophy, as one single tradition, as a system, and hence as a concept as such. In treating all differences in the history of philosophy as simply variations on a theme, or as specific instances or examples of something in general—a form of philosophy—is he not therein (a) creating a mythical (i.e., non-existent) problem, and (b) himself falling into the very trap that he apparently seeks to be rid of: metaphysics?[6] These complaints illustrate little understanding of Derrida however since:

(a) he is not unaware of this "danger"; (b) his strategy for overcoming the dominance of metaphysics openly claims to utilize those same tools; and (c) he has proposed a detailed argument explaining the significance of "metaphysics as such" for him in terms of specific issues by which this tradition can be said to be unifiable and homogenous. He does not thereby collapse all differences into the same, nor reduce the history of philosophy to a single structure. He does, however, insist that the identity of metaphysics, essentially, has not altered in certain respects since its inception with Aristotle. This entails a concept of metaphysics, or an Idea of metaphysics which provides the ground for all variations of the same as manifest within the tradition. It is this concept of Derrida's which we propose to examine here.

We should perhaps clarify a nomological difficulty at the outset. The term metaphysics, for Derrida, is often used interchangeably with philosophy as such. The same problem of the "as such" of each of these terms will be treated shortly, but first there are also other names for this concept. These include the following list: logos, logocentrism, the "name of God," positive infinity, onto-theology, infinitist theology, all monisms, all dualisms, indifference, infinite being, classical rationalism, the desire for a transcendental signified, the opposition between sensible and intelligible, the proper, the history of Reason, and language itself. This list, although nowhere collected as such by Derrida, permeates his work, and these terms circulate as if interchangeable with the concept of metaphysics as such. In addition, these concepts characterize his concept of metaphysics as properties or participants in a system. They permeate the concept, define it and circumscribe it. Metaphysics itself circumscribes a wider area yet, which includes: "all the Western methods of analysis, explication, reading or interpretation."[7] For Derrida, as for Heidegger, the "language" of the Western, occidental world is essentially the "language of metaphysics." This extends, for Derrida, back to the Pre-Socratics and includes the history of philosophy up to and including Heidegger. The totality of metaphysics' field of predominance is thus *à la fois* historical and also contemporary. Its range as synchronic includes all intellectual activity in the Western world. Nothing seems exempt from this coverage, nor could it be, for Derrida. This includes, as he himself has admitted, the work of deconstruction as well. But how could this be so? How could all variations in analysis, explication, reading and interpretation be "collapsed" or synthesized into one unifying totality? Derrida's synthetic approach must first be considered, in principle, as consistent with the claims of philosophy as such, any philosophy. This entails the idea of the Idea, a form, a concept, an *Eidos,* or an essence which persists over time unchanged and indeed as unchangeable. This "concept" is intrinsically repeatable, in history, but exists in eternity as in itself and is thus essentially unaffected by historical change. History manifests its appearance; eternity sustains its essence. We find this framework throughout philosophy, since its field is that of essences, of the "in general" being as such; indeed the realm of truth is just this. Thus in claiming that all particular manifestations of philosophy should entail an essence that is philosophy itself, or as such, which in turn grounds the possibility of philosophy in particular, or any specific system thereof (i.e., within the circumscription of a proper name, Hegel for instance), Derrida is being most faithful and respectful to philosophic tradition. Of course what is presupposed here is precisely that which we find. In order that one can "find" "philosophy as such," one must have a concept of philosophy already formulated which one in turn seeks within each particular version of the same. The origin of this "concept" is precisely the problem for Derrida, albeit in general. He will insist that "there is no third term," no concept as such, and certainly no Concept. But first we must explore the route he takes to arrive there. This process of the effacement of the origin, of the constitution of the concept, is also fundamentally metaphysical.

Derrida's notion of the concept of metaphysics as such is based on certain regularities or patterns of exclusion and inclusion within the tradition which incessantly repeat. The most significant of these is the "debasement of writing," which entails the elevation of speech, the organizing role of "presence" as the *archè* and *telos* of history, the separation of signifier and signified, and the role of the sign as essentially inessential. He thus claims:

> The history of (the only) metaphysics which has, in spite of all differences, not only from Plato to Hegel (even including Leibniz) but also beyond these apparent limits, from the Pre-Socratics to Heidegger, always assigned the origin of truth in general to the Logos. The history of truth, of the truth of truth, has always been . . . the debasement of writing, and its repression outside "full" speech.[8]

In a certain sense Derrida thus "creates" his concept of metaphysics according to the problem of writing. For Plato, for instance, writing was introduced as a threat to knowledge, to the mind, and especially to memory itself.[9] For Hegel, the "age of the sign" is the detour that is history;[10] it is on the way to Absolute Knowledge: the presence of truth to itself, of consciousness to itself, of the Concept to itself. The sign has always been, for metaphysics, a sign for something else and hence determined by what it is not. We shall trace this history in greater detail in the upcoming section but here we wish only to point out the most prominent examples of what Derrida considers the essence of philosophy itself. Of course this "debasement of writing" is also a sign for other things. It is the tip of the iceberg only and has ramifications that extend throughout all possibilities of thought and conceivability from the Greeks to the present for the Western world. Thus Derrida too commits the same "crime" in his explication of the problem. The problem of the sign is itself a sign of a larger problem. But in turn this expansion reveals the crucial role of the "sign" with respect to all possible implications within the structure of philosophy itself. Take, for instance, the concept of time. According to Derrida there has been only one since Aristotle,[11] which was finally consummated in the system of Hegel. This notion of time as a line, and essentially as a point which would return to itself in the moment of eternity both conditions and is conditioned by the metaphysics of presence which in turn entails and is entailed by the concept of sign as a detour between one presence and another; after the Fall and before the final enlightenment. This problem also moves into the realm of history and will be addressed shortly. The point here, however, is that: (a) the treatment of the sign in the history of metaphysics retains an essential character that sustains a unity of tradition and a system that fundamentally has no exceptions and indeed cannot have, by definition; and (b) Derrida's insistence on this issue as central in turn presents the "treatment of the sign" as itself a sign of other equally essential characteristics of this system, which furthermore all return to the concept of sign (or writing, for Derrida, since these terms are used interchangeably for the most part) to reveal its essentiality. He seems to consider the "sign" at once inside and outside of metaphysics.

Thus metaphysics as such is constituted by and constitutes a system of conceptuality. This system is what "allows for" the reduction of the sign according to Derrida and hence what sustains its condemnation as derivative and inessential:

> It is precisely these concepts that permitted the exclusion of writing: image or representation, sensible and intelligible, nature and culture, nature and technics, etc. They are solidary with all *metaphysical con-*

ceptuality and particularly with a naturalist, objectivist, and derivative
determination of the difference between outside and inside [my empha-
sis].[12]

The structure of this identity will also be examined in greater detail
shortly. At present we wish to illustrate simply that, for Derrida,
metaphysics as such entails a profound unity, an essential
homogeneity, but with respect to very specific issues and traits. It is
not a concept of metaphysics in general. This indeed would be impossible and Derrida would be the first to recognize such a problem. The
idea of unity is thus not founded on the unity of the Idea, even and
perhaps especially within metaphysics. There is an essential mediation
of the unity, which itself becomes effaced in the very success of the
production. This second level, as foundational, preliminary, essential,
yet hidden, is fundamental both within metaphysics itself (without Derrida) and for Derrida's treatment of metaphysics. It is this hidden mediation that allows for the constitution of the object as such, indeed of the
"as such"; that is, of the metaphysical concept and hence of the concept of metaphysics. For Derrida, all concepts retain an essential allegiance, by virtue of their form, to metaphysics as such. Thus the
concept of the concept, the ultimate unity, as the ultimate goal (also for
metaphysics) is the notion of God. Until this is reached (with Hegel) all
metaphysics is determined by this lack as its *telos:*

> The onto-theological idea of sensibility or experience, the opposition of
> passivity and activity, constitute a profound homogeneity, hidden under
> the diversity of metaphysical systems. Within that idea, absence and the
> sign always seem to make an apparent, provisional, and derivative
> notch in the system of first and last presence. They are thought of as
> *accidents* and *not as conditions* of the desired presence. The sign is
> always a sign of the Fall. Absence always relates to distancing from God
> [my emphasis].[13]

Thus Derrida elevates the notion of the sign and its treatment in all
metaphysical systems to the role of *essential* determinant for the concept of metaphysics as such. Paradoxically this would seem to confirm
that same structure, albeit substituting the notion of the sign as "the
condition of the desired presence" rather than simply as an "accident."
However this shift, if Derrida is successful, has ramifications that result in a re-structuring and re-thinking of this goal as such, which in
turn must reflect back on his elevation of the sign "in the service" of the
goal of presence as such.

Derrida's most convincing argument for the concept of metaphysics concerns the implicit choice of boundaries which is essential in either accepting or rejecting such a proposal. For instance, if one refuses to accept any form of unity of the tradition of Western metaphysics but rather insists on an essential difference from one specific system (i.e., Hegel's) to another (i.e., Plato's), one is therein presupposing a centralizing factor based on the "proper name."[14] Indeed on the myth of the proper name: the signature. This unity of the "work" of Plato (for example) is solely based on the name, the signing factor that states Plato wrote x, y and z. Therefore, there must be some essential "I think" that unites these works and makes them into a single whole: a project, an idea, an intention. Lurking behind this assumption is the notion of meaning as intrinsically related to intention, to a voluntarism that is not unfamiliar within the history of metaphysics. Indeed, the object of meaning has always been the meaning of the object: as a whole, as a unity, as a totality. As Derrida says,

> But to respect above all the philosophic specificity of this syntax (of metaphors) is also to recognize the submission of meaning to intention, to the truth of the philosophic concept, to the philosophical signified.[15]

Beyond the *'vouloir-dire'* (intention) of *'le nom propre'*, Derrida suggests there is a greater structural unity at work that provides a foundation for the system of thought which we tend to identify with a proper name.[16] The usage of particular metaphors, for instance, is not an accident or merely a convenience that one happens to find in particular philosophic texts, but rather points towards this underlying structure. The metaphors of the sun and the circle provide a key example of this for Derrida:

> Certainly the metaphors of the light and the circle, so important in Descartes, are not organized as they are in Plato, Hegel or Husserl.
>
> This metaphorics no doubt has its own specific syntax; but *as a metaphorics* it belongs to a more general syntax, a more intensive system whose constraints are equally operative in Platonism; and everything becomes clear in this sun, sun of absence and presence, blinding and luminous, dazzling.[17]

"En tant qu métaphorique" is the essential fold that Derrida insists upon within metaphysics itself. Metaphor is defined as inessential within the discourse of philosophy; as a "mere adornment," yet, as we will explain in greater detail shortly: (a) it appears systematically

within the tradition of philosophy; (b) particular metaphors reappear in different systems of thought yet function according to the same rules, and (c) the concept of metaphor—its essence—is an inextricably philosophical one. Thus we have "metaphor," for example, as a mere sign for something else (a lost presence, a future presence, a pure referent, a signified in itself) yet also engaged in a form of systematic appearance and reappearance, and indeed playing an essential role therein. The essentiality of something already defined as derivative and inessential is thus only discoverable beyond the limits of one system. This entails the linking of one philosophic system to another in terms of structure (and, paradoxically, an essentially philosophic one at that). The understanding of any concept is only possible in terms of analogy, in terms of differences, which nevertheless resemble each other. The idea of the idea in general, although Husserl insisted on the reverse,[18] is only discoverable for Derrida via specific instances of the idea from which one can deduce, reduce, produce, or reveal its essence. Thus a certain *Aufhebung* is implied here such that the constitution of the same via the differences retains *à la fois* identity and difference. The former is, of course, the essence of the latter; although the reverse is also true.[19] The final unity of the concept of metaphysics is not so final for Derrida, however. It is rather a sign for something else. This "absolute presence" will itself be interrogated, but first we must make the essential detour through the concept of history as the history of the concept, according to Derrida.

(d) History: Between Two Suns

> The metaphysical character of the concept of history is not only related to linearity but also to a whole system of implications (teleology, eschatology, *relevant* [conceptual syllogistic, via the Aufhebung] accumulation and interiorization of meaning, a certain type of traditionality, a certain concept of continuity, of truth, etc.).[20]

Derrida has reproached Foucault for not realizing the irony and essential abortion in the attempt to write a "history of madness," for precisely the above reasons. The notion of history, for Derrida, since it is itself a *concept* and thereby inscribed within the tradition and system of metaphysics, cannot be utilized apart from this "baggage" which gives it meaning. Thus the attempt to write a "history" of madness, for instance, must for Derrida be Reason's history of Reason's madness and not an account from the side of madness itself. History therefore is *always* Reason's domain,[21] and necessarily so for Derrida. It is this notion in general, its particular eruption in the Western world (albeit at different historical times), and its closure (also at various points along the line of time) which we intend to explicate here. The unity of metaphysics is thus identifiable and a function of this unity of history.[22] Indeed the history of metaphysics is essentially determined by the metaphysics of history, according to Derrida. Further, "it could not have been otherwise."[23]

The concept of history for Derrida is paradoxically both determined by metaphysics and yet a determinant of metaphysics and therefore of the Concept itself. The relation of the Concept to consciousness or knowledge itself is essentially historical and therefore: (a) teleological and (b) eschatological. Time is therein determined as a geneological relation between one full presence and another. Time is the time of history; that is, it is the continuous process of reappropriation from lost knowledge to regained knowledge. It is the movement of Truth itself, as it attains consciousness. In this movement the origin and *telos* are one and the same, yet both are absent. History fills this gap and progressively narrows it in the spiral of "relevance" (the *Aufhebung*) which provides knowledge of the object for the subject. It is therefore History which forms the essential "detour" from one "Sun" to another. As Derrida says, "History and knowledge, *istoria* and *epistème,* have always been determined . . . as detours for the purpose of the reappropriation of presence."[24] One can clearly see a legacy of Hegelian and Heideggerian thought at work here since, for Heidegger, Being has always been determined as presence and, for Hegel, history is essentially that of the Concept and for this Reason is necessarily circular and closed. Derrida's description, one should remember, is "for metaphysics," which means it is both history according to Derrida and according to the tradition of metaphysics. Indeed there can be no distinction here, according to Derrida.

The central figures for Derrida, regarding the determination of metaphysics and within its history as participants, founding members, and end points, are therefore of crucial significance as the representatives of this "unity of tradition." The origin of metaphysics (that is, the history of metaphysics) is, as one might expect with Derrida, multiple. There are, however, four particular points which are of exemplary significance. The earliest determinations of metaphysics began with the Pre-Socratics, he claims. From this era, we have received a notion that has persisted up to and includes Heidegger, and one which thereby installs the latter squarely within the metaphysics he would destroy. This characteristic concerns the origin of truth as the *Logos*. This has always been the truth of truth, or its meaning, and in addition the privileged role of the voice and the debasement of writing began here. The *phonè* as the locus of truth and the presence of consciousness to itself—immediately without worldly, empirical mediation—is what Derrida calls *phonologism:*

> ... the absolute proximity of voice and being, of voice and the meaning of being, of voice and the identity of meaning.[25]

Even Heidegger's thought sustains it, he claims. It is the *voice* of Reason that one "hears" when one "sees the truth." In addition, the shift from "inauthentic" to "authentic" being-in-the-world is a function of this desire for the pure presence of consciousness to itself. It is essentially a metaphysical opposition (presence/absence) therefore that orients the essence of Heidegger's thought, according to Derrida.

The notion of "presence" itself as central to metaphysics was inaugurated by Parmenides, Derrida claims. From Parmenides to Husserl the "privilege of the present, as evidence" is an essential trait in the history of metaphysics. In Husserl's "return to the things themselves" as his "principle of principles," we must remember that the basis of this claim was a metaphysical "prejudice" for the locus of truth in the pure presence of the things themselves to consciousness. For Descartes as well, for example, the "clarity and distinctness of ideas" immediately present to consciousness was the condition of the possibility of knowledge and truth. It was pure evidence itself.

The most important figure in the foundation of the unified tradition of metaphysics is certainly Plato; for Derrida,[26] Plato is responsible for the notion of idealization as objectivity and interiority. The locus of truth becomes the object, albeit an ideal object, and this could be known by the subject only via the inner light of Reason. There was also a certain interiority of objectivity brought into the world by Plato: the forms, and indeed the Form of form: the Concept. Thus it was Plato who began the "epoch of logocentrism," according to Derrida. As he says, it is "the epoch of onto-theology, . . . the philosophy of presence, that is to say, philosophy itself."[27] As we can see the original boundaries are already shifting somewhat for Derrida. The notion of presence as the locus of truth, although first installed by the Pre-Socratics, is herein regarded as authorized by Plato. The difference is simply one of degree and therefore in some respects inessential. Plato's formulation of the issue marks a crucial point in the development and indeed foundation of metaphysics for Derrida. The former's unification of the notion of presence and evidence with objectivity, ideality, and interiority, and above all (perhaps) with the Good—as the ultimate Good—is a turning point in the history of thought and in turn in the thought of History. All that is is essentially formal from that time on. The meaning of meaning is established in Plato's thought as objectivity, and this is indeed still the foundation for modern science. The ultimate pair of oppositional concepts which determines all others, according to Derrida, was also inaugurated by Plato: "The difference between the sensible and intelligible—with all that it controls, namely metaphysics in its totality."[28] This "epoch of the logos" is not, however, without an end and indeed perhaps a death, as we shall see shortly.

According to Derrida, the fourth major figure in the birth of metaphysics was Aristotle. The essential contribution he made, which did not change significantly until Husserl and even then lingered on in some respects beyond him to Heidegger, was the concept of time as a line, as linear. Although time is made up of individual points, together they form a line which admits of no gaps. The continuity of time and therefore of history are thus established. It is this line that Hegel folds back on itself into the circle which closes itself in Absolute Knowledge, but nevertheless the linearity of the line is therein maintained, even reaffirmed. It is with this notion of time, first as a series of points, and therefore essentially as a point, which inaugurates the *Now* and constitutes the presence of the present in Aristotle. Once again truth and evidence are situated in the moment of the now—the present, which is at once *this now* and *all nows*. The moment of truth is thus the intersection of the eternal Now with this now; it is the present indicative.

The end of the line, of history, of absence, of man, and of the sign (which has been reserved throughout the history of metaphysics as an absence in the service of a promised presence) is the culmination of metaphysics, according to Derrida, and this takes place with Hegel.

> He [Hegel] undoubtedly summed up the entire philosophy of the logos. He determined ontology as absolute logic; he assembled all the determinations of philosophy as presence; he assigned to presence the eschatology of parousia, of the self-proximity of infinite subjectivity . . . he had to debase or subordinate writing.[30]

Further:

> The horizon of absolute knowledge is the effacement of writing in the
> logos, the retrieval of the trace in parousia, the reappropriation of differ-
> ence, the accomplishment of . . . the metaphysics of the proper.[31]

Derrida's concept of metaphysics thus comes to a close with the appearance of Hegel's system, in particular with *The Encyclopedia*. The
epoch of metaphysics as *logocentrism* remains essentially unchanged
from Plato to Hegel, and the notion of the line of time *'n'a pas bougé'*
from Aristotle to Hegel, Derrida claims. With Hegel[32] therefore the
height of metaphysics is reached: the system is closed, finitude is essentially united with infinity, and all differences are essentially subsumed within one unity. It is precisely this collapse, this totality, this
closure of the circle, when the Presence of the origin is returned to in
the Presence of the *telos,* which in turn reveals the finitude of metaphysics as a whole, for Derrida. When the sign, the empirical world, the
detour that is history is ultimately effaced, as in Hegel, the movement
essential to metaphysics, albeit denounced as inessential, is paralyzed,
and the circle, or the egg (the metaphor of the world for Derrida as for
Bataille)[33] must begin to crack. Thus Derrida recognizes in Hegel both
"the last philosopher of the book and the first thinker of writing."[34] As
he says: "All that Hegel thought within this tradition, all that is except
eschatology, may be reread as a mediation on writing."[35] Writing for
Derrida is of course the notion of *différance,*[36] the excess, supplement,
that which exceeds the closure and capture by metaphysics. It is intrinsically absent. Thus Hegel is on the border, for Derrida, between the
end of metaphysics and the beginning of "something else" "which as
yet has no name"—(Grammatology?) There is little doubt that Hegel's
thought is what Derrida has in mind concerning the unity and history of
metaphysics as a unity, as the Concept, and in particular as the history
of the Concept. It was Hegel that first unified "metaphysics" as such
and made it into "a history," and indeed who first showed the essence
of essence as historical, and the essence of history as essential. The
key problem, however, which opens up this finality for Derrida, is
precisely that of eschatology. It is the Hegel's Achille's heel according
to Derrida. It is *death* that metaphysics has always claimed and intended to overcome, and it is the realm of the infinite, as also that of
Absolute Presence—the light of Eden and Heaven—that metaphysics
has always promised and moved towards. Hegel's system is the ulti-

mate *overcoming of death*—the *Aufhebung* of finitude itself—of man himself. The philosopher of Absolute Knowledge has solved all mysteries, and especially that of death. We will live forever. The catch is that the condition for infinity, for that promised eternal life, is precisely the sign. It is writing that is the gateway to infinity and not presence. The pure essence of *"s'entendre-parler"* is the ephemeral moment that can never become an object, and certainly not an object of knowledge. It has no longevity essentially. Only the sign: (a) is intersubjectively available, and (b) can constitute objectivity. We learn this from both Hegel and Husserl.[37] Language, for Hegel, is the element of truth and thus of the eternal. In this sense, then, the ultimate Presence of consciousness to itself is infinitely deferred, even in Hegel. The here and now is the realm of the voice, of immediacy and hence of falsity—at least with respect to the metaphysical tradition; that is, of the *epistème* itself.

The significance of this double edge of the Hegelian system for Derrida is crucial. Hegel thus reveals: (a) the closure of metaphysics, in the very production of its infinity and boundlessness; (b) the limits of the Concept; and hence, (c) the boundaries of philosophy itself, beyond which it cannot go. Philosophy as a totality thus becomes captive and in this finality is revealed: (a) as a finite system, but also (b) as one which can continue indefinitely. What lies beyond this closure extends to the realm of *différance,* for Derrida, and hence will be examined in greater detail in the following section.

Although Hegel is the apex of the triangle, or the final dot or moment in the circle that is history, that is metaphysics, that is philosophy, there are two other loose ends for Derrida that are of significance with regard to the limits of the at least centrally unified tradition of metaphysics. One is Husserl and the other is Heidegger. The fact that they are historical antecedents of Hegel is of little significance here. They represent folds in the tradition and also do not contradict Derrida's demarcation of the closure with Hegel since this finitude of the "system" is, as Derrida says, not its death: "That which is included within such a closure can continue indefinitely."[38] Husserl sustains the notion of presence as the criterion for evidence and truth despite his own contradictions on this point (which Derrida has demonstrated in his introduction to the *Origin of Geometry*). And Heidegger, as we have shown, returns to the phonological basis of the voice of Being, albeit unheard throughout the history of metaphysics.

The ultimate basis for Derrida's unification of the history of philosophy as a single tradition concerns a fundamental desire which he claims animates the totality of philosophy. This desire is for a "transcendental signified" which therein would be liberated from all worldly representation and any attachment to empirical signifiers, to language in particular. Not only are specific languages reduced in this act, but also language in general—the sign as such. The ultimate transcendental signified has of course always been God—"the name of indifference itself,"[39] that ultimate unity, omnipotence, omniscience that has no bounds, no limits and hence is essentially independent of all worldly, empirical form. He is the essential meaning of the notion of the transcendental signified; the essence of essence—indeed its ground of possibility. In the tradition of philosophy, God is represented metaphorically and necessarily so. This sign for the non-sign is presented in philosophy in general as the Light, or the Sun. Thus Derrida considers philosophy as heliotropic: incessantly turning towards the Light of truth, from one Sun to another: in search of the daylight, a photosynthetic plant that lives only within certain conditions of visibility and invisibility. The systematic appearance of these metaphors will be considered in greater detail, in terms of the "Grammar of Conceivability," in particular, but for the moment we wish only to point towards that *archè* which forms the *telos* for Derrida and for the history of metaphysics as such: that movement between one presence and another, that world whose changes are conditioned from one Sun to another.

> Philosophic discourse—as such—describes a metaphor which is displaced and reabsorbed between two suns. This end of metaphor is not understood as a death or dislocation, but as an interiorizing anamnesis *(Errinerung)*, a recollection of meaning, a sublation of living metaphoricity into a living property. Philosophic desire—irrepressible—to summarize-sublate-interiorize-dialecticize-master the metaphoric movement between the origin and itself, the oriental difference.[40]

Thus History, for Derrida, as for all metaphysics, is essentially (has always been and will always be) the "teleology of meaning."[41]

(e) The Grammar of Conceivability

> La langue nous empoisonne le plus secret de nos secrets, on ne peux même plus brûler chez soi, en paix, tracer le cercle d'un foyer, il faut encore lui sacrifier son propre sacrifice.[42]

Outline of the History of Metaphysics for Derrida

Pre-Socratics Parmenides Plato Aristotle   Hegel Husserl Heidegger

"origin of truth: logos"; "priority of the voice and the denunciation of writing"

"Priority of the present as evidence"

(a) "idealization as objectivity and interiority"
(b) "foundation of modern semiology"

(a) "apparent limits of the history of metaphysics"
(b) "the metaphysics of presence: unified tradition"
(c) "opening and accomplishment of phonologism (logocentrism)"

"the concept of time has not moved"

"the enigma of Now is mastered—the concept of time"

Metaphysics not only inhabits our language, according to Derrida, but also prescribes a "determined and finite system of conceptual possibilities." It is "a systematic chain and constitutes in itself a system of predicates. There is no concept of metaphysics in itself. There is a work [*un travail*] . . . on conceptual systems."[43] Metaphysics is thus a system of force, power, mastery, domination, violence and, above all, surveillance, for Derrida. Its territory includes all Western (occidental) languages and therefore all thought from this region of the world. There is apparently no escape from this "system" since metaphysics has itself "understood," included, and therefore dominated its other, and all possible others. The act of exclusion as "other" is therefore a more subtle act of inclusion,[44] since the "other," as understood by metaphysics, i.e., non-metaphysics, non-truth, non-philosophy, non-rationality, non-presence, non-essential, is captive within the system as a derivation from the proper; from the essential, true, etc. This framework provides the ground of the possibility of meaning in general and also of meaning for each "single term," word, or name in the system. The structure of this framework must now be examined in its particular manifestations and acts of domination and mastery, as Derrida understands these terms. It should be recalled, however, that despite this all-inclusive capture of thought by language and in turn by metaphysics, Derrida finds "within the system" an opening for the possibility of an "essentially" non-metaphysical thought. Of course this must be considered the "madness of the day,"[45] at least for the moment.

In striking contrast to the Anglo-Saxon notion of "ordinary language philosophy,"[46] Derrida insists that "ordinary language" is always already installed within the system of metaphysical conceptuality. That which it presupposes in its formulations and that which gives words, phrases, and the act of predication itself their meaning is essentially metaphysical. This means that in pretending (or insisting) that these constraints on the discourse do not exist, one falls victim to their commands, and all knowledge generated therein is necessarily in accordance with this ultimate command. Hence, metaphysics sustains its dominance and its hold on Western thought from within discourse, and most strongly in the cases where this is not taken into account. As he says, ". . . ordinary language is not innocent or neutral. It is the language of Western metaphysics and it carries not only a considerable number of presuppositions of all types but also inseparable presuppositions and for the little attention one pays to them, tied into a system."[47] This structure of presuppositions that are inseparable includes the preformulation of questions and answers according to a set of rules concerning the nature of questionability.[48] For instance, the question "what is. . . . ?" as we have shown, always installs the response within a definitive, essential, proper, and non-changing characterization. It is the question of the proper name. The question "why?" *(pourquoi?)* always presupposes the metaphysical notions of sign, origin, presence, absence, *telos,* and *archè*—and immediately so.[49] The instant one asks "why?" one is always already asking "what for?" which entails the philosophical notions of purpose, causality, destination, sender, receiver, and essentially the *sign* as a derivation from a more essential "non-sign"; its *telos* and origin.

The organization of the word itself is also taken into account by metaphysics. In order to be meaningful, a word must "stand for" something else; that is, it must signify a signified. The essential nature of the word is therefore *defined* as arbitrary; as a sign which is not essentially attached or linked to its referent. In Saussurian terms, which betray an inner link to classical metaphysics, for Derrida, the signified is independent of the signifier.[50] We should recall that philosophy is based, for Derrida, on the desire for the transcendental signified and, in addition, that he does not believe this to be actually achievable, although metaphysics insists on it. Thus the meaning of the word, that which it signifies, is severed from all essential relation to particular languages. It is this structure which provides the condition of the possibility for translation itself. Without an independent signified, one could not alter signifiers from one language to another. Thus metaphysics provides a theory of translatability which, if generalized to its highest level, turns into Chomskian universal grammar and, of course, ultimately a mathematics of meaning. Computer translation is already well installed in the business of realizing these aims.

For Derrida, however, the signifier and signified have an intrinsic relation the severing of which also violates the essential meaning of the term. The polysemic aspect of a term, for instance, is treated by metaphysics as inessential insofar as it will search for an underlying *unity* which serves to ground all differences. Derrida describes this movement of reduction in the following way:

> It [philosophy] will have doubtlessly sought for the reassuring and correct rule, the norm of this polysemy. It will have asked if a "tympan" [Derrida's exemplary term] is natural or artificial, if it is not founded ultimately on the unity of a fixed star, bordered, framed, surveying its

> margins as if a virgin, homogeneous, and negative space leaving its
> outside outside, without mark, without opposition, without determina-
> tion, ready as matter, master, *khora* to receive and to reflect the pat-
> terns. This interpretation will have been true, in fact the history itself of
> truth.[51]

Thus the structure of reducibility of all differences to an essence that is
the same, the center, and the form which inhabits their only apparent
multiplicity is inherent in the metaphysics of language, according to
Derrida. In the act of translation, it is this center that forms the possibility of the signified-in-itself: the meaning, the message without support from its means of transport, the end in itself. Thus a certain
violence is carried out in the name of the name. For Derrida, this
collapse of differences is suspect, since it is precisely the structure of
metaphysics itself. In addition, he will claim that no such center necessarily exists or is to be found. Instead what occurs in this formation of
the concept is an act of domination of one "concept" by another, or of
the many by the one. For instance, he cites the term *'pharmakon'*[52] as
used by Plato, particularly in the *Phaedrus*. This Greek term entails
both notions of remedy and poison at the same instant. It does not
choose between them. However, all translations of this term have
severed one from the other and installed either poison or remedy in the
English and French texts, for example. The duplicity cannot be toler-
ated within a notion of translation based on the unity of a central
signified. This theory, as we have shown, is essentially metaphysical.

> A name is proper when it has only one meaning. Better, it is only in this
> case that it is properly speaking a name. Univocity is the essence, or
> better the *telos* of language. This Aristotelian ideal has never been re-
> nounced by any philosophy as such. It is philosophy as such.[53]

The constitution of this "proper name," the univocal essence, is a
function of a system of oppositions within metaphysics which themselves betray a more original violence. It is precisely the constitution of
the Concept that is in question here. For Derrida, this is an essentially
violent act whereby a radical exclusion of making the inside pure and
the outside external and thus extrinsic occurs. This is an act, or perhaps *the act* of Mastery within and by metaphysics itself. "It is the
infinite mastery which seems to secure the instance of being (and of
the) proper for it; this permits it [metaphysics] to interiorize all limits as
being and as being properly its own."[54] We have already exposed the

paradox within the exclusion, albeit in spite of metaphysics. There are two sorts of excluding/including acts for Derrida, therefore, which interrelate and are mutually supportive of the metaphysical structure as a whole. One is a hierarchical organization of oppositions such that inside/outside, truth/falsity, intelligible/sensible, etc., are installed as parallelisms in a system where each numerator relates essentially to each other numerator and likewise for the denominators. The interdependence of numerators (essence, for example) with denominators (inessential) is by definition inessential. In addition, the conceptual pairs (binary oppositions in contemporary terminology) are related to other conceptual pairs in accordance with two essential pairs (instituted by Plato) which in turn are organized (defined) by one above all others. The opposition of sensible/intelligible is the key to the system as a whole, and the second, almost equally essential couple of couples include: interior/exterior; Good/Evil. From these three sets of oppositions we can quite simply derive all others which govern the history of Western thought. For Derrida, the most important of these pairs includes the following representative list (they are not in any order of priority, however, except the first three):

Intelligible	*Sensible*
Interior	Exterior
Good	Evil
essence	appearance
form	content
origin	copy
proper	improper
univocity	polysemy
presence	absence
mind	body
nature	culture
nature	history
presentation	representation
life	death
infinite	finite
conscious	non-conscious
general	particular
ideal	empirical
meaning	nonsense

signified	signifier
philosophy	mythology
being	not-being
identity	difference
truth	falsity
visible	invisible
speech	silence
reason	madness
epistème	*doxa*
God	man
speech	writing
philosophy	non-philosophy

The representatives of the hierarchical ordering of thought include, for Derrida: Aristotle, Descartes, Kant, Husserl, Heidegger. Thus the hierarchy of concepts can be revealed as a system of constraints of genres/species in which all forms of knowledge, of science, have a place. Some more essential than others. Philosophy, of course, forms and performs the foundation for all such systems. The paradoxes in the system will be addressed shortly in terms of the "secret," but one should recall that the terms "philosophy" and "non-philosophy," for instance: (a) are to be found inside the conceptual pairing, hence within the system, yet (b) the name of the system as a whole is of course: philosophy. This is no accident. In addition, some terms seem to be duplicates. For example, the concept of nature on one side is paired with "totally" different opposites on the other side. What can this mean with respect to the essential concept of Physics? Further, one can illustrate that some concepts on the "inessential" side, for example, can also be found on the essential side, albeit paired off with "other" others. How can a term be *à la fois* both essential and inessential? Is this not a violation of the system as such? One such term involves the notion of the sign as defined by signifier/signified. The signifier is considered inessential, yet this is a formal character; the signified is essentially "content," and content is defined in opposition to form and thus on the side of the inessential. Yet the signified is defined as essential. This confusion is not by accident either, as we shall explain shortly. The contamination implicated here is thus not without reason, as Derrida will insist.

A second formal characteristic animates the structure of metaphysics for Derrida, and this entails the notion of envelopment: "The whole is implicated, in the speculative mode of reflection and expression, in each part. Homogeneous, concentric, indefinitely circulating, the movement of the whole re-marks itself in each particular determination."⁵⁵ The representatives of this framework include: Spinoza, Leibniz, and Hegel. It is this quality that prescribes the limitlessness of metaphysics, its ultimate authority with respect to knowledge, and the closure that is total. There are no exceptions, no accidents, no chances, and no laughter. It is the determination of meaning itself according to the *logos*. It is also therefore the systematization of all particularity, since the meaning of the part is always already determined by the whole. The meaning of the whole being unquestionable, especially by the part, whose identity is therein determined. Membership in the system is a given, since existence, Being itself, is determined by this structure of presentation. To not be thus determined is to be non-sense, madness, non-existence, or nothing. All of which are essentially interchangeable terms. As we have shown, these non-inclusive terms for what the system seems to exclude are thus essentially determined by the system. It installs its own other "outside," but nevertheless as its own. Hence the outside is itself inside. It is the exterior *of* metaphysics. Its backyard, as it were, which is nevertheless surrounded by a fence—a barbed wire, an electrified one at that, with a guard at the gate: surveying the scene. Albeit a Kafkaesque description of the world of thought, Derrida insists this is not only a literary illusion but also a philosophic one. As he says: "Philosophy has always held to that: to think its other. *Its* other: that which limits it and that from which it rises in its essence, its definition, its production."⁵⁶ As we have shown, non-philosophy was included *in* the list of binary oppositions essential to philosophy itself. It thus captures its other and names it "other." This capture which names and incorporates, which allows for philosophy to "understand the whole," is essentially a movement of the *Aufhebung ("rélèvance")* for Derrida: "To think it as such (its other), to recognize it, one misses it. One reappropriates it, one disposes of it, one misses it or rather one misses missing it, that which with respect to the other, returns always to the same."⁵⁷ Thus Derrida claims all means of escape are *a priori* blocked and put out of play. Meaningfulness itself is always paid for by the currency, and only that currency, of metaphysics. To not pay the price is to be excluded by inclusion, and therefore displaced, devalued, abandoned, albeit remaining captive within that same system. Such has been done to the sign, Derrida insists. This inclusion and devaluation therein is a mode of effacement that is essential to the theory and practice of metaphysics. Indeed metaphysics' finest hour is represented by Husserl, for Derrida. The "return to the things themselves" is precisely this ultimate effacement of metaphysics itself in the act of its predominance. The "principle of principles," that which guarantees the truth of the things themselves is essentially a metaphysical one: the presence of presence to itself. That is, the evidence that founds truth presents itself without the sign, without a body, without the need for the empirical world (which was always only an example, for Husserl) immediately to a pure albeit transcendental consciousness. Nothing could be more profoundly governed by the presuppositions of metaphysics. For Derrida, the sign of this effacement *par excellence* is to be found concerning the effacement of the sign:

> One can efface the sign in the classical manner of a philosophy of intuition and of presence. This effaces the sign in deriving it, annuls reproduction and representation in making an unwarranted modification to a simple presence. But as it is such a philosophy—and in truth the philosophy and the history of the occident—which has thus constituted and established the concept as such of the sign, which is, since its origin and in the heart of its meaning, marked by this derivative or effacing will.[58]

There is thus an essential geneology for metaphysics and for all that falls within its scope, according to Derrida. The meaning of the sign is essentially determined and cannot be simply abandoned. Nevertheless Derrida does not simply accept it as given either, as we shall see shortly.

These two main features of metaphysics—(i) hierarchical ordering and (ii) envelopment of all—are also interrelated for Derrida. "These two types of appropriating mastery . . . communicate between each other."[59] Indeed they form a system of "total surveillance," he claims. The hierarchy is the means of including "all," of dominating and defining the other, of excluding it from essentiality; and the notion of the "totality" as closed is the precondition and thus basis for the movement of hierarchical organization. What to do with the other? The first step, as we have seen, has been to name it "other," and thus as inessential. What to do with the unknown? Approach it in terms of the known, in terms of language, in terms therefore of metaphysics. That is to say: appropriate it, include it within the system in one way or another. It is this prescriptive regulation of all thought and of all possibilities of thought as "meaningful"—that is for an other—which closes the system. It is therefore a finite system of principles with a potentially infinite range of possibilities. The genetic code forms a rather good analogy, on many levels, for this "model" of metaphysics, although Derrida does not rely on it. Instead he invokes the metaphor of the family: metaphysics is "an entire family of concepts"; it provides a ready and inescapable "inheritance" in Western thought; it is the dominion of the proper which is essentially that of the Father: the phallus.[60] It is Oedipus therefore that will threaten the system, or perhaps a Judas (as J. M. Rey has suggested). It is the copy, the representative, the non-original, dependent, derivative, indebted, guilty, inadequate, essentially false and evil son that will threaten the system. And necessarily so. Although essentially understood within the realm of the proper—the Father's house—the language of Being—the son, which is the Sign, *par excellence,* can therefore only rebel from within the dwelling that is called home but yet is not *"chez lui"* (his own), at least not essentially.

(f) The Trace of the Trace

White mythology—metaphysics has effaced in itself the fantastic scene which produced it and which remains nonetheless *active,* restless, registered in white ink, invisible design and recovered in the palimpsest.[61]

Derrida has called metaphysics the *"logos* that believes itself to be its own father,"[62] thereby implying: (a) that metaphysics has foundations, a heritage, an origin which is not within itself; that is, not metaphysics itself; and (b) that metaphysics, as a closed system, has effaced this ground and therein erased the trace of its essential heritage. It is this "past" of metaphysics that Derrida aims to reveal. It is the condition of the possibility of metaphysics itself, the origin of the Concept of the concept, and it is fundamentally the question of the determination of Being as Presence (Heidegger's question) which must now be addressed. As we have seen, this has not always been the case, in historical terms, since certain proper names, especially Plato, have been associated with its origin. In returning to these beginnings, however, as Husserl has shown with respect to the origins of geometry (which do not essentially lie with Galileo[63] but with structural, conceptual possibilities), we do not reach the essence of the problem. Since, according to Plato, he does not constitute the Forms, or the Concept, but rather merely uncovers them, he more precisely remembers them since all learning we should recall was for him a form of recollection.[64] Thus the nature of nature is given to philosophy as a ready-made discovery. We should be suspicious already of this "givenness" as the effacement of a process of constitution, as Husserl and Kant before him have shown. Thus Derrida's search for the origins of metaphysics is not essentially a historical one, although the signs of this effacement are certainly to be found in the historical manifestation of its beginnings. What this means is that one must begin to read metaphysics otherwise. It is this shift in perspective that we shall attempt to document here so as to reveal what Derrida has called "the trace of the trace,"[65] another name for what metaphysics has called "Presence." We should also recall that "presence" is the condition of the possibility and the ultimate criterion for *evidence* and therefore truth within the conceptual apparatus of the Western world, according to Derrida. Thus the stakes are rather high.

As we have shown, it is toward the limits of philosophy that Derrida turns in search of the exposure of the essential threads which constitute this discourse as a whole. Where the Concept no longer comprehends all, or where there is an apparent excess or inadequacy, an *inadequation* of form to content (in Hegelian terms), is where Derrida claims the roots of the system become somewhat visible. Since this comprehension is already (and always already) within the domain of metaphysics, the excess can only be determined in a negative way, or else with a neologism. Derrida uses both. One of his terms for this foundation is *différance:*

> . . . *différance* in its active movement—what is comprehended in the concept of difference without exhausting it—is what not only precedes metaphysics but also extends beyond the thought of being (of presence). The latter speaks nothing other than metaphysics, even if it exceeds it and thinks it as what it is within its closure.[66]

As is perhaps all too well known and reiterated as such, the term *différance* for Derrida is a combination of the terms *différer* (to differ) and *déferer* (to defer), but this in itself tells us little about its meaning. We insist that this entails a double conception of timing and spacing, a movement that allows for the constitution of the object-as-such, and hence for the constitution of the concept. It is textualization itself, in a certain sense. A better clue perhaps for the understanding of this term is from Husserl concerning the phenomenology of internal time consciousness. He claims that there is a fundamental "unnameable" movement which grounds the possibility of all that is made present to consciousness as such.[67] This is more than simply protention and retention, although it includes these aspects. Derrida's claim is that this essentially shifting, opening, spacing, and timing *à la fois* is the essential condition for metaphysical conceptuality and further that it is precisely this that metaphysics as such cannot comprehend. The rupture of the system, albeit from within, can never be comprehended from inside that system, he insists. As he says:

> Reason is incapable of thinking this double infringement upon Nature: that there is lack in Nature and that because of that very fact something added to it. Yet we should not say that Reason is powerless to think this; it is constituted by that very *lack* of power, it is the principle of identity. It is the thought of the self-identity of the natural being. It cannot even determine the supplement [another name for *différance*] as its other, as the irrational and the non-natural, for the supplement comes naturally to put itself in Nature's place. The image is neither in nor out of Nature. The supplement is therefore equally dangerous for Reason, for the natural health of Reason.[68]

Thus it is not the "Heraclitean flux" that Derrida is appealing to in his proposal of a ground for metaphysics. It is rather an essential gap inside the closure of the concept which is both an excess and an inadequation. But how is this possible and what proof can there be to substantiate such a claim?

Derrida insists that the system of metaphysical conceptuality entails a hierarchical ordering of binary oppositional concepts which are both recognized and not recognized within metaphysics. For example, the notion of the signified is considered as independent of the signifier; it is the "unbound ideality" that Husserl speaks of. However Derrida has shown in great detail that the constitution and recognition of the signified (of meaning itself) is a function of the signifier, of absence from that essential presence. If we examine the word "book," for example, we can divide it into signified and signifier without difficulty. Now if we examine only the signifier—the letters that form the word as a whole—we find the essence of this form is an ideality that this particular empirical example "book" partakes of. Each letter and indeed the word itself is a representation of the ideal letter *b*, etc., and the ideal word: "book." This is necessarily the case in order that this particular formulation can be *recognized* as the word "book." In order to be recognizable it must be repeatable, reiterable, citable, and hence must entail an *eidos* for which, as we have claimed, this particular instance is only a representation. Thus the essence of the "pure" signifier is always already a signified. In turn we can analyze the purely signified in a similar manner. The idea of "book" is essentially (metaphysics will claim) non-empirical, non-sensible, and purely intelligible. Yet the constitution of objectivity is only possible: (a) via language, which itself transforms the particular here and now into an eternal always; and hence (b) via the sign—or more precisely, the signifier. Without this "means" of separation of the object from this particular subject, it could never become an "object for anyone"; that is, never an object for science and hence could not possibly participate in the realm of truth, which is essentially public. Thus, at the heart of the possibility of the signified as such, we find the signifier. And the reverse is also true. This is not a particular instance of contamination and paradox regarding the relations of essence and appearance, of sensible and intelligible, but a fundamental, albeit effaced, condition for the possibility of metaphysics itself. As Derrida says:

> That the signified is originarily and essentially (and not only for a finite and created spirit) *trace,* that it is always already in the position of signifier, is the apparently innocent proposition within which the metaphysics of the logos, of presence and of consciousness, must reflect upon *writing as its death* and *its resource.*[69]

We shall examine the paradoxical conclusion of this discovery shortly, but first we must pursue the *différance* as a general phenomenon inside/outside metaphysics as a whole.

For Aristotle, as for the entire history of metaphysics, as we have shown, the time of evidence and of truth is the time of the present. It is the moment of the Now which is both here and now and yet also eternally Now. This is expressed in the form of the third-person present indicative of the verb to be: *is.* However, Derrida insists that the *now* is fundamentally non-existent, it is a constituted moment of time which essentially is non-temporal. In a certain respect, he is applying the investigations of Husserlian notions of time to the tradition of metaphysics as a whole. What this entails is a recognition of a fundamental absence within the moment of the present. That is, with the movement of consciousness from retention to protention, and back again, we have a result that is synthetic which forms that which metaphysics calls the Now: the Present. This essential moment for the understanding of truth is internally divided and essentially so. It is always a "recollection" of the past, albeit "held" in consciousness, and a movement toward the non-yet-present future. It is in short, extended.

Yet only spatial objects within metaphysics have the property of extension. This overlap, Derrida claims, is not by accident: "complicity, the common origin of time and space, the co-appearance as the condition of all appearance of being."[70] Paradoxically, and yet also necessarily for metaphysics, it is precisely this that Aristotle discovered, yet then recovered; that is to say effaced in order to constitute a metaphysics based on the point in time, of the Now as Present. As Derrida says:

> that which unfortunately will constitute the mainspring of metaphysics, this little key that opens and closes at the same time in its play the history of metaphysics, this clavicule where the entire conceptual decision of Aristotle's discourse is supported and articulated, it is the little word *ama*.
>
> *Ama* in Greek means "together," everything at once, both together, at the same time. This expression is initially neither spatial nor temporal.[71]

It is *Ama* that is *différance,* the trace, the supplement, the resource and threat to metaphysics. It is the spacing that allows for the constitution of the Present, and hence the truth, as metaphysics understands these terms. What this means is that the relation between the binary oppositions of metaphysics must be understood in a new way. The radical exteriority that allows for their identification as other than each other, as different, which therein constitutes within each side, the "same," must be re-thought. The foundation for this "complicity," this "secret relation," is the relation of "form" to Being, for Derrida. That is, of Presence to Truth, as an immediate relation of subject to object, of consciousness to the Concept. As we have seen, the Present is not essentially thus, and the object or the Form in itself is also a constitution as a function of the temporalizing spacialization that is the movement of *différance* itself. In terms of this revelation, Derrida asks:

> Thus what is the concept of form? How does it register phenomenology within the closure of metaphysics? How does it determine the meaning of being as presence, as the present? What is secretly communicated with this delimitation of the meaning of being which is to be thought essentially in the verbal form of the present . . . ? What does the complicity between the form in general *(eidos, morphè)* and "is" *(esti)* force us to consider?[72]
>
> In a sense—or a non-sense—that metaphysics will have excluded from its field, retaining nonetheless a secret and incessant relation with it, the form will be already in itself the trace *(ikhnos)* of a certain non-presence, the vestige of the "in-form," announcing—calling its other, as did Plotinus, to the whole of metaphysics.[73]

Thus the term "presence" is essentially, for Derrida, the trace of the trace. It is apparently metaphysical, yet also and essentially non-metaphysical, and it is the latter that of necessity has been effaced within the system in order to "propertize" the identity and name the presence-as-such. We shall return to this.

There is another fundamental place within metaphysics that he re-marks upon in terms of this complicity. This is the relation of philoso-phy to mythology, of philosophy to poesis, to imitation, and more precisely, of the *philosophème* to the *mythème:* to metaphor.[74] The notion of metaphor for metaphysics has always been determined by that "for which" it stands; for which it signifies, its referent as non-metaphorical. It is thus a derivative concept; indeed represents the concept of derivation as such. Metaphor is a displacement of meaning from its origin, from the literal meaning, and as such finds a place within philosophical discourse as a "mere adornment," as a heuristic addition that serves as an illustrative demonstration of a truth beyond itself. Its role is thus essentially self-effacing and self-effaced within philosophic discourse. Nevertheless, it appears within the latter and repeatedly, indeed, Derrida will claim, essentially. We must now trace this appearance, as it will reveal more precisely what Derrida insists takes the place of the essence of metaphysics as such.

> Philosophy as theory of metaphor will have been initially a metaphor of theory.[75]

The conditions of the possibility of philosophy as such, Derrida in-sists, are essentially metaphoric, although the concept of metaphor, it must be remembered, is essentially a metaphysical one. Thus there is an inextricable "zig-zag" process needed in order to understand either "term," since each is essentially understandable only in terms of the other. The notion of truth in philosophy has always been a function of visibility, of seeing by the Natural light of Reason in which we all partake as essentially constituted as Rational Animals. For Descartes, this meant the criteria of clarity and distinctness of ideas; for Plato it was a vision of the Forms themselves. This illumination of the truth to the eyes of consciousness, indeed of the mind itself, can be traced throughout the history of philosophy. Truth always appears; it always becomes visible; it is in effect always made present, brought to light. This is intrinsic to its meaning in philosophy. As Derrida says:

The opposition itself of to appear and to disappear, the entire lexicon of phainesthai, of alētheia, etc., of day and night, of visible and invisible, of present and absent, all of which is possible only under the sun. This, in as much as it structures the metaphoric space of philosophy, represents the nature of philosophic language. The appeal to the criteria of *clarity* and *obscurity* suffices to confirm that which we have announced earlier: all of this philosophic delimitation of metaphor is itself already constituted and produced by metaphors. How could a knowledge or a language be properly clear or obscure? [my emphasis].[76]

Of course the philosophic answer to this question must be the movement towards univocity, towards ideality as such, and therefore beyond the obscurity of poetic language and, in particular, of a metaphor. Thus Plato exiled the poets from the perfect Republic, and Husserl insisted on the exactitude of non-poetic, scientific univocal discourse for the truths of philosophy. It is this "precision" that would ensure "mutual understanding," a proper intersubjectivity and hence the possibility of universal truths—for anyone at any time. Thus language was to be purified, and metaphor, for instance, to be disposed of. This banishment of the other, as a threat to the purity of truth, Derrida has revealed as precisely the latter's resource at the same instant. It is thus the case with metaphor. Not only is the Sun the central metaphor around which the "orbit of metaphysics" revolves and toward which it incessantly turns as a "heliotrope," Derrida also claims that "the movement of metaphorization" is itself that of idealization or more precisely, the reverse is the case. As he says: "Above all, the movement of metaphorization (origin then effacement of the metaphor, passage from the detour of figures) is nothing other than a movement of idealization. It is understood within the master category of dialectical idealism, that is, the *Aufhebung* or the memory which produces signs, interiorizes them in raising, suppressing and conserving the sensible exteriority . . . it describes the space of the possibility of metaphysics."[77] This movement of metaphorization is essentially the movement of signification itself, which underlies both metaphorization and idealization. For the constitution of the ideal is only possible via the sign; that is, as an intrinsic relation of signifier to signified, no matter how radically one attempts to distinguish them. The other continually reappears within the same and must necessarily do so. It is "really there"; essentially. This is not to say, however, that the idea is essentially a metaphor, unless one is prepared to consider the notion of truth as essentially a construct; that is, as a *telos* and origin the reading of which is both always immediate and thus always mediated. One should recall that the essence of immediate presence is that spacing which is absence itself— the distance from one moment to the next, which is incessantly on the move. This mediation forms the essence of essence, which is to say, the sign as the detour on the way to truth, is precisely the truth of the truth. The metaphysics of metaphysics, if one prefers. But this is of course no longer metaphysics. Derrida's thought is focused on absence, on non-identity, on signifiers rather than signifieds-as-such, on "mythology" rather than "philosophy," and on the trace rather than the essence. Thus the trace of the essence, of the Concept, of metaphysics, is at once its essence and its non-essence. The trace is essentially non-essential. This means that Derrida's claims must be considered *outside* of metaphysical conceptuality in order to be understood. Yet he himself insists that the condition of the possibility of understanding is itself this metaphysical conceptuality. Thus the double bind is at once installed and hence can be overcome. It is essential to metaphysics that it master its other, indeed all otherness. The non-metaphysical, albeit effaced, origin of metaphysics will be effaced again, necessarily. As Derrida says: "According to a law, which one could formalize, philosophy always reappropriates for itself the discourse which delimits it."[78] In fact this essay is a part of that movement. Any attempt to understand Derrida's work is a movement toward its reappropriation by metaphysics, and thereby a movement, paradoxically, toward the former's recognition and thus destruction. If Derrida's work is essentially therein comprehended, it will be (a) discarded as merely parasitic and hence not essentially philosophical or (b) acclaimed as a giant step in the history of metaphysics as such. It could not be otherwise. However, at the risk of being Oedipus at the moment of facing the Sphinx, and considering the question, prior to formulating a clear and precise response, we have sought to present the concept of metaphysics according to Derrida as faithfully as possible. The tragedy will be, as Derrida himself recognizes:

> The heliotrope can always lift itself up. And it can always become a flower dried in a book.[79]

The ultimate risk is perhaps, as Bataille said of Hegel, "He did not know to what extent he was right."[80]

Section III
Re-cognizing Différance as the Apocalyptic Play of the World

IV

THE POST-SCRIPTUM
OF BEGINNING

A. Introduction

> The future is not a future present, yesterday
> is not a past present. That which is beyond
> the closure of the book is neither to be
> awaited nor refound. It is *there,* but *out
> there*—beyond—within repetition but
> eluding us there. It is there like the *shadow*
> of the book, the *third* between two hands
> holding the book, the *différance* in the now
> of writing, the movement between the book
> and the book, this other hand. . . .
>
> —"Ellipse"[1]

It might have been possible to think of *différance* as temporality itself, had this term not so thoroughly been usurped by the "metaphysics of presence" and the sense of Being as an eternal Now, which therein contains the sense of both past and future. It might also have been possible to think of *différance* as the spatiality of space, if this formulation did not immediately bring to mind the problematics of a transcendental aesthetic and the immediacy of intuitions for the possibility of the constitution of experience as such. As the "shadow" of the book, *différance* still falls victim to the "metaphysics of presence" in terms of the notion of absence, of the shadow of the light, and of the heliotropic orientation of metaphysics as such therefore. The "third," albeit between the two hands holding the book, can easily slide into the "third" of Hegel's dialectic and indeed of the triadic formulation that guides the teleology and eschatology of metaphysics in general once again. But what is "the movement between the book and the book"? "This other hand"? It is perhaps the difference between the repeated and the repetition, or between the origin and copy, or the time of the repetition, or perhaps its space. It is perhaps the "and" that both unites and divides the apparently identical. It is perhaps also the appearance, the appearing of the identical itself as different—as separated from itself by the conjunction "and." It is perhaps, further, the addition of the self-same to itself, therein making it fuller than itself with its own fullness; quite simply therein betraying its own excess. But why "this other hand"? To whom or to what does it belong? Can it belong? and why a hand? Why other? We could speculate upon the handiwork of the other in the following respect, if we consider the Heideggerian treatment of handicraft. The letting-emerge of the emergent. The surrendering of the craftsman to his craft—to the texture of the wood, to its feel, its moisture and its dryness, its grain. In short its particularity of the moment. It is the hand of the *"chemin,"* as distinct from the method or technique. It is the way of the non-repeatable and non-representable. But how can we here attempt to trace, track, or follow such a path which "leads nowhere," which "effaces itself," and which is designed (by design and non-design) to set us off its path? It is perhaps the letting-learn of the good teacher that we must address ourselves to and not look for a master-plan, or a key-concept, or a blazed trail in order to approach what Derrida calls: *l'a différance.* His own approach cannot be repeated. It is non-repeatable in its essence. In short, it has no "essence," no form as such, but is the way of an intervention that erupts in particular texts concerning particular issues. The difficulties of inscribing, describing, representing, speaking of, or writing about such a non-method should "make their presence felt" prior to the transcendental reduction we will attempt to perform in order to make present, albeit by an act of violence (that of language and writing itself), that which Derrida claims and insists cannot be made present. This is not, however, an *Aufhebung* of Derrida. Quite the contrary. We hope to leave Derrida's claims as such, as origin and excess of our exposé still very much alive and in transition.

In order therefore to "speak" of the "unspeakable," to represent the non-representable, and hence to "name" the "unnameable," we propose to treat *différance* as it relates analogically to force, the idiom, and thought as they relate to language, for Derrida. The leap in logic from *is* to *as,* or from a structure of identity (the name) to the structure of analogy (the metaphor) will also be exposed, as we move from a description of the limits of language to that of writing. Derrida's own work shifts from a focus on language as such to writing and then to inscription in general as habitation, and it is this movement we will attempt to trace here. Finally, we will approach our subject as such and attempt to describe its structure, which we perceive as subsisting over time in a determinate form. The notion of structure itself must be conceived, however, as being "under erasure," in the sense that it will have long since been overcome in terms of the limits of language; yet its formality will be seen to resurge within, albeit in spite of, *différance*. This paradox too will be addressed, wherein we may find ourselves returning to the problematics of force and form, or more precisely of force and language, wherein we shall begin. The difference between a circle and an ellipse is surely, as Derrida also must recognize, not that one returns to its origin and the other does not, but rather that one has *one* center and the other—the realm of *différance* to be sure—has *two*. It is precisely this elongation of the circle[2] and the doubling of its focus that we will be tracing here in so far as it is possible, and in particular, for us. A final word of caution before we embark might be that one should always recall the tradition of metaphysics in order to understand Derrida but then also always perform a transcendental reduction on it, put it under erasure, cross it out leaving it still (only just) legible. The recall will therein leave sufficient residue for us to at least point toward that which allows for the residue to settle and hence that which of itself *never* leaves a residue and hence *has* no remainder.

B. The Limits of Language

(a) The Language of Force

If structuralism is the language of form, then the language of force is a contradiction in terms for Derrida. Force and language in this context relate to each other as mutually exclusive and opposing terms. Hegel discussed this issue in terms of the tautological basis of the force of the concept in Kant, in particular with reference to the function and structure of the Understanding. He recognized, Derrida claims, that: "the explanation of a phenomenon by a force is a tautology" because "to speak of force as the origin of the phenomenon is without doubt to say nothing. When it is said, the force is already phenomenon."[3]

This relationship of the becoming-phenomenon of force is precisely that which illustrates the limits of language for Derrida, as for Hegel. The process of the making-present of the entity is thus, at the same instant, the making-absent of force. It is force itself that allows for the possibility of this making, but it is also that which can never itself (a) be made, or (b) be made present, or (c) be said in the saying. Force is indeed the "origin of phenomena" for Derrida, but to "speak of this" is to lose the "forcefulness" of force. The process itself is lost in the formalization by "speech." We should expand the notion of "speech" here to include language in general for Derrida and not reify or particularize his claims with regard to a "speech" as distinct from writing, or as distinct from "silence." As he says, further, with respect to Hegel: "But in saying this one must envisage *a certain powerlessness of language,* not of thought or force, to step outside itself to speak of its origin. Force is the other of language without which this here would not be what it is [my emphasis]."[4]

This "certain powerlessness of language" is that same limit that Derrida claims for all structures. That which forms its conditions of possibility, that which is the opening which necessarily exceeds it are by definition not capable of being understood from within that same structure or system. They form instead what one might term its "blind spot"—its shadow, its other side. There is thus a perspectival nature within the nature of structure introduced here such that it is intrinsically *not* all-inclusive, nor all-embracing. Structure as such, and thus language as structure, is prohibited therein from a certain omniscience. This prohibition is precisely the condition of its possibility, Derrida claims. In addition, the condition of the possibility of structure is itself a structure:

> If there are structures, they are possible as a result of this *fundamental structure* by which the totality opens itself and overflows to create meaning in the anticipation of a telos which we must consider here in its most indeterminate form. This opening is certainly that which liberates time and genesis (even coincides with them) but also that which risks enclosing the movement toward the future—becoming by giving it form. That which risks stifling force under form [my emphasis].[5]

There seems to be thus a certain "circularity" here in the proposition of a structure that founds the possibility of structures in general. The origin of the origin is the origin, in a certain sense and a certain nonsense. It is this tautology of which Hegel speaks and which he shows to be a function of the play of Force itself in its relation to the Concept— the *Begriffe*—the Notion. It is the play of play with its expression which, of course, is also one of the moments of its play. How can this be better (more clearly) expressed? We shall proceed slowly and necessarily unsteadily at this point.

Derrida speaks of "the blind origin of the work" with respect to the issue of the "operation of the imagination," and perhaps this will assist us in gaining some clarity for our problem here. As he says:

> In order to seize more precisely the operation of the imagination it is necessary therefore for us to turn towards the invisible interior of poetic freedom. We must divide ourselves in order to reunite in this night the blind origin of the work.[6]

There is thus a certain force of the imagination—its operation, its movement—which is not available to the realm of what philosophy terms "the visible," the "seeable" according to the light of Reason—the light of day. It is thus toward the night, darkness, shadow of non-reason that we must turn here. The need to separate ourselves from ourselves and to rejoin or reunite these two halves in this night is the path—dimly lit as it is—that we must follow here. The "blindness" of the origin is thus our "blindness" to "see" it. Indeed, it is not available to the "sensory" apparatus of sight at all. The meaning (sense) of this force is not to be a function of the light of Reason but of the non-light of non-Reason. It will be a "turning towards the interiority of poetic freedom." We should recall that philosophy had its origins in the making of prose from poetry—the prosaic comprehension of the world—of the poem. It has never claimed to be able to comprehend the making poetry of poetry, nor the interiority of this "liberty." This is perhaps instead Derrida's aim, although not his *"vouloir-dire,* in this context. It is more precisely a *Gelassenheit* of that which cannot of itself *Gelassen;* a letting-speak of that which cannot be said and perhaps a pointing toward that which can never be reached.

But more precisely what is the relation of force to language in terms of this attempt to "seize the operation of the imagination"? Derrida says it is a question "of an exit out of the world towards a place which is neither a place nor another world, neither a utopia nor an alibi. *Creation of a universe which is added to the universe . . .* and which says nothing other than the excess of the whole, this *essential nothing* from which everything appears and produces itself in language . . . and this is the possibility itself of writing and of literary inspiration in general [my emphasis]."[7]

"The creation of a universe that adds itself to the universe" is precisely the movement from the circle of philosophy to the ellipse of *différance.* But surely Derrida does not aim to *create* another universe, to "play God" by repeating identically what the "Original Prime Mover" has done. This is not, however, what is at issue here at all, despite appearances. One should note that it is a "second universe" that speaks of nothing but the *excess* from the first, from that which allows of no excess. In addition, the "second universe" is the one that *speaks* of this "essential nothing." The doubling here has become a doubling of itself, it seems, in the following respect. Surely the first universe is the world of form, of language, of "totality," and hence of the world as such. Indeed, of the as such of the world. However, the second universe also *speaks*—hence it is also a realm of language, form, etc. And therefore if force is that which exceeds language, it is still in absentia in this second universe. Is there not then a "third universe" which would be the non-said of the said (of the totality) and, yet again, a fourth which would mirror the second for the first, be analogous (if one prefers) and therein be the un-said of the un-said—the excess over and above (beyond) the said excess? And we might continue this process *ad infinitum,* since the excess by necessity intrinsically *exceeds*—even itself. The opening Derrida presents us with here in the "creation of a universe which adds itself to the first" is also reminiscent of the "inverted world" of which Hegel speaks in his criticism of Kant. In the "inverted world," all that is in the non-inverted (first universe?) is reversed. What is good in the first is evil in the second; what was a distinction in the first is transformed into an identity in the second; and vice versa; and so with the sweet and the sour, the north and south poles, and for all distinctions of opposition; that is, reversibility. The difference between Derrida and Hegel on this point, however, is crucial. Derrida's "second universe" is not Hegel's "inverted world," because (a) the "second universe" is not in a relation of opposition or inversion to the first; (b) the "second universe" and the first are never totalizable as one identical, self-same universe; and (c) the "second universe" is radically dissimilar to the first in that it speaks of the nothing which both exceeds and opens the possibility of the existence of the first. Thus the second universe is a radically first universe, but one that is unproclaimed as such. Quite simply, it is, Derrida will claim, the origin of the origin, plain and simple. This non-origin of origin will be examined in greater detail in terms of the scope of writing, but here we wish only to announce its non-presence in the space between Derrida and Hegel, which it is essential to maintain.

The force of force, for Derrida, is thus that it cannot be said. It is that which allows for the linguistic, but which intrinsically escapes the formality of the latter. There is therefore a certain "weakness" within the force of force, a certain powerlessness which is also a power. Force in general thus divides itself, for Derrida, at the instant of its description. It becomes either: (a) force as powerful or (b) force as powerless. This division and suppression of one side by the other is precisely that which makes force both (a) imperceptible and yet later (b) perceptible. It is perceptible *as* that which *has* been forgotten. We can see this most clearly in terms of Husserl's phenomenology, as he tries to explain in structural terms that which breaks free and in turn founds the structurality of structure. These moments are what Derrida calls "phenomena of crises" and "failures to reach goals."

> And when, in places, Husserl ceases to consider the phenomena of crises and failures to reach goals as accidents of genesis, as inessential, it is to show that *"forgetting"* is eidetically prescribed and necessary, within the notion of 'sedimentation', to the development of truth. To its unveiling, to its illumination [my emphasis].[8]

It is the forgetting of force therefore that allows for the constitution of the present as such, of the as such of the present, and therefore of the possibility of the immediately present to consciousness as such of what is called evidence or truth. It is the "principle of principles" of phenomenology that is at issue here and which Derrida insists is founded on a more primary, more ultimate, more original, but unspeakable foundation. It is "force" that is forgotten; it is "force" that cannot be captured *fully* in the moment of the "living present," the Now of evidence and of experience—transcendental or otherwise—in Husserl's phenomenology. Derrida continues:

> Now one would search in vain to find in phenomenology a concept which would permit one to think *intensity* or *force*. To think the power and not only the direction, the tension and not only the *in* of intentionality. Nothing is gained or lost except in terms of clarity and non-clarity, of evidence, of presence and absence for a consciousness, of capture or loss of consciousness.
>
> From whence come the difficulties to think genesis and pure temporality of the transcendental ego, to take account of the achieved or missed incarnation of the telos and of these *mysterious weaknesses* one calls crises.[9]

The issue here is obviously not the weakness(es) of Husserl or his phenomenology but rather of that which these limits are a sign for. For Derrida, this "break in the form" of form is not an accident but an essential structure—or rather an essential non-structure, or more precisely (and beyond metaphysics) an "inessential non-structure." We have almost pushed the most essential thereby outside of language; indeed we are approaching the issue here. It is not, therefore, that phenomenology simply needs other concepts or more of them, but that phenomenology as such is oriented on the basis of the evident as the "objective"—and immediately so. The objective is the structurable and, hence, is able to find its way at some stage into language. Thus Husserl insists on the condition of truth as intersubjectivity, and the constitution of the latter by writing. The putting-into-language as that which makes public—for anyone at any time—what is only then legitimately called: knowledge or science. Thus language and knowledge coincide profoundly here and hence also their shadows. The non-sayable and the non-true. This relation of language to the *epistème,* however, introduces our next section, which concerns language and the idiom and will thus be elaborated more fully there. The point here, however, is that there is a transformation which occurs in the process of putting-into-language which is: (a) made possible by force, yet (b) therein loses, forgets, buries, or suppresses that "same" force. As Derrida says: "To speak of force as the origin of a phenomenon is without doubt to say nothing."

In speaking of force, however, one might also be tempted to think in terms of Nietzsche and the two founding forces for all creativity and thus for the imagination as such. For Nietzsche, Apollo and Dionysius represent this original structure, and their struggle is reminiscent of that between metaphysics and its other, or sense and non-sense, order and disorder, the light of day and the darkness of night. One might, in addition, be tempted to understand force for Derrida as Dionysius for Nietzsche, but one should, however, resist such a temptation. We shall take a brief excursion therefore into this realm of intoxication in order to return to Derrida with perhaps a more sober, more clear, and more non-Nietzschean perspective.

We should recall that Apollo and Dionysius represent two principles of intoxication for Nietzsche, and they together provided for the "birth of tragedy" for the Greeks. The Apollonian principle "alerts above all the eye," and "acquires the power of vision," whereas for the Dionysian "the entire emotional system is alerted and intensified so that it discharges all its powers of representation, imitation, transfiguration, every kind of mimicry and playacting, conjointly." He is "continually transforming himself" and "represents bodily everything he feels. . . ."[10] It was therefore a function of the Apollonian principle or force that logic, science, rationality, forms, and structures came into being, and a function of the Dionysian that comedy and tragedy as such came on the stage. The Dionysian principle thus lends itself to "frenzy, hallucinations, endemic trances and collective visions." One might wonder if science as "white mythology" could not be considered a "collective vision" or an "endemic trance" for Derrida, and reasonably so. For Derrida, the two principles are not to be radically separated as one sets apart the oppositions of metaphysics. There is a certain game, a certain interplay from one side to the other and back again, which allows for the function of both "as" independent, and indeed as distinguishable. Thus one could not identify Dionysius with force and Apollo with language, to return to our subject at hand. The difference between them is also force, and therefore it cannot be localized or captured within one of the terms. Such is also the case with the relation of language to force, however. Indeed the two sets of relations are not identical but are *analogical.* A crucial distinction and a crucial relation. The relation in question here could also be described as that between Joyce and Husserl in terms of the question of univocity and equivocity of language, as Derrida has explored in his work on Husserl.[11] The issue is indeed interplay. It is the relation that exists, yet is prohibited. It is the transgression of form by force and the transgression of force by form. It is "force giving its place to the *eidos* (that is to say, to the visible form for the metaphysical eye)."[12]

Thus, just as the radical distinction between language and force has been made, so must it be overcome, but not forgotten. Language is not force, just as Apollo could never be Dionysius, nor a Husserl a Joyce; but the former could not exist without the latter, nor the latter be expressed without the former. The gap, or the inadequation of the form to the force, or of form to non-form is the abyss which goes by the name of *différance.* The space of inadequation is a space of movement, a spacing, and also a certain timing, a certain temporality. The "two universes" certainly do actually coexist, if Derrida is correct, but one cannot *speak* of both of them simultaneously. It is therefore one of the intrinsic limits of language which we speak in accepting the fact that we cannot, by definition, speak of it as such. Nor can we speak of anything as such in a profound sense, as we shall see shortly, but only point toward the "as such" with a netting that only catches the as such. The realm of the "as such," as we have seen is *not* the realm of which we are speaking. Yet, more precisely, it is the only realm of which speech can speak. The more precisely we aim towards our object the less clear it becomes. This too we must demonstrate as essential to our problem rather than a deliberate "confusing" of the issue. First, we must turn towards the idiom and the second limit of language.

(b) The Death of the Pure Idiom

> There was in fact a first violence to be named. *To name,* to give names that it will on occasion be forbidden to pronounce, such is the *originary violence of language* which consists in inscribing within a difference, in classifying, in suspending the vocative absolute [my emphasis].[13]

This "original violence" of language therein inscribed the possibility of taboo, of prohibition, and with this the possibility of law itself. To name is to distinguish—in effect, is to be born—to become separate, to be separated, to be is to be other, therefore, as primordially prior than to be the same. The condition of "sameness," uniting differences, is therefore a more radical difference. And the condition of difference is the name. The notion of an improper name is thus a contradition in terms. Therefore, Derrida calls the notion of *différance* a multiplicity of things. The appellations themselves he terms "nicknames strategically chosen." *Différance* is not, however, the idiomatic, so we shall proceed with some caution here. The other names of *différance* must be left as unannounced, therefore, for the moment.

The notion of naming, as a violence, is a violation of the idiom, of the purely unique, idiosyncratic, non-repeatable, non-representable. In the first instance we were concerned with that which language can *never* capture, whereas now we must deal with that which language, for Derrida at least, seems to kill. The "name" is the result of this process, not its beginning however. In the beginning the idiom lives, for Derrida, and thus it is killed with the installation of language as such:

> The death of absolutely proper naming, recognizing in a language the other as *pure* other, invoking it as what it is is the *death of the pure idiom* reserved for the unique [my emphasis].[14]

The paradox here is that, as we have seen with force, it is not possible for language to speak of its origin, of its other, of force. Thus what does "recognizing in a language the other as *pure* other" signify here? We should remark first that the term "pure" also appears with respect to the reference to the idiom. It is "the death of the *pure* idiom," not paradoxically, that of the idiom in general, but the *pure* form, i.e., not the impure idiom, or at least so it seems. What is at stake here is the issue of purity and impurity therefore, and much more so in fact than that of the idiomatic and the repeatable. What language kills is thus the *purity* of the idiom and it does this, also paradoxically, by "recognizing the other as *pure* other." In the movement from purity to impurity and from impurity to purity we can perceive perhaps the very movement of *différance* itself. As language names, that is installs itself, it therein makes the pure idiom impure and makes an impure other *purely* other. What this entails is a radical dislocation and reorganization of "things." It is precisely the constitution of the object as object; of the constitution of the concept as concept; that is, of the concept as such. It is the making-proper of the name. (One should recall that *propre* in French means proper and also clean in English.) But how can the making-impure of the idiom be the same as the making-pure of the other? This is precisely the founding act of metaphysics, according to Derrida, in that the other becomes excluded from the House of Being as such— that is, from the Same. Indeed the radical distinction of same and other, identity and difference, Being and non-Being is inaugurated here. One should also remark that Derrida speaks of "the death of *absolutely proper* naming," which is not the *death of* absolutely proper naming but rather that death that ensues by virtue (or vice) of the process of *absolutely proper naming*. The banishment of the other from the same is what is in question here. And the ensuing death of the pure idiom. But how can an idiom be impure? Is an idiom not essentially *only* an idiom? What sort of *other* could or does the idiom have which could contaminate it? The generality of language itself seems to be the only answer to such a question. That which "contaminates" the pure idiom must be universality. The pure idiom, as Derrida says, is that which is "reserved for the unique." Yet after the advent of language, *nothing* is reserved for the unique. The idiom is contaminated with generality—is overcome yet sustained—since it is not the death of the idiom as such of which Derrida speaks, but of the "pure idiom," to repeat. Thus it is a death which is not a death at all. The pure idiom surely must die, but what is sustained is a certain sort of (albeit contaminated) idiom. But much of this argument hinges upon the distinction between the "pure idiom" and "the idiom as such," or the "idiom in general." One might justifiably wonder at such a distinction and question its legitimacy perhaps. We shall attempt to clarify this apparent confusion. First, the idiom as such, or idiom in general must by definition be the most general form of the term idiom. It is from the idiom-in-general that one can then derive various types of idioms. Such types might include: biological idioms (mutations, for instance) physical idioms (the unpredictable in the physical universe), and indeed *pure* idioms. That pure idioms resemble idioms in general is only the case if one insists on a metaphysical definition of the "in general" as radically excluding its other and therein becoming "pure." This need not be done, we insist, and in particular with reference to Derrida, *should* not be done. When he speaks of the pure and the impure and most oppositions in general, he does so with an eye to their "secret relationship." It is not for nothing that he refers to the oppositions of metaphysics as "copulating concepts." Thus we insist on the distinction between the "pure" and the "in general."

Returning to the idiom, language therefore kills something. As we have said, it kills the purity. But surely this is a paradox in that language, it seems, can only speak of the universal; that is, is it not language itself which installs the purity, as we have shown with the "pure other"? How can language at the same instant perform two opposing and seemingly mutually exclusive operations? Perhaps, for Derrida, there is no such "thing" as language in general. That is, language itself is neither pure nor an object, but that which allows for the possibility of objects. But in saying this it seems that we have shifted language now into the realm of force; that is, as a precondition for and hence one step removed from the "object" as such.

This emergence of the "object as such" might also be called that of the idiom as such—or perhaps, the "pure idiom." But we have shown that "language is the *death* of the pure idiom." How then can language be at once the condition of the life and death of the pure idiom? Simply because language is the condition of the possibility of the pure and the impure. It is language itself that makes things into things by making them proper; that is, with names, and hence with certain properties, certain qualities that are henceforth inscribed therein, by definition. Thus language is the condition of the possibility of the *pure*-in-general, or of purity as such and thus also for the pure idiom. This is not simply sophistry but a chain of necessity which will point towards what Derrida calls (nicknames) différance. We are also pointing toward another limit of language here which, although first emphasized by Hegel, was perhaps first thought by Plato, who said that "writing is the condition of the law." Once written, the law will exist for all and for all times, and one can continually refer to it and not depend on subjective and fallible memories. For Hegel, a more profound relation is revealed when he refers to the order of language as the order of truth:

> And the unutterable—feeling or sensation—far from being the highest truth, is the most unimportant and untrue. If I say "the individual," this individual, "here," "now" all are universal terms. Everything and anything is an individual, a "this," and if it be sensible, is here and now.[15]

And for Derrida, we have the death of the pure idiom by the movement of language whose function is to "name" and therein make proper. But still a paradox emerges, and this entails: (i) that the idiom-in-general "exists" prior to language, and (ii) tnat the impure idiom "exists" after language (within it and perhaps in spite of it), and thus (iii) there is another impoverishment or inachievement, intrinsic to language, and therefore another of its limits can be revealed. The first problem, concerning that which antedates language, must point us towards an indescribable abyss. The notion of being-before-language is non-sensical intrinsically—just as "nature" as such is non-sensical. The concept of nature exists only in relation to its others: culture or history. The idea of a pure nature, prior to the advent of culture, cannot be sustained except by the forgetting of the origin of the notion itself. This has indeed been done however, in Western thought, and thus should not be seen as inconceivable. But the process of the effacement of the constitution of such a construct should perhaps now be considered and taken into account. It is the forgetting that Derrida has shown even Husserl to have inscribed in the process of history, as eidetic, as we mentioned earlier. Therefore, with respect to language and the idiom, we must wonder about the "pure idiom" as being even possible "prior" to language. Is it not simply a function of language, of distinction, of naming, of separation that anything such as the "pure idiom" or the "unique" could exist? Of course, to say that something exists already begs the question here, since for Derrida, "to exist" is "to be an entity," and hence to already be "inscribed": to be named. As we said, to be named is to be born. Nevertheless, we must wonder about the nonplace for the "pure idiom" in the context of which Derrida speaks. We propose that the "pure idiom" is an *a posteriori* concept which perhaps points beyond language rather than back, behind it—posthistorically, rather than prehistorically—and which therefore is a *product* of language, albeit exceeding the latter. Oedipus and the master/slave dialectic in Hegel must immediately come to mind in this context, although both paradigms must also be resisted. We must *pursue* the *chemin* of Derrida here without prescriptively imposing ready-made paradigms and interpretations on his thought. The thought of *différance* is emerging, albeit slowly, perhaps painfully, in this process and one must take the time for its appearance. Thus the question of the "return of the idiom" to overthrow language, its Father, or Master, must be ruled out of order at this juncture—also the very one when it appears and seems to be relevant.

If the "impure idiom exists after language," our second query above, a certain relation of language to the impure idiom seems to be presupposed here. One might even reduce language as such to the impure idiom as such. But there is no *after* of language. Language resists temporality intrinsically. It persists over time. Therefore, unless we "return" to an age of silence as the "time of the cry," prehistory, which is evidently not possible, the issue of the "afterwords" of language seems essentially a non-issue. Finally, with respect to the inachievement of language, its impoverishment, it seems we have found something substantial. Language, in its act of naming, aims to make pure the impure—to make things proper; that is, to produce things themselves. However, it must of necessity fall short of its goal (also a parallel situation to that of Husserl aiming towards absolute univocity, and Joyce towards its inverse.) What language cannot do, therefore, is kill the idiom as such. What it does is kill the "pure idiom . . . reserved for the unique." In a word, language is powerless to destroy the idiomatic, although it surely contaminates it, changes its identity by giving it or assigning it one that is fixed within a system of others, defined by differences themselves, and so on, in a chain of signification. Thus in a very profound way, the violence of language is a limited violence— inherently. It aims toward the in general in general, but it can never achieve such a goal. Just as Leibniz's mathematization of the universe must necessarily fall short of an algebra for everyday life. The excess in the system is precisely where the idiomatic appears and reappears, even if only for an instant. It is the life of language that it itself can neither kill nor speak of. But once again, the idiomatic is not force, although it is perhaps what Derrida calls "the force of force" and the "force of weakness." It is perhaps that which "with no force of its own forces force." And in this movement and this process language can say nothing. Indeed, it is the "nothing" that language cannot say.

(c) The Thought of Language

If we accept the limits of language thus far described in terms of force and of the idiom in general, then how must one consider what Derrida terms *la pensée* with respect also to language? The thought of language must of necessity exceed language, exceed its object and indeed the "object form" in general. Thought, for Derrida, is precisely this *excess*. Far from being therefore indescribable (unsayable), however, we propose to move once again toward our issue via metaphor, via the structure of analogy rather than identity. In addition, we hope to show that this structure is the foundation of "identity" insofar as the same is always the same *as*. But first we must distinguish Derrida's "thought" from that of Heidegger, which is at first glance *not dissimilar:*

> 'Outside the economic and strategic reference that Heidegger justifies in giving to an *analogous but not identical transgression* of all philosophemes, *thought (la pensée)* is here for me a perfectly neutral name, the blank part of the text, the necessarily indeterminate *index* of a future epoch of *différance* [my emphasis].[16]

Derrida admits therefore to an analogous relation to the "same term" in Heidegger's work. Analogous must mean: (i) similar but not identical; and hence (ii) having the same structure (form?) but with different contents. In a certain respect therefore the term "thought," for Derrida, performs the same function in his work as it does in Heidegger's, though they define the term differently. For both it is that which exceeds metaphysics and therefore, in the same breath, "all languages of the West." Metaphysics and language are thus profoundly synonymous for both thinkers. In addition this "excess" also extends beyond "all polemics" which take a "stand" or a "side," "one track" on an issue. Thinking, for both Derrida and Heidegger, provides an essential opening which draws one towards the abyss of the unknown, of the enigmatic, and hence of the "as yet unnameable." Yet Derrida calls thought "a perfectly neutral name" in this context. Surely a slip of the tongue (pen), since, as we know from Derrida himself, "the name is not neutral"—it is that which profoundly violates and kills the "pure idiom." However, Derrida continues to situate his claim in terms of textuality, and it is here that he breaks from Heidegger. For the latter, we should recall, thinking is simply "being drawn into what withdraws." It therefore defies all relation, all formalization, all law and all method, as technique. For Derrida, however, "thought" is an index. (Indeed he speaks of "thought" and not "thinking," one should also remark.) "The blank part of the text . . . where the whites take on importance" is surely the enigmatic, but not the enigmatic in general as for Heidegger. We shall not be rid of the analogical relation of Derrida to Heidegger so easily, but for the moment let us focus more precisely on Derrida's claims as such. Thus, Derrida continues:

> In a certain sense, "thought" means nothing. Like all openings this *index* belongs within a past epoch by the face that is open to view. This thought has no weight. It is, in the play of the system, that which never has weight.[17]

The metaphor of weight here is not without allusions to Nietzsche, we suspect, and to the issue of gravity, the gay science, and the movement beyond good and evil. But we will only suggest such a reference at this point. Thought, for Derrida, seems to be situated on the border between the "system" and that which lies "beyond it," yet is also in a certain sense precisely that beyond. "It has no weight" for the scales of Reason. That is, of language. As an "index" it is a pointer, a sign-post along the *way* that is not a method. But is this not also a contradiction in terms? Only in an absolute sense, we insist, and it is this absolute positivity, so characteristic of science, metaphysics, and language, which we are aiming to expose here as its limit. Beyond such positivity one finds, instead of theses and/or antitheses, hypo-theses. That is, the realm of the possible. Indeed that of the possibility of possibility is precisely thought, for Derrida, we claim. The opening is not "not-yet," but already; it is the *"déjà pas encore,"* but not that of Hegel. It is not a usurping or capturing or speaking, in an exact sense, of the possible. It is a pointing towards that possibility of possibility. Just as "infinity" always exceeds the "totality," for Levinas, thought always exceeds that same language it uses to express itself.

We find this relation more precisely explained by Derrida with reference to what he terms "the imagination." As he says: the imagination "is the freedom which only shows itself in its works. These are not *in* nature but they live nowhere else but in our world."[18] Thus the imagination is to be found in a certain sense behind or beneath that which it produces. It is not, however, the "author" of the work in this sense, but something instead which can never be made present. It is "the enigmatic origin of the work as indissociable unity and structure."[19] But can we not decipher this "enigmatic origin" and reveal it, bring it to the light of day, understand it reasonably; in short, speak of it? Derrida will insist that this is structurally impossible. Since language is the language of structure, the idea of possibility, the not yet *and* already in structures intrinsically escapes. This is because "the freedom of the imagination consists precisely in this: that it *schematizes without concepts*."[20] It is evidently the Kantian imagination of which he speaks here. It is that which allows for the unity of sensibility and the concepts of the understanding that is at issue. Kant himself admitted to these same problems in treating the imagination.

> This schematism of our understanding, in its application to appearances and their mere form, is an art *concealed in the depths of the human soul,* whose real modes of activity nature is hardly likely ever to allow us to discover, and to have open our gaze. This much we can assert: the image is a product of the empirical faculty of reproductive imagination; the schema of sensible concepts, such as figures of space, is a product and as it were a monogram, of pure a priori imagination, through which and in accordance with which, images themselves first *become possible.* These images can be connected with the concept only by means of the schema to which they belong. In themselves they are never completely congruent with the concept [my emphasis].[21]

It is well known that Kant was not adverse to the recognition of unavoidable mystery and therein the limits of knowledge, the *epistème,* and of course Reason. But Derrida parts company with his predecessor in the phrase "an art concealed in the depths of the human soul," although he would certainly agree with the remainder of this phrase. The imagination for Derrida is not a "property" of humanity in the sense of metaphysics' determination of "man as the measure of all things." As with Heidegger, such "humanism," anthropomorphism, and ethnocentrism must be ruled out. Thus the imagination transcends the locus of the "human soul" for Derrida, as distinct from Kant. Further distance from Kant will also become evident as we proceed in terms of the "subject" of "experience" and the transcendental aesthetic, in particular with regard to the "constitution" of space and time, for Derrida, as distinct from Kant's "simple acceptance of them *a priori*." But more on this must be delayed at this stage. Derrida's imagination, it seems, betrays a profound relation to that which he calls thought, which "never has weight *in* the system." The notion of thought, as we have seen, is an "opening" from within the system or structure, which points toward its "exterior." In this sense, it contains a certain force, indeed that very force which language itself cannot contain. In short, thought as imagination is a power, albeit unrecognized by language, but one which allows for the possibility of language or representation as such. As Derrida says:

> *Imagination is the power* that allows life to affect itself with its own re-presentation. The image cannot represent and add the representer to the represented, except insofar as the presence of the re-presented is already folded back upon itself in the world insofar as life refers itself to its own lack, to its own wish for a supplement. The presence of the represented is constituted with the help of the addition to itself of that *nothing* which is the image, announcement of its dispossession within its own representer and within its own death. The property of the subject is merely the movement of that representative appropriation. In that sense imagination, *like death,* is representative and supplementary [my emphasis].[22]

The power of the imagination, its force, is therefore the force of death. It is the economy of an exchange, a "dispossession" that is announced in its very movement. More precisely, the imagination is itself a movement, for Derrida, but one that is not without its own laws of motion. It is only "free" within very particular limits. Its liberty, as he says, is *not* to show itself except in its *works;* that is, its products, its effects, its results. The term "liberty" for this characteristic might easily be shifted to its opposite, but this is not the issue here. The point is that the movement of the imagination is constrained *itself* by an economy of presence and absence. Is this the economy we know so well as that of classical Western metaphysics? And further, is this precisely the economy of language itself for Derrida? To make present one thing at the expense (price, cost) of making absent something else? It would seem so. But is this formulation "beyond metaphysics," or does it not also betray a fundamental link at the level of presuppositions for Derrida's thought of the imagination? We must proceed cautiously here since we may easily fall back into the "abyss" of metaphysics. The "absence" of the imagination is the absence of *death,* a radical absence, which therefore is not the absence "of something." It is a space that allows for the appearing to appear—to be represented in its presentation. Therefore the image as the "image of death" is precisely that "nothing" which was never "something" and can never become "something." As Derrida says: "Imagination is at bottom the relationship with death."[23] Death must be considered in its structural and therefore metaphoric sense here, for Derrida, since it represents a "radical absence" of both subject and object in the process of the *appearance* of both. Further, we must point to the significance of "death" as the abyss, as the radically unknowable (for us and for Derrida) and hence as that which will always escape formalization. The work of the imagination is therefore always only in relation to this, and therefore also to thought or that which "means nothing." But thought is not the same as death or the imagination for Derrida, and certainly thought and the imagination must also be distinguished. "The blank part of the text" is not imagination certainly, but it is Derrida's metaphor for thought, and may well be for death also. As we said earlier, it is "where the whites take on importance," in particular for Mallarmé, whose poetic productions put the "whites" to "work" in his play with language. First, the text is not a book, for Derrida, but rather exceeds this totalization. The book is surely a text, but the reverse is not and cannot be the case. What this means for thought is that the "text," as inscription, leaves spaces, indeed constitutes spaces within itself in order to "be a text." It constitutes openings in itself which exceed itself. The text is not, precisely speaking, the spacing; the text is that which allows for spacing, and yet spacing is that which allows for texts. But more on this later. It seems that the text, in terms of thought, opens the possibility of the latter; it opens the openings, yet does not control them. In the same way, the "image," in a certain sense, is "death," for Derrida. The outline is never closed in on itself, or it would not demarcate a form and hence a content. But the outline of the image opens itself to other images—to thought itself—to the possible. As Derrida says:

> Imagination alone has the power of giving birth to itself. It creates nothing because it is imagination. But it receives nothing that is alien or anterior to it. It is not affected by the 'real'. It is pure auto-affection. It is the other name for *différance* as auto-affection.[24]

Just as thought "means nothing," the imagination for Derrida, "creates nothing." Each is the condition of the possibility of the other in this sense. But their relationship is also much more intimate. Both thought and the imagination are in a profound respect immune or transcendent from that which they produce—their own effects, it seems. Since the imagination "alone has the power of giving birth to itself," it is not produced by its products (i.e. works of art). Further it "receives nothing that is alien or anterior to it." In a more radical sense, it seems that nothing *could* be anterior to imagination. It is that which always pre-exists that which exists. It is always therefore anterior to that which is. (To be, for Derrida we should recall, means "to be an entity.") With reference to thought, for Derrida, we should perceive a striking similarity in structure here. Thought is "radically other" than that which "presents" it or indeed represents it. Thought also receives nothing that is alien or anterior to it. It is a realm that paradoxically is both closed and open. It is closed in on itself in that it cannot be captured, cannot be formalized or totalized. In a word, it cannot be spoken, only spoken of, or spoken from. Exactitude, objectivity, and hence language as such will always be inadequate in the formalization of thought. But thought is a realm that is also "open" to language in a relation of overlap, of excess, and hence of inadequation once again. It marks the *index* in the "old system" (metaphysics) of the "as yet unnameable": the epoch of *différance*. It is, as we have shown, a signpost but, in so being, effaces itself. Thought is not within language, but it is, as Derrida says, "nowhere else." This sense of being-in-exile outside of the house of Being that is language is perhaps the play of language itself: its force, its weakness, its form in general, and *its* idiomatic structure reserved for the unique. But in describing language as such, Derrida insists that the term language itself must be overcome. In a certain respect, by illustrating the "limits of language," one has therein already stepped outside of "that same structure." Language, as inadequate to force, the idiom, and thought, has shown itself to be a structure more expansive than language as such, yet still representable by that term. This expansion of the realm of that which formalizes, or inscribes the differences is therefore a crucial step in the recognition of that which has exceeded first the literal category of language as such and now, as we shall see, the metaphoric expansion to inscription in general as *writing.*

(d) From Language to Writing

Although it may seem that the notion of writing, as a particular organization of language as such, should therefore be considered within the concept of language, Derrida insists that language as such is a subset of a wider notion of writing as such. Writing is to be considered for him therefore as a certain structure wherein language itself is inscribed. Thus for Derrida: "the *name of language* is beginning to let itself be transferred to, or at least summarized under the *name of writing*. . . ."[25] What is interesting here is that the notion of the *name* remains that which links yet divides language from writing. The "name" is precisely that which language is in control of. It is the property of language and indeed the "proper" of language, as we have shown. Yet Derrida insists on a shift *beyond* language but via this same "property"—from one to another. How can "writing" therefore exceed the limits of language? Indeed it does not, in a certain sense, but rather it illustrates a certain form of the formality or structure of language as such. Thus the paradox here is similar to the problem of a "science of writing" as a "necessary yet difficult task," since science is itself dependent on writing for the constitution of its object—indeed of objectivity as such. But the shift from the name of language to the name of writing allows for that which exceeds language to at least be pointed towards. Derrida explains the importance of this shift in the following way:

> The secondarity that it seemed possible to ascribe to writing alone affects all *signifieds* in general, affects them always already, the moment they enter the game. There is not a single signified that escapes, even if recaptured, the play of signifying references, that *constitute* language. The *advent* of writing is the advent of this play . . . [my emphasis].

And further:

> Writing thus comprehends language.[26]

But what is "this secondarity" for Derrida? It is precisely the derivative formulation that metaphysics (Western thought) has ascribed to the sign. The sign as determined as a sign for something else; the sign as without a proper place, without a proper identity; as self-effacing and as an *in*essential detour "from one full presence to another"; as the passage through history towards the truth—the non-sign. It is *this* "secondarity" which Derrida claims "affects all signifieds in general." Thus, he says, "the signifier is always already in the place of the signified" and "from the moment we have meaning, we have nothing but signs." The reference as such exists nowhere and indeed is simply an effacement of its own constitution via the sign system it denies. More of this later when we approach the incessant, indefinite, and infinite play of the supplement in terms of the structure of *différance*. At this point, the structure of the signified as such must be addressed as it leads us from language to writing, for Derrida. But what is this "game" he speaks of? It is the game of the "world"; it is the world "playing with itself"; it is the "initial doubling" that allows for all representation and hence, in turn, all presentation as such. Metaphoric to be sure, we can only make suggestive remarks here to point toward that which seems to be within the "said" (written, for Derrida) and which as we should now recognize, must always remain essentially unsaid. Nevertheless, he continues, "there is not a single signified that escapes, even if recaptured, the *play* of signifying references that constitute language." We must recognize here that a shift in levels has been instituted such that "writing as such," as this "play of signifying references," is now claimed to be that which *constitutes* language. Thus writing is more fundamental than language at this point and not interchangeable with it. Further, he says the former *comprehends* the latter. This is surely a sort of *Aufhebung* on his part such that language is itself "captured" here in a system of circulation, of exchange, an orbit that extends beyond itself. The significance of this "capture" by writing must now be addressed. Derrida explains this "comprehension" and inclusion of language by writing in the following way:

> One says language for action, movement, thought, reflection, consciousness, unconsciousness, experience, affectivity, etc. Now we tend to say *writing* for all that and more. To designate not only the physical gestures of literal pictographic or ideographic inscription, but also the *totality of what makes it possible;* and also, beyond the signifying face, the signified face itself. And thus we say writing for all that gives rise to inscription in general [my emphasis].[27]

Thus the *Aufhebung* of language by writing moves to the level of the conditions of the possibility of the former by the latter. This is therefore not properly an *Aufhebung* in the sense that Hegel uses this term. The "conditions of possibility" of a system in their relation to that same system must radically *exceed* that which they describe, or inscribe, according to Derrida. Thus "comprehend" here must be considered not as an expanding "circle or orbit," as a "greater area" of understanding, but as a more profound, more primordial level of interpretation. The term "writing" itself will be overcome in the same way as we proceed.

For Derrida, the term writing can be seen also in terms of athletic, political, and military organization: "One might also speak of *athletic* writing, and with even greater clarity of *military* or *political* writing in view of the techniques that govern those domains today."[28] These "types" of writing surely do not refer to pamphlets on the subjects, but rather to a certain formalization of athletics, of the military, and of politics. Athletic writing, for instance, should be considered that repetition that is "the formation of form" itself. The training that produces the athletic. It is thus in a certain sense a form of technology about which we are speaking here. It is the *technique* that is writing in a certain sense. It is that which is intrinsically repeatable and that which "governs" the formation of form. It constitutes the objectivity of the object—in all fields—but most obviously in that of the sciences perhaps. This is why the comprehension of what Derrida calls "writing" is structurally impossible from within the domains of science and philosophy. As structures, these fields must betray a certain "incompetence" to comprehend their own "conditions of possibility," and indeed therefore their own origins. As we have said earlier, the origin of philosophy is not intrinsically philosophical, nor can that of science be scientific. Indeed it is this certain "exorbitant" chance that allows for the possibility of systems in general. As Derrida says:

> Indeed we must comprehend this *incompetence of science* which is also the *incompetence of philosophy,* the closure of the *epistème.*
>
> This common root, which is not a root, but the concealment of the origin and which is not common because it does not amount to the same thing except with the unmonotonous insistence of difference, this *unnameable* movement of difference itself, that I have strategically nicknamed trace, reserve or *différance,* could be called *writing* only within the historical closure, that is to say within the limits of science and philosophy [my emphasis].[29]

We should recognize several things here. First, that with the shift from language to writing we have (a) not moved outside of the realm of "science and philosophy" and yet (b) have moved "outside" the realm of language (another name for philosophy as such, we should recall). Thus one might justifiably ask "*where* are we at this juncture?" The most accurate response must be "nowhere," but this will not help to clarify things very much. More precisely, the shift from language to writing is, in a certain way, the putting of language as such (and therefore philosophy or metaphysics) under erasure. It is the very exposure of language to its limits. Yet we speak of this, and therefore use language, and hence metaphysics. Indeed Derrida himself names the "unnameable"—albeit with a multitude of "nicknames" which must bear some family resemblance. Yet, as he says, the "common root" (a philosophical presupposition, to be sure, for all differences in order to constitute the "same," the "object," the "identity"—in short, the "proper") is not a root. We have therefore nothing substantial with the term writing, and therefore it slides into "trace," "reserve," *"différ-*

ance," as we move "beyond the historical closure" of "science and philosophy." We are indeed moving into the realm of those excesses that language could not capture: force, the idiom, and thought. We are thus exceeding the property of the proper and have begun to speak of the "forbidden territory" here, or perhaps of that which is not a place at all but rather a *space:* the spatiality of space, more precisely. But first the shift *to* writing is also a shift *of* writing, for Derrida.

Writing, we should recall, is the condition of the possibility of language, but it is therefore also a certain condition of impossibility. The possibility of language is certainly the possibility of the proper, of the making-pure, of the constitution of the object, of the name-in-general, and therefore of the concept—indeed of the Concept of the Concept. Therefore the "condition of its impossibility," to repeat, must undo or put in check the achievement of these same ends. A certain conflict is thus at work here, or a certain tension: two contradictory commands that nevertheless produce the possibility of language, since it does, at least appear to, exist. An apparent double bind seems therefore to be the essential structure of what Derrida calls writing. But this is not actually the case, since a double bind, by its very installation as such, therein *paralyzes* all movement. There is "no exit" absolutely from such a structure. But this is hardly that which Derrida is describing with his term "writing." Indeed nothing could be further from his thought here. Instead, this tension intrinsic to writing is a *movement,* unceasing, which produces effects, one of which we might name language. This movement is "kept in motion" by the very opening we described earlier as force, the idiom, and thought. Therefore that which founds the "closure" also keeps it open to a future that is not, as he says, the "present future," but always potentially at least radically other (death itself, perhaps). The double bind is thus exceeded in the very movement that is writing itself. What this presupposes, of course, is a certain space of temporality—a spacing itself which shifts the ground and hence the ground of itself. Indeed it has "no proper place," as we should recall. Thus writing is what Derrida calls the "supplement *par excellence,*" in the sense that it is never full, yet always too full and overflowing its own bounds. We shall describe this paradox in greater detail later in terms of the structure of *différance* itself, but here wish simply to re-mark the place where the "proper" is shifted (according to its own grounds) to the "non-proper," or *displaced* as Derrida says:

> If supplementarity is a necessarily indefinite process, *writing* is the sup-
> plement *par excellence* since it proposes itself as supplement of supple-

ment, sign of sign, taking the place of a speech already significant, it *displaces* the proper place of the sentence, the unique time of the sentence produced *hic et nunc* by an irreplaceable subject, and in turn enervates the voice. It marks the place of the initial doubling [my emphasis].[30]

That writing is not a replacement for speech, nor modeled thereon, is clearly explicated by Derrida with reference to Husserl, to Heidegger, and to the problems of phonologism.[31] The locus of the phonè as that of pure presence of consciousness to itself has been treated in terms of the "concept of metaphysics for Derrida" in the preceding chapter and will be considered again with reference to the constitution of subjectivity, for Derrida, shortly. At this point it must be recalled simply that "speech," "living speech" of the "living subject," cannot be invoked as more primordial than writing, or more proper. Since language itself is a function of "the play of writing," speech too must be seen to be derivative in this context. As Derrida says, this "displacement enervates the voice" and "displaces the unique time of the *pronounced* sentence." It is not for nothing that Derrida speaks of the "death sentence" as the structure of the sentence as such. But that too will be treated in greater detail later.

Why writing is the *"supplement par excellence"* for Derrida must indicate a certain definition or precision of this term "writing." As he says: "To write: is to know that what is not yet produced in the letter lives nowhere else, does not await us as a perscription in some *topos ouranos* (τοπος ουρανος) or some divine understanding. Meaning must wait to be said or written in order to become that which is to differ from the self that it is: the meaning."[32]

Thus writing "contains" a radical originality, a radical institutionality, a radical founding, a radical creativity in its essence. Its essence is rather that it does *not* "contain" this, but lets the to-be-written be written. It is difficult (perhaps impossible) to describe this process, since the to-be-written is the not-yet-written and hence the not yet *existent* for Derrida. It is perhaps thought, the idiom, or force, but it is not yet an "object of thought" or, more precisely, inscribed within the system of differences which gives us that which we call: meaning. Thus writing constitutes meaning for Derrida, or more precisely, the condition of the possibility of meaning as such (in particular and in general). Unlike Plato, he insists that the "said" exists nowhere prior or apart from the saying; that is, the said-as-inscribed. In other terms, this means that the signified as such does not exist for Derrida except in the effacement of its essential relation to the signifier as such. It is the business of philosophy to precisely make such a division and to efface therein the *constitution* of the "object" *as* object. As the extension (thought) beyond the closure of philosophy and science, the term "writing" attempts to include precisely this "unthinkable" aspect. We should not, however, confuse writing in Derrida's sense with the transcendental ego and its acts of object-constitution for Husserl. Phenomenology, Derrida insists, remains trapped within a metaphysics of presence and is therefore powerless to comprehend that which, in essence, can never be made or become "present to consciousness." It is this presentation to consciousness as such that circumscribes what Husserl calls evidence, the condition of the *epistème,* and truth. Precisely *why* writing exceeds "consciousness as such" requires an exposition of what, for Derrida, is essential to the constitution of subjectivity—a certain absence—that which (a) was never present, and (b) will never be present. But we will approach this issue in greater detail within the horizon of that which we call the "principle of death" within the structure of *différance.* At this point, we have sought only to show the *necessity* of the transgression from language as such to the term *writing,* for Derrida. The significance of this shift cannot of necessity be totally justified at this point, but in the attempt to *follow* the path of Derrida, we have sought to expose a certain structural shift which entails the inclusion of that which language as such could not accept, describe, or comprehend. We thus approach the abyss which Derrida calls "the original valley":

> Writing is the moment of this original valley of the other in being. Moment of depth also as fall. Instance and insistence of the serious *(grave).*[33]

V

THE SCOPE OF WRITING

(a) From Writing to Arche-Writing

> I use words to mean anything I want them to mean.
>
> *Alice's Adventures in Wonderland*

Far from repeating such a radical gesture as Alice in her effort to be master of the situation and hence of the signification of *her* words, Derrida's usage of the term "writing" as an expansion from "language" has nonetheless already exceeded its own proper meaning. This excess must now be recognized and not simply pointed towards by metaphor as in the previous section. We cannot with "writing" extend our thought to the space of an originary inscription, or a non-derivative articulation not dependent on the "experience," "will," work or intention *(vouloir-dire)* of a present consciousness immediately present to itself. The term writing is limited in its essence to this derivation. Yet that which Derrida is aiming to describe proceeds beyond and indeed attempts to explain the possibility and constitution of such a "presence." As he says, in using the term "writing" one remains "necessarily within the domain of science and philosophy"; that is, within the domain of the *Logos*. In order to move his discourse towards the "roots," "origins" (which are of course at the same time "non-roots" and "non-origins") of *Logos* itself, it is necessary to *not* utilize terms, if possible, that will immediately, by definition, usurp the excess (efface it) in giving meaning itself to the discourse. Yet, to be meaningless is not as such Derrida's aim, needless (perhaps) to say. The issue is to show the conditions of the possibility of *Logos* and hence of truth, as these terms are understood within the tradition of Western thought, or metaphysics itself. It is not however a simple step outside of metaphysics (which would also be outside of language) that is required here. It is also more than the simple "putting under erasure" of the "concept of writing" as such. That which Derrida aims toward is more than a "sort of writing," or something that both is and is not a writing. The limits of writing are inscribed in its relation to speech (as other than speech) and in relation to the subject (author) as the "writ*er* of writ*ing*." Both of these relations must be put in question in order to follow Derrida at this point. We can no longer assume them nor allow them to "control" our discourse or our analysis here. Therefore, we propose to indicate the significance (paradoxically perhaps) of the shift from "writing," for Derrida, to that space of "arche-writing." Derrida explains the move in this way:

> The "rationality" . . . which governs a writing thus enlarged and radicalized, no longer issues from a logos. Further it inaugurates the destruction, not the demolition but the desedimentation, the deconstruction of all the significations that have their source in that of the logos. Particularly the signification of truth.[1]

It is significant to note that Derrida still employs here the term *rationality,* albeit in quotation marks. That which "governs a writing thus enlarged" is therefore comparable to a "rationality," but is not a rationality. It is not *Logos* that governs its own constitution and therefore not *Logos* that founds the conditions of the possibility of "truth," for Derrida. But of course it is *Logos* that governs truth as such. The distinction allowed by the usage of quotation marks is precisely what is at issue here, and it will become crucial to understand the shift that occurs when one speaks of the difference between "rationality" and rationality, for example. This is not a transcendental reduction but also not dissimilar to it. In the reduction, certain paralysis of usage occurs, a certain bracketing, a certain exclusion, but one which Husserl himself admitted "changed nothing." For instance, he reduces the "life-world" in order to approach the constituting structure of the transcendental ego. Derrida, of course, does not focus on such issues except in order to reach beyond or beneath them. The parallel here is that, where Husserl sought to explore the conditions of the possibility of the constitution of the object-as-such (for consciousness as such), Derrida seeks to explore the conditions of the possibility of constitution of the as such by Reason itself. One might reasonably expect therefore that his discourse cannot be subjected to the dictates of Reason in its effort to extend to its (necessarily non-reasonable) conditions of possibility. But we must proceed with caution here, since it is a journey that paradoxically requires that Reason be invited to come along—but always and necessarily *a posteriori*. Derrida, too, insists explicitly that the "need for Reason" cannot be avoided, but that its usurpation of our approach must be resisted "as long as possible." The danger is always that in making such an attempt the discourse will simply become "meaningless" and leave no trace before being therein comprehended (as incomprehensible) by Reason. Therefore, with the phenomenological reduction as our model here, we must describe the process at the same instant as it is exposing itself in the description. Yet this task in intrinsically impossible, just as the performance of a transcendental reduction on the transcendental reduction. Thus the structural limits of description make themselves felt. With this we move towards what Derrida calls arche-writing.

> From then on, to wrench the concept of the trace from the classical scheme, which would derive it from a presence or from an originary nontrace and which would make of it an empirical mark, one must indeed speak of an originary trace or *arche-trace*. Yet we know that that concept destroys its own name and that, if all begins with trace, there is no "originary" trace.[2]

The term "trace" here is "another name" for that which Derrida calls "writing," we should recall. The paradigm is the same however in the shift from trace to arche-trace, as from writing to arche-writing. It is the extension of the same concept to utilize it "strategically"; that is, structurally rather than "literally." That is, the movement from writing to arche-writing is the shift from writing as such to that which is "like" writing, only more so in a way and hence not "writing," properly speaking, at all. What is happening here, we suggest, is the shift from the *is* structure of the *Logos* to the *as* structure of that which founds it, for Derrida. We are performing the same gesture in describing "writing" in terms of the term "trace," but we must show the necessity of this displacement which "puts things in place," as we proceed to deepen or extend our analysis here. But why is this the "concept that destroys its own name" here? And is this also *true* for "writing" in its move to "arche-writing"? This problem presupposes a certain notion of the concept as synonymous with the "name": that is, the "proper name," the notion of identity itself, as excluding difference (its other). Yet how can a concept destroy its own name? If *it* is doing the destroying here, then is it not also the *victor* in the end of the "battle of the proper name"? The battle here is not dissimilar (in structure) to that of the master/slave dialectic for Hegel. The difference is, of course, that for Hegel the constitution of the concept is the *result,* not the beginning, and the beginning is the non-concept or that which is not yet named, but will be. For Derrida, the opening of the battle is the concept in struggle with itself. This presupposes a certain duplicity within that which admits of no duplicity. A certain double already there, yet unacknowledged, unrecognized. Indeed it is in the "end" the recognition of this inner duplicity as essential to the concept which destroys it, for Derrida. Therefore the destruction is not of the "name as such," in a certain sense, but of the name of the "concept"; that is, of the "concept as name," of the concept as the proper name of the name, as its sense, its meaning, its prescriptive circumscription and limit. We transgress these limits with Derrida and arrive at a more originary origin. Also only *a posteriori,* since of course we are *already* within the realm of the *Logos*—or the world according to Reason. The problematics of the origin of origin as an essential non-origin will be addressed with respect to the trace as such in the upcoming section. Of course, the issue will be that the trace-as-such is also a contradiction in terms and does not, indeed cannot (properly speaking) exist.

Yet Derrida retains the "proper" in his movement beyond Reason and not only as the legacy or face of the past that "allows itself to open to the future." The "proper" is essentially irreducible, we suggest. As he says, the issue is concerning a *"rationality"* which *"governs* a writing." We are certainly not free of structural constraints in this formulation. Quite the contrary. We are moving towards an *ultimate law,* an ultimate structure which itself has no other. (The same problem as concerns Derrida in terms of the Absolute Spirit or *Geist* in his criticism of Hegel, by the way.) Although still using the "old names," Derrida explains the significance of this structure and of its primordiality in terms of science, the *epistème,* and objectivity as such:

> Writing is not only an auxiliary means in the service of science—and possibly its object—but first, as Husserl in particular pointed out . . . , the condition of the possibility of ideal objects and therefore of *scientific objectivity.* Before being its object, writing is the condition of the *epistème* [my emphasis].[3]

Thus the question of writing cannot, due to structural constraints, answer to the question of truth. It cannot answer to science: to linguistics (for example), which makes of it an object-of-study. An "ology." This is why, as Derrida says, Grammat*ology* is still within and therefore falls victim to the system of Western thought known as metaphysics, or in short: *Logos*. Thus we will not speak here of Grammatology. It is that which gives rise to "ology" that we wish to speak of. But what sort of primordiality is this, and how can its existence be proven or established, rather than simply described and posited as such? Can one prove or disprove Derrida's claims as such? Are they weighable on the "scales of Reason"? Or do they not exceed and put those same scales in question? As he says, the "thought of the *différance* [another name for arche-writing] is that which in the play of the system *never* has weight." It is that which falls through the net of *Logos*—yet it is not simply force, the idiom or thought, as we described earlier. We are dealing with a *structure* here, albeit one which includes the above triad of elusive problems. Derrida explains:

> *Arche-writing,* at first the possibility of the spoken word, then of the "graphic" in the narrow sense, the birthplace of "usurpation" . . . this *trace* is the opening of the first exteriority in general, the *enigmatic relationship* of the living to its other and of the inside to an outside: *spacing* [my emphasis].[4]

He further claims that arche-writing is the "articulation of the living on the non-living." But first how can we describe the *possibility* of the spoken word, its preconditions, without moving immediately into a psychology of speech, or perhaps a transcendental psychology of the spoken as such? Husserl had similar problems in distinguishing transcendental phenomenology from transcendental psychology, as we know. But the *subject* of speech is not at all the issue here. We must rule out the notion of speech as the property of a subject, or writing as that of an author, or movement as a result of a "Prime Mover." With such formulations we must arrive at Nietzsche's notion of the will which ultimately wills itself—not unlike Geist either fundamentally— and thus return to a metaphysics of Being and Presence and the problems of consciousness as it relates itself to an object which is fundamentally "its" object. It is beyond such a will to power and the power of the will that Derrida is pushing us here. The "possibility of the spoken word" is the possibility of spacing and timing, the possibility of "articulation in general," as "habitation," he claims. "Indeed we speak of inscription in general, in order to make it quite clear that it is not simply the notation of a prepared speech representing itself, but *inscription within speech* and *inscription as habitation* always already situated."[5] We might justifiably return to the inscriptions of "Now is the noon" and "here is the tree," as Hegel's opening words in the movement towards Absolute Knowledge. What escaped him here, Derrida claims, is the *movement of writing* itself. He described everything else, but paradoxically did not or could not explicate that which pushed his discourse onwards to everchanging formulations. It was more than *Geist,* as we shall see presently.

Yet how are "inscription in general" or arche-writing to be understood as the foundation of *Logos* (albeit denied and effaced therein)? What is "inscription in general" for Derrida? And is this not in itself a contradiction in terms? Indeed we might suggest first that it is *necessarily* a contradiction in terms. The problem of contradiction or, more precisely, of non-contradiction as one of the two founding principles of philosophy as such, is the issue here. (The other founding principle being that of analogy, as Aristotle explicated at some length, also paradoxically, as we shall see later). That which is a "contradiction in terms" is more exactly a contradiction within *a* term. It is the "concept that destroys its own name," as we discussed earlier. The need to adhere to this principle of philosophy here must also be suspended, at least for the moment. The "term," "word" for Derrida, is precisely that which *houses* its own contradiction, its own destruction (according to philosophy). It is the locus of the *violence* that suppresses (makes mute, speechless) its other, which nonetheless lives within the term— albeit illegitimately for the *Logos.* We might well ask what else lives under the roof or within the house of Being, which Heidegger called language or metaphysics as such. That which does not "properly" exist there but also "exists nowhere else," Derrida claims. But concerning "inscription in general," why is this a contradiction in terms for Derrida and yet also against Derrida? Because inscription is intrinsically non-general—there can be no such "thing" as "inscription in general," or which is the same thing, inscription as such. The terms "in general" and "as such" belong inextricably to the system of thought controlled by metaphysics. It is *Logos* that constitutes the possibility (at one level at least) of the "in general," of the "as such." We must keep this opening in mind as we proceed further along Derrida's path, and search for further hidden "forks" in the road leading *back* (onwards) to Reason.

More precisely for Derrida, the possibility of inscription in general, or *all* signification, is a function of *différance* (another name for arche-writing) in the following sense:

> Différance is also the *production* of these differences, of this diacricity
> from which linguistics comes from Saussure and all the structural sci-
> ences which have taken it as their model have reminded us that they
> were the condition of all signification and of all structure [my empha-
> sis].[6]

Thus we should realize several things here. First, *différance* is a productive and therefore active movement, and second that its products
are the "differences" of which Saussure speaks in describing the possibility of meaning in general in language. Meaning is that "space" *between* the terms, their relations and interrelations within a "chain of
signification." Thus we are not to focus on the terms as such, but on
their relations to one another. That is precisely: their *differences*
wherein their meanings lie. Yet how are these differences produced as
such, aside from simply the movement of language as such? As we
have shown, Derrida extends the issue beyond language, and thus the
problem of meaning in general must be treated in terms of inscription in
general, and in terms of the production of differences in general. Yet
what allows for this production, we repeat? First, we must remark that
meaning is here seen as an effect, a result, a product, an *a posteriori,*
and not self-originating. Although it may be true for Derrida, as for
Merleau-Ponty, that "we are condemned to meaning," it is precisely
this condemnation as such—the fall of thought into the *Logos*—which
is in question here. One might initially be tempted to view the production of differences as result of the "Same," in a classically metaphysical
formulation. From the One we arrive at the many. Indeed the many
(differences) are considered, by Hegel for instance, as products of the
One and hence in the end must return to the One: return from the
"detour of differences" back to that realm of the Same—the essential
condition of their appearance as such. This is not the case for Derrida
however. Writing for him is instead, as arche-writing, radically originary. This means that nothing *precedes* it, nothing founds it, and nothing ultimately controls it. Paradoxically, it is this ultimate power which
allows it to "fall victim" to the structure and structurality (the formation of form) which characterizes metaphysics. We shall explore later
this excess, which is simultaneously a lack, in terms of its economy. At
present it is crucial to point out that arche-writing, for Derrida, is that
"structure" which, for example, allows for the possibility of a description of something which Hegel called *Geist.* It is the condition for such

a name as such, and yet also that which exceeds it. More precisely, Derrida describes the constitution of differences by *différance* (arche-writing) as an *inaugural movement:* as that which institutes for the first time that which did *not* exist prior to that movement:

> It is because it is *inaugural* that writing is dangerous and anguishing. It does not know where it is going; no wisdom keeps it from this essential precipitation towards the meaning that it *constitutes* and which is initially its future.
>
> *It is not however capricious except by cowardice.* There is nonetheless no insurance against this risk. Writing is for the writer, even if he or she is not an atheist, but if one is a writer, a maiden voyage and without grace [my emphasis].[7]

Thus we return to "writing" as our model for "arche-writing." Evidently Derrida is speaking on two levels (at least) here in his description. In both senses, we have a notion of a *blindness* which is intrinsic to the structure/movement of writing as such. Its lack of direction is its freedom and its danger; it is that which opens the possibility of writing and yet potentially, at least, closes off the possibility of a future radically other (not a future present) than the present or the past. Writing thus "makes" a difference, at the same time as it produces differences, or meaning as such. Meaning here, it should be recalled, must be understood in Husserl's sense of the term as "object," as the structure of the intention *(vouloir-dire)*. In addition, we should add, writing therein produces *identities:* or those 'objects' which we can and indeed do name. Writing therefore *à la fois* produces or constitutes that which we cannot any longer consider writing, or even arche-writing. Writing, in its movement, therefore creates a shift which alienates, isolates, or exiles itself from its own recognition. Writing effaces itself in its "being-written." This is so because "writing as such" does not exist, is not an entity, and can never become an object, nor therefore an "object for science." Neither can one develop a phenomenology of writing, since it necessarily eludes that which Husserl called experience—the immediate presence of the object to consciousness. All of these last terms must be seen in this context as necessarily obsolete.

Derrida speaks of writing, or in particular of arche-writing for us, at this juncture, as a sort of opening to *exteriority* as such. Later he will consider it in terms of the spatiality of space: that movement which is spacing itself, which grounds the possibility of what Kant has described as the "*a priori* intuitions of [both] space and time." But first, what is this "exteriority" for Derrida? Does this term itself not also situate our issue *within* that same metaphysics we had sought to leave behind, or exceed? Indeed Derrida speaks of the movement of writing as a *descent,* yet also the movement of thought into metaphysical formulations as the "fall" of thought. How are we to understand these metaphors, classical as they are, for a "fall" from one place to another? The issue here for Derrida is the following:

> Writing is the issue as the fall of meaning out-side of itself: metaphor 'for-otherness-in-view-of-otherness-here-down', metaphor as metaphysics where being must hide itself if one wishes the other to appear.[8]

As one might expect, the descent of one "side" is simultaneously the ascent of "another," of the same thing. Writing for Derrida is here very similar to the movement of *Geist* which Hegel describes. But in reverse. It is the fall of *meaning* outside of itself: which is to say the shift from meaning to non-meaning, but not to a simple nonsense, as we mentioned earlier. The fall of thought into "metaphysics" is a parallel but reversed movement therefore. This movement is also, however, a function of the movement of arche-writing or *différance* as such. It takes no sides in the struggle between "identity" and "difference." It constitutes both simultaneously and as complimentary, or in struggle, if one prefers. Thus one might perceive the constitution of meaning by (according to) the *Logos* as a fall of non-meaning into meaning. And in addition, one might conceive the therein-constituted meaning as further (or later) being capable of (or inescapable from) a fall subsequently into non-meaning. One might be tempted to sum up this double process in the words of the Anaximander fragment—but one should not, we suggest. Nietzsche's translation of this fragment, subsequently retranslated into English runs as follows:

> Whence things have their origin, there they must also pass away according to necessity; for they must pay penalty and be judged for their injustice, according to *the ordinance of time* [my emphasis].[9]

The "justice" he imposes on this movement is too akin to the Reason and logic of metaphysics, we suggest, and the Ultimate Good as the ultimate expulsion of difference from the same. Instead we are perhaps closer to that which Nietzsche referred to as "beyond good and evil," and the difficulty of judgment as such. The double movement *allows* for the notions of good and evil as such; it therefore allows for *ethics* as such to be constituted *a posteriori* to the structure of metaphysics.

Derrida is not unaware of this danger as a danger and as a freedom, as we have already intimated in terms of writing in particular. But for history in general, he also admits:

> To recognize writing in speech, that is to say *différance* and the absence of speech, is to begin to think the *lure*. There is *no ethics* without the *presence* of the other, but also and consequently, without *absence,* dissimulation, detour, *différance,* writing. The arche-writing is the origin of morality as of immorality. The non-ethical opening of ethics. A violent opening [my emphasis].[10]

This violence, as we have shown, is the violence of the proper name. But we have also shown that this violence is not so much a death as a contamination; that which makes "purity" and "impurity" possible. It is thus a short step to the recognition of the conditions of the possibility of ethics (in general) as also, at the same instant, the conditions of the impossibility of ethics. The presence of the other, indeed the presence of the subject to itself, as the condition of ethics, is precisely that which Derrida has revealed as the myth of metaphysics—indeed that which constitutes the possibility of metaphysics—but also that which is fundamentally false. (What false could mean in this context must remain necessarily unclear and imprecise.) The simultaneous condition of ethics here is the presence and absence of the other, of the subject to itself: in short of *mediacy*—of *différance* and of writing. It is this presence/ absence relation which is precisely that movement of arche-writing itself. But we shall explore this in greater detail shortly. For the moment we must recognize: (a) that we have not here overcome the need or the possibility of an ethics, but (b) that we must turn towards a radically new foundation for the same, one which is of necessity beyond metaphysics as such. The terror instilled in such an approach is described by Derrida himself in the following admission: " . . . writing cannot be thought outside the horizon of intersubjective violence."[11] Indeed we call each other names—both properly and improperly—in order to have what we call society and what Husserl called intersubjectivity. It is the possibility of the constitution of intersubjectivity as such that the question here and thus necessarily the limits of metaphysics in this regard. We have always already transgressed them, but it is perhaps Derrida who is one of the first to attempt to describe such a transgression (a) as necessary but thus also (b) as past. The age of metaphysics. The epoch of *différance* is—as with thinking—"that which we know we have not yet begun." Perhaps.

We must now address that which Derrida calls the trace, as yet another name for arche-writing, another name for *différance*. It is with the trace however, in particular, that we shall approach what Derrida points towards as the "radical past," which is radically other than the present part, as we shall explore presently.

(b) The Radical Past: The Trace

> If the trace refers to an *absolute past,* it is because it obliges us to think a past that can no longer be understood in the form of a modified presence, as a present-past. Since past has always signified present-past, the absolute past that is retained in the trace no longer merits the name 'past' [my emphasis].[12]

The radical past of the trace is therefore not a past that has been "forgotten" in the sense that it was once present. It is neither a sort of "future" that can be made present, or brought into "consciousness." The "form" of the trace exceeds both possibilities, for Derrida. It is, however, not absent-as-such, since this too would necessitate the relation of the trace to the present as its other, which is also not the issue to be treated here. Thus how are we to localize this nebulous "concept," which indeed is not a concept as such, if it intrinsically escapes all preconditions for formalization? We intend first to examine the roots of this notion for Derrida as they appear in Husserl, Levinas, and Freud. The similarity of the "trace" to temporalization as such, for Husserl, to "the trace of the other" for Levinas, and to the "magic writing pad" for Freud will be examined initially here. We hope in this process to illustrate the profound though subtle differences between Derrida's "trace" and *"les traces des autres."* The movement from Husserl to Levinas to Freud, and finally beyond Freud by a "return" (which is not a return) to Husserl also parallels that of Derrida himself on this issue, we suggest. His own work began with the opening in Husserl which pushed him beyond the latter's own phenomenology, properly speaking, and is at present (1981) concerned with the unconscious in Freud, as beyond that which Freud himself formalized due to the latter's reliance on metaphysical presuppositions and preoccupations. Levinas occupies a central position in this transition only in a figurative and symbolic sense, since he *à la fois* puts in question "the metaphysics of presence," with his treatment of the relation of totality and infinity, yet in the end returns to an Absolute Presence as the absolute foundation that allows for this absence which exceeds all possibilities of totalization.

Levinas is therefore significant for Derrida: (a) in terms of the concept of the trace itself, and also (b) in terms of the former's simultaneous recognition of the limits of metaphysical closure and his reciprocal reversal and self-effacement in the return to a metaphysical foundation. We should also recall that the "overcoming of Husserl" is simultaneously a borrowing from him as well. Derrida thus never performs a critique of those he "overcomes," since his tools of operation are borrowed precisely from each position therein treated. This paradox of a non-method, as deconstruction presents itself, will also be examined here as the development (which is not a development) of the notion (which is not a notion) of the trace as such (which does not exist as such). This double movement is precisely that which Derrida has expressed above in his usage and subsequent discrediting of the term "past" to describe the relation of "trace" to the present. But as with Derrida, we cannot move directly to our "object" of discussion, or we shall expose all too soon that "it does not exist" and therein short-circuit or abort that which we herein shall be attempting to conceive.

(i) Husserl and the Time of the Trace

> We must then situate as a simple movement of the discourse the phenomenological reduction and the Husserlian reference to a transcendental experience. To the extent that the concept of experience in general—of transcendental experience in Husserl in particular—remains governed by the theme of presence, it participates in the movement of the reduction of the trace.
>
> But that must come to terms with the *forces of rupture.*
>
> In the originary temporalization and the movement of relationship with the outside, as Husserl actually describes them, *non-presentation* or depresentation is as "originary" as presentation. That is why a thought of the trace can no more break with a transcendental phenomenology than be reduced to it [my emphasis].[13]

This "originary temporalization" for Husserl, we should recall, is the "movement of protention and retention (of consciousness)" which constitutes temporality itself. This movement is what constitutes the "Now" according to Husserl, and it is the condition of the possibility of the very space/time of evidence and truth itself. It is the "Now" in which perception as such occurs, but the "Now" is not itself a perception. It is a constitution which allows for the possibility of perception. We can describe it always only "after the fact." But what is the relation of the trace here, for Derrida, to this movement of temporalization in

Husserl? Why is it that the trace can "no more break with transcendental phenomenology than be reduced to it"? And if this is the case, how can we situate the trace in terms of this same phenomenology? Can one be inside and outside of phenomenology at the same instant? Derrida says yes. It is the non-necessity of "making a choice" which is at issue here. But first the trace and temporality must be shown as similar yet not reducible to each other.

As consciousness constitutes the Now for itself, it extends itself as protention towards the not yet Now and "holds" this in itself. As "time itself" shifts, the protended becomes a retention and a new protention takes its place. As the moment of the Now, the protended and retained "as not yet past" are synthesized into the *present*. Therefore the notion of presence is here revealed as a constitution of the not-actually-future (beyond the present) and the not-yet-past (after the present). As Husserl says of retention in particular: ". . . it is already clear that the retentional 'content' is, in the primordial sense, no content at all."[14] The notion of "contents" of consciousness (or perception) is founded on this movement from protention to retention and its synthesis into the Now, and therefore neither retentions nor protentions can be properly named "contents" or perceptions. They are perhaps proto-perceptions, but this helps little in the comprehension of this process. Indeed the process itself is, even for Husserl in a certain sense, incomprehensible. As he says:

> We can only say that this flux is something which we name in conformity with what is constituted, but is nothing temporally "objective." It is absolute subjectivity and has the absolute properties of something to be denoted *metaphorically as "flux,"* as a point of actuality, primal source point, that from which springs the "now," and so on. . . . In the lived experience of actuality we have the primal source point and a continuity of *reverberation. For all this, names are lacking* [my emphasis].[15]

Even Husserl, as we have seen, must "resort" to the metaphoric as his means of pointing toward that for which "all names are lacking." This "absolute flux" is, however, considered to be absolute subjectivity in the sense, we suggest, of the absolute of subjectivity. Certainly the constitution of the present by the subject is an effaced, and indeed self-effacing process. We are "always already" in the Now, in the moment of the present it seems. It is only when we consider a "something" that is extended in time, that we are able to catch a glimpse of this protentive-retentive primordial synthetic process.

It is not for nothing therefore that Derrida calls the trace (which is analogous to that which for Husserl "all names are lacking") the originary non-origin of origin. Origin, we should recall, is embedded in the signification of a simplicity, a unity, a certain primordiality that is founded on the one. Yet, as Husserl has shown, there is a certain movement or flux beyond this oneness that allows for its constitution. This movement might plausibly be seen as the movement of the trace itself. As Derrida says: "the instituted trace cannot be thought without thinking the retention of difference within a structure of reference where difference appears as such."[16] Further: "The trace . . . articulates its possibility in the entire field of the entity, which metaphysics has defined as the being-present starting from the occulted movement of the trace. The trace must be thought before the entity."[17] Yet several paradoxes must immediately appear at this point which include: (i) if the trace must be thought *before* the entity, as the movement of the flux before the Now, then how can one name it as movement, which is already an "entity," a name, a something; and (ii) how can this movement (apparently ultimately singular as it is) be considered the non-origin of origin (pure and simple)? Or is there an "other" for the trace? Does it divide itself? or multiply itself or dissimulate itself? Indeed Derrida will answer that the movement of the trace is necessarily *"occulted."* It removes itself from the "scene of writing" in its simultaneous constitution of it. Yet how is this possible, and why is it considered a non-origin if in fact it is a more primordial one, if Derrida and Husserl are correct here? The problem is more than one of terminology here— yet also that. The movement of protention and retention (to return to Husserl, our model here for the moment) is at one and the same instant *a* single movement and yet also a double movement. What this means, in a certain sense, is that it has always already begun. That is, one does not "begin" with a protention that recedes into the background and becomes a retention, and then another protention, etc. The retention is always *already there* in a certain sense, and hence the protention is always in terms of an already "retained" retention. The protention is thus in a certain sense a "result," an effect, and so therefore is the retention. What this involves is to not conceptualize the process within a framework of classical metaphysics—i.e., of cause and effect, or more precisely, of linear causality: or in short, of Newtonian mechanics. We must put that formalizing apparatus in brackets at this point. What is at issue is rather that which "cybernetics" today more precisely understands. This is a double or "circular" causality, such that a mutual, reciprocal adjustment occurs the result of which is a *zero* or steady state. In metaphysical terms what this means is that the "present" is a result; the starting point for truth and evidence is a *product.* That in short the "origin" is not, in a more radical sense, the origin. Indeed one could move in two directions at this point. One would be to change the meaning of "origin" so as to make it no longer a simple unitary formulation (to be realized as double, as reflexive). Or one could accept the current definition and refer to that which founds the origin as a "non-origin." This confusion is what Derrida has attempted to "put in place" with his reference to the notion of trace as an arche-synthesis which becomes the "origin of origin." As he says:

> The trace is not only the disappearance of origin—within the discourse that we sustain and according to the path we follow it means that the origin did not even disappear, that it was never constituted except reciprocally by a *non-origin,* the *trace,* which thus becomes the origin of the origin [my emphasis].[18]

In its relationship to the sign, as distinct from the symbolic, the trace is what Derrida will call the "becoming-sign of the symbol." The same process of occulation or self-effacement occurs in this case, he claims. The difference between a sign and a symbol, as taken from Husserl, requires that the symbol retain a certain "natural relationship" or intrinsic connection to that which it symbolizes. In Saussurean terms, this means a certain intrinsic, non-separable relation of signifier to signified. The "becoming-sign of the symbol" is thus, for Derrida, the separation of a signifier from signified, such that the possibility of a transcendental signified (essence, *eidos,* concept as such) is therein constituted. The movement of the trace is that which allows for this shift that is also we should recall the foundation of philosophy as such, in particular with reference to Plato and the formation of the Forms. Indeed the idea of the "as such" is precisely this "having-become sign of the symbol." The *sign* is thus also representative in its essence, of: (a) an essence that is not itself and hence (b) of the lack which it itself is. The symbol does not have such a function. It cannot have, by virtue of its very structure. Such a lack, or space, has not yet been constituted. Is it not ironic therefore that Derrida terms "animality" that form of life wherein the "symbolic" is not yet an issue, or has not yet been constituted. It is where immediacy still reigns and the *différance* has not yet opened the realm of repetition, of representation, nor therefore of the symbolic.[19] The difficulty here should be recognized as one of contextual variation rather than an essential stumbling block in the understanding of the difference between sign and symbol for Derrida. When he speaks of "animality," it is in relation to "humanity" as such, and in this context the symbolic represents the possibility of representation. It is to be considered in general with respect to the nonsymbolic. The distinction of sign and symbol is properly "beyond animality" as an issue, as a whole, since the symbol in its relation to the sign, although more "animal" than "human" (in the classical sense of these terms), is still nonetheless a "human" quality. It is still in the realm of representation, but in a different sense than that of the sign. The symbol *represents* that immediacy we illustrated as "characterizing" animality, but it *is not* that same animality. The symbolic, in its immediate intertwining of signifier and signified, is thus not "animality" as such but in a certain sense "represents" that animality as such. As we shall illustrate more fully later, it is not possible for "humanity" to be "immediately related" to itself. The relation to itself is always already a function of the trace, of *différance,* which also therefore opens the space of representation and repetition. In short, the space of what Husserl calls "internal time consciousness," although the trace is not identical to this, for Derrida. He parts company with Husserl on this matter in a very profound way, although never absolutely, and hence never in opposition (as such) to Husserl.

> The concept of the trace is thus not equivalent to that of retention, of the becoming-past of that which had been present. One cannot think of the *trace*—and hence of *différance*—starting from the present or from the presence of the present.[20]

It is true in the end that Husserl's formulation of retention and protention as the constituting movement of temporality itself returns ultimately to a foundation of the present. That which is "retained" in the retention *was* originally "present" for consciousness, even though, evidently, not present as such. The problem is that consciousness as such is still the ultimate filter of that which allows itself to be constituted in what is later called "perception." For Derrida, we should recall, "perception as such does not exist."[21] What this means is that the "role" of retention in this process must be seen as radically dissimilar to that which it plays for Husserl. Derrida relies here on what Levinas will call the *"trace de l'autre,"* which was never present, and also on what, for the moment, we will call that which is "unconscious," as it plays its part in the constitution of consciousness. The non-conscious is not capable of being held in the grasp of phenomenology as such, of the Husserlian variety at least, since consciousness (whether transcendental or empirical) is always the gateway to that which will become "its" object. In this sense Husserl is still trapped in what Nietzsche called the "stamp of being on becoming." As Derrida says: "As the phenomenology of the sign in general, a phenomenology of writing is impossible. No intuition can be realized in the place where the 'whites' indeed take on an importance."[22] Levinas too realized this, as we shall explore now.

(ii) Levinas and "La Trace de l'Autre"

Derrida seems to have acknowledged his debt to Levinas on numerous occasions, including the recent article entitled, "En ce Moment Même dans cette Ouvrage Me Voici."[23] Yet he is not within the orbit of Levinas's thinking at the most fundamental level. The similarity is described by Derrida himself in the following admission:

> I relate this concept of the trace to what is at the centre of the latest (1963) work of Levinas and his critique of ontology: the relationship to the illeity as to the alterity of a *past* that was never and can never be lived in the originary or modified form of presence. Reconciled here to an Heideggerian intention . . . this notion signifies . . . the undermining of an ontology which, in its innermost course, has determined the meaning of being as presence and the meaning of language as the full continuity of speech.[24]

We must therefore consider that which "is at the centre of Levinas's latest (1963) work" in terms of "the trace of the other," since it is in this essay in particular that Levinas describes most clearly that which he considers the term "trace" itself to signify. He begins with a consideration of the "Me" as the term of identification *par excellence* and hence the origin of all phenomena of identity as such. The Me is what constitutes the identity of identity in traditional metaphysics, he claims. It is as Kant insisted, the "I think" which unites all *a priori* intuitions *a priori*. And so with Descartes. Even Hegel situates the role of "my consciousness" at the center of the movement of knowing itself. It is this center that Levinas, as with Heidegger, hopes to displace. The space for the "Other" as other must be inscribed therein he claims. It is the Other as *"le tout autre,"* not *my* Other, and therefore not dominated by the subject-object formulation as the object-as-immediately present formulation which characterizes metaphysics as such. Levinas thus insists upon a place for the "unknown" as unknowable. A place where infinity will always exceed totality as such.[25] Totality might here be considered the movement of consciousness towards its "object" in an effort to appropriate it. To name it, for Derrida. Infinity is that which is *intrinsically* unnameable. That which will never, can never be appropriated. It is *"le tout autre."* But this is not an "out there," a spatial beyond which "infinity" in this sense refers to. It is "the most immediately" present (to use Heidegger's formulation) and therefore that which necessarily escapes us (to use Hegel's formulation). Levinas himself explains this movement in the following way:

> The heteronomous experience that we are searching for would be an attitude which cannot be converted into a category and for which the movement towards the Other is not recuperated in identification, and does not return to its point of departure.[26]

But what is this *"départ sans rétour"?* It is that which *exceeds* the formulation of totality, yet is to be found paradoxically "within" this. What is in question here is thus a certain interiority as a certain exteriority. Indeed the metaphysical opposition of interior/exterior is "powerless to comprehend" this issue. As Levinas says, in terms of the Same, the Other is that which in the Same never returns to that same Same. It is the Other in the Same which is left unsaid in the saying; it is the "blank part of the text" as both *part of* of the text and, in a certain sense, *apart from* the text. It is, in Derrida's terminology, the *margins* of philosophy, and not *of* philosophy. It is that Other which philosophy will never understand, never assimilate, and never radically be rid of in its expulsion of the Other from the Same. It is, for Levinas, the following:

> The work radically considered is in effect a movement of the Same towards the Other which never returns to the Same.[27]

We should beware of this capitalization in Levinas's discourse as an indication of where Derrida will part company from him. The *"Même"* and *"Autre"* are here necessarily the same as such and the other as such. An important consideration to keep in mind as we proceed.

Levinas shifts the notion of the Other to the schema of a temporality where the other becomes the Radical Past. It is that which is/was/will never be present-as-such. His basis for this shift is in terms of an *inheritance* of the "Me" which "I must accept and recognize" and of an influence/responsibility on/of the "Me" which "extends beyond my death." It is in this sense that the Me is situated temporally with respect to "others" for Levinas. What mediates his discourse is surely a notion of ultimate responsibility and hence ultimate guilt, in Heidegger's sense of the term. The "Absence of the Other" is not my fault, but it is surely "my responsibility," Levinas tells us. The other is thus a sort of burden that the Me must carry, albeit an absent other. The not-yet others and the already-having-been others are surely not present-with-me, but their burden and influence on me is therefore all the heavier. One must include "them" in that which one calls the "Me" and therein recognize their distance from me: indeed, more precisely, my distance from them. They will never be present-as-such with me. This is structurally essential for Levinas. He thus seems more concerned with others-in-general than the others *with* which I cohabit the earth at the time of my life. He turns therefore toward a radical and generalized responsibility that Derrida has shown[28] profoundly misses "my responsibiity" as such, in particular: that is, in terms of my life. Responsibility in general is a more subtle way of evading that same responsibility as such and must be recognized as such a reversal. Responsibility as such is thus a more profound, the most profound perhaps, form of *irresponsibility* and avoidance of being-with others in the very claim to be "more radically" with and respectful, indeed reverant, of others as others-in-general. The Absent Other is not in this sense a past or future generation for Derrida, as it seems to be here for Levinas. The latter states his position on this rather clearly in the following:

> To be for a time which would be without me, to be for a time after my time, for a future by which the famous "to-be-for-the-dead," to-be-for-after-my-death" would not be a banal thought which extrapolates its proper duration but the passage to the time of the Other.

And further:

> This is ethics itself.[29]

Not for Derrida, as we have shown. However the similarities must still be pursued here. Levinas continues with his description of the other as trace; indeed the trace of the other as trace, and in terms of that which he names *le visage*. We should point out first that *le visage* is not translatable into English as simply "the face" without a violent (in this context) reduction of its meaning. *Le visage* is "a facing" more precisely; it is an opening of the face and is therefore expression as well as face as such. *Le visage,* for Levinas, is thus the opening for the possibility of ethics. It is that calling of the Same to the Other which he describes, paradoxically to be sure, as an *imposition:*

> The face [*le visage*] imposes itself on me so that I cannot be deaf to its call nor forget it—I wish to say that I can not cease to be *held* responsible for its misery. Consciousness thus loses its first place [my emphasis].[30]

The condition of this displacement of consciousness from itself—the first place—is thus a certain guilt as it looks into the face of the other. The guilt is a function of the misery it sees there. Such a model for the condition of intersubjectivity as a foundation for an ethics must be somewhat suspicious, we insist. The face of the "other" is surely not intrinsically a miserable face for which one holds oneself necessarily responsible. The gesture is indeed one of a certain humanity here, without doubt, but as a general relation of self and other it cannot be sustained, we insist. Even for Derrida, the excess of the "other" is not a plea for help by the helpless, but a joy, a play, an enjoyment that seeks to be shared. It is the opening of desire, not of guilt. However the structure of the trace is what we must return to here as our primary concern. The beyond of *le visage* is what Levinas calls the trace, as "the trace of the other." It is what exceeds the said, and indeed the sayable. It is "the entire Infinity of the absolutely other-escaping ontology."[31] Derrida would agree thus far. Further, Levinas claims:

> The trace is not a sign like any other. But it also plays the role of the sign. . . . it signifies outside of all intention to make a sign and outside of all projects to which it could be aimed.

Further we have an authenticity at stake here:

> The authentic trace, on the contrary, disorders the order of the world. It appears as super-imposition. Its original significance designs itself in the impression which is left by that which had wanted to efface its traces in the care to accomplish a perfect crime, for example. That which has left traces in effacing its traces, not having wanted to say anything or do anything by the traces that were left. It has disordered the order in an irreparable way. It has absolutely passed. To be inasmuch as to leave a trace is to pass by leaving, to absolve oneself.[32]

Thus we have the most precise convergence of Derrida and Levinas. The radical past emerges again as the "never-to-be," never-having-been present (to consciousness as such). It disorders the order; it destroys the possibility of the "perfect crime" (which is metaphysics' intent, for Derrida). The "perfect crime" would be the possibility of leaving "no trace" whatsoever. For the past to be "over" totally once it is past. Paradoxically, to not leave the possibility of a retention. Yet it is the retention as present-past which we sought to overcome in our advancement from Husserl to Levinas here. The significance of the trace is here the difference between the past and the radical past; it is that which is "not caught" in the retention, yet that which the retention as being retained signifies. It is the intrinsic signification, representation, repetition which is being signaled here, although Levinas does not speak in such terms.

He describes the "same movement" or structure instead in terms of the other as "person," as "personal," and hence the excess (which is the trace) as the relation of the Me to that opening which penetrates my selfness and opens me to that which is "not me." But the other is profoundly another me here. It is not otherness as such of which Levinas speaks. It is the "face" of the other. It is the *eyes* of the other into which I gaze and realize "my limits" in the very act of extension of myself. I cannot, in a profound sense, return to the other of "my" past and save him. He has already drowned. He is already "not here." This structure is therefore essentially one of a guilt that is thus instilled by a certain helplessness of the Same to reach the Other. The tragic is therein inscribed for Levinas, and in an irreducible fashion; the Other has been lost or is "not yet" for him. The Other is therefore not reachable.

For Derrida, the implications of this "movement of the trace" are radically dissimilar at this point. His focus is not on the "humanism" latent in Levinas's description and therefore exceeds the notion of "Other" as another me. The "Other" as *"tout autre"* for Derrida is thus more general, paradoxically, than for Levinas. The excess of the "Other" is therefore extended to that which is not "modeled" on the "me"; for instance, the animal, the sign, and "the play of the text of the world." We shall return to this extension shortly, but first the point at which Derrida most radically separates himself from Levinas must be made evident. This is in terms of that which ultimately orients *"la trace de l'autre."* It is once again, as one might expect, *Presence.*

Levinas returns to his point of departure (also paradoxically) via the works of Marcel and Buber, wherein God is brought into the discourse as its foundation, in a similar manner to that of Descartes. It is the condition of the *"tutoiment"* as an intimate approach to the Other which Levinas situates *in* the notion of Presence. Indeed the "Presence of God" is a function of the "trace of the other." The Presence of God is, as we know, precisely that presence which does not appear yet makes its "presence known" or indeed felt. As Levinas tells us: "He only shows Himself by His *trace,* as in chapter 33 of Exodus. To go towards Him is not to follow His trace which is not a sign; it is to go towards Others who stand in His trace."[33]

We should recall that for Derrida one of the aims of deconstruction is the "desedimentation of onto-theology" and that "the name of God is the name of indifference itself." Thus Levinas has returned to metaphysics, in spite of his apparent departure from it, in situating the "trace of the other" as a function of the "Same"—as indeed capitalized. The sense of the Same can be easily seen here as that of the One; both philosophy's and theology's goal of description, yet also (until Hegel at least) that which it could never reach. It is not surprising therefore that Levinas is aiming toward an extension beyond Hegel with his notion of "infinity" as beyond all totality. Paradoxically again, he returns to a "totality," albeit never conceivable as such, which is founded on the Presence of Consciousness to itself (albeit perhaps God's own). This totality in the end exceeds even "infinity"; indeed also *in* Levinas's senses of these terms. For Derrida, however, a certain distance must be taken from these claims as shown earlier. What must be saved, however, is the notion of the trace and the notion of a past that "was never present" and will never return to the present (or to itself). The movement of the trace is therefore inscribed within Levinas yet in turn, in effect, effaced also therein. It is in this opening that we can situate Derrida, yet must therefore extend our own description beyond that "overlap" with Levinas. The closure which Levinas implicitly begins with and explicitly finalizes his claims with is not acceptable to Derrida, and therefore neither is it possible for us to reduce the trace according to Derrida to the trace according to Levinas. The differences must therefore be recognized as more profound than the apparent similarities. Thus we move on toward that which Freud has called the "unconscious" and the *"scène de l'écriture,"* according to Derrida.

(iii) Freud and the Written Trace

> With the alterity of the unconscious, we have to do not with modified horizons of the present—past or future—but with a past which has never been present and which will never be.[34]

Derrida's reading of Freud in terms of the trace attempts to reveal a structure which was (a) described by Freud in his writing; yet (b) was not known as such by Freud himself due to his reliance on metaphysical concepts to explicate his findings. In spite of this discrepancy, or perhaps due to it necessarily, Derrida points toward the notion of the trace, or writing as arche-writing, in Freud as both used by him and as that which "uses him." This is not a simple reflexivity of the written and the writer, however, but a more profound structure which Derrida insists is at the root of both the dream and wakefulness, at the heart of metaphysics as such, and that which allows for the constitution of what we call the "present-as-such" or consciousness, as distinct from the unconscious. This structure is neither conscious nor unconscious, therefore, but that movement which allows for this distinction. It is the "movement of the trace" as it (a) inscribes itself and (b) therein effaces itself. The double aspect of this movement was described by Freud himself in terms of what he called "psychic writing," and it is this "origin" to which we must now turn in order to understand Derrida's simultaneous reliance on and abandoning of this same formulation.

Freud's concern with the notion of trace began with his earliest writings, which focused on the problem of memory. "Memory," he said, "has a capacity for being permanently altered by single occurrences."[35] The difficulty here (which remains Freud's concern thirty years later) is, as Derrida points out, "the necessity of accounting *simultaneously* . . . for the *permanence of the trace* and the *virginity of the receiving substance,* for the engraving of the furrows and for the perennially intact bareness of the perceptive surface: in this case the neurones." "It would seem," Freud continues, "therefore, that neurones (the basis of memory) must be both *influenced* and *unaltered,* unprejudiced [my emphasis]." The difficulty here is the problem of writing in *one* term or place or topology (metaphoric or otherwise) *two* seemingly contradictory possibilities. In terms of classical metaphysics, the difficulty is insurmountable. The principle of non-contradiction rules out immediately the housing of "A" and "−A," or as in this case, the "permanence of the trace" and the "virgin, unaltered surface" within one term. Yet memory as such seems to exhibit such qualities, Freud insists. Freud thus shifts the model to a twofold structure such that *some* neurones "retain no trace" while *others,* at a "deeper" level, retain all traces. The trace here is thus considered as virtually synonymous with memory itself. The trace for Freud, at this point, is little more than the opening of memory to storage, to the constitution of a *reserve* of experiences which in turn play a role in all "future," that is, "new, virgin" ones. It is this constitution of a "reserve" as the work of the trace which will become significant for Derrida, as we shall see shortly.

The crucial aspect of the twofold structure for Freud centers around a notion of "differences of force," such that the "trace itself" is a result of a difference in force rather than a determined plentitude. As Derrida says: "Memory thus, is not a psychical property among others; it is the very essence of the psyche: *resistance,* and precisely thereby, an *opening* to the effraction of the trace."[36] The "difference" here which allows for the constitution of memory is between the "forces of resistance" and the "forces of breaching." In some cases the resistance is too strong and the trace is forgotten, while in others the breaching overcomes this resistance and a memory trace is implanted, or imprinted. Thus the force of repetition itself makes itself felt here since its power is precisely that of "breaking through" the forces of resistance.

Derrida translates this process in terms of the idea of deferral and of Freud's subsequent concern with *Thanatos* and *Eros* in terms of the pleasure principle and its being overcome by the reality principle. As he says: "All these differences in the production of the trace may be interpreted as moments of deferring. In accordance with a motif which will continue to dominate Freud's thinking, this movement is described as the effort of life to protect itself by deferring a dangerous cathexis, that is, by constituting a reserve."[37] We shall see that this "reserve" in its effort to "protect life" is paradoxically also the principle of death as *différance.* It is that which allows for the constitution of an economy which makes life "livable." Yet, *différance* in this sense is also that which opens life's intimate, though deferred, relation to death. It is that which allows Derrida to say that "life *is* death (deferred)." More precisely, the notion of the trace, as utilized at this juncture in Freud, contains the notion of life's simultaneous protection and threatening of itself by virtue of its capacity for repetition which is: (a) that which constitutes a reserve, a memory; yet (b) also considered the "death instinct," in the sense that the "compulsion to repeat" is a compulsion to "master." Thus Derrida says: "Life must be thought of as *trace* before being determined as presence." But we are already ahead of ourselves here. The problem of presence as a result for consciousness will arise again shortly. At this point we must turn towards the non-origin of origin as Derrida finds it in Freud.

We should recall that this more primordial foundation which is simultaneously a non-foundation was also found in Husserl and Levinas, according to Derrida. But with Freud we approach a deeper connection in terms of the problems of writing and the trace as such with respect to the "dream-work."

Freud's concern with dreams relies heavily on written, that is scriptural, metaphors which are themselves modeled on hieroglyphic rather than phonetic forms of inscription. This is no accident, Derrida insists, since the dream work is not comparable to anything we might term translation from one "language" to "another." Nor does the interpretation of dreams allow itself to be based on such a process. The "origin" of the dream is not "in" the unconscious, no more than it is "in" consciousness, Freud tells us. It is instead a fundamental non-origin. This process therefore is revealed as an idiosyncratic structure such that "each dreamer invents his own grammar."[38] There is no standard "code" for the interpretation of dreams, since the meaning of each particular symbol therein is inscribed in terms of the subject in particular and his/her own particular biography and psychic foundations. The train in Freud's dream is therefore not identical to the train in Derrida's, for instance. The meaning of each term is not translatable from one context to another, but rather is strictly and irreducibly localized in each particular context. This "situatedness" of each term is more typically characterized in hieroglyphic, symbolic script than in languages of the "West" (phonetic), since the signified in the latter has been severed from the signifier in order that the notion of meaning as such, in accordance with metaphysical demands, could be established. It is therefore this "originary" writing that dreams "represent" which will be of concern to Derrida. It is the "inaugural movement," which does not represent a full presence but which in turn allows for its constitution. We must pursue the dream work therefore in order to perceive that which, according to Derrida, is the "common root" of both dreams and wakefulness—indeed it is the space of *différance* where there are no differences.

As we have shown, the "conscious text" of the dream is not a translation from an "unconscious one" but is in a certain sense already "original," if we can still rely on this word to signify something for us. As Derrida says, "the notion of text here extends beyond the choice of 'conscious' or 'unconscious' to something more fundamental."

> The conscious text (recounted by the dreamer) is thus not a transcription, because there is no text present elsewhere as an unconscious one to be transposed or transported. For the value of presence can also dangerously affect the concept of the unconscious. There is then no

unconscious truth to be rediscovered by virtue of having been written elsewhere. There is no text written and present elsewhere which would be subjected, without being changed in the process, to an operation and a temporalization . . . which would be external to it, floating on its surface. There is no present text in general, and there is not even a past present text, a text which is past as having been present. The text is not conceivable in an originary or modified form of presence. The unconscious text is already a weave of *pure traces,* differences in which *force and meaning* are united—a text nowhere present, consisting of archives which are always already transcriptions.[39]

The notion of the "nowhere" of the text in terms of this topography (which is ultimately not a topography) of Freud's model for the dream work and its interpretation must now be addressed. Freud himself proposes the well-known model of the mystic writing pad as a structure analogous to that which he earlier called "psychic writing." This "writing pad" shows what Derrida has claimed as the fundamental *absence* of the text to be precisely a Freudian notion, and indeed one which Freud himself had some difficulty to respect in his formulation as *description* of the process itself. This model includes therefore the "work of consciousness," just as it explicates the foundation of the possibility of dreams and therefore the "work of the unconscious." Just as memory "breaches" this distinction, so too does the notion of "psychic writing" as demonstrated by this model. The "mystic writing pad" is composed of a wax slab, a sheet of wax paper and a thin celluloid sheet which covers the paper. If one is to inscribe "something" upon the pad, one uses a stylus, not a pen or pencil or anything which contains ink. A certain pressure and a certain formation of form are all that are required since the "letter" or inscription becomes visible by a process of reversal. With pressure exerted on the celluloid, the wax slab becomes imprinted, and this inscription in turn is "sent" back up to the original celluloid via the mediation of the wax paper which "picks up" the inscription from the wax slab. In order to "erase" the inscription, all that is needed is to lift the celluloid on which it appears from the wax paper and it is "cleared," as if new once again. The "stain" or the imprint, however, remains on the wax slab and cannot be erased. Neither can it ever become visible, however, except in "certain lights." In brief, this is the model Freud and, in turn, Derrida use to explicate a process of the psyche they both see as foundational. We propose here to suggest a few problems in terms of this same model which both seem to overlook. First, the double movement of "memory" as: (i) the permanent imprint of the trace, and yet (ii) the constantly virgin opening to new impressions seems to be a function only of "external" influences. Indeed the subject is herein "written upon" before it realizes or indeed recognizes (as a form of repetition always after the fact) that which it writes. What this model implies therefore is (a) a certain passivity of the subject in terms of its relation to the "external" world, and indeed a certain division between internal and external which we suggest is inadequate; (b) a certain manipulation therefore of the subject by the "world as such," and (c) a certain lack of responsibility of the subject to its inscription, which is indeed prescriptive in terms of its action. The subject is, in short, in this model necessarily a "victim." Its actions are always already inscribed by the "other"; indeed by otherness itself. The "imprinting" so well explicated in terms of the world to consciousness does not return full circle or ellipse such that the subject also inscribes itself upon the world, which in turn inscribes itself upon the subject. Is it not this reflexivity or "circular causality," characteristic of cybernetics, which Derrida himself is aiming towards with his notion of *différance* as economy? The exchange in terms of the "writing pad" model seems however to be short-circuited.

In addition there seems to be a strange sort of economy where nothing is lost between the wax slab and the "appearance of the inscription" on the celluloid sheet of consciousness. Indeed Freud admits of the problem of a scratch or tear in the wax paper which can in turn lead to a loss of the imprint in consciousness. But have we not therefore returned to a metaphysical notion of a primordially "good" nature, a perfectly functioning structure, a total adequation of imprint and imprinted: in short, a full presence which is in turn *damaged* through usage. Usage here must be considered life itself: the lived relation of the subject to the world, wherein the "wax paper" has the possibility and indeed danger of being damaged. It seems therefore that a certain Fall is depicted here, such that the resulting imprint in consciousness has little chance of ever fully containing the "actual" imprint itself except in the earliest days of childhood. Indeed is this structure not precisely that which Freud has explored in terms of infantile sexuality and primordial forms of repression? It is this process—of the tearing and scratching (also interesting sexual and scriptural metaphors) of the wax paper—which is *essential* to the actual function of consciousness as beyond the pleasure principle. Indeed the "scratching and tearing" seem to precisely represent the principle of reality for Freud. This is also a violent and violating structure which however (paradoxically) is what "saves" or "protects" the subject. Protects it from what? Ultimately, for Freud, as for Derrida (it seems) from itself. The "imprinting of the subject by the world" is therefore seen as a fundamentally neutral process, on the one hand, yet also a violent and violating process. It is precisely the relation of the trace to memory. It is therefore the *double movement* of *protection* and *violation* which is in question here. Derrida thus pursues the issue at this point in terms of this double movement which metaphysics as such "is powerless to comprehend." Yet as he says: "the machine which even Freud recognizes, as its limit, does not run by itself. The machine is dead. It is death."[40] Thus we return to the relationship to death as the subject's relation to representation, which is the foundation of its "psychic structure." Yet Freud says: "There must come a point at which the analogy between an auxiliary apparatus of this kind and the organ which is its prototype will cease to apply. It is true too, that once the writing has been erased, the Mystic Pad cannot 'reproduce' it from within; it would be a mystic pad indeed if, like our memory, it could accomplish that."[41] Thus, Derrida says, Freud opposes a writing of memory to a more primordial writing in the soul—an essentially "unforgettable" writing—and thus he steps within the realm of metaphysics, in spite of himself, and returns to Plato's structure of this duplicity of good and bad writing.[42] With such an objection, Derrida aims to keep open the aspect of the non-origin, of the textuality of texts (conscious and unconscious) and hence of a certain "being-imprinted" of the subject by the world. Indeed, so does Freud, but he returns to the problem of the responsibility of the subject and of the non-responsibility of the machine. Indeed, it is a question here of the *will* which is at stake. For Derrida, there is a fundamental identity between the "subject" and the machine in terms of the problem of nonresponsibility. This is not to submit the subject to a certain sort of technological structure or mechanization, but rather to illustrate: (a) the limits of the subject in terms of its power, and indeed more precisely in terms of its will to power; (b) the hidden notion of humanism[43] lurking within Freud's discourse; (c) the role of death in the constitution of the subject and the object; indeed of man and machine; and (d) the structure of the subject as also not fundamentally different from that which Derrida calls "animality"—that undifferentiated relationship to the symbol as non-representative, non-translatable, and fundamentally within the sphere of the idiomatic and non-repeatable. Thus the classical Aristotelian distinction of man and animal is under fire here, and so is the contemporary problem of the distinction of man and machine. Indeed, if man is the "rational animal," then the machine "is a better man than we are." It is programmed and has more than instant recall of all that is inscribed therein. The sphere of animality too—where representation has not yet encroached—is not unlike that sphere of what Freud calls the "dream work" or "psychic writing." The dreamer, we should recall, always "invents his own grammar," and dreams, Freud tells us, are fundamentally "untranslatable." They retain an irreducibly idiomatic and idiosyncratic (non-repeatable and non-representable) dimension. Animality as such, Derrida tells us. Thus with the notion of the trace, we are forced here to rethink the divisions of consciousness/unconsciousness, and far beyond this psychoanalytic sphere (yet perhaps its "repressed" presuppositions) the ultimately metaphysical distinctions of animal, man, and machine. Indeed, Derrida is not attempting to make man into either a machine or an animal, but rather to show the limits of man in precisely these terms. We must now turn therefore beyond the notion of the trace as such to writing, for Derrida, as it inscribes, he claims, the absence of both subject and object as its fundamental preconditions.

(c) The Absence of Subject and Object: Inscription as Such

The "subject," for Derrida, is comparable to the Master, to the Father, to the author, to the agent, indeed to an ultimate causality and, in this sense, does not exist. The "object," likewise for him, is considered as the thing-in-itself, as the "effect" of a cause, as a referent "about which" language speaks and hence also, in this sense, does not exist. These determinations of the meaning of subject and object as such are precisely those of metaphysics. Therefore, for Derrida, it is of crucial importance to recognize this duality as, in a certain sense, a myth and therein to inscribe, beyond metaphysics, a new radically other notion of both subject and object as always already inscribed; indeed as results or effects themselves of that which he calls arche-writing, *différance* or, in this context, the "play of supplementarity." It is his unraveling of the metaphysical notions of both subjectivity and objectivity which we shall attempt to explore here, together with the subsequent replacement by the (indeed always already there) structure of absence, which founds the possibility of their presentation as such. In Derrida's words:

> Nothing—no present and in-different being—precedes the difference and spacing. There is no subject that would be its agent, author, and

master of the difference and to which this here would overcome eventually and empirically. Subjectivity—as with objectivity—is an effect of *différance*.[44]

As with Heidegger therefore, Derrida insists upon a limit to what metaphysics has inscribed as "humanism." And as with Husserl, Derrida insists upon a more primordial process (a transcendental kinesthetics) which inscribes the object as object: that is, objectivity as such. Beyond Heidegger, however, Derrida will claim that *différance* is that which opens the distinction and subsequent problematic of the relation of Being to beings; that ontological difference which for Derrida is *not* so primordial. Beyond Husserl too (as we have shown), Derrida insists on a certain non-retention which is the basis of that which later *(après coup)* comes to be known as the retention, in its relation to protention, and then, subsequently, as that "fundamental movement of subjectivity itself." This too is therefore an "effect" of *différance* and not to be considered an ultimate foundation. Indeed, we already know that for Derrida the *différance* (which is writing) extends beyond such a conception of foundation or origin. Thus we shall proceed here from the limits of humanism and the authority of the author as parallel for Derrida and Heidegger, and from the non-objective constitution of the object as parallel for Derrida and Husserl, to a realm more akin to Nietzsche, wherein we find the Abyss inscribed and indeed the Abyss of inscription itself, which Nietzsche himself did not discover, Derrida will insist. Nietzsche too always ultimately remained trapped within the metaphysics of presence in his profound opposition to this formulation. The "death of God" is, as Derrida says, not the issue here, since with this notion we find ourselves reduced simply to being the "other" of metaphysics—a certain "negative theology" as Dufrenne has pointed out, although inappropriately applying such a criticism to Derrida rather than Nietzsche. Finally, in opening the space of the Abyss (which is ultimately and always already within metaphysics), we shall proceed to show its effacement is thus also structurally inscribed. Indeed how the opening itself is necessarily always already concealed in the production of what metaphysics names the *subject* and the *object*.

(i) Heidegger, Humanism, and Beyond

Heidegger's concern with humanism is an attempt, unlike Derrida, to "put man in his place" in terms of a certain severance from his traditional identity with the animal world. The definition of man as "rational animal" is a focus on this *link,* Heidegger insists, and does not "do justice" to what is more primordially the "essence of man." The notion "rational animal" contains man as a subset of "animal," with his singular distinguishing quality being that of Reason or rationality. This comprehension of man effaces that which is most essential, Heidegger claims, and therefore must be rejected. Since humanism in general from the Roman era to Marx, including all Christian versions of the same, has relied on this essentially metaphysical determination of man, it too must be rejected in all its forms. Thus Heidegger claims to *elevate* the status of man to its "proper" place:

> The unique proposition is rather that the highest humanist determinations of the essence of man still do not express the *dignity proper to man.* In this sense, the idea which is explained in *Sein und Zeit* is against humanism. If one thinks against humanism it is because humanism does *not* situate the *humanitas* of man at a *high enough* level [my emphasis].[46]

Heidegger seems to elevate "man" to an even higher position than do the humanists, who already have made man in a certain sense "the measure of all things" and the "for which" (end) of all projects in the world and/or beyond it as such. Yet how is it possible that the "highest" could be considered yet "higher"? The key to this issue is to be found in what Heidegger considers the "essence of man," which humanism as such has effaced. This "essence" includes the following aspects: (a) a certain "throwness" into the world; (b) having a *world,* as distinct from simply an environment or a surrounding; (c) having a language and, in a certain sense, "being had" by language; (d) the singular quality of *"ekstasis,"* which allows for the clearing which opens the possibility of the "coming" of Being and thus the way to the "truth of Being" and its destiny; and ultimately (e) to be the "shepherd" of Being, which is not a Mastery nor Slavery, but a guidance in the same instant as it is a letting be of (i) the essence of all things in the world, and (ii) the essence and destiny of Being as such. These qualities of "man" have been forgotten in the history of the West, for Heidegger, due to the predominance of metaphysics, as it has usurped our language and hence our possibility of thought. The thought of possibility, indeed "called thinking,"[47] the poetizing of Being by itself via man, has been not only forgotten therefore but, in a certain "authentic" sense, has not yet even begun. It is this inauguration of a new relation of man to Being that Heidegger's thought is pointing towards, we suggest. In this process, it is worthy of note that he focusses on *"Dasein"* or "human existence," which is not to be confused with what metaphysics has called the "subject." As he says: "The essential greatness of man certainly does not reside in the fact that he is the substance of being as 'subject' of this here, to dissolve in the all too glorious 'objectivity' as a trustee of the power of Being—the being-present of being."[48]

We can see here that Heidegger equates the "making-subject" of man with the "making an object" of him at the same instant. It is this which we have "rightly" done with studies of animals and other living things, he claims, but this is precisely why man and animal must be radically separated. In addition, the non-subjectification of man portrays a more radical understanding of his "essence" for Heidegger in that "it is not man that decides" when it comes to issues of Being as such. Being is beyond man and beyond the traditional will-to-power, will to objectify, to comprehend, to capture and to master. Thus Heidegger relies on the notion of the *destiny* of Being in order to submit man to this ultimate constraint on his relation to the world, to himself, and indeed ultimately of Being itself. Thus it has been the destiny of Being to have been forgotten in the metaphysical understanding of the world to date. The possibility of being "called to thinking," to being open to the Being of beings is for Heidegger a function of (a) a certain "passivity" of man and yet also (b) a certain recognition of his own limits and indeed his ultimate, not-to-be-outstripped limitation: death itself. The authenticity of *Dasein* in its relations to the world, itself and to Being is a function of its relation to death itself—indeed its *own* death, or as Heidegger says: being-towards-death. But we should recall once again that Heidegger is not concerned here with the "subject" of man, nor with his subjectivity, but rather with a more primordial condition for this same subjectivity and indeed that which when "recognized as the essence of man" will overcome this "will to mastery," the effects of which we should see in the terms, the division and the ultimate identity of subject and object.

For Derrida, as we know, the issues are not dissimilar with respect to the "subject and object" from Heidegger's portrayal of them. However, there are also some fundamental differences to be acknowledged. Indeed in some respects, Derrida uses Heidegger in order to step outside of the circumference of the latter's perspective. This movement, we should recall, is essential to the work of deconstruction in its simultaneous borrowing and distancing from a position/text on which it feeds. It is thus with Heidegger.

The first objection by Derrida, and perhaps the most serious, concerns Heidegger's reliance on the traditional metaphysical concepts of essence and appearance, the former containing a certain primordiality denied to the latter. The "essence" of man is at stake here, and indeed, it is the "forgetting" of this *essence* which concerns Heidegger. This conceptual opposition, also represented by presence and absence (of the truth) orients in addition Heidegger's distinction of authenticity and inauthenticity; indeed the issue of the *truth* of Being is precisely founded on metaphysics as such. We have not yet arrived at Nietzsche for whom "truth is a useful error." This would be a step back into *"technè"* for Heidegger, no doubt, wherein the notion of truth would be "in the service of something." Yet Heidegger opens the way to a *technè* of Being, such that man is "in the service of" the destiny of Being. This *reversal* is not radical for Derrida, it seems, since he claims that the problem of the ontological difference between Being and beings is not deep enough. It is this relation which, when realized (indeed by man), will reorient and indeed resituate man and put him in his proper place, above "animals" and below Being. Although this hierarchy is not explicitly put in question by Derrida, with reference to Heidegger, we should recall that animality for the latter is "not to be outstripped" and thus not severed from the notion we call "man." Derrida does not rely on the "essential" in his analysis, but rather on what Kant called "the conditions of the possibility" of things. Things indeed, as a result. Such is the "primordial and forgotten difference" in Heidegger's thinking, for Derrida. Thus Derrida turns away from the "proper," "essence" of things to that which he considers makes them possible. Indeed he turns to *différance* as that movement which opens the possibility of the *difference* between Being and beings and, in turn, Heidegger's subsequent analysis of this issue. Being is thus itself a "result," for Derrida, and not the most primordial. It is the *movement* of "presence and absence" of Being—its Destiny, according to Heidegger, which is to be the issue for Derrida. Not Being as such in its being-present or absent for man. In a certain sense, therefore, we step back from the center of man, which Heidegger, although recentering or decentering in one sense, has established as the focal point for the destiny of Being: indeed its *shepherd*. For Derrida, however, the play of the supplement which ultimately dislocates the "proper" and hence the possibility of formulations such as "the essence of man" is of greater significance.

> Supplementarity, which *is* nothing, neither a presence nor an absence, is neither a substance nor an essence of man. It is precisely the *play* of

presence and absence, the *opening* of this play that no metaphysics or ontological concept can comprehend. Therefore this property of man is not a property of man; it is the very dislocation of the proper in general [my emphasis].

Further in relation to man the animal, with rationality as an adjective:

. . . its (the supplement, *différance*, writing) play *precedes* what one calls man and extends outside of him. Man calls himself man only by drawing limits excluding his other from the play of supplementarity: the purity of nature, of animality, primitivism, childhood, madness, divinity. The approach to these limits is at once feared as a threat of death and desired as access to *a life without différance* [my emphasis].

Thus he says:

Writing will appear to us more and more as another name for this structure of supplementarity.[49]

"A life without différance" is for Derrida, we should recall, "pure presence itself"; it is that which metaphysics claims we have lost and which must be regained. It is the *telos* of history; it is precisely that history is teleological, for metaphysics. And this "ultimate presence" of consciousness to itself as its own "object," as an ultimate subjectification of the object and objectification of the subject, is, as Hegel has shown, Absolute Knowledge. It is death itself. And it is thus that we will be forever denied access to it, in spite of its most profound paradoxical proximity to us. Thus Heidegger turns toward being-toward-death as the index of man's authenticity in his relation to himself. Is death simply subsumed and hence forgotten amidst "idle chatter," or is it squarely and individually, indeed idiosyncratically, "faced"? The answer to this question will answer the question of the authenticity of man. Indeed the entire history of metaphysics can be considered to be simply "idle chatter" in its fundamental forgetting of death as such. Metaphysics has always included death as a means, a way, and hence as a sign. Indeed the "sign" is also in question here. But death as such has never been addressed as such for Heidegger. It has been forgotten in eschatology—in a teleology of presence, which is simultaneously the "destiny of the absence" of Being. Thus teleology as such is also to be overcome for Heidegger, since it submits the object to the will of a subject in the relation of *technè* or technology. Being as such will forever escape technologization, Heidegger tells us, and it is in this (our) age, therefore, that it recedes even further from sight.

But Derrida will object here to this relation of "presence and absence" in terms of visibility and invisibility," albeit of Being itself as it "comes" into language. These metaphors orient the totality of metaphysics, Derrida insists, and center one's thinking on the Sun/light of Reason itself.[50] The "visible," although not a function of the light of Reason (explicitly for Heidegger), is nonetheless subjected in this "metaphoric" formulation to the constraints of a metaphysics which presupposes a certain light according to which "things" become visible. Indeed a certain relation of the "face to the sun" is also presupposed here. A certain simultaneity of temporal relations is also set firmly in place. The "seen," the "visible," in short the "made visible" by Being for man, for Heidegger, is thus ultimately a vicious metaphysical circle Derrida claims. The paradox is the following therefore for Derrida:

> And if Heidegger has radically deconstructed the authority of the present for metaphysics it is to lead us to think the presence of the present.

It is thus the constitution of the "presence" as such which is in question here. Yet, as Derrida goes on to say:

> The ontological distance of *Dasein* from that which it is as ek-sistanz and from *Da* to *Sein* this distance which appears initially as ontic proximity should be reduced by the thought of the truth of Being. From whence the dominance in Heidegger's discourse of the entire metaphorics of proximity, of simple and immediate presence, associating with the proximity of Being. The values of nearness, shelter, home, service, security, voice and hearing.[51]

Thus from the "betrayal by metaphor," Derrida explicates a shadow in Heidegger's discourse itself which situates it squarely *within* the metaphysics of presence which the latter would "destroy" by the "sense" of his words.

Nevertheless in terms of our "subject" here, which is indeed the overlap of Derrida's and Heidegger's positions, we should insist that the notion of "subject" as such, with its counterpart "object" as such, are to be abandoned here for the following reasons: (i) they are results of a process which itself is effaced in the very achievement of *their* constitution; (ii) the conditions of their possibility must therein be analyzed in order that (a) the role of writing in its relation to that which we call its "author" can be more clearly understood; and (b) the role of the written "object" can be understood more precisely as that simultaneous result of a process which extends beyond what we call the subject. Thus we situate the power of constitution otherwise in this formulation. The "subject" for Derrida is not "man as such," since man as such does not exist. What exists is a movement of supplementarity which allows for such notions to be established and which in turn defies existence (to be) in terms of that result which therein rules out the possibility of the recognition of this "more primordial process" which "is" not.

Thus Derrida focuses on a fundamental inscription of the "subject," which is not within its control. It is, as Heidegger said of *Dasein,* "thrown" into the world; it is also thrown into "inauthenticity," by the very destiny of Being. Rather than appealing to destiny, however, Derrida turns to a "play" of *différance,* which opens the possibility of destiny and non-destiny of that non-teleological, non-oriented orientation. *Différance* is "overtaken" by the destiny of Being in the latter's very process of self-effacement and forgetting within the tradition of metaphysics. Thus without the "power" of the subject we have a structure already "at work" here in which we must *a posteriori* "situate" that which we retroactively call "the subject," and *a fortiori*—the "object." As Derrida says, *différance* is:

> an operation which is not an operation, which can be thought neither as passion nor as the action of a subject upon an object, nor starting from an agent, nor beginning from a patient, nor beginning from nor moving towards any one of these terms.[52]

Thus the "causality" of *différance* is authorless, and indeed ultimately without authority. It is in a certain sense haphazard. It is chance itself as it simultaneously appears and is effaced within the discourse of Reason. Thus Derrida refers to it as "play" rather than "work," the latter having always been submitted to a system of *technè,* and hence of a *telos* of Reason as such:

> The concept of play [*jeu*] is beyond this opposition [empirical/logical]; it announces at the dawn of and beyond philosophy, the unity of *chance and necessity* in a calculus without end.[53]

The irony of a "calculus without end" should not turn us back to Hegel, however. We should recall that *différance* is not without its "rationality," its own sort of "order." It moves, therefore, according to a pattern which indeed is capable of being formalized, indeed lends itself to a formalization which would nonetheless remain "beyond" the closure of metaphysics. We have thus left Heidegger far behind us at this juncture. What Derrida is exposing here is a structure or play which itself takes on the form of an "economy" which, in Heideggerian terms, opens the possibility of thinking (a) the truth of Being, (b) the essence of man, and (c) their ontological difference and thus relation that metaphysics has systematically forgotten. Yet Derrida's move is, in a certain sense, not so radical with respect to his treatment and indeed "distrust" of the notion of the subject. As he himself recognizes:

> Before being . . . that of Heidegger, this gesture was also that of *Nietzsche* and of *Freud* both of whom placed consciousness and its assured certainty of itself in question.

Further, as he says for Nietzsche:

> . . . consciousness is the *effect* of forces to which essence, the track and methods are not proper to it. Force itself is never present.[54]

Neither is the trace itself, nor arche-writing, nor *différance,* we should recall "ever present." Thus we have seen that Derrida's approach to and subsequent withdrawal from Heidegger can be summarized in the following paradoxical respect. First, Derrida, too, claims to *extend* the range of that which we call "man" to expose the interrelations of "human existence" with animality, divinity, childhood, madness, and other forms of "excluded otherness" from the concept of "man as such." This is not, as we have seen, the *elevation* of "man" from the description as "rational animal," as it is in Heidegger. The extension is not in accordance with a "proper essence" of man, but rather with the notion of "proper essence itself" and its inapplicability in a profound sense. The second movement Derrida makes, also parallel to but radically differing from Heidegger, is in terms of the subsequent *limits* on "human existence" in accordance with a certain "thrownness" (indeed perhaps a throw of the dice) which situates "man" *within* structures and forces—indeed the play of *différance* and supplementarity itself, which he does not (a) authorize nor therefore (b) control. It is *différance* that gives birth to man, for Derrida, not the reverse. And it is *différance* that opens the space for the conditions of the possibility of Heidegger's problematics. Thus we insist that the distinction between Derrida and Heidegger is as radical and profound as that between Hegel and Kant, for instance. Of course the analogy here is limited to a similarity of analogies (analogy of analogy) and the similarity of the names as such. Indeed it is the differences which open meaning here; it is the relations of the names, rather than their full plentitudes, which we have sought to illustrate. Indeed this formulation could easily be situated at one level, within the Heideggerian discourse, yet at another, more profound (in a certain sense) within the Derridaean. Of course in the end it is neither and accepts neither totally. But first we must turn to the "object," which like the 'subject' herein addressed does not properly speaking exist, for Derrida.

(ii) Husserl, the Transcendental Ego and Death

In Husserl's exposure of the "objectivity" of the object as a result of a fundamental constitutional activity on the part of the "subject," he in turn was forced to rely on a more primordial form of "subjectivity." It was this "form" which, as ultimately the condition of the possibility of form itself, he termed the transcendental ego. We shall explore the movement of his thought in this context from the ego to the transcendental ego, to the intersubjective constitution of a world as "the world as such," to objectivity as such, to the leap to inscription as its precondition, and in turn Derrida's analysis of the latter as it undermines all that led Husserl toward it. For Derrida, the fact that inscription is the ultimate basis of "objectivity" presupposes a certain absence of both subject and object; indeed "my death" as writer is therein inscribed for him. It is thus that our study of the transcendental ego and its effects in the world which give us a "world" will lead to the exposure of the notion of death for Derrida as a more primordial foundation. Indeed as a non-foundation, to be sure, as we have already illustrated with *différance* as such. Thus the notion of absence here of both subject and object must be seen as "internal" and inscribed within their names as such. Their absence is thus, as distinct from Heidegger, not a former aspect, or grounding aspect in as much as it houses and is housed by them, albeit effaced within the tradition of metaphysics. It is this "parasitic" relation, as exposed by Derrida, which will also mark the difference between the latter's position and Husserl's, to say nothing of Heidegger.

Husserl turns from the ego, in the world, to the transcendental ego after the reduction, in an effort to comprehend the conditions of the possibility of the "intentional object" as constituted by a subject. The object as such is always, therefore, a result for him: an intended meaningful result. But for the ego-in-the-world, this process happens largely "behind his back"; it is, in short, effaced. The ego finds a world always already there. As he says:

> The objective world is constantly there before me as already finished, a datum of my living continuous objective experience and even in respect of what is no longer experienced, something I go on accepting habitually. It is a matter of examining this experience itself and uncovering intentionally the manner in which it bestows sense, the manner in which it can occur as experience and become verified as evidence relating to an actual existent with an explicable *essence of its own* which is not my own essence and has no place as a constituent part thereof, though it nevertheless can acquire sense and verification only in my essence [my emphasis].[55]

Thus we find a double movement here wherein the ego (a) *finds* a world, yet (b) is also responsible for its constitution, and yet further (c) the object as such has an existence, indeed an essence, that is radically *independent* of that "same subject." The difficulty in understanding this give and take of the power of the subject for Husserl can be overcome if one shifts to a notion of *levels* of subjectivity, or indeed reduces the ego in the world and therein "finds" a transcendental ego. The preconditions for the possibility of such a shift are, as we know from Derrida's analysis,[56] not reducible. But first we must "find" the transcendental ego at work.

In order to find not only a world but *the world* as such for anyone (within the limits of normality, as defined by Husserl, amazingly enough), the constitution of the transcendental ego must, as transcendental, be somewhat beyond the differences from one ego to another at the empirical level. Indeed we have, in a certain sense, an ego-in-general here. In Husserl's terms, we have "a certain harmony of the monads." He says so explicitly: "Consequently the constitution of the world essentially involves a 'harmony of the monads.' . . ."[57] Indeed we have more than a simple harmony here, since the transcendental ego or essence of each empirical ego (with respect to the constitution of objects as such) is indeed an essential structure in which each ego as ego participates—necessarily. It is, in a certain sense, the ego as such. Thus we have the possibility of a "certain harmony of the monads"; indeed for science as such, or more precisely perhaps, a world as such for us all. Nevertheless, Husserl admits of a certain gap or difference from one ego to another, in spite of this common foundation. The "other," he says, "can never become an immediate experience for me." He is always and necessarily so, immediately perceived.

We have an ontological *abyss,* therefore, which paradoxically opens the possibility of society as such: or in Husserl's terms, of intersubjectivity as such.

The basis of intersubjectivity is thus a certain identity and a certain difference between the monads. Since they are ultimately harmonious, the force of identity in general overcomes the force of difference. Husserl explains it in the following manner in his consideration of society as such as:

> An Ego-community, which includes me, becomes constituted (in my sphere of ownness, naturally) as a community of Egos existing with each other and for each other—ultimately a community of monads, which moreover (in its communalized intentionality) constitutes the *one identical world.* In this world all Egos present themselves, but in an objectivating apperception (mediately) with the sense 'men' or 'psychophysical' men as worldly objects [my emphasis].[58]

Thus along with the possibility of becoming a subject in the world, one becomes at the same instant "an object for others." Sartre as we know[59] has made much of this as a fundamental violence of one subject against another. But we shall remain with Husserl instead for the moment, as he becomes relevant for Derrida.

We have found thus far that intersubjectivity is a condition for the possibility of a world, indeed of the world as such, and that in turn the condition for intersubjectivity has been ultimately a certain "identity" of structure of the monads—indeed the transcendental ego as such. But Husserl continues here with what may appear to be a profound reversal, since he turns towards the conditions of the possibility of intersubjectivity in terms of the constitution of the object as such, as an object for anyone, as within the sphere of inscription. The voice, albeit the locus of "primal" evidence for the immediate relation of the ego to itself is not sufficient for the constitution of the object for anyone. My death kills also my voice, and thus the voice of evidence must transcend such an absence. It is here that science, the world of objects, and ultimately the world of truth as such for now, the past, and the future, requires a *written trace* which "makes objective" what the subject learns to be true. Thus Husserl speaks of the sedimentation of science and tradition and the inheritance one is born into. He also thus warns of the dangers of such "worldly inscription"[60] in that the "original intention," the guiding *telos,* can therein (over time) be lost or forgotten. But, he says, the text as such is not (as worldly) a danger as such to truth. The ideality of the object is radically independent of its inscription. In this context he speaks of the "theoretical" possibility of the total destruction of the world as making no difference in terms of the ideality of the "objective." The latter transcends existence as such, although it requires the latter for its "coming into existence." As essential effacement, to be sure.

If we return now to our transcendental ego and its constituting structures, we find a certain absence and indeed limit of its transcendence has been inscribed therein. With respect at least to the "sense and verification" of the objective world as such, the transcendental ego is in a certain sense insufficient. Necessary indeed, but insufficient. The transcendental ego as such is always already in a transcendental community of egos (parallel to the empirical one to be sure), which Husserl himself calls the "transcendental We"—indeed a transcendental intersubjectivity which forms its precondition. Yet the condition for transcendental intersubjectivity is clearly the "harmony" presupposed for the monads; or, in short, the transcendental ego. There thus seems to be a certain double primordiality here or else a certain effacement which allows for such a duplicity to appear as such. It is here that we find Derrida's analysis as an opening to precisely this effacement. What is effaced is not only the empirical, limited perhaps, finite world, but also finitude itself—the very limit of the ego (in either sense) which shifts its constitutional abilities from the "structure of intentionality as such" to those forms of inscription for anyone at any time known as *writings*. In addition, Derrida claims that death is here not only an accidental problem which writing comes to supplement or fill in for the subject, and indeed for all subjects as such, but rather the *structural condition of the possibility of writing as such*. He explains the reversal of priority and the "effacement" in Husserl in the following way:

> The absence of intuition—and hence of the subject of intuition—is not only tolerated by the discourse, it is required by the structure of signification in general despite the slight attention that one usually pays to it. It is radically required: the total absence of the subject and the object of an enunciation—the death of the writer and/or the disappearance of the objects he was able to describe—does not prevent the text from meaning *(vouloir-dire)*. This possibility, on the contrary, gives birth to meaning *(vouloir-dire)* as such, gives it to be understood and to be read.[61]

This "structural necessity" also goes *a fortiori* for Derrida for his notion of writing in general or arche-writing, but first we must pursue what he calls the total absence of the subject, or death itself. It is not however, in a certain sense, death in general which is in question here—in the sense that one would write for posterity, as Levinas suggests. Death, in this case, is specifically the death of the writer in the very process of writing. It is not for nothing that Derrida says of writing that it is "toujours une question de vie et de mort." In this context we should recall that which Plato/Socrates complained of with respect to writing as such and the intrinsically absent author, indeed the author as its father, master, originator, etc.

> You know, Phaedrus, that's the strange thing about writing which makes it truly analogous to painting. The painter's products stand before us as though they were alive, but if you question them, they maintain a most majestic silence. It is the same with written words; they seem to talk to you as though they were intelligent, but if you ask them anything about what they say, from a desire to be instructed, they go on telling you just the same thing forever. And once a thing is put in writing, the composition, whatever it may be, drifts all over the place, getting into the hands not only of those who understand it, but equally of those who have no business with it; it doesn't know how to address the right people, and not address the wrong. And when it is ill-treated and unfairly abused it always needs *its parent* to come to its help, being unable to defend or help itself [my emphasis].[62]

It was for this reason that Socrates argued for the *voice* of Reason as the voice of the Father—the presence of the subject to his own words in terms of a certain responsivity and a responsibility. It is as if in the speaking one is not temporally, spatially, or meaningfully separated from one's own speech. Thus the possibility of explication, of challenge, and of the defense of the child by its father is inscribed in such a structure. These are precisely the qualities, as benefits, which writing lacks, and it is for these reasons that it is considered dangerous not only to memory but also to meaning itself. If one asks it what it means, it just goes on repeating the same thing over and over again, we repeat. Thus in terms of the Platonic tradition Husserl, in his recognition of writing at least as the condition of the scientificity of science, seems to have overcome many metaphysical obstacles. (However, it is also Plato who later says that writing is the condition of the possibility of the law; in particular social and political law, but also law in general. We shall return to this.)[63] The problem with Husserl's recognition, for Derrida, is that it does not recognize the conditions of possibility of writing as such except by a return to radically and violently imposed and presupposed metaphysical notions such as "the essential harmony of the monads," and the bracketing of the conditions of the possibility of the bracketing process (the transcendental reduction as such), and the essentially transcendental basis for the ego as such which therein effaces that which for Heidegger and Derrida is "not-to-be-outstripped": death. Indeed it is the subject's relation to death—his own and in general—which is the basis for the constitution of subjectivity as such, for Derrida. But first we must return to that which, for Derrida, allows the written to be written as such. As he says:

> *My death* is *structurally necessary* for the pronunciation of 'I'. That I could also be alive and that I am certain of that comes after the negotiating *(marché)* of meaning *(vouloir-dire)* and this *structure* is active, it sustains its original efficacy even when I say 'I am alive' at the precise moment when, if that is possible, I have a full and actual intuition of it [my emphasis].[64]

Thus for Derrida, beyond "writing" (in the traditional sense of the term), the condition of meaning in general, as in general, and always already thus, is "my death." In order that my speech means something, it must be inscribed within *the* world *as such;* indeed language already does this, as we have shown, and thus in a certain sense, "my death" (in particular, or anyone else's as well in their speech) is always already inscribed. My speech leaves me in the instant of its formulation and in a radical sense never returns. It is already transposed into the "for others" formulation which is the essence of speech itself. Thus Derrida poses the problem of auto-affection in Rousseau, in particular,[65] as always already mediated. My relation to myself is therefore for Derrida always already within the currency and system of exchange of my relation to others. Indeed the former is a product of the latter, as Freud among others has clearly illustrated. Thus we overthrow at one blow the distinction between speech and writing, as explicated in the *Phaedrus,* and the "essential harmony" of the "essential monads" as the precondition for the constitution of objectivity as such, the world as such, and science in particular, for Husserl. The subject, be it transcendental or otherwise, is always already inscribed, for Derrida, within a system of exchange which is always already public (for others) and which presupposes the "structural necessity of my death" in order to "make sense." Sense or meaning is thus essentially public or collective as well, in this sense. The problem of the idiom or the idiomatic in general must reappear therefore as enigmatic essentially. How is it possible to constitute the "idiom" or the idiomatic for me or the other? Is this not ruled out of order to begin with within Derrida's formulation here?

We should recall that the idiomatic, for Derrida, is to be situated within the notion of the untranslatable, unrepeatable, and non-representable. In addition it is the idiomatic, idiosyncratic which defines his notion *à la fois* of the *sacred* and of *animality* as such. It seems therefore that, in the expansion of the notion of man from being other than "animal" and other than "divine" to an inclusion of these qualities within the sense of the idiomatic, we must transgress that which he calls the meaningful as such. Indeed this is precisely where we are. The notion of meaning has always been inscribed as "objective" or, in a certain sense, the meaning of the object. That which *cannot be objectified,* that is not situated within the *"Logos"* system of exchange (logocentrism as such) cannot be said, and *a fortiori* cannot be written. It extends beyond the limits of language, as we have shown. But we are not in a realm where these limits precisely do not apply. We have extended the field beyond the subject, beyond the object, beyond the sayable as such, beyond the as such and therefore must approach what Derrida himself has called, in distinct terms, animality on the one hand and divinity on the other. The irony of their profound similarity (identity) must herein be addressed in particular as this relates to Nietzsche's formulation of the same. For Nietzsche, as we know, the "death of God" was required in order to liberate the "essence" of man, which contained a not-to-be-outstripped form of nature he called bestiality. We now propose therefore to address once again the parallels to Derrida's position as the latter overlaps with Nietzsche, but also the precise and profound distinctions therein.

(iii) Nietzsche and the Abyss of Inscription

The convergence of animality and divinity within what Derrida would call man is only partially convergent with Nietzsche's position on this issue. As we have said, Nietzsche insisted on the death of God as such as the precondition for the last man to become the "over-man"—the ultimate creator of value and things himself. Indeed to become his own Father, which would therein eliminate the Father of Fathers: *Logos* itself. In this context Nietzsche claims that "truth is a useful error," but that it certainly does not as such (that is as philosophy has understood from Plato and Socrates' time) exist. There is thus no Absolute truth or essence to things for Nietzsche, at least not that we can know. All we can know are interpretations, and it is force and the "herd instinct' of the 'rabble' (collective repetition as such) which will make what the creators will into truths-for-others. Indeed force is, for Nietzsche, the basis of the constitution of science itself, and therefore of its overcoming. In proposing a world of will and force (which might ultimately be the same thing), Nietzsche inaugurates a notion of the irreducible duplicity of forces and, hence therein, a notion of contradiction which cannot be outstripped. It is at this point that Derrida's position converges somewhat with Nietzsche's, as we have seen in terms of the relation of *différance* to that of the forces of Apollo and Dionysius. In terms of the absence of subject and object as a result of force as such, Derrida admits the following fraternity with Nietzsche:

> If *différance* is recognized as the obliterated origin of absence and presence, major forms of the disappearing and the appearing of the entity, it would still remain to be known if being, before its determination into absence or presence, is already implicated in the thought of *différance*. And if *différance* as the project of the mastery of the entity should be understood with reference to the sense of being. Can one not think the converse? Since the sense of being is never produced as history outside its determination as presence, has it not always already been caught within the history of metaphysics as the epoch of presence? This is perhaps what Nietzsche wanted to write and what resists the Heideggerian reading of Nietzsche; *différance in its active movement*—what is comprehended in the concept of difference without exhausting it—is what not only precedes metaphysics but also extends beyond the thought of being. The latter speaks nothing other than metaphysics, even if it exceeds it and thinks it as what is within its closure.[66]

Indeed Nietzsche too spoke "nothing other than metaphysics" in what was more precisely an attempt to speak of its other. Where Nietzsche fell back into metaphysics was in his attempt to separate himself too radically from it. To set himself apart from and against metaphysics. Indeed he attempted to install the "Abyss" between himself and metaphysics—the Abyss of death itself, and in particular, the death of God. As Nietzsche says:

> Before God! But now this God has died. You higher men, this God was your greatest danger. It is only since he lies in his tomb that you have been resurrected. Only now the great noon comes, only now the higher man becomes—Lord.[67]

Thus the condition for becoming the Father is to kill the Father, or at least, as in this instance, to find that he is already dead. Indeed, in a certain sense, has always already been dead—it was just that we did not know this. We "blinked," as Nietzsche says.

Thus we have Oedipus within Nietzsche and, in addition, a movement not unlike that which we find in Hegel (the ultimate metaphysician, for Derrida, we should recall). In the "death of God," man is at once *more essentially man* for Nietzsche and yet also *no longer man* as such. He becomes God; he becomes that same oppressor he would revolt against. In short, he becomes the Master. But this is not for all men equally, Nietzsche insists. It is for "those who would hear his words" and then "abandon him to his chilly heights." The overman follows no one except himself. And himself he despises, since he is at base a work of nature, a result of forces which are beyond his control. The will to power is thus forever submitted to a "play of forces" to which even the overman is necessarily blind. It is thus that Nietzsche creates and destroys his overman—yet he would kill God. It is thus also that God is sustained. Was it not in Christianity, for instance, that man finds God *within;* that man is always already essentially God? Was it not in Plato that man, as finitude as such, has his essence in infinity as "Godliness" as such? It is thus that Nietzsche remains trapped within the metaphysics he would destroy, and it is thus that he paradoxically preserves (in Hegelian fashion at that) the same God he would destroy.

Derrida argues that the "Nietzschean demolition remains dogmatic and like all reversals, a captive of that metaphysical edifice which it professes to overthrow." Yet he considers Nietzsche to have "intended" (a strange word for the Derridaen discourse) to speak of the *différance,* to speak of the conditions of presence and absence. In fact, he has (a) fallen into the Abyss and, indeed, (b) covered it up (before and after his own leap therein). Has not Nietzsche thus buried himself, we might well ask? No, Derrida insists, it is his writing as such that will save him from a total effacement of having said "nothing at all."

We thus return to the question of writing for Derrida. As with Nietzsche, Derrida has claimed that "reading and therefore writing, the text were for Nietzsche 'originary operations' with regard to the sense that they do not first have to transcribe or discover, which would not therefore be a truth signified in the original element and presence of the *logos,* as *topos noetos,* divine understanding, or the structure of *a priori* necessity."[68] It is this "fall" into writing of the writer which Nietzsche recognized as within the structure of writing as such. The writer "blinks" when he writes and opens his eyes only afterward, if at all. It is thus that Nietzsche's *writing itself* tells us more about writing than that which he wrote about writing. It is the "forgetting of the self," the Dionysian principle, which ultimately orients the writing of writing. Yet *différance* or writing, for Derrida, is also that space between the Apollonian and Dionysian principles. It seems therefore that this "space" is governed ultimately by the Dionysian principle. But first, what sort of space is this? It is the space of writing itself, Derrida insists—the space which is at once a distance and an absolute proximity. It is, in a certain sense, the distance of/from that which is called the "absolute proximity." In short it is the Abyss. Without a subject or an object—indeed their absence as the preconditions (structural necessities a priori), writing is cast adrift, it seems, and is subjected to the process of objectification. In short, as we have shown, writing falls into the *Logos* at precisely this moment where the Father, the writer, its *Logos* is exiled from it (or killed, as with Nietzsche). The difference between the death of God (*Logos* ultimately) and the "structural necessity of his absence" is the crucial issue with respect to the fundamental difference between Derrida and Nietzsche. The decentering of the *Logos* is not the end of *Logos* for Derrida, and the Abyss of writing is not one without end or without foundation. There is always an ultimate ground for Derrida, even though this can no longer be called the ultimate ground, or origin. Indeed it is precisely the non-origin of origin of which we speak. Decentering the *Logos,* or making the absence of subject and object a structural necessity, opens the possibility (a) of inscription itself, as we have shown, and (b) of meaning itself. Absolute freedom to say anything at all without an invisible "point of orientation" (officially outside of the system) is the ultimate slavery and ultimate capture of what purports to be non-metaphysical—indeed anti-metaphysical—by metaphysics itself. Thus the master/slave dialectic in Hegel can be applied precisely to Nietzsche, yet not at all to Derrida. The making of a hypo-thesis is not reducible to the stepping into the ring of a polemic. In a word, Nietzsche's passion was perhaps too much for him. Yet Derrida finds *différance* at the heart of Nietzsche's writing:

> Nietzsche *has written what* he has written. He has written that writing—and first of all his own—is not originally subordinate to the logos and to truth. And that this subordination has come into being during an epoch whose meaning we must deconstruct.[69]

As we have shown, it seems that Nietzsche's writing, as radically opposing the *Logos,* therein falls victim to it all the more. Yet Derrida insists there is more to Nietzsche than this. That which exceeds his claims, that which in a certain sense could not be said, was written in the "form" of the writing itself. Indeed Nietzsche seems to have contradicted himself on most counts.[70] Every issue for him could be both affirmed and disconfirmed; those he loved he also hated; the essence of tragedy carried with it a certain comedy; the reciprocity of life and death and indeed the "transvaluation of all values" illustrate, to a certain extent, that which Derrida is here emphasizing, we suggest. Indeed writing itself is not capable (Nietzsche's or Derrida's most obviously, but also *all* writing, Derrida will claim) of being totalized into a unified and not self-contradictory whole. In fact the demands of philosophy, of *Logos*—the principle of non-contradiction—is *intrinsically* violated by the very structure of writing, Derrida claims. "Writing denounces itself," he says. Thus we have an abyss within the very structure of writing itself such that the totality (interpretation, reading) of a text is never a full presence of the object itself, nor of the subject to its object *a fortiori*. The essential mediation of writing by temporality and spatiality (its *a priori* conditions, for Derrida, as we shall see later) is what dislocates the proper, the correct from itself. For Husserl, we should recall, it is *only* in writing that the constitution of scientific objectivity, indeed objectivity as such, is possible. Yet Derrida herein insists that: (a) logocentrism which would make the text into an object, and reading into a form of totalization towards the "intention" *(vouloir-dire)*, meaning, essence, center of the text, can never accomplish its task completely; and (b) that writing itself has an intrinsic structure which (i) within metaphysics is self-destructive; and (ii) beyond metaphysics, entails an infinity of meanings and readings. The opening of writing is thus the space of the Abyss, for Derrida, the Abyss which is infinity itself. It is this that the *Logos* (as Nietzsche also no doubt recognized) has killed in its usurpation of infinity for itself. As Derrida says: "God is the name of indifference itself," and this must be overcome. But as we have shown, his tools are different from those of Nietzsche although not dissimilar. Derrida openly claims to borrow[71] his tools from metaphysics, openly admits that "man" for him is not the "overman" of which Nietzsche speaks; yet at the same time he insists that metaphysics as such, as dominated by the name of God, the Father, the *Logos,* must be overcome, and that writing is indeed a radically inaugurating and originating activity. It is precisely the origin of the origin—which can never be simply an origin nor a non-origin. The Nietzschean discourse, in its defiance of a non-contradictory totalization, opens the space of inscription itself as understood beyond the "blink," which is also intrinsic to Nietzsche's discourse as such. Yet perhaps Nietzsche knew this too and yet refused to speak of it. We should recall that, for him, "a wise man never says all that he knows"— it would be too dangerous. We should also recall that for Nietzsche, not unlike Derrida in a fundamental way (which thought might perhaps make the latter himself blink):

> When one speaks of *humanity,* the idea is fundamental that this is something which separates and distinguishes man from nature. In reality, however, there is no such separation: "natural" qualities and those called truly "human" are inseparably grown together. Man, in his highest and noblest capacities, is wholly nature and embodies its *uncanny dual* character. Those of his abilities which are terrifying and considered inhuman may even be the fertile soil out of which alone all humanity can grow in impulse, deed and work [my emphasis].[72]

We might also recall that for Derrida writing and textuality as such can be considered as a seeding, sowing, indeed a disseminating process.[73] One ploughs the fields to set up furrows, lines of demarcation, and one seeds them only after they are ploughed. Some take root, others do not, but the important aspect of this metaphorical structure is that the seeds be sown. The "inhuman" basis of humanity, for Nietzsche, is precisely what frightens us all in terms of our humanity. It is the Abyss into which perhaps we have thrown madness, childhood, abnormality, animality, divinity, or the sacred as such, in our process of the fabrication of man as such, not realizing that in the same process (a) we have therein thrown *ourselves* into the Abyss, as Nietzsche did in his "reversal" of the problem; and (b) we have effaced the fact or fundamental truth (if these words still mean anything after Derrida) that we have always already been in the Abyss—this *same* Abyss. That the "other" (we would exclude) is always already within us—be it the other as sacred or the other as bestiality (not so easy to accept perhaps). The Abyss of which we speak therefore is not something "out there," something which we can leap over, face, or avoid. Just as we are neither the subjects we think we are nor the objects others make of us, so too writing for Derrida is not simply this inscription here. Yet it is precisely that and nothing else besides. Writing too is always already within the Abyss and yet also carries with it the radical inauguration of the Abyss itself. Writing is precisely this spacing which opens the Abyss—the Abyss, we repeat, where we are not where we might be or have been (only). We must now therefore turn to the structure of writing, or *différance,* or the supplement, as Derrida uses these terms, in order to open wider the gaping (w)hole we have now found ourselves in the midst of. A final warning before we leave *Logos* too far behind us here on the solid rock that has recently turned into an immanent volcano. In approaching the "written" as such here, in its movement as movement, we risk being able to "say nothing" about it. The Abyss, we should recall, is, although the condition of speech itself, the unspeakable. However, we propose to examine its *form* in the upcoming section and its movement as one that incessantly *repeats. Différance* is thus, we suggest, (a) not subject to its own laws, yet (b) lends itself to its own objectification. The reason for this may be more than Derrida's *admitted* "borrowing" from metaphysics. As long as his discourse makes sense to us, it is possible to formalize it. As long as the *différance* of which he speaks remains a truth for us, we should be able to find it not only "at play" in Derrida's writing, but also and necessarily so—*at work.* Thus we shall attempt to describe that which is necessarily an object for us, yet not an object for Derrida. If we succeed we must therein illustrate Derrida's position as both (a) true and yet also (b) false. If this is established, the also paradoxical result must be that with such a *duplicity* we will have illustrated precisely that which Derrida has called "the movement of *différance.*" Further, to avoid as many misunderstandings as possible, we hope in this process (a) to avoid contradicting ourselves and to therein limit the play of *différance* in order to be credible and conceptualized at all, yet (b) to take the risk of being a subject and making an object only by virtue of and on the condition of this very play of *différance* which opens our discourse and which must, if Derrida is correct, overturn it. As Derrida says:

> *Différance* produces what it forbids, makes possible the very thing that it makes impossible.[74]

VI

THE STRUCTURE OF
DIFFÉRANCE

A. The Limits of Economy

Although the notion of a "structure" of *"différance"* may seem a contradiction in terms, given our preceding analysis of both structurality and *différance,* precisely as the latter necessarily exceeds the former, what we propose here is not a reversal of that position. Instead, since *différance* is the principle of repetition itself, of representation, of death, and of economy as such, the condition of the possibility of presence and absence, the proper and the improper, and, as we shall see, of temporality and spatiality as such (beyond Kant's transcendental aesthetic), we propose that *différance* as such in its effects or traces therein itself *performs* the same process which "it" attributes to others. That is, in short, *différance* itself, as the nonrepresentable principle of representation, itself repeats. It (a) allows for the possibility of repetition and in turn (b) itself repeats *as a form* in all its various effects. The fact that we have a plurality of effects of this principle already indicates a certain similarity between the differences. Although our method here is precisely within the field of metaphysics, we find nonetheless that the structure of *différance,* paradoxical perhaps as this may appear, lends itself to a certain representation within the domain of metaphysics and, more specifically, within the realm of language. In this analysis, we will not have transgressed Derrida's claims which we began with concerning language and force, the idiom, and thought. Indeed we shall attempt to remain consistent with them, in order to explicate the structurality which allows for those differences to appear. *Différance* is thus not force, nor the idiomatic, nor thought as such, but rather a more primordial movement which, as Derrida says, "not being a force of its own, nevertheless forces force." As we may recall, *"différance"* is a "strategic nickname" of that which is necessarily unnameable in the sense of having a proper name. This does not mean that *différance* "goes without saying" or that it "remains in the shadow of language and speech" as the unsaid. Indeed Derrida himself proposes to nickname *"différance"* the "trace," the "reserve," "arche-writing," and the "supplement," for example. Thus *différance* as such does not remain in the shadow of "presence" or the presentable. It is pointed toward albeit always by a sort of impropriety.

In addition, as we have shown, Derrida claims there is a certain "rationality" (although no longer adhering to the structure of the *Logos*), a certain order, a certain principle, indeed a certain structure that repeats, which the movement of *différance* as such *exhibits*. It is this structure of repetition which itself repeats (in all its effects) that allows for us to trace its movement and to reveal it as such. Although Derrida says that *différance* does not *exist,* we should recall that to "exist" for him means "to be an entity," in Husserl's intentional sense of this phrase. Since *différance* can never be an object but rather is the condition for the possibility of all objects, one cannot "properly speaking" speak of its existence. Nevertheless *différance* "exists nowhere else" but within the structure of the entity as such. As we have shown, *différance* is the *abyss* itself which is not "out there" but rather that rationality which we find housed within all interiority as such, for us, within the subject (as absence) and within the object (as a certain spacing). As Derrida says:

> An entire theory of the structural necessity of the abyss will be gradually constituted in our reading; the *indefinite process of supplementarity* has always already infiltrated presence, always already inscribed there the space of repetition and the splitting of the self. Representation in the abyss of presence is not an accident of presence; the desire of the presence is, on the contrary, *born from the abyss* . . . of representation, from the representation of representation, etc. The supplement itself is quite exorbitant, in every sense of the word.[1]

The supplement is of course simply "another name for *différance*." This "always" which Derrida refers us to here regarding the "already infiltrated presence" and the "already inscribed space of repetition and splitting of the self" is precisely the point at which we find the "form" of *différance* as such. It has "always" already done various things in the world. It is thus in a paradoxical sense "omnipresent" by its very absence, since we see its "effects" everywhere. Indeed all that we see are its effects. Thus Derrida here has (perhaps deliberately, perhaps in spite of himself) illustrated a concept which is not properly speaking a concept, a word which is not properly speaking a word, and a movement which is not properly speaking a movement. Yet, once we have put the term proper under erasure, we can see more clearly what it is that *différance* as such is—in the proper sense of the term. More precisely, one can therein exhibit that which allows for all form (as always already there) as itself a form and perhaps necessarily so.

Although Derrida claims that the supplement is "exorbitant" with respect to the orbiting of metaphysical bodies around the sun, he also admits to the following precisely metaphysical properties of that which would call itself "exorbitant." First we have *différance* as a *concept of economy,* indeed the most general concept of economy as such:

> It is the concept of economy and since there is no economy without *différance,* it is the most general structure of economy itself [my emphasis].[2]

Indeed we have the admission here that *différance* is, as such, a structure—the "most general structure of economy" as such. We shall return to this in our treatment of the "play of supplementarity" in the upcoming section concerning precisely the issue of economy. At the moment, it is crucial to point out Derrida's systematic rejection of the structurality of *différance* and yet his subsequent reliance on the same notion for its description.

He admits, however, that *différance* is not to be considered *"astructurale"* or in opposition to structurality or form as such. Indeed we cannot be "radically other," according to Derrida, without falling back precisely and squarely into the universe of metaphysics as such. Yet we can see clearly in the following formulation that Derrida would use the term structure in this context only "under erasure"; that is, saying *à la fois* yes and no to the same term:

> Differences are the effects of transformations and from this point of view the *theme of différance* is *incompatible* with the static, synchronic, taxonomic, ahistoric, etc., motif—of the *concept of structure.* But it goes without saying that this motif is not the only one to define structure and that the production of differences, the *différance, is not astructural;* it produces *systematic* and *ruled* transformations which up to a certain point open the space for a structural science [my emphasis].[3]

Thus Derrida is not "anti-structure" or anti-structuralism, but would nonetheless separate himself from any notion of structure which excludes the movement of temporality and hence a certain spacing as such. We shall see more precisely why in the following section concerning the space/time of *différance,* but here we must simply insist that the notion of *structure as such* does not exist for Derrida. One might use the same term "structure" otherwise, therein saving it and his analysis from falling back into metaphysical determinations and presuppositions as such.

More precisely Derrida defines his *usage* of the term structure, as distinct from that of 'structuralism' for instance, with respect to that which he "names" *différance. Différance,* we should recall, is the condition of the possibility of the "play" of presence and absence as such—of entities, of vision, or metaphysics, and of the world as such. Thus structure, in this context, refers us inextricably to this "always already there" play of *différance,* as each in turn limits the other:

> Originary *différance* is supplementarity as *structure.* Here structure means the irreducible complicity within which one can only *shape or shift* the play of presence and absence: that within which metaphysics cannot think [my emphasis].[4]

We shall return to the "thinkability" of *différance* in terms of Reason and Nature with respect to the "play of supplementarity" in the next section on economy, but here we must realize that Derrida's notions of "structure" and of *différance* remain inextricably intertwined. The "play" of the *différance* is not free of its *own* constraints. It has always only two "options," and even these are strictly regulated according to the "principle of economy." Presence and absence for him thus interrelate in a structural, economic fashion. This is not a haphazard chance-determined affair, however. As he says, "one can *only* shape or shift" this play, one can never escape it. We have, therefore, uncovered a certain system based on a certain incompatibility of a simultaneous "presence and absence" of that which "exists"; indeed of existence itself. This seems indeed to be founded precisely on what metaphysics has called the "principle of non-contradiction." For instance, if x is present, it cannot at the same time and place also be absent, and vice versa. Derrida, we suspect, and we should not be surprised, would agree with such an analysis. Indeed it is precisely this which we suggest he is trying to illustrate. Where *différance* itself lives, he will also claim, is *outside* of this either/or structure, but *not dissociable* from it. *Différance* allows for this structure to exist as such.

Thus *différance* is not radically separable from metaphysics, but

rather itself involves an "inextricable complicity." Indeed we will claim
that an economic contract is at stake here which allows for the means
and mode of production as such: the mode being *différance;* the means
of course being metaphysics as such. It is, in short, the two together
which produce that which we might call "the play of the world."
Further, in economic terminology, one might realize metaphysics to be
the principle of capitalization, of property, and of inclusion/exclusion
therefore, whereas *différance,* being without a force of its own and
having no proper name, nevertheless allows itself, by default as it
were, to be submitted to the violence of metaphysics. But is history,
this history in particular (of metaphysics as such), not over? Has Hegel
not already demonstrated this sufficiently and necessarily? Indeed Derrida believes it to be over, yet metaphysics is certainly not exhausted as
yet by the process. Indeed one finds capitals and property and univer-
salization by the "in general" or the concept to be still very much alive
in the world—physically and metaphysically, today. However, we find
différance appearing also at this post-historical juncture and indeed
therein threatening this predominance of metaphysics. It is the "structure of *différance,*" which is not, we should recall, the "return of the
repressed."⁵ *Différance as such* never appears and thus does not return. There are no "returns" on such an interest, Derrida insists.

Nevertheless as a final word of introduction to the structure of *différance* as the economy of the play of supplementarity, as the "principle
of death," and as the condition of the possibility of a "new transcendental aesthetic," we should consider the relation of *différance* to
the machinery of Hegel's *Aufhebung* and the dialectic as such. At one
point in the interviews of *Positions* Derrida claims that, if one had to
define *différance,* it might be "that process which 'destroys' (indeed
aims to destroy) the Aufhebung." Derrida himself realizes, however,
that this is "not possible as such."⁶ The *Aufhebung* is indestructible in
terms of any attack one could mount *against* it. As we know, all polemics can be immediately subsumed, consumed, and integrated into the
system according to Hegel, and thus *"forgotten."* The concept will win
against any opponent which purports to be (or to have) the Anti-
concept, or indeed the "Anti-Christ," as we have seen from
Nietzsche's experience. Instead therefore, in realizing this "indestruc-
tibility" of the *Aufhebung,* Derrida proposes the notion of *différance* as
a sort of "chance interruption," as the laughter which upsets the system,⁷ which intervenes and in a profound way sets the machine (albeit
slightly) off course. However, as with all mechanized processes (if we

can consider the *Aufhebung* to be such), a slight deviation is more profound than a large and therefore immediately noticeable one. And further, as Derrida says: "the machine as such (as yet at least) does not run by itself." For Derrida there is always a reserve or a remainder which the *Aufhebung* cannot integrate. It is the "non-representable," which is of course usurped by "being-represented" anyway—the violence of the name, as we have shown, which Hegel too was well aware of. Nevertheless, Derrida aims with *différance*—which is exorbitant, unnameable, and can never be made present, which escapes all formalizations, as do force, the idiom and thought with respect to language—to make a *fold* in the process of systematizing and the all-inclusiveness of the *Aufhebung*. In short, to point toward the Abyss which Hegel knew existed yet which he justified himself in overcoming by referring to this realm as the "realm of the false." "The unutterable" was for him quite simply the "untrue." Thus it could be "overcome." But for Derrida, this economy of the *Aufhebung* must be seen as an effect of an economy which extends beyond such a violence:

> By this placing in relation of the restrained economy and the general economy one *displaces* and one *reinscribes* the project of philosophy itself, within the privileged space of Hegelianism. One *folds* the *Aufhebung*—the *'relève'*—to write itself otherwise. Perhaps, quite simply, to write itself. Better, to take account of its consummation of writing [my emphasis].[8]

The "consummation of writing" is precisely the return of the Concept to itself in the Absolute Knowledge of History itself: or, in short, the end of History. It is the return of presence to itself and is thus the end of the "sign," the route, the passage, the detour which is more than history—temporality itself. Thus the paralysis of Hegel's system is felt in terms of the collapse of all differences into the Same, or which for Derrida is the absolute presence of presence, absolute life, or absolute death. It is the movement of death that is the movement of the *Aufhebung* as it captures its other along its path to the sunlight.[9] Its forgotten moment is, however, Derrida insists, the moment of writing itself, which is the hidden support and therefore hidden opening within the "absolute process" itself. It is writing which *allows* for this movement and yet which is also denounced and effaced as the *Logos* purports to be always already there: or, in short, to be "its own father."

Différance, however, does not claim to "out-father" the father of Nature and Reason itself, but rather to open the space for the mother.

Différance gives birth to Reason; it is the condition of its possibility and its "impossibility" in terms of Reason's claim to be its own absolute foundation. The movement of Reason is therefore finite, since it is the mother, or indeed the *structure of maternity* more precisely, that which Reason cannot "comprehend," which will be made evident in the final hour, the final stroke of Reason in its attempted usurpation of the world. Just as each system has its blind spot or its point of orientation, for Derrida, so too each system is founded upon that which is intrinsically "not comprehensible" or "integratable" within that same system. Such is the Mother for this same *Logos*. Again, however, we have the problem of the absent father in this structure, but that is, as Derrida says, "perhaps always the case." After all, as he says, "the condition for the possibility of writing (in all senses of the word) is precisely *patricide*."[10] We have never left Oedipus, therefore, but have returned to find not only the *tragic* aspect of the death of the Father, and thus his subsequent return, but also the *comic* aspect of the highest form of love, perhaps the model for all love in general, as precisely that which is excluded from society's notion of legitimacy in order therefore to sever the latter from a nature which never existed. In short, we have found incest, again. We have found Oedipus in the bed of his father, and of course with the woman who is *à la fois* his wife and his mother. Perhaps, as Derrida says with respect to *différance,* in the end one "does not choose." Although one is forced to conclude, the debate itself is, however, interminable. It is thus that we approach the graphic of supplementarity as that which for Derrida is the "economy of *différance.*"

(a) *Différance* as Economy

For Derrida, as we have shown, the notion of *différance* is the "concept of economy as such," the most general form of economy. It is indeed that which allows for the *movement* which we call economic, he claims. The notion of economy is thus for Derrida a more primordial "ground" than that of traditional philosophy, which is concerned with static forms, structures, substances, and essences as such. The Platonic forms do not move, we should recall. Thus with Derrida we turn toward a universe (indeed a second one) of movement, of forces, of play, which also nonetheless contains or exhibits a certain "calculus" and a certain "system." In shifting, however, from a "substantial" universe to one that is essentially in motion, Derrida proposes a certain "dislocation of the proper," a certain "inappropriateness," which is essential to *différance* as such. As he says:

> *Différance* is not a process of propriation in any sense whatever. It is neither the positive (appropriation) nor the negative (expropriation) but the *other*. From this point it seems, yet we are marking the necessity of a process to come, it would be no more than Being a species of *Ereignis*.[11]

It is thus no accident that Derrida uses the term *"différance,"* which is not a "proper" term. *"Différance,"* as a word, does not properly speaking exist; neither does *différance* as such for Derrida. We have thus a good example of what Derrida calls the inextricable relation of signifier and signified, at the same time as we have a description of that process. *Différance* is both signifier and signified here. One can also realize in this "example" the structure of *différance* as such as the economy which produces the same, the name, and the proper, but which itself is none of these. *Différance* is a composite term made up of the two proper words: to differ and to defer (as we have mentioned above), and together for Derrida they form *différance* (the ending being better translated perhaps as differ*ing* in English). The problem, however, is that the essential impropriety of *"différance"* is therein lost since "differing" is a quite appropriately recognized official word. Nevertheless "differing" sustains the notion of the process of *movement* which Derrida aims to describe here. But the movement is a sort of oscillation more than a unilateral, or one-dimensional, uni-directional process. Indeed it is the movement between the thought of differing and defering; the former being related to spatiality, the latter to temporality. Both include a notion of opening, of a promise, of an extension, of a postponement, of a detour, of a repetition, of a substitution, of a representation, and indeed of a sort of *doubling* that exists over the extension of space and time. But the two terms nevertheless, in spite of this apparent commonality of root, cannot be collapsed into one whole without the *eclipsing* of one aspect by the other. If one thinks of differing, the notion of spatiality is brought into mind; if one thinks of deferring, likewise for the notion of temporality. But the two juxtaposed within one concept leave one impotent to consider both simultaneously. Instead, phenomenologically, what seems to occur is a vibration, or oscillation back and forth between one and the other. As one comes into view, the other recedes into the background, and vice versa. This is precisely what Derrida names *différance*—in all senses of the term. In fact, he opens the way to a new sort of phenomenology of writing, although he insists this is not possible. The presence-absence oscillation and the simultaneous unthinkability of the two terms represent the problem. The difficulty of a phenomenology of writing would thus be that which is "put in the shadow" when the "other" comes to light (into view, into consciousness) is necessarily eclipsed from consciousness as such. Thus phenomenology cannot describe its own shadow.

Derrida insists further that "the name of *différance*" is not a proper name. For him it "menaces the proper as such." As we have shown, the "essence" of *différance* (its proper character) does not exist as such. As Derrida says concerning the "term" and the "process" of *différance:* (which are as we know inseparable),

> Older than Being itself, such a *différance* has no name in our language. But we "already know" that if it is *unnameable* it is not tentative because our language has not yet found or received this name, or because it is necessary to search in another language, outside the finite system of ours. It is because there is no name for that—not even essence or Being, not even that of *"différance"* which is not a name, which is not a pure nominal unity and dislocates itself ceaselessly in a differing chain of substitution.[12]

Thus Derrida proposes a theory of the proper name and its correlate: the intrinsically "improper" name. The name is the locus not only of language but also of Reason, *Logos,* and metaphysics as such. It is for being "in search of a name" that Derrida reproaches Heidegger and the latter's reliance on the notions of the proper and the essential in his "overturning" of humanism as such. It is the structure of authority and power of the "proper" that Derrida hopes to (a) reveal and (b) escape from or overcome. Yet *différance,* as such an economy of play with presence and absence, has of itself no power. It is precisely this element which is denied to this movement since it does not "constitute" itself in these terms. Instead it "submits itself" to the domination of metaphysics and the system of the proper, and it is this "weakness" which is of crucial significance for Derrida:

> *Différance* is not. It is not even a being-present . . . It *commands nothing,* rules over nothing and in no way exercises any authority. It does not announce itself by any capital. Not only is there no kingdom of *différance* but it *foments* the subversion of all kingdoms [my emphasis].[13]

It is, as Derrida says elsewhere: *"la force de la faiblesse."* But, more precisely, what is this *différance* which we find structures itself in the form of an economy that is always elusive, always on the move, that has no place in the system of signs which circumscribe the "meaning-ful"? As we know, Derrida shifts "interminably" from one term to another when he refers to *"différance,"* and we should examine the paradoxical implications of such a move. Since for him *différance"* is in a certain sense a "nickname" for that which essentially cannot be named, other nicknames too are possible. The notion of a nickname we might recall is oriented towards a naming in situation, a naming accord-ing to circumstances, a usually context-specific term which, if removed from that particular environment, makes no sense. It is thus with the nicknames of *"différance"* (which is also one, we should not forget). These include, as we have shown: the trace (in terms of a relation to Freud and Levinas), writing (in relation to Saussure, concerning the system of differences wherein the spaces or gaps between the full terms are shown to be the locus of meaning), *différance* (in relation to Heidegger's and Hegel's albeit differential usage of the term differ-ence), the reserve (in relation to Freud and Plato), and the supplement (in relation to Rousseau and his usage of this term, which Derrida shows to be a demonstration of the very notion of supplementarity as such, in spite of Rousseau, to a certain extent). Thus we find the names of this "process"—this fundamental economy—to be context-specific nicknames; yet also, in spite of their differences, all seem to be naming "the same thing." Of course *différance* is not a thing and is certainly not to be found within the orbit of what metaphysics calls the "same." Nevertheless, have we not uncovered here a certain *concept* of *différ-ance* which transcends specific situations, circumstances, and texts? After all, is it not Derrida himself who claims that the "proper name" is not a reliable index for that which we call a "textual system"?[14] That "Freud" wrote *x,* does not therefore sever *x* essentially from *y* that Plato, for example, wrote long before. Instead, for Derrida, as we know, there is a more fundamental structure (metaphysics itself in this case) which links one context-specific text (Freud) to another (Plato). The proper name is thus an unreliable index for what he calls the *context* of a *text.* It is thus that Derrida is able to trace from one "text" to another various systems of metaphors which, in relation to the struc-ture of metaphysics, profoundly link them together into one tradition. Indeed we are dealing with the issue of *levels* of textuality here and relative value differences accordingly. Nevertheless is it possible, ac-cording to Derrida's own "system of interpretation," to view the differ-ences between "supplement," *"différance,"* "reserve," "trace," and "writing," for example, as related only to the proper name of the author which, as we know, no longer legitimately houses its ultimate authority?

Derrida admits to a certain structural identity, however, between the play from one "nickname" to another and the play of *"différance"* (for example) as such. The "indefinite replacement of signifiers" is precisely the process of substitution which he claims characterizes *différance* itself. Yet he also admits to a certain *"point of orientation"* for the whole system, which necessarily remains vague and unnamed, which is the "blind spot" that can never be named without "the whole game being terminated and collapsing" therein. This "point of orientation" is here not simply one signifier among others, but the locus of the signified as such, it would seem. He explains the paradox of the "exiled centre" in the following manner (in particular with reference to his analysis of Rousseau and the supplement):

> Within the play of supplementarity, one will always be able to relate the substitutes to their signified, this last will be yet another signifier. The fundamental signified, the meaning of the being represented, even less the thing itself will never be given to us in person, outside the sign or outside the play. Even that which we say, name, describe as the prohibition of incest does not escape play. There is a point in the system where the signifier can no longer be replaced by its signified, so that in consequence no signifier can be so replaced, purely and simply. For the *point of nonreplacement* is also the *point of orientation* for the entire system of signification, the point where the fundamental signified is promised as the terminal point of all references and conceals itself as that which would *destroy at one blow the entire system of signs*. It is at once the spoken and forbidden by all signs [my emphasis].[15]

We must interrupt at this point for an instant only. What is this "point of non-replacement" for Derrida, which is also the "point of orientation"? The non-replaceable, non-representable, which allows for representation and replacement; indeed the play of *différance* itself. Do we not here have the idiom, the subject, the writer, the non-authorized authority, the illegitimate father, who in fact has never left his text? Do we not have the "child which is the father of the man" here? Do we not have the "madness" which Reason thinks it has excluded from the house of being or language itself? Do we not have that intrinsically unsayable, the point of the non-blink of the eyes in that face of the other which is also our own, which we know has never left us? We might indeed be in the Abyss, and it may indeed be in us, as Derrida says; and there may indeed be an intrinsic and inextricable relation of signifier to signified, but does this not also translate, at this point of non-return, of non-replaceability, non-representability, and non-substitutability, into the relation of author to text? That precisely effaced relation by metaphysics itself; that "*logos* believing itself to be its own father" and yet also effaced by Derrida in his emphasis on the non-proper, the non-authority, the "*force de faiblesse*" of *différance* itself. *Différance,* as we have been shown by Derrida himself, does not rest upon nothing. It comes to a halt, a stop, indeed perhaps to an abyss in the system, in the calculus—which never goes full circle, nor full ellipse, and thus never returns totally. Is it not this that Derrida himself has pointed towards throughout his work? The essentiality of the non-return. The "fold in the *Aufhebung*" is precisely the "false," as Hegel said. It is the idiom of the "me"; the non-replaceable point of orientation of all totality. Derrida continues, we propose, to describe this very relation at the same moment as he effaces it therein. For example:

> Language is neither prohibition nor transgression, it couples the two endlessly. That point which *does not exist,* it is always elusive or what comes to the same thing, *always already inscribed* in what it ought to escape or ought to have escaped, *according to* our own indestructible and mortal desire [my emphasis].[16]

It is surely not the "sign as such" of which Derrida speaks here. "That point which does not exist" could only be the "me" of my writing which is (a) always already no longer "mine," as we have shown, yet (b) no one else's. That this "me" does not exist is simply a return to the recognition of the non-entity, non-objectifiable, and hence non-subject (in metaphysical terms) that I am. As we have shown too, it is not *différance* which is "always already inscribed" in the system it would escape—but it is the "me," as the subject of metaphysics, as the thrown *Dasein,* who is tossed into a relation of submission to the very thing he would command—the text of life itself. Such is the play of the world, for Derrida according to *différance,* we suggest. And such is the tragic: "according to one's own indestructible and mortal desire." That will to power which is at once installed and overcome is that which we call the "subject." It is thus that Derrida turns toward the notion of *différance* as the "play of that dangerous supplement." For a world as such, the "danger" could not exist. The danger instead is realizing that we have here a notion of writing which is "beyond good and evil"—and which thus opens the space and the conditions of the possibility for both. This space is the *space of repetition,* which we shall see is both:

(a) the space of imitation, respect, repetition as teleologically oriented towards the "master"; and yet also (b) the space of repetition as mockery, as disgust, as subversive, as humorous.

A final note before we turn to "that dangerous supplement." The division of repetition into the space of imitation on the one hand and of mockery on the other is not reducible in this duplicity to a simple relation to the space of good and evil respectively. Instead the "space of evil" is to be found as the "other side" of both aspects respectively. The "will to power," which allows the slave to repeat and in the end overtake and become the Master, is no less a movement of "evil" than the space of mockery and irreverence. The first is the space of the "serious," the second the space of the "comic." These relations become immediately very complex, as we have indicated, and thus we must return to a more simple basis of exposition—that which is (both) logically (and illogically) prior to the division of "good and evil" as such: "the play of supplementarity."

(b) The Play of Supplementarity

The notion of the supplement is, for Derrida, analogous to that of *différance* and therefore exhibits similar structural and functional relationships. We shall attempt to describe here, not only the economic structure which links the "play of the supplement" to the "economy of *différance*" or the notion of economy as such, but also to show the social, political, ethical, and necessarily non-ethical dimensions of this notion of supplementarity. For Derrida, it describes in a text "what a text is," and "in writing what writing is"; but we should recall the notions of a text and of writing are for Derrida no longer to be considered materially, or literally. They are not only metaphoric, as we have shown, but illustrate an essentiality of metaphor itself in "the play of the world" as text and as arche-writing. We should also recall that the "supplement" here is and is not interchangeable with the notion of *différance*. In some respects, the "play of supplementarity" describes more precisely the structure of *différance* itself, as we shall demonstrate; yet in other respects the "play of the supplement" is one "form" or process of function among others which characterizes the notion of *différance* for Derrida. Perhaps these are at the deepest level the "same," but we propose here to approach this issue "as if" they are not. The results of this analysis will, we hope, speak for themselves and let the unsaid and of course the unsayable remain as such. The paradox is of course that it is precisely this "remainder" which we are attempting to describe here. Nevertheless one can always, as Derrida says, shape or shift the "play of presence and absence," although one can never escape from it as a whole. Thus we will approach the structure of the "play of supplementarity" *as* the structure of the economy of *différance*.

(i) The Structural Dimensions

Derrida explicates this structure in terms of its systematic appearance and disappearance (presence and absence) within the texts of Rousseau. His focus on Rousseau here is both: (a) one example among others, and yet (b) the example *par excellence* for all other examples—the model for exemplarity itself. This is also the case with his *"fil conducteur"* of analysis—the supplement itself. He explains the situation in the following manner:

> In certain respects, the theme of supplementarity is certainly no more than one theme among others. It is in a chain, carried by it. Perhaps one could substitute something else for it. But *it happens* that this theme describes the chain itself, the being-chain of a textual chain, the structure of substitution, the articulation of desire and of language, the logic of all conceptual oppositions taken over by Rousseau. . . . It tells us in a text what a text is, it tells us in writing what writing is. . . [my emphasis].[17]

Thus, in a profound respect, Rousseau represents for us here the entire schema of "conceptual oppositions" (of metaphysics no doubt), and the "supplement," as a term, a process, a function, an operation, indeed as a certain economy, represents that which is (a) *made present* and perceptible by this structure of conceptual oppositions, and yet also (b) *made absent* by this same structure—indeed by the structure of the same, or identity, of the proper. We must recall here the important distinction which Derrida makes between the text and the book.[18] The former admits of no center, of no totality once and for all, and of no essential mediator. The latter is, of course, the reverse and admits of only one proper meaning, theme, point, etc. Thus we are dealing here with Rousseau's text, which is in some respects one text among others, but in other respects the text of all texts—representing therein textuality itself. Derrida explains his choice in terms of a certain chance: "it happens that . . ." and thus leaves his decision here outside the "system"; indeed the point of orientation is always in exile, he tells us. So we must begin on the inside in order to find that outside which we already know is always already the interior of the interior itself.

For Derrida we thus find that:

> Rousseau inscribes textuality in the text. But its operation is not simple. It *tricks* with a gesture of effacement, and strategic relations like the relationships of force among the two movements form a complex design. This design seems to us to be represented in the handling of the concept of the *supplement.* Rousseau cannot utilize it at the same time in all virtualities of its meaning. The way in which he determines the concept and in so doing lets himself be determined by that very thing he excludes from it, the direction in which he bends it, here as addition, there as substitute, now as the positivity and exteriority of evil, now as a happy auxiliary, all this conveys neither a passivity nor an activity, neither an unconscious nor a lucidity on the part of the author. Reading should not only abandon these categories—which are also the founding categories of metaphysics—but should produce the *law* of this relationship to the concept of the supplement [my emphasis].[19]

We must consider carefully the implications of this important passage in Derrida's text. First, he claims that there is a certain "trick" at work here in the gesture of textuality itself, indeed in the inscription of textuality as such in the text. Yet how can one inscribe such a formulation? Is not "textuality" as such always already inscribed, and necessarily so, in that which we call a text? Is textuality not the essence and property of the text as such? How could we have a text without textuality already inscribed therein? But Derrida seems to be aiming toward something other than the "essence" of a text, properly speaking. There is no such thing for him as we have shown. Thus if the text is without an essence, what could textuality mean in this context? It is precisely this which the "play of the supplement" describes, Derrida claims. First, as he says, its operation is "not simple." This implies not simply that it is difficult or complex, but that it is not *unitary.* The "operation" *of* textuality, its movement as such, is thus divided and indeed contains opposing dimensions, at least two of which we can describe. Derrida himself says we have "two movements within this operation" we call textuality. As we know from the preceding analysis, these are the movements of presencing and absencing—or appearance and disappearance. Together they form a "complex design" or pattern we call the text. More specifically Derrida claims these two opposing movements which are housed *à la fois* within the term and play of the supplement, include the following notions:

> . . . the concept of the supplement . . . harbours within itself two
> significations whose cohabitation is as strange as it is necessary. The
> supplement *adds itself,* it is *a surplus,* a plentitude enriching another
> plentitude, the fullest measure of presence. It cumulates and accumu-
> lates presence. It is that the art, *technè,* image, representation, conven-
> tion, etc., come as supplements to nature [my emphasis].[20]

(The evident social and political implications will be addressed in due
time in the upcoming section. We wish here to follow the structure as
such of the supplement, for the moment.)

The second movement, which is as primary as the first, entails the
following:

> But the supplement supplements. It adds only *to replace.* It intervenes
> or insinuates itself in-the-place-of; if it fills it is as if one fills a void. If it
> represents and makes an image, it is by the anterior default of presence.
> Compensatory and vicarious, the supplement is an adjunct. . . . . As
> substitute, it is not simply added to the positivity of a presence, it
> produces no relief, its place is assigned in the structure by the mark of
> an emptiness.[21]

Further, he claims, there is always "a supplement at the source." Thus
the *two movements* which Derrida claims produce the operation of
textuality itself seem to (a) contradict one another; (b) paralyze one
another; and thus (c) produce the conditions of the *impossibility* of
each other at the same instant. This is precisely the case for textuality,
we insist. The "play of the supplement" is this mutual exclusion of its
"own" other; not unlike the "work of metaphysics," we might add. The
difference, however, which is of crucial significance, is that the supplement does not *"banish"* or exclude its other, it merely overshadows it.
One aspect comes into view as the other "discretely slides into the
background." The "other" in this play remains therefore essential, active, and still within the scene of that which we call textuality. Derrida
continues:

> This second signification of the supplement cannot be separated from
> the first. Each of the two significations is by turns *effaced* or becomes
> discretely vague by the presence of the other. But their *common func-
> tion* is shown in this: whether it adds or substitutes itself, the supple-
> ment is exterior, outside of the positivity to which it is superadded.[22]

Thus the structure of the "strange" economy becomes evident. However, what this "operation" or "play" seems to involve or invoke is the

double bind of the simultaneity of "presence and absence." Indeed
Derrida points toward precisely this in terms of the supplement adding
itself (a) as an addition to a full presence, and thus already paradoxical;
and (b) as a substitute for a presence which was *never* there. As we
have shown, presence is always a result of a prior constitution, in
which the Abyss (or absence itself) is simultaneously effaced and included (consumed by writing, as Derrida says). Thus the irony appears
of the supplement which would add itself superfluously (seemingly) or
add itself as a copy without there ever having been an original. In both
cases we have a situation of "mistaken identity," and it is perhaps this
which Derrida refers to as its "common function." The first case,
where presence already purports to be full, reveals that it was not;
indeed it *needs* a supplement to present itself *as* that full presence.
Hence we have the institution of a certain illegitimate entry here. The
supplement slides into place within "presence" and must remain there
hidden, essential, yet always unannounced. When the absence of Presence becomes "known," the game will be up, as Derrida says, and
indeed as Hegel announced without knowing it. In the second case, the
irony must also be felt as unavoidable. Where "presence" is lacking,
the supplement arrives to take its place. Yet (a) presence was *always
never* there, and hence (b) the supplement is thus radically originary
and indeed can therein (and should be) mistaken for that same presence
it would re-present. It is the substitute without difference at this stage.
Yet, if one realizes that the supplement is indeed a supplement, and not
that originary presence, once again "the game will be up." So the
supplement as a substitution must purport to be that presence it substitutes. Indeed has not "presence as such" always already been this?
Derrida says yes.

The difficulty of "thinking" or conceiving of this movement which
seems to efface itself, and necessarily so, according to the predominance of the metaphysics of presence and of the concept as such, as
pure and simple, must now be addressed. Derrida is profoundly aware
of this difficulty, as we have shown, with his reliance on various
methods for the "shifting" and "shaping" of this play of presence and
absence. Such methods have included: bracketing (as per Husserl),
putting the term under erasure (as per Heidegger), nicknames, using
inverted commas to shift from the *is* to the *as* structure, and indeed of
metaphorization of the issues in an attempt to point toward that which
"cannot essentially be said." Yet, as we know according to Derrida
himself, "from the moment we have meaning, we having nothing but

signs."²³ Yet, "la chose même se dérobe toujours."²⁴ The "noumenal realm" is precisely that "blind spot" which the system cannot include, or comprehend. And further, it is "blindness to the law" that allows for the constitution, is the constitution, and is the result of the constituting movement of the supplement itself. But we propose to shift the play of metaphors here, and instead of *looking* for the supplement we shall instead *listen* for it. Since our eyes and, in particular, our vision has been always ready organized for us by Reason itself, as distinct and opposed to Nature itself, we cannot depend on it to give us a reliable impression of this "essentially non-essential" concept which is not a concept. In the exploration of the "play of the supplement," we too are trapped within its play. What this means is that we can only present "x" at the expense of not presenting "not x"; or, more precisely, we make absent the "other half" of that which we aim to speak about the instant we set the pen to the page. Looking "between the lines" here will of course not suffice since that space is the space—albeit allowing for articulation—of inarticulation itself. Thus the difficulty arises phenomenologically, yet, of course, is also beyond this formulation of it. Derrida explains the problem in the following manner:

> The supplement is what neither Nature nor Reason can tolerate.
>
> Blindness to the supplement is the law. And especially blindness to its concept. Moreover, it does not suffice to locate its *functioning* in order to 'see' its meaning. The supplement has no sense and is given to no intuition. We do not therefore make it emerge out of its strange penumbra. We speak its reserve.
>
> Reason is incapable of thinking this double infringement on Nature; that there is lack and because of that very fact something is added to it [my emphasis].²⁵

As we know, Rousseau had precisely these problems. If Nature is full presence, how is it possible that Reason comes to supplement that fullness? And indeed is not Reason itself always already that full presence? Yet can Reason substitute for Nature? Is Nature not already a result of the movement of Reason, as Hegel has shown? And so on. This *structure,* indeed the *function* or, more precisely, the *"play* of the supplement"* (that principle of repetition itself) repeats. It is not only the formation of form itself, as Derrida has shown, but is also the "informing of itself"—that formula which opens itself to non-formalization yet also to a very particular form of formalization. The paradox here is that what we have uncovered in the "play of the supplement" seems to be essentially that "play" which allows for the constitution of the concept as such. Is the concept not the house of an interminable opposition of forces, which although never equal never allow for neither the absolute death of one nor therefore the absolute life of the other? The enslaving of the one side by the other for the sake of "presentation," in order to constitute an origin as if radically originary, and thus the hidden dimension behind and within all presence makes itself felt over time. Since it is "over time" that the Master will be overcome by the slave which "officially" at least, does not, properly speaking, exist. We already know the structure of this dependency is essential to the Master as such, for Hegel. But for Derrida, it seems we have returned to this same notion of the concept, although via the detour, via the absence, via the slave, via that *illegitimate* contradiction which can never be radically overcome. As he says:

> Something promises itself as it escapes, gives itself as it moves away and strictly speaking it cannot even be called presence. Such is the constraint of the supplement, such exceeding all the languages of metaphysics, is this structure *almost* inconceivable to Reason.[26]

Indeed it is the structure that allows for the constitution of Reason as such. It is the phenomenology and the non-phenomenology of *Geist*. It is indeed that structure which can never be made "present" to "consciousness" and thus never ultimately phenomenogical. It is only *almost* inconceivable to Reason in this context, rather than totally inconceivable, since, as we have shown, there is always a trace of the "play of the supplement" left or to be found in each text. It is never totally effaced, nor totally presentable of course. It is illegitimate, but not absent as such.

More precisely the "play of the supplement" for Derrida, as it allows for textuality as such, performs a certain dance or a certain mockery with the concepts of Reason. It oscillates back and forth between oppositions, never resting long within the arms of any one in particular. As we have shown, the "play of the supplement," as dance, is what Nietzsche has called the "dance of the pen" (which Derrida notes one can only do while sitting down). The walk, as teleologically oriented, is reserved for the philosopher, but the repose of the seated writer is one that, as we know, is not a leisure. The "dance of the pen" is that participation in writing by a writer which draws him/her into the realm of madness. The process of inscription itself, we suggest, (which would not be surprising at this point) is a process of madness itself. Perhaps the "play of the supplement" could be considered the structure of madness. That double bind which paralyzes all movement. Yet, with an absolute double bind and with an absolute madness, one could not write; indeed any form of inscription would be impossible. Instead the writing of writing or the textuality of the text *participates* in madness, but always and necessarily so, ends up on the side of Reason. The text is always ultimately in the form of a book, although, as we should recall, it is never totally captured therein. The reduction of a text to the book should be tempered therefore with the recognition of what Derrida calls the difference between "the book and the book" with which we began this analysis. That *difference* is possible only because of *différance,* or more precisely, because of the "maddening play of the supplement":

> The supplement is *maddening* because it is *neither* presence *nor* absence and because it consequently breaches both our pleasure and our virginity.[27]

It is not for nothing, therefore, that Derrida speaks, albeit metaphorically, of the "play of the supplement" as having a not dissimilar structure and function to that of the hymen.[28] Thus we must enter into the social and political dimensions of such a structure.

(ii) The Social and Political Dimensions

> The child will know how to speak when one form of his unease can be substituted for another; then he will be able to slip from one language to another, slide one sign under the other, play with the signifying substance; he will enter into the *order of the supplement,* here determined (with Rousseau) as the human order: he will no longer weep, he will know how to say, "I hurt" [my emphasis].[29]

With the "play of supplementarity," one shifts therefore from the "pleasure principle to the reality principle," from the order of Nature to that of Reason, from animality to humanity, and from a certain impotence of immediacy to the potency of being-at-a-distance; indeed to being in society as such. The child, although inscribed at birth into the order of Reason by being properly named (usually), does not, Derrida claims, enter into "the order of the supplement" until he knows how to "no longer weep" but *instead* how to say "I hurt." Thus the repression and conversion of the immediate and the incommunicable, meaningless feelings (in this case) and the transformation of the child into a "human being" as such—a *member* of the society and civilization as such. One does not begin therefore in the "order of the supplement," but rather one enters into it at the instant one enters into *language.* The speech of the child, once uttered, severs him radically from that original "animality." Yet Derrida insists:

> Without childhood, no supplement would even appear in Nature. The supplement is here both humanity's *good fortune,* and the origin of its perversion. The health of the human race. . . .[30]

The notion of an "originally good Nature," as in Rousseau, is not that to which Derrida is referring us here. It is rather a "nature" prior to good and evil, where the "innocence" and incapacities of the child make themselves felt and society comes to its aid. Society responds, in short, to the child when it is able to say "I hurt." It cannot not respond. The cry instead can be overlooked, misunderstood, overheard, submerged, and it falls victim ultimately to its own incomprehensibility. As we have shown, meaning is for Derrida ultimately a *collective* affair. The meaningless of the supposed full presence of innocent childhood thus makes its irony felt as we realize the "play of the supplement" here. But also, ironically, it seems that the "play of the supplement" opens the doors to "the work of Reason" and hence to the conceptuality of metaphysics as such—indeed as the only schema of conceptuality we know. Derrida is well aware of this, as we know:

> The supplement will always be the moving of the tongue or acting through the hands of others. In it everything is brought together: progress as the possibility of perversion, regression toward an *evil* that is not natural and that *adheres to the power of substitution* that permits us to absent ourselves and act by proxy, through representation, through the hands of others. Through the *written.* This substitution always has the form of the sign. The scandal is that the sign, the image, or the representer become forces and make 'the world move'. This scandal is such, and its evil effects are sometimes so irreparable, that the world seems to turn the wrong way [my emphasis].[31]

Thus Derrida considers "the play of the supplement," that "power of substitution," to be the essential opening which allows for the constitution of society as such, yet also that very danger and threat which exposes it to its own destruction. When the "representer" becomes a force of its own, the child attains maturity, only with the structure of a freedom which is always already "beyond good and evil." The freedom of responsibility necessary to learn that same responsibility is also the freedom of irresponsibility. In terms of society and history as a whole, we thus have the "play of the supplement" as a "play of life and death" as such. Yet as we know, the supplement produces its own antidote, in a certain respect, and sets up its own opposing and therefore limiting *force*. It is not on the loose here, but rather exhibits a certain restraint, and indeed constraint on itself as such. It is subject to its own law, in short. Thus the "play of the supplement" opens the space of truth and falsity, of rhetoric and logic, of literature and philosophy, and at the same instant, or perhaps a little later, closes it. It is the space of *articulation* as such. It is thus the space both of the *Bible* and of *Mein Kampf.* It is the space of political representation—of democracy and of Divine Right. It is the space of elections and yet also of dictatorship: the dictatorship of the proletariat and of the fascists. The opening of supplementarity as such is, as Derrida says, "of a certain madness," and hence a certain "non-ethical" opening of ethics. There is thus no conception of an original Fall from the original Good for Derrida here, but rather the notion of an always already *double universe*—the play of history and society being that of presence and absence which seems in the long run to always be ultimately reciprocal. The problem is that our lives contain an essential finitude and thus the *return* of the "play of the supplement" may not be seen as it moves "full circle" or full ellipse in our lifetimes. Nevertheless Derrida insists upon a certain economy in the long run:

> The logic of the supplement—which is not the logic of identity—allows for the acceleration of evil to find at once its historical compensation and its historical guardrail. History precipitates history, society corrupts society, but the evil that links both in an *indefinate chain* has its natural supplement as well: History and society produce their own *resistance to the abyss* [my emphasis].[32]

It seems that the abyss must mean evil here for Derrida, yet this is not simply the case, we suggest. Rather it is metaphysics as such which has defined evil as the exterior and excluded from the notion of "presence" as the locus of the Good, the true, the evident and ultimately the interior. Yet Derrida insists that evil is to be found *within society* as such, within history as such and indeed "no where else." This is not an argument for the retrieval of evil, nor of its propagation, as some[33] (whose motives we shall not address here) have suggested concerning Derrida's work. Instead what he shows here is a notion of society as such and history as such, which are submitted to this *law of textuality* as such, which he has called the "play of the supplement." This "logic," this "rationality," this "economy" is that which governs the "play of the world" for Derrida, and its hazardous aspect must be recognized. As we shall see in the next section, this is *death* itself. And this is not the work of the devil, but rather that necessarily never-present "play of the supplement." Thus the tragic cannot ultimately be separated from the comic, but the reverse is also true.

The domain of Reason as such has always been that of a certain, though limited, *violence.* Its guardrail has been the "play of the supplement" itself. But this violence of the name and of inscription (as such) into a world whose meaning is governed by the "play of signification," which kills the pure idiom, which escapes yet is dependent on the "play of forces," is "not to be outstripped," Derrida claims. One offers oneself up for the sacrifice at the same instant that one offers one's son in the ultimate "belief" in a certain truth beyond the immediately present or available one. Indeed the secret is that this is the precondition and unavoidable prescription for all inscription as such. It is the violent rupture that cannot be avoided which opens the path to all reproduction. It is indeed perhaps, as Derrida has suggested, the opening of the hymen itself where that *original incest* gave way to the birth of what we call society as such. It is thus that Derrida points to that always after-Babel situation of language and indeed the myth of the original tower itself. The transcendental signified is nowhere to be found for Derrida, we should recall. That which opens the possibility of language as such is already that which necessitates the production of speech, indeed writing, of language*s* as such. There never was and will never be *one* language, for Derrida. This should be already more than evident at this point. The structure of *différance* itself denies such a possibility. Yet we have philosophy and thus we have the attempt. It will be thwarted from its own absolute accomplishment, Derrida claims, and thus its own *finitude* will always be *infinitely deferred.*

It is not so however for that which we have called here: "the point of orientation" of the system. This point is (a) subject to the law of the supplement, of "play," as Derrida calls it, yet (b) aims to disrupt the law itself. It is that *rupture* perhaps which the system (be it metaphysics or the "play of supplementarity" perhaps) as such can never fully comprehend or integrate. It is that opening which allows for repetition but which is not repetition itself. As we have shown, the structure of the "play of the supplement" exhibits itself as play. The supplement supplements, as Derrida says. Thus what is the exorbitant of the exorbitant itself? We must approach the "beyondness" of the "beyond good and evil" aspect of writing or the "play of the supplement," as we call it here, in order to better portray this "blind spot" in the "play of the supplement" itself.

(iii) The Point of Orientation: Ethics

> Society, language, history, articulation, in a word supplementarity, are born at the same time as the prohibition of incest.[34]

Indeed we would add that the instant *before* this birth, or indeed the condition of its possibility is the performance of what cannot yet be called incest. It is the end of the virginity of nature and its simultaneous constitution. It is Oedipus once again in bed with his mother who, with the constitution of society as such, becomes his wife. Of course the recognition of the former aspect is always too late. He is always already married to this "double" woman. Indeed it is always woman who received the blame for the duplicity in society. A duplicity Derrida claims, which is intrinsic—its condition of possibility and that which at the same time is capable of threatening it with non-existence. The castration of Reason is not however performed by the woman; it is, as we have shown, Oedipus who performs such a feat, albeit for the sake of, in place of, as a sign for woman herself. Thus Oedipus plays the roles of both Father and son, and of both mother and father. He is essentially therefore *asexual*—or perhaps bisexual, if this term can still be meaninful for us. Such is the structure of the "non-ethical opening of ethics" for Derrida, we suggest.

As with Nietzsche, Derrida finds himself in a situation which is essentially beyond "good and evil." He thus speaks of arche-writing as a "writing beyond good and evil." This is not, however, an abdication from the issue of ethics but rather, as Heidegger and others have shown, a square facing of the issue of this necessarily *contemporary* problem we call ethics. How can ethics, which was always based on a particular notion of consciousness which we now know to be a "serious" joke (Reason's), continue to exist? Yet, how can we abandon ethics as such? Neither choice is open to us according to Derrida's analysis, we suggest. But neither is the option of assuming a certain guilt and a certain tragedy to the "play of the world," and thus a certain resignation or passivity. We are beyond the metaphysical choice of activity/passivity as well at this juncture. Indeed we have found that that which allows for the constitution of society is a certain vulnerability of the "self," the child (in us all) to the "demands" of the other—be that a present or absent other. The child is inscribed—like it or not—in society, and it is forced to learn, insofar as it is able, to transform its *immediate* wants (a) into *future* desires, and (b) into a scriptural, linguistic form capable first of being spoken, but later and ultimately of being written. The child is, in short, forced to recognize not only the *"fort/da"* of its mother (or perhaps this relation is more applicable with respect to the father/mother relations respectively to the child) but also of *itself.* It's own death is what the child must learn to inscribe, in order that it have its own life—in the society as such. This is neither in itself good nor evil, but rather can be made into a good thing or an evil one depending, as we know, on circumstances. Depending precisely on the *context,* the situation in particular; or *particularity as such.* As we know, for Derrida, the realm of particularity is that which Reason or language as such cannot describe. Reason speaks only Reason, or more precisely, only the "in general." The "this here" is always already *also* the "that there." The *Da* is always already most profoundly *Fort.* It is this that the child must learn. And thus we have arrived again at the "writing" which is necessarily "beyond good and evil." Thus we have also pointed towards that space within the word, that *Abyss* within which the subject (a) defines an ethical orientation, but which (b) illustrates the ultimately unethical or evil structure within "ethics" itself, as "ethics itself," or *in general.* No ethics in general is any longer possible because, in fact, it was *never* possible. Ethics as such is always already unethical. The person in general does not exist. "I," as I speak or write my name, do not therein any longer exist. It is this that it seems to us Derrida's analysis is pointing towards: that *specificity* which he names both the sacred and animality. (Animality is, in Derrida's sense of the term, the non-repeatable and non-representable.) In short, radically exterior to that realm of the supplement. It is thus that the realm of ethics must be shifted to a realm which does not admit of an *ethics as such.* Ethics, in this situation, we suggest, is intrinsically *situated.* There is no context in general,[35] as Derrida says. The term itself negates its own possibility. That is, it requires for its meaning that it be situated. Thus ethics, as situated, can never be written. In the writing, we not only violate ethics as such, but also require our own death as such. Ethics is not to be based on the martyrdom of Reason, for Derrida, we suggest. Instead the irreducibility of the signifier/signified relation, before the symbol becomes sign, must be the *locale* of what perhaps we can only term being-ethical. Once inscribed, it becomes its own opposite and necessarily so as we have shown. The "object" of man is no longer an ethical object, by definition. It must be admitted here, however, that Derrida does not write on ethics as such and nowhere has formulated these ideas in any systematic fashion. But we propose that this too is also intrinsic to the situation. Derrida's work, for the most part, exhibits a profound identity and inextricable complicity of signifier/signified, and such is the case with this issue in particular. Nevertheless a general structure emerges, and it is this "form" of that which is necessarily without form which we have sought to point towards here. We recognize, however, that it is something which can be made neither present or absent, but which *opens the space for this play.* The latter being the "play of supplementarity," as we have shown, and the former, we suggest, is the "point of orientation"—that "blind spot," which even the "play of the supplement" cannot describe. And necessarily so.

(c) The Principle of Death

Heidegger claimed that ". . . in Dasein there is always something *still outstanding,* which, as a potentiality-for-Being for Dasein itself, has not yet become actual. It is essential to the basic constitution of Dasein that there is constantly something *still to be settled.*"[36]

Freud insisted that "children *repeat* unpleasurable experiences for the additional reason that they can *master* a powerful impression far more thoroughly by being active than they could by merely experiencing it passively. Each fresh repetition seems to strengthen the mastery they are in search of."[37] And further: "The manifestations of a *compulsion to repeat* exhibit to a high degree an instinctual character, and when they act in opposition to the pleasure principle, give the appearance of some 'daemonic' force at work."[38]

And *Derrida* claims that "What writing itself, in its nonphonetic moment, betrays, is life. It menaces at once the breath, the spirit, and history as the spirit's relationship with itself. It is their end, their finitude, their *paralysis.* Cutting breath short, sterilizing or immobilizing spiritual creation in the *repetition of the letter,* in the commentary or the exegesis . . . it is the *principle of death* and of difference in the becoming of Being."[39]

As we know, that which is "still to be settled" for *Dasein* will never be actually, and that repetitive attempt to be master of the situation—to control the *Fort/Da* of life itself—will be forever frustrated as the real-

ity principle necessarily installs itself. But how is it that "writing itself
. . . betrays life"? How is it to be understood as the "principle of death"
which we find in the repetition of the letter, the commentary, or the
exegesis? We propose to analyze this fundamental structure of *différance* for Derrida, first in terms of his relation to Freud and Heidegger
on this issue, and second (in each context) as he diverges radically
from their positions. Once again we must approach *différance,* and
here in particular the "principle of death," in an indirect fashion. Aside
from its pretentious aspects, it would also be ludicrous to propose an
analysis of the "structure of death itself." As Bataille said: "Concerning death there is evidently nothing to be said." But concerning our
relation to this Abyss—that principle of all principles, perhaps—there
is, as we shall explore presently, much to be said. Heidegger's notion
of *Dasein's* Being-towards-death shall lead us toward that which is not
to be outstripped, that essential structure of "human existence" which
no "authentic" theory can overcome (or bury). Eschatology is not
allowed in this domain therefore. And with Freud we shall explore that
"other" instinct which counteracts *Eros*—*Thanatos* itself—as that
"compulsion to repeat," which in appearance seems to be the work of
some "daemonic force." As we have shown previously, Derrida's work
is *not* an attempt to open the doors to "evil itself" or to justify,
rationalize, nor certainly not to welcome that which the Western world
has named evil. However, this too is "not-to-be-outstripped," as we
turn towards the "good" of our preference. One is a function of the
other, as we shall see, and the doorway which opens us to that which
we call good is simultaneously the same one which exposes us to the
dangers of evil. Of this aspect Derrida, as we have shown, is well
aware. He says: "Writing is the evil of representative repetition, the
double that opens desire and contemplates and binds enjoyment. Writing represents (in every sense of the word) enjoyment. It plays enjoyment, renders it present and absent. It is play."[40] We shall return to the
play of play as beyond the comic and the tragic, but first a short, but
necessary, detour through the "Abyss" for Heidegger, as it relates to
that for Derrida.

(i) The "Abyss" for Heidegger

Heidegger's concern with *Dasein* is based on an attempt to come to
terms with Being as such. Toward this end, he seeks to understand and

explicate the "essential structure of *Dasein.*" This structure includes: a care-structure, the moods, the situatedness of Being-in-the-world, and indeed a certain thrownness therein. But the principle aspect of *Dasein's* essence is a certain *lack,* a certain indebtedness, which is also a certain Abyss intrinsic to its Being-in-the-world. Yet *Dasein* has a way of concealing its own essential nature from itself in the mode of Being-in-the-world, which Heidegger calls "inauthenticity." In such a mode (which seems ontologically *prior* for Heidegger), *Dasein* does not reflect on death but rather relates to it in terms of "idle chatter" : that speech which says nothing, which clouds, covers up, and effaces the very possibility of thought itself. So *Dasein* lives inauthentically, yet, in this fashion, does not realize its own potential. This potential, Heidegger claims, is an authentic Being-towards-death—a certain genuine *Angst* which *Dasein* realizes in facing the Abyss, which it knows therein it can never know without losing itself as *Dasein.* Upon entry one pays the price of life itself, and it is thus the inevitable distance *Dasein* must live with in its authentic relation to death. In short, it must face its own *powerlessness* in the face of death itself. It reflects on itself therefore most profoundly in facing death, as if facing a mirror which never lies. The truth of *Dasein* is thus revealed via this pain of death. Indeed it is, as Derrida says, the "death sentence." Heidegger explains the paradox in the following manner:

> The "ending" which we have in view when we speak of death, does not signify Dasein's Being-at-an-end, but a Being-towards-the-end of this entity. Death is a way to be, which Dasein takes over as soon as it is. . . .[41]

And further:

> Any Dasein always exists in just such a manner that its "not yet" belongs to it.[42]

In addition, for Heidegger, this movement towards authenticity of *Dasein,* which is its "ownmost potentiality," is also a movement of *isolation,* and indeed *in* isolation. The "idle chatter" of the crowd continues, yet *Dasein,* in this particular case, absents itself from it. In such a process the individuating factor of death itself becomes evident for *Dasein.* One dies alone; one faces one's death alone; and thus the Being-in-the-world which is essential to Dasein is threatened. It is "in-the-world" only for a while, only for a time, only on the condition that this be a *finite* relation. As Heidegger says concerning this essential authenticity of Dasein:

> When it [Dasein] stands before itself in this way, all its relations to any other Dasein have been undone. This ownmost non-relational possibility is at the same instant the uttermost one.[43]

And further:

> Dying is *essentially mine* in such a way that no one can be my representative . . . [my emphasis].[44]

And thus Heidegger returns to a notion of "my proper death," which is no one else's, to a certain non-representability of death. No one can "take my place," and neither can I take someone else's. We thus approach what Derrida has called *différance* as the principle of repetition, or representation, and of the non-proper, albeit from the other side.

We should recall that for Derrida there is a *point* in the signifying chain which nicknames *"différance,"* for which the signified can never be made present. We have analyzed this point of no return as that point of orientation which is the subject (albeit effaced in Derrida's position). It is this "point of no return" which we must now face in terms of Heidegger's exposé, and beyond it in terms of Derrida as such.

Derrida insists that the "master name" in the supplementary series is "death" itself. It is that *signifier* whose signified is always already denied it. It points toward the beyond itself, and yet paradoxically is that which allows for the constitution of what is here and present as such. As Derrida says:

> . . . the *master name* of the supplementary series: death. Or rather, for death is nothing, the relationship to death, the anguished anticipation of death. All the possibilities of the supplementary series, which have the relationships of metonymic substitutions among themselves, indirectly name the danger itself, the horizon and source of all determined dangers, the *abyss* from which all menaces announce themselves [my emphasis].[45]

A strange name to be sure, for Derrida—the "master" name. But this term too is a name which is not a name; indeed is one which destroys itself. Since the "master name" has no content and can never have, it is the name of the "unnameable" itself, of that which can never be named—essentially. Thus the Abyss here, as represented by death, in turn returns to represent all that is intrinsically unknowable (and thus unnameable). It is that "representation" for all which would *menace* life itself (death of course being the ultimate menace) and thus is both inside and outside of the representation. In a paradoxical way therefore death is (a) non-representable, yet is (b) the condition for all representation. It is the abyss which allows for repetition, and which kills (menaces) the repeater and the repeated in that same process. But we shall return to this issue in greater detail in terms of Derrida's relation to Freud. For the moment we must return to the "work of death" or, more precisely, of the "subject's relation to its own death" and the effects which this brings.

As we know from Heidegger, the result of "facing death" for *Dasein* was a recognition of an essential aspect of its own Being which it now knows it could never know: a certain painful authenticity, in short. But for Derrida, the relation of the "subject" to its own death is what allows for the "very constitution of its subjectivity":

> As the subject's relationship to its own death, this becoming is the constitution of subjectivity. On all levels of life's organization, that is to say, of the economy of death. All graphemes are of a testamentary essence. And the original absence of the subject of writing is also the absence of the thing or the referent.[46]

Thus the subject, in facing its own death, in short—in writing—therein constitutes his own subjectivity. What this means is that death, as distinct from Heidegger's view of it as an isolating factor (for *Dasein* which is not to be identified with the term "subject," however), is a certain unifying factor. A certain aspect of the self which is shared, and indeed forms the basis of human collectivity. As we know, for Derrida, the subject is not a master, a radical creator (as Nietzsche would insist), but rather always situated within limits, as a result. Consciousness, for Derrida, is a product as we know, an effect, in short, of the play of *différance;* and thus is *intrinsically* collective, as is meaning, its vehicle. Thus, in a certain respect, death as a principle—indeed *the principle* of writing itself (although it absents the subject and object as such) is also that very element which allows for their constitution. It allows for that *writing* which is *à la fois* the becoming conscious and unconscious of the subject—the making present and absent of the object. The "original absence" of which he speaks here is simply the recognition of that which earlier we spoke of as the "radical inauguration" that characterizes writing. The act of writing being, in a certain respect, always "behind the back" of the "subject" who writes and the "object" written about. Writing, as we know, is the condition of their possibility in any meaningful way. Thus writing gives birth to meaning, but also, and necessarily so, Derrida claims, menaces it with death. This relation to death is a function of that principle of repetition we spoke of earlier and must now return to, via Freud and what he refers to as the "death instinct" or *Thanatos.*

(ii) Freud and the Principle of Life and Death

Freud was never convinced that a "death instinct" actually exists, but he did propose several hypotheses on the matter, which we shall attempt to explore here. He suggested that all organic matter (life in all its forms) was perhaps originally inorganic and that it strove during the span of its life to return to that earlier state. It was this "striving to return" which Freud defined as the nature of *instincts* in general. As he says, an instinct is

> . . . an urge inherent in organic life to *restore* an earlier state of things. . . . an expression of the *inertia* inherent in organic life. . . . an expression of the *conservative* nature of living substance [my emphasis].[47]

Thus life seeks to make life easier for itself—in short, to die. The aim of life is thus, in a peculiar way, death. But we have an additional force at work here that opposes itself to this "will to death," a force which is called the *life instinct,* the sexual instincts, and later *Eros* itself. This is not reducible to the pleasure principle, however, but instead is radically opposed to it. Thus the life instincts divide into two aspects: (i) the pleasure principle, always deferred and mediated by (ii) the reality principle—the repression and deferral of the former. The reality principle is thus not the same as the death instinct, although not dissimilar, as Derrida has shown.[48] But first this detour that is life, for Freud, exhibits in its inertia, in its "compulsion to repeat," that same "death instinct" of which we spoke earlier. The paradox here is that the "compulsion to repeat" which characterizes the death instinct is also the same principle which characterizes the life instinct and allows the subject to "master the situation" and to become no longer a passive victim of the *fort/da* of life, but rather its active producer. It is thus via the *principle of repetition* itself that the *life and death* instincts in Freud are manifested as two opposing forces. The common force itself, at once Erotic and Daemonic, is that compulsion to repeat, which simultaneously saves us from death—for the moment—and condemns us to it ultimately.

Thus Derrida parts company with Freud. This principle of repetition Freud speaks of is precisely the "principle of death" for Derrida. But, as we have shown, for the latter "life [is] death deferred." Just as all metaphysical oppositions turn into their opposites over time and space which is writing, so too life becomes death for Derrida. But can one say that death becomes life (also as Derrida's "logic" here seems to suggest)? Indeed we have already said it—death is that which allows for the constitution of subject and object. But how is this possible, since it seems to destroy them at the same instant? For Derrida, we should recall, there is a certain *spacing* involved in the notion of *différance* which requires a certain time and indeed *timing* as such. All does not occur in the blink of an eye nor in the "moment of vision" that opens the way to Heidegger's authenticity. Indeed the "principle of repetition" which death represents can also be called the principle of imitation: that repetition crucial to all learning, and yet that which kills all originality. In terms of art, Derrida thus explains this notion:

> *Imitation* is . . . at the same time the life and death of art. Art and death, art and its death are comprised in the space of alteration of the originary iteration; of repetition, reproduction, representation; or also in space as the possibility of iteration and the exit from life placed outside of itself.[49]

Thus we find that (a) one can never, properly speaking, repeat, reproduce, or represent anything at all; yet (b) one always only repeats, represents, and reproduces. The "origin," as we have shown, is a result of this process and not, radically or precisely speaking, an origin or foundation. This is also the case with the "principle of death." It is the end as *telos* of all life, yet is never directly aimed towards, can never be directly faced, and is always approached in the detour which is time and space of history itself. Life's history. A finite history, as Hegel among others, has shown. Thus death upsets the circle of totality which would complete man, which would allow him to "settle things," and to master the "compulsion to repeat" itself. It is death that is the model for the fundamentally *non-closable* opening, and thus for all openings as such. It is that which opens man, *Dasein*, or the subject to its own otherness, which can never be named as such, never be included in a system called "knowledge," and never be controled by its other principle called *Eros*. As Derrida says it "opens the space of calculation, of grammaticality, of the rational science of intervals (those differences we call identities as such) and those 'rules of imitation', that are fatal to energy.'"[50]

The law is always, for Derrida, a function of writing and is thus always already condemned to its own death. In the end, as we shall see, writing is unfaithful to itself and indeed kills itself. This is its principle, which we shall see it remains ultimately faithful to in its unfaithfulness. (Perhaps these categories too have exhausted their usefulness in this context.) This paradox of writing is thus, as the "principle of death," that it must (a) include itself as its first and last victim, yet (b) therein vindicate itself as correct, except, as Derrida says, "we will have arrived at a knowledge which can no longer go by that name." The danger is therefore:

> The supplement transgresses and at the same time respects the interdict. This is what also permits writing as the supplement of speech, but already also the spoken word as writing in general. Its economy *exposes and protects us* at the same time according to the play of forces and of the differences of forces. Thus the supplement is *dangerous* in that it *threatens us* with death [my emphasis].[51]

And thus we inscribe our own death with each movement of the pen. The subject which no longer *needs* to exist, (and so *a fortiori* for the object) is thus reduced. It abdicates and decenters itself in the act of writing, and, as we know, *all acts* are ultimately constituted, authorized (and hence unauthorized) by writing itself. Since writing is ultimately the "principle of death," it is also ultimately perhaps unknowable as such. But the "as such" structure of knowledge is precisely what is in question here. And thus it is that the "principle of death" opens the circularity of "knowledge" and "names" as such. That always "unknowable" is what for Kant, we should recall, *allowed for the knowable.* The noumenal realm seems thus to be reinstated in Derrida's analysis as not a simple "out there" of space itself, as metaphysics would have it, but rather as the intimate relation of the "subject" to spacing itself as it simultaneously constitutes and is constituted by that which we will now refer to as *timing* or temporalization itself. This is also what Derrida will call *spacing,* as involving more precisely the *spatialization of time itself.* These are not *a priori* intuitions, however, as they were for Kant, but rather the conditions of the possibility of the *a priori* itself. We shall thus examine this aspect of *différance* for Derrida as it necessarily defies the formulation of "a new transcendental aesthetic."

B. Postface: A New Transcendental Aesthetic?

Derrida opens the possibility of a new transcendental aesthetic in terms of his notion of *différance,* yet closes it again on the same page.[52] As we know, *différance* is for him the space of inscription, or articulation, of meaning, of form, and thus forms the condition of the possibility of the spatiality of space and, at the same instant, the temporality of time. Kant was forced to submit to the "forms of space and time as such" as *a priori* conditions of the possibility of experience in general. The experience of the "out there" was always already "in space," and of the "in here" for "the subject," as the "transcendental unity of apperception," was always already "in time." His deduction in the transcendental aesthetic briefly runs as follows. He attempts to isolate, from the concepts of the understanding, those pure *a priori* intuitions which always necessarily inhabit our experience. As he says:

> In the transcendental aesthetic we shall, therefore, first isolate sensibility by taking away from it everything which the understanding thinks through its concepts, so that nothing may be left save *empirical intuition.* Secondly we shall also separate off from it everything which belongs to sensation, so that nothing may remain save *pure intuition* and the mere *form* of appearances, which is all that sensibility can supply *a priori* [my emphasis].[53]

Thus Kant seems to move by a method of subtraction and ever-increasing isolation of parts from the mixture of sensibility with the understanding—that which he calls knowledge—to a realm of empirical intuition as such, which is then "reduced" (via the bracketing procedure) to pure intuitions which he says take the *form* of "the mere form of appearances, which is all that sensibility can supply *a priori.*" We know from Hegel's critique of precisely this process that what Kant forgot systematically throughout this procedure was his metaphysical (indeed borrowed from the understanding itself) notion of *form* as such. The form is not lost as one proceeds by subtraction to arrive at those "pure *a priori* intuitions." It is rather presupposed and indeed cannot be left behind, in order to follow Kant here. The notion of form seems therein to transcend both categories of "sensibility"—either empirical or pure—and of the "understanding" itself (wherein we know it has its proper place as well.) Thus Hegel reproaches Kant for imposing and indeed presupposing a certain form (of form itself) on his findings, such that his results are always already preformulated. He can arrive nowhere but where he began. That the "force" of the "understanding" is precisely this escape from its conscious reduction was what initiated our excursion beyond the realm of language as such for Derrida and toward that realm of force as such which can never be informed without also being at once excluded and yet also always *inadequately* represented. Kant called it the realm of the dangerous, the awesome, and the sublime.[54] But not the realm of the origin of space and time, which, as we shall see, is precisely where Derrida advances beyond the possibility of a new transcendental aesthetics.

On the one hand he claims:

> A new transcendental aesthetic must let itself be guided not only by mathematical idealities but by the possibility of inscriptions in general, not befalling an already constituted space as a contingent accident, but producing the spatiality of space.[55]

Thus we cannot admit to the non-possibility of "mathematical idealities" since indeed we do have them, by some means. Yet the notion of the mathematical ideality as a *model,* or indeed as the model *par excellence* for the production of idealities in general—Hamlet, for instance—must be rethought, Derrida suggests. As we know, for Husserl as well, there was a transcendental realm, beyond experience as such, which admitted of a certain ontological structure which therein allowed for the constitution, not only of geometry and such like forms, but also of a life-world and all its various dimensions not reducible to mathematical form. In addition, as we know, Husserl focused on the role of writing, in particular with respect to the "origin of geometry," as an essential element in its constitution as an "object for anyone, at any time," indeed as an ideal object. Yet Husserl also insisted that all "worldly representations" of ideal objects could be destroyed in fact, empirically, and this would or could change nothing with respect to the essential ideality of those same ideal objects. They were thus (a) dependent upon writing for their constitution within intersubjective time and space, yet (b) once constituted as such became radically independent of that same form which once served to house them. Thus the "origin" of the origin is effaced, Derrida claims. But first, he recognizes the important shift made by Husserl which advances from Kant's transcendental aesthetics to a realm of transcendental kinesthetics:

> The *Husserlian project* not only put all objective space of science within parentheses, it had to articulate aesthetics upon a transcendental kinesthetics [my emphasis].[56]

Yet, in spite of the movement of consciousness in the constitution of temporality as such, which thus opens the possibility of spatiality as such (also a Kantian priority of time over space, of interior over exterior, and ultimately of subject over object), Husserl eventually had recourse to the metaphysical notion of the present (the time of all evidence) as always a combination of present past and a present future that would thus produce the present as such. This is, as we have shown, not radical enough for Derrida, since the "abyss," that inner space, or spacing, which allows for the constitution of temporality as such, in Husserl's sense, is still effaced in this process. That same spacing, or spatiality, is collapsed within the ultimately dominating form of the present. Just as Kant used *form* both prior to his "reduction" to the "pure forms of intuition *a priori*" and indeed in the latter formulation, so does Husserl begin and end with the notion of a *present* that is purely and simply the essence of consciousness. Nothing escapes it (that is of any importance) Fink tells us.[57] That which is unconscious has no place in transcendental phenomenology. Indeed it plays no part, therefore, in the formulation and indeed preformulation of science, truth, knowledge, or evidence itself. Derrida does not agree, as we have shown. That which can never (in the past or the future) enter consciousness as such is precisely that which allows for its constitution as such. It is, in short, the "structural necessity of the abyss."

We thus move beyond Kant, Husserl and Hegel in this domain and turn to Derrida's claims as such.

> Origin of the experience of space and time, this *writing of différance*, this *fabric of the trace,* permits the difference between space and time to be articulated, to appear as such, in the *unity* of an experience (of a "same" lived out of a "same" body proper [my emphasis].[58]

As we know, *différance* is that movement (a) which allows for the formation of form itself, and (b) which will eventually overturn and unravel that same production. *Différance,* in short, is always on the move and does not come to a halt once something is produced. And as we know, *différance* is, in a profound way, an "unauthorized" movement—without plan, without design, without motive. Yet it is "that force which forces force"—the "force of preference" itself. Thus we have space and time as such conceived here as results of this productive process. We experience the "effects" and "results" of *différance,* and these are precisely those "forms of all intuitions" which Kant described. But they seem to betray a certain commonality of root in Derrida's analysis, and it is this which we must explore more fully now.

For Derrida there is a certain spacing intrinsic to all articulation. He insists that spatiality as such is (a) a result of *différance,* yet also (b) its fundamental opening as such. The movement of *différance* is, in short, both the collapsing of spatiality into moments of identity, ideality, or the "sameness" we call an object, or Heidegger called a clearing, and the opening of spatiality within all ideality, which leads it to its own "overcoming" or unravelling. The "first" movement here is the production of the possibility of meaning as such for Derrida. It is the realm of the "differences" between "full" terms, wherein the space gives both *à la fois* a certain contextual significance. Thus Derrida says:

> It is the systematic play of differences, the traces of differences, of *spacing* by which the elements relate to one another. This spacing is the production, simultaneously active and passive—of the *spaces* without which the 'full' terms would not signify. This is also the *becoming-space* of the spoken chain that one calls temporal and linear; becoming-space makes writing possible and all correspondence between speech and writing, all passage from one to the other [my emphasis].[59]

Thus the spacing which is the work/play and effect of *différance* allows for the moments of meaning we call speech and writing as such. Evidently one cannot write or speak the totality of one's message within the "instant" or the "blink of an eye" as such. Evidently one cannot and does not run all of one's words together in speech or in writing to form one *single* term. Evidently one does not write one letter on top of another in the process of writing or enunciate all letters of a word at once in the process of speaking. The time it takes to enunciate, to articulate, in either form, is the process of spacing which is irreducible within the production of meaning itself. This may seem to be a trivial point, but with the notion of spacing also comes that of *context* and the difficulties which must ensue in terms of a spatio-temporal demarcation of the latter. Where does a context begin or end? Derrida will say always—in context. Quite simply, the notion of *context as such* cannot and indeed does not exist. There is no such thing as a context-in-general, by definition. Yet the term exists as such. So one must define context as such always according to the context.[60] The text-context relation here shall illustrate that movement of *différance* Derrida terms *habitation*—that inscription in general which is always already situated, although indeed paradoxically. As Derrida says:

> Indeed we speak of inscription in general, in order to make it quite clear that it is not simply the notation of a prepared speech representing itself,

but *inscription within speech* and *inscription as habitation always already situated* [my emphasis].⁶¹

But what could inscription as habitation entail here in this context? Precisely, we suggest, the question of context itself. As is well known and generally all too flippantly expressed, the meaning of a term is (largely) determined by its context. For Derrida it is not possible to decontextualize a term and save its meaning as such. Indeed to "free" a concept, an ideality, of its chains of inscription—the 'sound-image' as such. As we have shown, the signifier and signified are thus, for Derrida, inextricably intertwined. The "becoming-sign of the symbol" is never complete, and thus the radical separation (of signifier and signified) as the "transcendental signified" can never, for language, ever be more than an Idea in the Kantian sense—and perhaps should be left external to our discussion here, which is not "moving in that direction" as its *telos.* Thus the situation of inscription is that "chain of signifiers" which always already entail a certain chain of signifieds and thus a texture, a "fabric" (as Derrida says) of signification. The removal of one thread would destroy the entire tapestry of course, to pursue the metaphor slightly further. But the notion of context seems to be even more precisely situated than this general demarcation. Indeed it is for Derrida. The opening of a text, in particular, and the usage of a particular term always already situate that term in that time and space of the text. If, as is usually the case, the "same term" (which is by definition an impossibility for Derrida) appears later in the time/space of the text, one can be sure that its meaning is no longer the "same" as before. In this sense one can never repeat the "same thing" for Derrida. It is always already otherwise. What we have in the "second instance" of the "same term" is, more precisely speaking, an "exact homonym"; indeed a word that may sound and look the same, but whose meaning is radically altered due to contextual shifting, indeed due to the play of *différance* itself. Thus one might be tempted to suggest that there is perhaps a notion of a transcendental signif*ier* in Derrida's position, such that the meaning—the signified aspect of a term—may alter but its form, but not its body. Perhaps. But the point here is that: (i) the notion of context is contextually determined itself and cannot be discussed in general, except in negative terms; and (ii) the play of *différance* at once constitutes the context of a term and therein its meaning, and also shifts that same context so as to therein already alter and defer its meaning as such. Derrida has given us sufficient examples of this process through his deconstructive practices. We might consider Husserl and the notion of the living present as it is undercut yet sustained by his later notion of internal time consciousness and that "unnameable movement"; we might consider Condillac and "good and bad" metaphysics; we might consider Plato and "good and bad" writing; we might consider Hegel and the simultaneous constitution and unravelling (which he effaced from himself) of the Concept; we might look at Heidegger and his simultaneous adherence to and attempts to destroy metaphysics as such; and we might finally consider Derrida himself.

For the latter, as we know, "writing denounces itself." Writing or *différance,* as that movement of spatiality and temporality itself, makes repetition (a) impossible as we have shown, yet (b) also all that we ever have. Of course repetition is therein used in two different senses of the term; indeed it is perhaps always already more than *one* term.

We thus turn toward the notion of writing, for Derrida, which, as we have shown, he uses interchangeably with trace, arche-writing, reserve, the play of the supplement, the movement of *différance,* and so on. He also slides, it seems to us, back and forth from the term writing as "this inscription here" to a notion of writing as inscription anywhere and at any time: indeed as he says, inscription in general. His justification of such a move is to show that he is referring to a "sort of writing" which is also prior to "speech" as such and which is not a representative thereof but which radically originates that same possibility. Yet, he claims that writing (in general) is the "articulation of the living on the non-living"; it marks the "dead time" within the present that was always already there.

We suggest that "writing" in this *double role* for Derrida is more than simply an innocent metaphor; in fact this duplicity is essential to its usage. And further, we suggest that "writing" is not severable from its "original" context as written inscription; indeed this "borrowing" allows for the constitution of a *model* which is then transplanted from the "empirical" plane of this writing here to one which can only be considered, if not metaphysical (inscription *as such*), at least, in the sense that Kant used the term—transcendental. Writing as *différance,* in its ontological role, thus appears to us much in the way that "form" appeared to Hegel when he read Kant on the "forms of *a priori* intuitions." Derrida seems thus to *transplant* the form of writing in particular out of its particularity into a realm of the *in general,* where it not only sustains the same form but, in taking on a transcendental character (beyond empirical intuition as such), it returns to organize and preformulate all experience as within that same form. Derrida seems to acknowledge this transcendental aspect of his "theory" when he refers to the "originally non-intelligible sphere" which he calls that of writing, indeed arche-writing, the intelligibility of which "remains to be seen," just as Kant's "*a priori* forms of intuition" extend beyond knowledge as such to a realm which organizes the conditions of its possibility.

Derrida formulates his position in the following manner, with respect to what could only be called an "arche-reading" that would *parallel* and yet transform "arche-writing":

> The space of writing is thus not an originarily intelligible space. It begins to become so from the origin, that is to say from the moment when writing, like all the work of signs, produces repetition and therefore ideality in that space. If one calls *reading* that moment which comes directly *to double* that originary writing, one may say that the space of pure reading is always already intelligible, that of pure writing always still sensible [my emphasis].[62]

Is not the "reading" which is that "moment which comes directly to *double* that originary writing" precisely that which we (and Derrida also, we suggest) call metaphysics itself? We should recall that we began, in our search for Derrida's *différance,* with the opening of the possibility of a "double universe," that movement from the "circle" of metaphysics (with one sun) to the "exorbitant" orbit of *différance,* "which comes directly to double" that origin—which Derrida claims is not an origin (pure and simple). One might justifiably ask where are we at this juncture? Have we returned to a space, indeed the movement which produces spatiality itself, and indeed therefore the movement which would allow for, account for, and open the possibility of not *one* universe, but *two?* It would seem so. That second universe was first shown to be the realm of *différance* itself, the realm of the "still sensible," in Kant's sense of the term, which we have paradoxically shown exists also at the highest of transcendental heights. Yet now we arrive at "another" formulation of a "second universe" which is that space of "reading" which makes intelligible, indeed formulates, informs, articulates the first "only sensible," although more "original" universe. This space of reading as always *a posteriori* to that space of writing seems to be a slight paradox, however, in terms of that which we formerly addressed as the "second universe." More precisely, have not these terms been *inverted* in this second usage as compared with the first? Indeed. And necessarily so. If we have explicated anything at all concerning the movement of *différance* for Derrida, it should have been at least the necessity of this inversion. Although we insisted that the "inverted world" of which Hegel spoke with reference to Kant was not simply reducible to the realm of *différance* for Derrida, it should now be clear why Derrida's position can "no more be severed from this notion than be reduced to it." Derrida, it should be recalled, situated his own work in the same way with respect to Husserl's phenomenology. We suggest it might be more appropriately situated with reference to what Hegel called "Force and the Understanding." Although not therein reducible to force as such, *différance,* as we have shown, is not dissimilar to it. The "play of the double universe" is itself both a movement of force and a movement of play, we insist therefore. Since one sun is that of metaphysics, and the other is that of *différance*—or is it not perhaps the moon of which Derrida speaks, which has no light of its own, which has the power of eclipsing the sun periodically, and which lights that part of the world which the sun by its absence cannot reach—do we not have two forces at work here? Hegel would say yes, and we know the immediate result of such a formulation. Names in this case mean everything. Perhaps it is thus that *différance* has no proper name and exceeds all conceptualizing as such, yet can it therein exceed all transcendental formulation of the same? We have suggested that it cannot.

But if we have gone "full ellipse" in this process in the explication of *différance* to show that it is (a) precisely what it claims it is not, yet also (b) is not precisely that which it claims to be, have we not therein established both the existence and non-existence of *différance* as such? Has Derrida said anything else? It was he who from the beginning claimed (a) *différance* does not *exist;* (b) it has no proper name; and (c) it cannot be said as such. "We can only point towards it with a silent movement of the finger." We would add only one thing in this context, and this concerns that "other hand" which Derrida spoke of in our opening citation. Perhaps now when we re-read this "same" piece of writing, its meaning will have changed for us. Perhaps this time that "other hand" will present itself for us. If it does, it will surely be the result of nothing but the uncanny movement of *différance* itself. If it does not—what more can be said?

> The future is not a future present, yesterday is not a past present. That which is beyond the closure of the book is neither to be awaited nor

refound. It is *there,* but *out there*—beyond—within repetition but elud-
ing us there. It is there like the *shadow* of the book, the *third* between
two hands holding the book, the *différance* in the now of writing, the
movement between the book and the book, this other hand . . . [my
emphasis].[63]

NOTES

Introduction

1. Immanuel Kant, *Prolegomena to Any Future Metaphysics,* trans. L. W. Beck (Indianapolis: The Bobbs-Merrill Company, Inc., 1950), p. 126.

2. Jacques Derrida, *Of Grammatology,* trans. Gayatri C. Spivak (Baltimore: The Johns Hopkins University Press, 1974), p. 50.

3. This claim is well known as one of the mainstays of Kant's entire system of thought. In the *Prolegomena* he says, for instance: "We know not this thing as it is in itself but only know its *appearances;* namely, the way in which our senses are affected by this *unknown something.* The understanding, therefore, by assuming appearances, grants the *existence* of things in themselves also" (p. 62, my emphasis).

4. This claim is made by Derrida with specific reference to Husserl, but it can apply equally well in this context, we suggest. See in particular, *La Voix et le Phénomène* (Paris: PUF, 1967), p. 117.

5. This is also well known as a central issue for Kant, and he says explicitly what is at stake for him in this question is the following:

> How is nature itself possible? This question—the highest point that transcendental philosophy can ever reach, and to which as its boundary and completion, it must proceed—really contains two questions. How is *nature in the material sense,* that is, as to intuitions, or considered as the totality of appearances, possible; how are space, time and that which fills both—the object of sensation—possible generally? . . . How is nature possible *in the formal sense* as the totality of rules under which all appearances must come in order to be thought as connected in experience? [PAFM, p. 65; my emphasis]

6. Jacques Derrida. *La Vérité en Peinture* (Paris: Flammarion, 1978), pp. 23–24, my translation. Despite the possible implications here that deconstruction thereby overturns or even revolutionizes institutions, we insist that this is not the case. The impact of deconstruction is instead yet to be decided in the same sense that it makes no claim to be progress-oriented nor destructive as such, but to reveal the limits intrinsic to that which claims instead to be universal. For more on Derrida's influence on the institution of the media see Gregory L. Ulmer's review of *La Carte Postale* (*Diacritics* 11 [Sept. 1981]: 39–56).

7. Kant, *PAFM,* p. 132.

8. Ibid., p. 115.

9. Ibid., pp. 76, 96, 98, and 102.

10. Ibid., p. 13.

11. Ibid., p. 9.

12. Ibid., p. 75.

13. Ibid., p. 115.

14. Ibid., p. 21.

15. Jacques Derrida, "Tympan," in *Marges de la Philosophie* (Paris: Editions de Minuit, 1972), p. ix, my translation.
16. Jacques Derrida, *OG*, p. 3.
17. Ibid., for instance, pp. 79, 86, 162, 163, 244; and *Positions* (Paris: Editions de Minuit, 1972), pp. 13, 29, 46, and 50.
18. Kant, *PAFM*, p. 21.
19. Ibid., p. 19.
20. Ibid., p. 13.
21. Ibid., p. 75.
22. Ibid., p. 115.
23. Ibid., p. 102.
24. Ibid.
25. Ibid.
26. Ibid., p. 116.
27. Ibid., p. 60.
28. Derrida, *MP*, p. 73, my translation.
29. Kant, *PAFM*, p. 81.
30. Ibid., p. 97:

> In Nature there is much that is incomprehensible; . . . but if we mount still higher and go even beyond nature, everything again becomes comprehensible. For then we quit entirely the objects which can be given us and occupy ourselves merely with Ideas, in which occupation we can easily comprehend the law that reason prescribes by them to the Understanding for its use in experience, because the law is reason's own production.

For more on this notion and on Derrida's of "Reason believing itself to be its own father," see Jean-Luc Nancy's analysis, "La Voix Libre de l'Homme," *Les Fins de l'Homme* (Paris: Editions Galilee, 1981), pp. 163–84.
31. Kant, *PAFM*, p. 76.
32. See in particular Derrida's essay on Kant, "Parergon," in *VEP*, p. 43.
33. Kant, *PAFM*, p. 76.
34. Ibid., p. 93.
35. Ibid., p. 46.
36. For more on this notion, see Derrida's contribution to the study of Hegel, most notably in his text, *Glas* (Paris: Editions Galilee, 1974). In particular see pp. 217, 250–57.
37. See Derrida's essays in *MP* titled, "Tympan," "Le Supplément de Copule," and "La Mythologie Blanche."
38. Kant, *PAFM*, p. 65.
39. See Derrida's essay on Kant titled, "Parergon," in *VEP*, pp. 28–34.

I. The Principles

1. Jacques Derrida, *Positions* (Paris: Editions de Minuit, 1972), p. 129, my translation.
2. Jacques Derrida, Of Grammatology, trans. Gayatri C. Spivak (Baltimore: Johns Hopkins University Press, 1974), p. 162.
3. Ibid., pp. 10, 14, 24, 60–62, 67, 68, 70, 149, 158–64, 258–60, 307, 312, 314, for instance. For more on the notion of "law" in Derrida, specifically with reference to his relation to Plato, see "La Leçon de Calcul" by Denis Kambouchner in *Nuova Corrente* 28 (1981): 87–100.

4. Derrida, *P,* p. 112. For more on Derrida's notion of "deconstructing the idea of the book" with respect to that which cannot be reduced simply to commentary (as our analysis here is aiming to illustrate), see Philippe Venault's article entitled "cela s'appelle digraphe" in *Magazine Litérraire,* 1974.

5. Derrida, *OG,* p. 24. For more on this notion of "borrowing from metaphysics" in Derrida, see Francois Wahl's article entitled, "Mort du Livre?" in *Quinzaine Litérraire,* 15–31 October 1967.

6. Derrida, *OG,* p. 99.

7. Derrida, *P,* p. 67.

8. Derrida, *OG,* p. 70.

II. Deconstructive Gestures

1. Jacques Derrida, *Of Grammatology* trans. G. C. Spivak (Baltimore: The Johns Hopkins University Press, 1974), p. 39. For a good summary of the process of deconstruction as "desedimentation," see Robert Laport's essay, "Une Double Stratégie," in *Ecarts—Quatre Essais à Propos de Jacques Derrida* (Paris: Fayard, 1973).

2. Derrida, *OG,* p. 33. For more on the issue of the circumscription of domains, be they sciences or objects, see Derrida's article, "The Law of Genre," in *Critical Inquiry* 7 no. 1 (Autumn, 1980), trans. Avital Ronell.

3. Derrida, *OG,* p. 2. For more on Derrida's concern with exteriority as a more radical interiority see Luce Fontaine de Visscher's article, "Des Privilèges d'une Grammatologie," in *Revue Philosophique de Louvain,* 1969.

4. Derrida, *La Voix et la Phénomène* (Paris: Presses Universitaires de France, 1967), p. 100, my translation.

5. Derrida, *VP,* p. 102.

6. Derrida, *OG,* p. 39. For a rigorous comparison of the "similar themes" developed in *Of Grammatology* and *La Voix et Le Phénomène,* see René Scherer's article, "Clôture et faille dans la Phénoménologie de Husserl," in *Revue de la Métaphysique et de la Morale,* no. 73 (1968).

7. Derrida, *OG,* p. 31.

8. Derrida, *VP,* p. 40. For a good summary of Derrida's analysis of Husserl in *VP* with respect to its relation to Joyce's *Ulysses,* see Bernard P. Dauenhauer's article, "On Speech and Temporality," in *Philosophy Today* (Fall 1974): 171–80.

9. Derrida, *VP,* p. 23.

10. Derrida, *OG,* p. 26.

11. Derrida, *VP,* p. 27.

12. Derrida, *OG,* p. 29. For more on Derrida's analysis of Saussure, see Bertil Malmberg's article, "Derrida et la Sémiologie: Quelques notes marginales," in *Sémiotique* 211 (1974): 189–99.

13. Derrida, *OG,*p. 83–86.

14. Ibid., p. 4.

15. Derrida, *VP,* p. 24. For more on this issue for Derrida, see J. N. Mohanty's article, "On Husserl's Theory of Meaning," in *Southwestern Journal of Philosophy* 5 (1975): 229–45.

16. Derrida, *VP,* p. 25.

17. Ibid. p. 9–10.

18. Ibid., *VP,* p. 31.

19. Derrida, *OG,* p. 34.

20. Ibid., p. 39–40.

21. Ibid., p. 40.
22. Derrida, *VP,* p. 6.
23. Ibid.
24. Ibid., p. 79.
25. Ibid., p. 21.
26. Ibid., p. 104.
27. Ibid., p. 73.
28. Derrida, *OG,* p. 56.
29. Ibid., p. 40.
30. Derrida, *VP,* p. 56–57.
31. Ibid., p. 109. For more on the "general strategy" of Derrida's work concerning such contradictions, see Bernard-Henri Levy's text, "Derrida n'est pas un gourou," in *Magazine Littéraire,* 1974.
32. Derrida, *OG,* p. 46. Although the "validity" of Derrida's choice of example is not our present concern here, it is for Peter Steiner in "In Defense of Semiotics: The Dual Asymmetry of Cultural Signs," in New Literary History (1981): 415–35.
33. Derrida, *OG,* pp. 30–31.
34. Ibid., p. 30.
35. Derrida, *VP,* p. 63.
36. Ibid.
37. Ibid., p. 14.
38. Ibid., p. 75.
39. Derrida, *OG,* pp. 30–31.
40. Ibid., p. 40.
41. Ibid.
42. Ibid., p. 32–33.
43. In his recently published article, "My chances/Mes Chances: A Rendez-vous with some Epicurean Stereophonies," translated by Avital Ronell and myself in *Taking Chances,* ed. Joseph H. Smith and William Kerrigan (Baltimore: The Johns Hopkins Press, 1984), Derrida says the following concerning Freud's treatment of the superstitious person compared with "the man of science":

> Precisely at this point it is even more difficult for Freud to sustain this limit which separates him from the superstitious person since they both share the *hermeneutic compulsion.* If the superstitious person throws himself [*projette, projiziert*], if he throws himself outwards and towards the 'motivations' that Freud claims to be looking for internally, if he interprets chance from the standpoint of an "external" event at the point where Freud reduces it or leads it back to a "thought," it is because essentially the superstitious person does not believe, any more than Freud, in the solidity of the spaces circumscribed by an occidental sterotymy. He does not believe in the contextualizing, framing and not actual limits between the psychic and the physical, the inside and outside, not to mention all of the other connected oppositions. [p. 25]

44. Derrida, *OG,* p. 29.
45. Ibid.
46. Aristotle, *Metaphysics,* trans. Richard Hope (Ann Arbor: University of Michigan Press, 1952), p. 83.
47. Derrida, *OG,* p. 39.
48. Ibid., p. 43.

49. Ibid.
50. Ibid., p. 42.
51. Ibid., p. 45.
52. Derrida, *VP*, p. 107.
53. Ibid., p. 58.
54. Ibid., p. 70.
55. Ibid., p. 71.
56. Derrida, *OG*, pp. 30–31.
57. Ibid., p. 73.
58. See, in particular, Derrida's essay, "La Pharmacie de Platon," in *La Dissémination* (Paris: Editions du Seuil, 1972), p. 86. For the English version see, *Dissemination*, trans. Barbara Johnson (Chicago: University of Chicago Press, 1981).
59. Derrida, *VP*, p. 117.
60. Ibid., p. 75.
61. For more on this notion of the "two economies," for Derrida, see his essay, "De l'économie restreinte à l'économie générale—un hégélianisme sans réserve," in *L'Écriture et La Différance* (Paris: Editions du Seuil, 1967), translated by Alan Bass in *Writing and Difference* (Chicago: University of Chicago Press, 1978).
62. Derrida, *VP*, p. 5.
63. Ibid., p. 58.
64. Ibid., p. 62.
65. Ibid., p. 92. For further analysis of Derrida's relation to Husserl concerning the role of metaphysics in the latter's phenomenology, see Jean Catesson's article, "A Propos d'une pensée de l'intervalle," in *Revue de la Métaphysique et de la Morale*, no. 74 (1969), pp. 75–90.
66. Derrida, *VP*, p. 68.
67. Ibid., p. 32.
68. Derrida, *OG*, p. 56.
69. Ibid., p. 39.
70. Ibid., p. 72.
71. Ibid., p. 39.
72. Ibid., p. 58.
73. Ibid., p. 57.
74. Ibid. For more on Derrida's concern with writing, see Claude Perruchot's article entitled: "The Liberation of Writing," trans. Harriet Watts, in *Boston University Journal* (Fall 1974), pp. 36–44.
75. Derrida, *OG*, p. 62.
76. Ibid., p. 43.
77. Ibid., p. 52.
78. Derrida, *VP*, pp. 98–117.
79. Ibid., p. 5.
80. Ibid., p. 99.
81. Ibid., p. 113.
82. Ibid., p. 111.
83. Derrida, *OG*, p. 46. In "Political and Historical Ideas in Contemporary American 'Left' Criticism" (forthcoming in *Boundary 2*), Edward Said claims that "deconstruction attempts to master all other methods." The deconstruction of the "entire tradition" is hardly equivalent to the mastery or the domination of the same, we insist. Instead, deconstruction, we claim, is concerned

with the *limits* and *presuppositions* of this tradition and all its methods of analysis and interpretation, etc. Usurpation, in this context, cannot therefore be subsumed within Said's characterization of deconstruction as mastery, we suggest.

84. Derrida, *OG,* p. 46.

85. Ibid., p. 37.

86. Ibid., p. 92.

III. The Object of Deconstruction

1. Jacques Derrida, *Positions* (Paris: Editions de Minuit, 1972), p. 14, my translation.

2. Plato, "Parmenides," *Collected Dialogues of Plato,* ed. Edith Hamilton and Huntington Cairns, trans. Cooper et al. (Princeton: Princeton University Press, 1961), pp. 928–929, paragraphs 133–35.

3. Edmond Jabès, Interview with Maurice Partouche, *Le Monde,* August 2, 1981, p. ix.

4. Jacques Derrida, "Supplément du Copule," in *Marges de la Philosophie* (Paris: Editions de Minuit, 1972) p. 211; trans. Alan Bass, *Margins of Philosophy* (Chicago: University of Chicago Press, 1982).

5. Jacques Derrida, "Tympan," *MP,* p. ix.

6. See Lionel Abel's article, "Jacques Derrida: His 'Difference' with Metaphysics," *Salmagundi* (Winter 1974).

7. Jacques Derrida, *Of Grammatology,* (Baltimore: The Johns Hopkins University Press, 1974), p. 46.

8. Ibid., p. 3.

9. See, in particular, Plato's "Phaedrus," *CDP,* pp. 520–21 (275a,b):

> And so it is that you, by reason of your tender regard for the writing that is your offspring, have declared the very opposite of its true effect. If men learn this, it will implant forgetfulness in their souls; they will cease to exercise memory because they rely on that which is written, calling things to remembrance no longer from within themselves, but by means of external marks.

See also 275d,e; and 276a,b.

10. Derrida makes this claim with specific reference to Hegel's *Encyclopedia* and the *Aesthetics* in his article entitled "Le Puits et la Pyramide", *MP,* pp. 81–83. We have also explicated this notion in terms of Hegel's *Phenomenology of Spirit* in an article, "The Semiotics of Hegel and Nietzsche," *Carleton Journal of Philosophy* (Winter 1979).

11. See, in particular, Derrida's essay, "Ousia et Grammè: Note sur une Note de *Sein und Zeit,*" *MP.* This essay is an analysis of Heidegger's critique of Hegel in terms of a traditional, that is Aristotelian, notion of time.

12. Derrida, *OG,* p. 71.

13. Ibid., p. 283.

14. For more on Derrida's analysis of the signature and the proper name, see "Signature Evènement Contexte," *MP.*

15. Derrida, "La Mythologie Blanche," *MP,* p. 318, my translation.

16. See also Derrida's essay, "La Mythologie Blanche," *MP,* p. 304.

17. Derrida, *MP,* p. 319, my translation.

18. See, in particular, Husserl's *Logical Investigations,* Investigation II, concerning "Locke's Universal Triangle," where he refutes the claim made by

Locke concerning the prerequisite of a multiplicity of examples of the same thing in order to constitute its ideas as such as based on the principle of analogy. For Husserl, instead, the ideal unity is itself contained in each instance of a thing, and one need not find "another" in order to deduce it by analogy. This paper here, in order to be identifiable as such, already entails the idea of paper as such. We should recall that one of Derrida's earlier works, "Archaéologie du Frivole," which introduces Condillac's *Essai sur l'origine des Connaissances Humaines* (Paris: Editions Galilée, 1973) attempts a sympathetic reading of the same.

19. See also Heidegger's, *Identity and Difference,* trans. Joan Stambaugh (New York: Harper and Row, 1957). Derrida's notions of the relations of these terms draw heavily from Heidegger and, in particular, from this text.

20. Derrida, *P,* p. 77.

21. See, in particular, Derrida's essay, "Cogito et l'histoire de la folie," *ED,* pp. 51–99.

22. See Derrida's comments in *Positions,* pp. 77–81, where he further explicates this essential relation of the notion of history, as a concept, to the tradition of metaphysics as determining the notion of conceptuality as such.

23. Derrida, *OG,* p. 3.

24. Ibid., p. 10.

25. Ibid., p. 12.

26. See also Derrida's essay, "La Pharmacie de Platon," *D.*

27. Derrida, *OG,* p. 12.

28. Ibid.

29. See Derrida's analysis of the problem of presence in *La Voix et le Phénomène* (Paris: Presses Universitaires de France, 1967); in particular see Chapter 5: "Le Signe et le Clin d'Oeil," pp. 67–77.

30. Derrida, *OG,* p. 24.

31. Ibid., p. 26.

32. See also Derrida's essay, "Le Puits et la Pyramide," *MP.*

33. See also Derrida's essay, "La Pharmacie de Platon," *D,* p. 99:

> The configurative unity of these significations—the power of speech, the creation of being and life, the sun (which is also, as we shall see, the eye) the self-concealment—is conjugated in what could be called the history of the egg or the egg of history. The world came out of egg. More precisely . . . [my translation].

34. Derrida, *OG,* p. 26, pp. 103–105.

35. Derrida, *OG,* p. 26.

36. For further clarification of this notion, see Derrida's essay, "Différance," *MP.*

37. For Hegel's claims here, see in particular, the *Logic,* trans. William Wallace (Oxford: Clarendon Press, 1975), p. 31:

> Now language is the work of thought: and hence all that is expressed in language must be universal. What I mean or suppose is mine: it belongs to me—this particular individual. But language expresses nothing but universality; and so I cannot say what I merely mean.

For Derrida's concern with Husserl with respect to this issue, see the former's introductory essay in *L'Origine de la Géometrie,* trans. Jacques Derrida (Paris: Presses Universitaires de France, 1974), pp. 83–88, 90–92, 94, 96, 97, 103.

38. Derrida, *P,* p. 23.
39. Derrida, *OG,* p. 71: "Only infinite being can reduce the difference in presence. In that sense, the name of God, at least as it is pronounced within classical rationalism, is the name of indifference itself."
40. Derrida, *MP,* p. 321. For more on Derrida's concern with philosophy and literature in general, see his interview with Lucette Finas in *Quinzaine Littéraire,* 16–30 November 1972, in an article entitled "Jacques Derrida: Avoir l'Oreille de la Philosophie."
41. Derrida, *MP,* p. 323. Concerning the controversy between Derrida and Foucault on this issue, see E. M. Henning's article, "Foucault and Derrida: Archaeology and Deconstruction," *Stanford French Review* (Fall 1981): 247–64. For another perspective on this "debate," see Edward Said's article, "The Problem of Textuality: Two Exemplary Positions," *Critical Inquiry* (Summer 1978): 673–714.
42. Jacques Derrida, *La Carte Postale* (Paris: Aubier-Flammarion, 1980), pp. 240–41. We have discussed the possibilities of translating this passage with Derrida and, due to the multiplicities of levels of meanings involved here, have decided to abstain from the reduction of the same which any translation would necessarily invoke. For instance, *la langue* is not sufficiently translated as language, nor tongue, since both apply equally well. Also the Saussurian distinction between *langue* and *parole* is certainly implied here although unstated as such. In addition, the problem of the translation of *chez soi* and *le foyer* with respect to what Derrida calls burning. He situates his discourse here between various contexts or situations which are not reproducible or representable in the English language, or at least we could not perform the task. Where is the fire no longer able to burn? There is evidently no simple answer to such a question, and thus translatability itself is put into question; indeed the presupposed structure of translatability is therein revealed. For more on Derrida's position with respect to translation, see his text, *L'Oreille de l'Autre* ed. Claude Lévesque and Christie MacDonald (Montréal: VLB Editeur, 1982).
43. Jacques Derrida, "Les Fins de l'Homme," *MP,* p. 141. For further development of this problematic, see also the recent text, *Les Fins de l'Homme— A Partir du Travail de Jacques Derrida* (Paris: Editions Galilée, 1981). See in particular Derrida's essay, "D'Un Ton Apocalyptique adopté naguère en Philosophie." This text deals with a notion of textuality as structurally apocalyptic and the way in which this relates to the problem of the end of metaphysics, philosophy, and the notion of man therein determined.
44. See in addition Derrida's essay, "Tympan," in *MP.*
45. This is the title of a presentation which Derrida gave in Toronto at the University of Toronto, October 1979. The main issue here is an analysis of an essay by Blanchot, "La Folie du Jour," which concerns the double bind of constituting an account that would be comprehensible of something that is not reasonable and therefore intrinsically unaccountable. It is forthcoming as a publication by Derrida.
46. See in particular the works of J. L. Austin and J. R. Searle. For Derrida's response to this tradition of "ordinary language philosophy," see his essay, "Signature Event Context," *MP,* and also "Limited Inc a b c . . . ." in *Glyph* 2 (1979): 162. This latter essay is a response to Searle's criticism of Derrida which is to be found in *Glyph 1* (1979): 151 and is entitled, "Reiterating the Differences: A Reply to Derrida." For the most recent response by Searle to Derrida, see his review of Jonathan Culler's text, *On Deconstruction,* in *The New York Review of Books,* November 7, 1983, pp. 73–78. Searle's article is

entitled, "The World Turned Upside Down." Gayatri Spivak has recently ana-lyzed this "debate" which "never really took place" in her article, "Revolutions that have as yet no Model: Derrida's Limited Inc," in *Diacritics* (December 1980). For more on this issue as a whole, see Stanley Fish's article, "With the Compliments of the Author: Reflections on Austin and Derrida," *Critical In-quiry* (Summer 1982): 693–721. And for another perspective, see Jonathan Culler's article, "Convention and Meaning: Derrida and Austin," *New Literary History* (1981): 15–30. In addition, see Edmond Wright's article, "Derrida, Searle, Contexts, Games, Riddles," *New Literary History,* (1982): 463–77.

47. Derrida, *P,* p. 29.

48. See also Heidegger's text, *What is Philosophy?* (New Haven: College and University Press, 1956). Derrida draws heavily from this text with respect to these issues.

49. See Derrida's essay, "Speech and Writing According to Hegel," trans. Alphonso Lingis, in *Man and World* 11 (1978): 116–127.

50. The main source for Saussure's position here is *Course in General Lin-guistics,* trans. W. Baskin (New York: Fontana/Collins, 1959). See in particular Part I—"General Principles: The Nature of the Linguistic Sign," p. 65. Der-rida's treatment of Saussure can be found in *OG,* pp. 27–73.

51. Derrida, *MP,* p. xxiv.

52. Derrida, *P,* p. 58–59. For a more detailed account of this issue, see Derrida's essay, "La Pharmacie de Platon," *D.*

53. Derrida, *MP,* p. 295.

54. Ibid., p. xiv.

55. Ibid.

56. Ibid., p. i.

57. Ibid., p. ii.

58. Jacques Derrida, *La Voix et le Phénomène* (Paris: Presses Universitaires de France, 1967), p. 57.

59. Derrida, *MP,* p. xiv.

60. Derrida develops this relation of the logos to the phallus with respect to Lacan, Freud, and Nietzsche in his text, *Eperons: Les Styles de Nietzsche,* trans. Barbara Harlow (Chicago: University of Chicago Press, 1978).

61. Derrida, *MP,* p. 254.

62. See Derrida's text *ESN.*

63. See also Husserl's *Crisis of European Sciences,* trans. David Carr (Evanston: Northwestern University Press, 1970), pp. 23–60.

64. See in particular Plato's "Meno," *CDP,* pp. 353–85.

65. See also Derrida's essay, "Ousia et Grammè," *MP,* p. 76:

> Presence is thus the trace of the trace, the trace of the effacement of the trace. Such is for us the text of metaphysics, such is for us the language that we speak. It is to this single condition that metaphysics and our language can make a sign towards their proper transgression [my trans-lation].

66. Derrida, *OG,* p. 143.

67. See Husserl's *The Phenomenology of Internal Time Consciousness,* trans. J. S. Churchill (Bloomington: Indiana University Press, 1964). In par-ticular, see "The Temporally Constitutive Flux as Absolute Subjectivity," sec-tion 36.

68. Derrida, *MP,* p. 149.

69. Ibid., p. 73.
70. Ibid., p. 65.
71. Ibid., p. 64.
72. Ibid., p. 202.
73. Ibid., p. 206.
74. See also Derrida's crucial essay on this, "La Mythologie Blanche," *MP,* pp. 247–324.
75. Ibid., p. 303.
76. Ibid., p. 299.
77. Ibid., p. 269.
78. Ibid., p. 211.
79. Ibid., p. 324.
80. Jacques Derrida, "De l'Economie Restreinte à l'Economie Générale— un Hégélianisme sans reserve," *ED,* p. 369. The original citation reads: "Il [Hegel] ne sut pas dans quelle mésure il avait raison."

4. The Post-Scriptum of Beginning

1. Jacques Derrida, "Ellipse," *l'Ecriture et la Différence* (Paris: Editions du Seuil, 1967), p. 436; trans. Alan Bass, *Writing and Difference* (Chicago: University of Chicago Press, 1978), p. 300.
2. See in particular Derrida's essays, "Ellipse," *ED;* "Ousia et Grammè," *MP,* p. 60; "La Mythologie Blanche," *MP,* pp. 315, 319, 320, 324.
3. Jacques Derrida, "Force et Signification," *ED,* my translation.
4. Ibid., pp. 9–49.
5. Ibid., p. 44.
6. Ibid., p. 17.
7. Ibid.
8. Ibid., p. 46.
9. Ibid.
10. Friedrich Nietzsche, *Twilight of the Idols* (Harmondsworth: Penguin Books, 1968), p. 73, trans. R. J. Hollingdale.
11. Jacques Derrida, "Introduction" to *l'Origine de la Géometrie* by Edmond Husserl (Paris: Presses Universitaires de France, 1974), pp. 104–106.
12. Derrida, *ED,* pp. 9–49.
13. Jacques Derrida, *Of Grammatology,* trans. G. C. Spivak (Baltimore: Johns Hopkins University Press, 1974), p. 112.
14. Ibid. p. 110.
15. G. W. F. Hegel, *Logic,* trans. William Wallace (Oxford: Clarendon Press, 1975), p. 31.
16. Derrida, *OG,* p. 93.
17. Ibid.
18. Derrida, *ED,* p. 16.
19. Ibid.
20. Ibid.
21. Immanuel Kant, *Critique of Pure Reason,* trans. Norman Kemp Smith (New York: St. Martin's Press, 1965), p. 83.
22. Derrida, *OG,* p. 184.
23. Ibid.
24. Ibid., pp. 186–87.
25. Ibid., pp. 6–7.
26. Ibid., p. 7.

27. Ibid., p. 9.
28. Ibid.
29. Ibid., p. 93.
30. Ibid., p. 281.
31. See in particular the following texts by Derrida: *La Voix et le Phénomène* (Paris: Presses Universitaires de France, 1967) concerning Husserl; and, concerning Heidegger, see: "Ousia et Grammè," "Les Fins de l'Homme" in *MP*, and in *OG* see pp. 12, 69; and see *Positions* (Paris: Editions de Minuit, 1967).
32. Derrida, *ED*, p. 21.
33. Ibid., p. 49.

5. The Scope of Writing

1. Jacques Derrida *OG*, p. 10.
2. Ibid., p. 61. For more on this notion of arche-writing in Derrida see C. Singevin's article, "Pensée, Language, Ecriture et Être" in *Revue Philosophique* 162 (1972): 129–248.
3. Derrida, *OG*, p. 27.
4. Ibid., p. 70.
5. Ibid., p. 290.
6. Derrida, *P*, p. 17.
7. Derrida, *ED*, p. 22.
8. Ibid., p. 49.
9. Martin Heidegger, "The Anaximander Fragment," in *Early Greek Thinking*, trans. David F. Krell and F. A. Capuzzi (New York: Harper and Row, 1975), p. 13.
10. Derrida, *OG*, pp. 139–40.
11. Ibid., p. 127.
12. Ibid., p. 66.
13. Ibid., pp. 61–62.
14. Edmund Husserl, *The Phenomenology of Internal Time Consciousness*, trans. James S. Churchill (Bloomington: Indiana University Press, 1964), p. 53.
15. Ibid., p. 100.
16. Derrida, *OG*, p. 46. For an analysis of Derrida's relation to Husserl on this issue, see Christopher McCann's article, "Jacques Derrida's Theory of Writing and the Concept of the Trace," *Journal of the British Society of Phenomenology* 3, no. 2 (May 1972): 197–200.
17. .Derrida, *OG*, p. 47.
18. Ibid., p. 61.
19. Ibid., p. 242. Derrida says here that "the concept of animality . . . in its specific functions must locate a moment of life which knows nothing of symbol, substitution, lack of supplementary addition, etc., everything in fact whose appearance and play I wish to describe here. A life that has not yet broached the play of supplementarity and which at the same time has not yet let itself be violated by it: a life without *différance* and without articulation."
20. Derrida, "La Différance," *MP*, p. 22, my translation.
21. See, in particular, Derrida's work on Husserl in *VP*, pp. 72–76, concerning the relation of perception to non-perception.
22. Derrida, *OG*, p. 68.
23. This article was first published in *Textes pour Emmanuel Levinas*, ed. François Laruelle (Paris: Editions du Seuil, 1981).

24. Derrida, *OG,* p. 70. For Levinas's response to Derrida's early article, see "Tout Autrement," *L'Arc* 54 (1973): 33–37.
25. See in particular Levinas's major work: *Totality and Infinity,* trans. Alphonso Lingis (Pittsburgh: Duquesne University Press, 1969).
26. Emmanuel Levinas, "La Trace de l'Autre," *Tijdschrift voor Filosophie,* no. 3, (September 1963), p. 609.
27. Ibid., p. 610.
28. See in particular the following essays by Derrida: "Violence et Métaphysique," *ED,* and "En Ce Moment Même en Cet Ouvrage Me Voici," *TPEL.*
29. Levinas, *TVP,* p. 611.
30. Ibid., p. 615.
31. Ibid., p. 619.
32. Ibid., p. 620.
33. Ibid., p. 623.
34. Derrida, *OG,* p. 22. For Derrida's most recent work on Freud concerning this issue, see *La Carte Postale* (Paris: Aubier-Flammarion, 1980) pp. 277–437. For several good analyses of this work, including Derrida's responses and comments on each, see *Affranchissement—du transfert et de la lettre* (Paris: Editions Confrontation, 1982).
35. Derrida, "Freud et la scène de l'écriture," *ED,* p. 200, my translation.
36. Ibid., p. 201.
37. Ibid., p. 202.
38. Sigmund Freud, *The Interpretation of Dreams,* trans. James Strachey (New York: Basic Books, 1965), p. 386.
39. Derrida, *ED,* p. 211. For more of Derrida's treatment of this issue as it relates to the work of Jacques Lacan, see the former's essay, "Le Facteur de la Verité," *LCP,* pp. 439–524, and *Eperons: Les Styles de Nietzsche* (Chicago: University of Chicago Press, 1978). For an analysis of the differences between Lacan and Derrida, see Norman N. Holland's article, "Re-covering the Purloined Letter," *The Reader in the Text,* ed. Susan R. Suleiman and Inge Crosman (Princeton: Princeton University Press, 1980), pp. 350–70.
40. Derrida, *ED,* p. 227.
41. Ibid., p. 27.
42. See, in particular Derrida's work on Plato concerning this issue of the double nature of writing in "La Pharmacie de Platon," *Dissémination* (Paris: Editions du Seuil, 1972).
43. See Heidegger's *Lettre sur l'Humanisme,* trans. Roger Munier (Paris: Aubier, Editions Montaigne, 1964). For Derrida's analysis of this, see his article, "Les Fins de l'Homme," in *MP.*
44. Derrida, *P,* p. 40.
45. Mikel Dufrenne, *Le Poétique* (Paris: Presses Universitaires de France, 1973). See in particular the essay, "Pour une Philosophie non-Thélogique," pp. 7–57.
46. Martin Heidegger—*LSH,* p. 78.
47. Martin Heidegger, *What is Called Thinking?,* trans. J. G. Gray (New York: Harper and Row, 1968).
48. Heidegger, *LSH,* p. 77.
49. Derrida, *OG,* p. 244.
50. Concerning the significance of the metaphors of the sun and light within the history of philosophy, see in particular Derrida's essay, "La Mythologie Blanche," *MP.*

51. Derrida, "Les Fins de l'Homme," *MP*, p. 156.
52. Ibid., p. 9.
53. Ibid., p. 7.
54. Ibid., p. 18.
55. Edmund Husserl, *Cartesian Meditations,* trans. Dorion Cairns (The Hague: Martinus Nijhoff, 1973), p. 106.
56. Derrida, *IOG*, p. 11.
57. Husserl, *CM*, p. 108.
58. Ibid., p. 107.
59. See Jean-Paul Sartre's *L'Être et le Néant* (Paris: Gallimard, 1943).
60. See Edmund Husserl's *Crisis of the Human Sciences,* trans. David Carr (Evanston: Northwestern University Press, 1970).
61. Derrida, *VP,* p. 104.
62. Plato, "The Phaedrus", *CDP,* p. 521.
63. See in particular Plato's *Laws, CDP,* p. 1446. See also Derrida's *OG,* p. 292.
64. Derrida, *VP,* p. 108.
65. Derrida, *OG,* pp. 97–268.
66. Derrida, *OG,* p. 143. For more on Derrida's current position on Nietzsche, see the recently published text, *L'Oreille de l'Autre* (Montreal: VLB Editeur, 1982), pp. 11–125. This text is being translated and will appear in the near future as *The Ear of the Other* (New York: Schoken Press).
67. Friedrich Nietzsche, "Thus Spake Zarathustra," in *The Portable Nietzsche,* trans. Walter Kaufman (Harmondsworth: Penguin Books, 1976), p. 398.
68. Derrida, *OG,* p. 19.
69. Ibid.
70. Derrida, *ELSN,* pp. 38, 40, 50, 54.
71. See Derrida's own characterization of deconstruction as a strategy involving the borrowing of terms and the double structure of eastration and mimesis in *Positions,* p. 112. In addition, see *OG* on the borrowing process as a form of parasitic habitation: pp. 24 and 60. Here he is concerned with the "exhaustion" of the concept borrowed as strategically necessary for the operation of deconstruction.
72. Nietzsche, *PN,* p. 32.
73. Derrida, *OG,* p. 219. Here Derrida claims: "Languages are sown. And they themselves pass from one season to another." This section deals in particular with Rousseau's essay, *The Essay on The Origin of Languages,* trans. John H. Moran and Alexander Gode (New York: Fredrick Ungar Publishing Co., 1966).
74. Derrida, *OG,* p. 143.

6. The Structure of *Différance*

1. Jacques Derrida, *OG,*. 163.
2. Derrida, *P,* p. 17.
3. Ibid., p. 39.
4. Derrida, *OG,* p. 67.
5. See, in particular, Herbert Marcuse's *Eros and Civilization* (Boston: Beacon Press, 1955), pp. 11–20. Here he deals with the Freudian notion of the origin of violence as the social repression of instinctual urges which are not considered acceptable or normal behavior within society as such.

6. In a discussion with Derrida (November 1981) concerning this issue and his explicit claim in *Positions* about wanting to "destroy the Aufhebung," he admitted that "the Aufhebung as such is indestructible" but, nevertheless, that it can be "interrupted" so that it never returns full circle. Indeed, it does not in fact anyway, according to Derrida's textual studies as he exposes this fallacy with his deconstructive practices.

7. See, in particular, Derrida's essay, "De l'Economie Restreinte à l'Economie Générale—un Hégélianisme sans Réserve," *ED*, p. 367.

8. Derrida—*MP*, p. 21.

9. See H. S. Harris's text, *Towards the Sunlight—Hegel's Development* (Oxford: Clarendon Press, 1972). See also Derrida's analysis of the metaphysics of light, sun, and vision, which he claims plays an *orienting* role in the history of philosophy in his essay, "La Mythologie Blanche," *MP.*

10. See Derrida's essay, "La Pharmacie de Platon," in *D*, pp. 84–95.

11. Derrida, *MP*, p. 27. For more on Derrida's notion of *différance* as an economy, see Claude Levesque's text, *L'Etrangeté du Texte* (Montreal: VLB Editeur, 1976), pp. 117–200.

12. Derrida, *MP*, p. 28. For a brief summary of Derrida's notion of *différance* as it relates to other contemporary work in France, see Annette Lavers's article, "Man, Meaning and Subject, A Current Reappraisal," *Journal for the British Society for Phenomenology* 1 (1970), pp. 44–49.

13. Derrida, *MP*, p. 22.

14. Ibid., p. 304.

15. Derrida, *OG*,. 266.

16. Ibid., p. 121.

17. Ibid., p. 163.

18. Ibid., pp. 6–26, 86.

19 .Ibid., p. 163.

20. Ibid., p. 144.

21. Ibid., p. 126.

22. Ibid., p. 145.

23. Ibid., p. 150.

24. Derrida, *VP*, p. 117.

25. Derrida, *OG*, pp. 147–48.

26. Ibid., p. 154.

27. Ibid.

28. See, in particular, Derrida's essay, "Living On: Border Lines," *Deconstruction and Criticism* (New York: The Seabury Press, 1979), pp. 77, 100–101, 154–55.

29. Derrida, *OG*, p. 246.

30. Ibid., p. 147.

31. Ibid.

32. Ibid., p. 174.

33. See, for instance, Roger Poole's article, "Structuralism Side-Tracked," *New Black Friar*, June 1969; Emmanuel Levinas's article, "Tout Autrement," *L'Arc* 54; Michel Foucault's article, "Mon Corps, Ce Papier, Ce Feu," *L'Histoire de la Folie* (Paris: Gallimard, 1972); Mikel Dufrenne's essay, "Pour une Philosophie Non-Thélogique," *Le Poétique;* and perhaps the most critical essay by John R. Searle, "Reiterating the Differences: A Reply to Derrida," *Glyph 1*,1977.

34. Derrida, *OG*, p. 266.

35. See, in particular, Derrida's essay, "La Structure, le signe et le jeu dans la discours des sciences humaines," ED, pp. 409–428.
36. Martin Heidegger, *Being and Time,* trans. John Macquarrie and Edward Robinson (New York: Harper and Row, 1962), p. 279.
37. Sigmund Freud, *Beyond the Pleasure Principle,* trans. James Strachey (New York: Norton and Co., 1961), p. 29.
38. Ibid., p. 25.
39. Derrida, *OG,* p. 25. For an analysis of the role of death in language for Derrida as compared to Wittgenstein, see Marjorie Grene's article, "Life, Death and Language—Some Thoughts on Wittgenstein and Derrida," *Partisan Review* (1976): 266–79. For another comparison of Derrida and Wittgenstein, see David B. Allison's article, "Derrida and Wittgenstein: Playing the Game," *Research in Phenomenology,* no. 8, 1978, pp. 93–109.
40. Derrida, *OG,* p. 312.
41. Heidegger, *BT,* p. 289.
42. Ibid., p. 287.
43. Ibid., p. 294.
44. Ibid., p. 297.
45. Derrida, *OG,* p. 183. For more on Derrida's relation to Heidegger, see David Wood's article, "Derrida and the Paradoxes of Reflection," *Journal of the British Society for Phenomenology,* 11, no. 3 (1980), pp. 225–37. See also Robert D. Cummings's article, "The Odd Couple: Derrida and Heidegger," *The Review of Metaphysics* 34, no. 3, (Mar. 1981): 487–521. For another article by David Wood on the question of style as it relates to Derrida and Heidegger, see "Style and Strategy at the Limits of Philosophy: Heidegger and Derrida," *The Monist* 63, no. 4 (October 1980): 494–511.
46. Derrida, *OG,* p. 69.
47. Freud, *BPP,* p. 30.
48. Jacques Derrida, *La Carte Postale—de Socrate à Freud et au-délà* (Paris: Aubier-Flammarion, 1980). See, in particular, his essay, "Spéculer sur 'Freud'," pp. 277–437.
49. Derrida, *OG,* p. 209.
50. Ibid., p. 66.
51. Ibid., p. 155.
52. Ibid., pp. 290–91. Derrida's closure of the possibility of a "new transcendental aesthetic" with respect to the notion of *différance* concludes in the following manner:

"Nevertheless in spite of the Kantian revolution and the discovery of pure sensibility (free from all reference to sensation) to the extent that the concept of sensibility (as pure passivity) and its contrary will continue to dominate such questions, they will remain imprisoned in metaphysics. If the space-time that we inhabit is *a priori* the space-time of the trace, there is neither pure activity nor pure passivity." [P. 291]

For more on this issue of the need for transcendental questions, according to Derrida, see, "Philosophie et Communication," in *Actes du Congrès de l'Association des Societés de Philosophie de langue Français* (Montreal: Editions Montmorency, 1973). In particular, see Derrida's discussion with Paul Ricoeur (pp. 393–431).
53. Kant, *CPR,* p. 67.
54. See, in particular, Kant's *Critique of Judgment,* trans. J. H. Bernard

(New York: Hafner Press, 1974). The section, "Analytic of the Sublime" (pp. 82–181), is particularly relevant here.

55. Derrida, *OG,* p. 290.
56. Ibid.
57. See the Appendix in Husserl's *Crisis,* p. 385, by Eugen Fink.
58. Derrida, *OG,* p. 65.
59. Derrida, *P,* p. 38.
60. Derrida, *ED,* pp. 409–28.
61. Derrida, *OG,* p. 290.
62. Ibid., p. 232.
63. Derrida, *ED,* p. 436.

BIBLIOGRAPHY

By Jacques Derrida

Books

1962 Translation and Introduction to Edmund Husserl, *L'Origine de la geometrie*. Paris: Presses Universitaires de France. 2nd ed., 1974. ET: *Edmund Husserl's Origin of Geometry: An Introduction*. Tr. John P. Leavey. New York: Nicolas Hays, 1977.

1967 *De la Grammatologie*. Paris: Minuit. ET: *Of Grammatology*. Tr. Gayatri Chakravorty Spivak. Baltimore: The Johns Hopkins University Press, 1967. Ch. 2 of the ET, "Linguistics and Grammatology," was published in *Sub-Stance*, no. 10 (1974), 127–81.

La Voix et le phénomène: Introduction au problème du signe dans la phénomenologie de Husserl. Paris: Presses Universitaires de France. 2nd ed., 1972. ET: *Speech and Phenomena: And Other Essays on Husserl's Theory of Signs*. Tr. David B. Allison. Evanston: Northwestern University Press, 1973.

L'Ecriture et la différence. Paris: Seuil. ET by Alan Bass, Chicago: University of Chicago Press, 1978.

1972 *La Dissemination*. Paris: Seuil.

Marges de la philosophie. Paris: Minuit.

Positions. Paris: Minuit.

1974 *Glas*. Paris: Editions Galilée.

1976 *L'Archéologie du frivole: Lire Condillac*. Paris: Denoel/Gonthier. Rpt. of 1973 Introduction to Condillac's *Essai sur l'origine des connaissances humanies* (Paris: Editions Galilée).

Eperons: Les Styles de Nietzsche. Venice: Corbo e Fiore. Rpt. and tr. into English, Italian, and German of the 1972 "La Question du style." Also: Chicago: University of Chicago Press, 1978. Tr. Barbara Harlow.

1978 *La Vérité en Peinture*. Paris: Flammarion.

1980 *La Carte Postale*. Paris: Flammarion.

1982 *Affranchissement du transfert et de la lettre*. Paris: Editions Confrontation.

L'Oreille de l'autre. Montreal: VLB Editeur, 1982.

Articles

1959 "'Genèse et structure' et la phénomènologie." In *Entretiens sur les notions de genèse et de structure*. Ed. Maurice de Gandillac et al. Paris: Mouton, 1965, pp. 243–60. Discussion, pp. 261–68. Rpt. in *L'Ecriture*.

1963 "Force et signification." *Critique* 19, no. 193 (June 1963), pp. 483–99, and no. 194 (July 1963), pp. 619–36. Rpt. in *L'Ecriture*.

"Cogito et histoire de la folie." *Revue de Métaphysique et de Morale* 68 (1963): 460–94. Rtp. in *L'Ecriture*.

1964   "A propos de *Cogito et histoire de la folie*." *Revue de Métaphysique et de Morale* 69 (1964): 116–19.
"Edmond Jabès et la question du livre." *Critique* 20. no. 201 (February 1964): 99–115. Rtp. in *L'Ecriture*.
"Violence et métaphysique, essai sur la pensée d'Emmanuel Levinas." Revue de Métaphysique et de Morale 69 (1964): 322–45 and 425–73. Rpt. in *L'Ecriture*.

1965   "La Parole soufflée." *Tel Quel*, no. 20 (Winter 1965), pp. 41–67. Rpt. in *L'Ecriture*.
"De la Grammatologie." *Critique* 21, no. 233 (December 1965): 1016–42, and 22, no. 224 (January 1966): 23–53. Rpt. and adapted in *De la Grammatologie*.

1966   "Le Théâtre de la cruauté et la clôture de la représentation." *Critique* 22, no. 230 (July 1966): 595–618. Rpt. in L'Ecriture.
"La Structure, le signe et le jeu dans le discours des sciences humaines." In *L'Ecriture*. ET: "Structure, Sign, and Play in the Discourse of the Human Sciences." In *The Structuralist Controversy: The Languages of Criticism and the Sciences of Man*. Ed. Richard Macksey and Eugenio Donato. Baltimore: The Johns Hopkins University Press, 1972 (1970), pp. 247–65. Discussion, pp. 265–70.
"Freud et la scéne de l'écriture." *Tel Quel*, no. 26 (Summer 1966), pp. 10–41. Rpt. in *L'Ecriture*. ET: "Freud and the Scene of Writing." Tr. Jeffrey Mehlman. *Yale French Studies*, no. 48: *French Freud: Structural Studies in Psychoanalysis* (1972), pp. 74–117.
"Nature, culture, écriture (de Levi-Strauss à Rousseau)." *Les Cahiers pour l'analyse*, no. 4 (1966), pp. 1–45.

1967   "De l'Economie restreinte à l'économie générale: un hégélianisme sans réserve." *L'Arc: Georges Bataille*, no. 32 (May 1967), pp. 24–44, Rpt. in *L'Ecriture*, ET: "From Restricted to General Economy: A Hegelianism Without Reserve." Tr. Alan Bass. In *Semiotext(e)* 2, no. 2 (1976): 25–55. "La Forme et le vouloire-dire: note sur la phénomènologie du langage." *Revue Internationale de Philosophie* 21, Fasc. 3, no. 81 (1967): 277–99. Rpt. in *Marges*. ET: *Speech and Phenomena*, pp. 107–28.
"La Linguistique de Rousseau." *Revue Internationale de Philosophie* 21, Fasc. 4, no. 82 (1967): 443–62. Slightly changed in *Marges* as "Le Cercle linguistique de Geneve." "Implications: entretien avec Henri Ronse." *Les Lettres Francaises*, no. 1211 (6–12 December 1967), pp. 12–13. Rpt. in *Positions*.

1968   "Le Puits et la pyramide: introduction à la sémilologie de Hegel." *Hegel et la pensée moderne* (Seminaire sur Hegel dirigé par Jean Hyppolite au College de France, 1967–68). Ed. Jacques d'Hondt. Paris: Presses Universitaires de France, 1970, pp. 27–84. Rpt. in *Marges*.
"La Pharmacie de Platon." *Tel Quel*, no. 32 (Winter 1968), pp. 3–48, and no. 33 (Spring 1968), p. 1859. Rpt. in *Dissemination*.
"OUSIA et GRAMMÈ: note sur une note de *Sein und Zeit. L'Endurance de la pensée*. Ed. Marcel Jouhandeau. Paris: Plon, 1968, pp. 219–66. Rpt. in *Marges*. ET: "'*Ousia and Grammè:* A Note to a Footnote in *Being and Time*." Tr. Edward S. Casey. In *Phenomenology in Perspective*. Ed. F. Joseph Smith. The Hague: Nijhoff, 1970, pp. 54–93.

"Sémiologie et grammatologie: entretien avec Julia Kristeva." *Information sur les sciences sociales* 7, no. 3 (June 1968): 135–48. Rpt. in *Positions.* Also rpt. in Julia Kristeva, Josette Rey-Devobe, and Donna Jean Unicker, eds. *Essays in Semiotics: Essais de sémiotique.* (Approaches to Semiotics 4) The Hague and Paris: Mouton, 1971, pp. 11–27.

"La 'Différance.'" *Bulletin de la Société Francaise de Philosophie* 62, no. 3 (July–September 1968): 73–101. Discussion. pp. 101–120. Rpt. in *Marges.* Also rpt. in *Theorie d'ensemble.* Paris: Seuil, 1968, pp. 41–66. ET: *Speech and Phenomena,* pp. 129–60.

"The Ends of Man." *Philosophy and Phenomenological Research* 30, no. 1 (1969): 31–57. Tr. Edouard Morot-Sir, Wesley C. Puisol, Hubert L. Dreyfus, and Barbara Reid. Rpt. in *Marges.*

1969   "La Dissémination." *Critique* 25, no. 261 (February 1969): 99–139, and no. 262 (March 1969): 215–49. Rpt. in *Dissémination.*

1970   "D'un Texte à l'écart." *Les Temps Modernes* 25, no. 284 (March 1970): 1545–52.

"La Double Séance." *Tel Quel,* no. 41 (Spring 1970), pp. 3–43, and no. 42 (Summer 1970), pp. 3–45. Rpt. in *Dissémination.*

1971   "La Mythologie blanche (la métaphore dans le texte philosophique)." *Poétique,* no. 5 (1971), pp. 1–52. Rpt. in *Marges.* ET: "White Mythology: Metaphor in the Text of Philosophy." Tr. F.C.T. Moore. *New Literary History* 6, No. 1 (Autumn 1974): 5–74.

"Signature, événement, contexte." *La Communication II,* Actes du XVᵉ Congrès de l'Association des Sociétés de Philosophie de Langue Française. Université de Montréal. Montréal: Editions Montmorency, 1973, pp. 49–76. Discussion, pp. 393–431. Rpt. in *Marges.* ET: "Signature Event Context." Tr. Samuel Weber and Jeffrey Mehlman. In *Glyph: Johns Hopkins Textual Studies,* Vol. 1 (Baltimore, 1977), pp. 172–97.

"Positions: entretien avec Jean Louis Houdebine et Guy Scarpetta." *Promesse,* nos. 30–31 (Autumn and Winter 1971), pp. 5–62. Rpt. in *Positions.* ET: *"Positions." Diacritics* 2, no. 4 (Winter 1972): 35–43, and 3, No. 1 (Spring 1973): 33–59.

"Les Sources de Valéry: Qual, Quelle." *MLN* 87, no. 4 (May 1972): 563–99. Rpt. in *Marges* as "Qual, Quelle: les sources de Valéry."

"Le Supplément de copule: la philosophie devant la linguistique." *Langages* 24 (December 1971): 14–39, ET: "The Copula Supplement." Tr. David B. Allison. In *Dialogues in Phenomenology.* Ed. Don Ihde and Richard M. Zaner. The Hague: Nijhoff, 1975, pp. 7–48. Also: "The Supplement of Copula: Philosophy *Before* Linguistics." Tr. James Creech and Josue Harari. *The Georgia Review* 30 (1976): 527–64. This translation is to be rpt. in the forthcoming *Textual Strategies: Criticism in the Wake of Structuralism,* ed. Josue Harari.

1972   "Tympan." May 1972. In *Marges.*

"La Question du style." *Nietzsche aujourd'hui?* I: *Intensités.* Paris: Union Générale d'Editions, 1973, pp. 235–87. Discussion, pp. 288–99. Rpt. of a Modified Version in French and *ET* by Barbara Harlow in *Epérons.* Excerpts of another *ET* by Reuben Berezdivin published in *The New Nietzsche: Contemporary Styles of Interpretation,* ed. David B. Allison. New York: Dell Publishing, 1977, pp. 176–89.

"Avoir l'oreille de la philosophie." *La Quinzaine Littéraire,* no. 152.

(30 November 1972), pp. 213–16. This interview with Lucette Finas is rpt. in Lucette Finas et al., *Ecarts: Quatre essais à propos de Jacques Derrida*. Paris: Fayard, 1973, pp. 303–12.

"Hors livre." In *Dissémination.*

1973   "Glas.: L'Arc: *Jacques Derrida*, no. 54 (1973), pp. 4–15. Excerpts of this appeared in *La Quinzaine Littéraire*, no. 172 (1973), pp. 23–36.

"L'Archéologie du frivole." In Condillac, *Essai sur l'origine des connaissances humaines*. Ed. Charles Porset. Paris: Editions Galilée, 1973, pp. 9–95. Rpt. under separate cover as *L'Archéologie du frivole: Lire Condillac.*

1974   "Mallarmé." In *Tableau de la littérature française: DeMadame Stael à Rimbaud*. Paris: Gallimard, 1974, pp. 368–79.

"Le parergon." *Digraphe*, no. 2 (1974), pp. 21–57.

"Le Sans de la coupure pure (Le parergon II)," *Digraphe*, no. 3, (1974), pp. 5–31.

1975   "Economimesis." In Sylviane Agacinski, Jacques Derrida et al. *Mimesis des articulations*. Paris: Aubier-Flammarion, 1975, pp. 55–93.

"Le Facteur de la vérité," *Poétique*, no. 21 (1975), pp.96–147. ET: "The Purveyor of Truth." Tr. Willis Domingo, James Hulbert, Moshe Ron, and Marie-Rose Logan. In *Yale French Studies*, no. 52: *Graphesis: Perspectives in Literature and Philosophy* (1975), pp. 31–113.

"+ R (par dessus le marché)." In *Derrière le Miroir*, No. 214, (May 1975) (Paris: Maeght Editeur), pp. 1–23.

"Signéponge." In *Francis Ponge*. Colloque de Cerisy. Paris: Union Generale d'Editions, 1977, pp. 115–44. Discussion, pp. 145–51.

"Entre Crochets." *Digraphe*, no. 8 (April 1976), pp. 97–114.

"Ja, ou le faux-bond." *Digraphe*, no. 11 (March 1977), pp. 83–121. This is the second part of an interview with Derrida. The first part is "Entre Crochets."

"Pour la philosophie." *La Nouvelle Critique*, no. 84 (1975), pp. 25–29. Rpt. as "Response a *La Nouvelle Critique*." In *Qui a peur de la philosophie?* Groupe de Recherches sur l'Enseignment Philosophique (GREPH). Paris: Flammarion, 1977, pp. 451–58.

Response to Questions on the Avant-Garde. *Digraphe*, no. 6 (October 1975), pp. 152–53.

"La Philosophie et ses classes." In Qui a peur de la philosophie. GREPH. Paris: Flammarion, 1977, pp. 445–50. An extract of this. "La Philosophie refoulée" was published in *Le Monde de l'Education*, No. 4 (1975), pp. 14–15.

1976   "Pas I." *Gramma: Lire Blanchot 1*, nos. 3–4 (1976), pp. 111–215.

"Signéponge." *Digraphe*, no. 8 (April 1976), pp. 17–39. This is a different fragment from the identically titled one listed under 1975. Both are extracts from a work now published as *Signéponge/Signsponge*. Tr. Richard Rand. New York: Columbia University Press, 1984.

"Où commence et comment finit un corps enseignant." In *Politiques de la philosophie*. Ed. Dominique Grisoni. Paris: Bernard Grasset, 1976, pp. 55–97.

"Où sont les chasseurs de sorcières?" *Le Monde*, 1 July 1976.

"Fors: Les mots anglés de Nicolas Abraham et Maria Torok." Preface to Nicolas Abraham and Maria Torok. *Verbier de l'Homme aux Loups: Cryptonymie*. Paris: Aubier-Flammarion. 1976, pp. 7–73. ET: "FORS:

The English Words of Nicolas Abraham and Maria Torok." Tr. Barbara Johnson. *The Georgia Review* 31, no. 1 (Spring 1977), pp. 64–116.

1977 "L'Age de Hegel." In *Qui a peur de la philosophie?* GREPH. Paris: Flammarion, 1977, pp. 73–107

"Scribble." Preface to Warburton. *Essai sur les hieroglyphes.* Paris: Aubier-Flammarion. To appear Fall 1977.

1979 "Living On." In *Deconstruction and Criticism.* New York: Seabury Press, 1979, pp. 75–176.

1980 "celle comme pas un." Preface to *L'Enfant Au Chien-Assis.* Jos Joliet, Galilée, 1980.

1980 "The Conflict of the Faculties." Unpublished; for Conference at Columbia University, New York, May 1980 (on Kant).

"The Law of Genre." *Critical Inquiry,* no. 1 (Autumn 1980): 55–81. Tr. Avital Ronell.

1981 "Téléphathie." *Furor* 2 (February 1981): 3–41.

"Les Morts de Roland Barthes." *Poétique* 47 (September 1981): 269–92.

"Les Tours de Babel." Unpublished text (on Benjamin).

"D'un ton apocalyptique adopté naguère en philosophie." In *Les Fins de L'Homme.* Paris: Galilee, 1981, pp. 445–86.

"Geschlecht—différence sexuelle, différence ontologique." *Research in Phenomenology,* Vol 13, 1983, pp. 68–84.

"The T-I-T-L-E-E-R." *Substance,* no. 31 (1981), pp. 5–22. Tr. Tom Conley.

1982 "Comment Juger Jean-Francois Lyotard." Colloque à Céricy, 1982 (on Lyotard). To be published.

1984 "Mes Chances/My Chances." In *Taking Chances.* Ed. Joseph Smith and William Kerrigan. Baltimore: Johns Hopkins University Press, 1984. Unpublished text, for Conference on Psychoanalysis, Washington, D.C., October 1982.

On Jacques Derrida

Books

The special volume of *L'arc: Jacques Derrida,* no. 54 (1973) will be referred to as *L'Arc.*

The special section of *Les Lettres Françaises, Grand Hebdomadaire Littéraire, Artistique et Politique,* no. 1429 (29 March 1972), devoted to Derrida, will be referred to as Les Lettres.

Les Fins de L'Homme—Colloque de Cérisy. Ed. Jean-Luc Nancy et Philippe Lacoue-Labarthe. Paris: Galilee, 1981.

Ecarts. Lucette Finas, et al. Paris: Fayard, 1973.

L'Etrangeté du Texte. Claude Levesque. Montreal: VLB Editeur, 1976.

Saving the Text. Geoffrey H. Hartman. Baltimore: The Johns Hopkins University Press, 1981.

Marxism and Deconstruction. Michael Ryan. Baltimore: The Johns Hopkins University Press, 1982.

Deconstruction Theory and Practice. Christopher Norris. London: Methuen, 1982.

Herméneutique et Grammatologie. Jean Greisch. Paris: Editions du CNRS, 1977.

Research in Phenomenology. Issue no. 8 on Derrida.

Boundary 2. Fall, 1979.
Oxford Literary Review. Vol. 3, no. 2, 1978.
Reading Deconstruction Deconstructive Reading. G. Douglas Atkins. Lexington: Kentucky University Press, 1983.
Deconstruction: Theory and Practice. Christopher Norris. London: Methuen, 1982.
The Deconstructive Turn. Christopher Norris. London: Methuen, 1983.
Deconstructive Criticism. Vincent B. Leitch. New York: Columbia University Press, 1984.
Derrida on the Mend. Robert Magliola. West Lafayette: Purdue University
Applied Grammatology. Gregory Ulmer. Baltimore: Johns Hopkins University Press, 1985.

Articles

Abel, Lionel. "Jacques Derrida: His *'Difference'* With Metaphysics." *Salmagundi,* no. 25 (Winter 1974), pp. 3–21.
Allison, David Blair. Translator's Preface to Jacques Derrida's *Speech and Phenomena: And Other Essays on Husserl's Theory of Signs.* Evanston: Northwestern University Press, 1973, pp. xxxi–xliii.
———. "Derrida's Critique of Husserl: The Philosophy of Presence." Dissertation, Pennsylvania State University, 1974.
Altieri, Charles F. "Northrop Frye and the Problem of Spiritual Authority." *PMLA* 87 (1972):964–75.
Ames, Vah Meter. "Art for Art's Sake Again?" *The Journal of Aesthetics and Art Criticism* 33, no. 3 (1975):303–07.
Anquetil, Gilles. "*Glas,* le nouveau livre de J. Derrida." *Les Nouvelles Littéraires,* no. 2457 (28 Oct.–3 Nov. 1974), p. 9.
Backes-Clement, Catherine. "La Dissémination: la méthode deplacée." *Les Lettres,* 4–5.
Bandera, Cesareo. The Crisis of Knowledge in *La Vida Es. Sueño." Substance,* no. 7 (Fall 1973), pp. 24–47.
Barthes, Roland. "Letter to Jean Ristat." *Les Lettres,* 3.
Beigbeder, Marc. "La Grammatologie de Jacques Derrida." In *Contradiction et nouvel entendement.* Paris: Bordas, 1972.
Benoit, Jean-Marie. "Le Colosse de Rhodes, quelques remarques à propos de *Glas* de Jacques Derrida." *L'Art Vivant,* no. 54 (December 1974–January 1975).
———."L'Inscription de Derrida." *La Quinzaine Littéraire,* no. 182 (1974), pp. 18–19.
———. " 'Présence' de Husserl." *Les Etudes Philosophiques* 4 (1969):525–31.
Bertherat, Y. Book Review of Derrida's *L'Ecriture et la différence. Esprit* 35, no. 10 (October 1967), pp. 698–700.
Beyssade, Jean-Marie. " 'Mais quoi ce sont des fous': Sur un passage controverse de la 'Première Méditation.' " *Revue de Métaphysique et de Morale* 78 (1973):273–94.
Bonnefoy, Claude, "La Clôture et sa transgression." *Opus International* 3 (1967).
Bothezat, T. "Lecturer to Visit Baltimore." *The Sun* (Baltimore), 2 Feb. 1968.
Bouazis, Charles. "Théorie de l'écriture et sémiotique narrative." *Semiotica* 10 (1974):305–31.
Bové, Paul, "Introduction—Nietzsche's Use and *Abuse of History* and the Problems of Revision: 'late-comers live truly an ironical existence.' " *Boundary 2* (Winter 1979): 1–15.

Boyer, Philippe. "Déconstruction; le désir à la lettre." *Change: La destruction*
     1. No. 2 (1969): 127–48. Rpt. in *L'Ecartée*. Paris: Seghers-Laffont. 1973.
————. "Le Point de la question." Change: *L'Imprononcable, l'écriture
     nomade*, no. 22 (1975) pp. 41–72.
Brague, Remi. "En Marge de 'La pharmacie de Platon' de J. Derrida." *Revue
     Philosophique de Louvain* 71 (May 1973): 271–77.
Broekman, Jan M. *Structuralism: Moscow—Prague—Paris*. Tr. J. F. Beekman
     and B. Helm. Boston: D. Reidel, 1974, pp. 91–94 and 101–04.
Brykman, Genevieve. Book Review of Derrida's *La Dissémination*. *Revue
     Philosophique de la France et de l'Etranger* 164 (1974): 256.
Buci-Glucksmann, Christine. "Déconstruction et critique marxiste de la
     philosophie." *L'Arc*, pp. 20–32.
Catesson, Jean. "A propos d'un pensée de l'intervalle." *Revue de Métaphysi-
     que et de Morale* 74 (1969): 74–90.
Caws, Peter. "The Recent Literature of Structuralism, 1965–70."
     Philosophische Rundschau 18, Heft 1–2 (1972), pp. 63–77.
Chatelet, F. "Mort du livre?" *La Quinzaine Littéraire*, no. 37 (1967), p. 14.
————. "Qui est Jacques Derrida? La Métaphysique dans sa clôture." *Le
     Nouvel Observateur* (Special Littéraire), 20 November–20 December,
     1968.
Chumbley, Robert. " 'DELFICA' and 'LA DIFFERANCE': Toward a Nerva-
     lian System." *Sub-Stance*, no. 10 (1974), pp. 33–37.
Cixous, Helene. "L'Essort de Plusje." *L'Arc*, pp. 46–52.
Clemens, Eric. "Sur Derrida: Alternance et dédoublement." *TXT*, Cahier no. 5
     (1972).
Clement, Catherine. "A l'écoute de Derrida." L'Arc, pp. 16–19.
————. "Le Sauvage." L'Arc, pp. 1–2.
Corvez, Maurice. "Les Nouveaux Structuralistes." *Revue Philosophique de
     Louvain* 67 (1969): 582–605.
————. La Crise du signe et de l'imperialisme: Trotsky/Derrida." *Scription
     Rouge*, No. 5 (September–November 1973).
Cross, Derek. Review of Derrida's *Introduction* to Husserl's *Origin of
     Geometry: Review of Metaphy* (September 1979), pp. 168–172.
————. Review of *Writing and Difference*. pp. 172–74.
Culler, Johnathan. "Commentary." *New Literary History* 6, no. 1 (Autumn
     1974): 219–29.
————. *Structuralist Poetics: Structuralism, Linguistics, and the Study of Lit-
     erature*. Ithaca, New York: Cornell University Press, 1975.
————. "Convention and Meaning: Derrida and Austin." *NLH*, (Summer
     1981): 15–30.
Cumming, Robert Denoon. "The Odd Couple—Heidegger and Derrida." *The
     Review of Metaphysics* 34, no. 3 (March 1981).
Daix, Pierre and François Wahl. "Qu'est-ce que le structuralisme?" *Les Lettres
     Françaises*, no. 1268. (29 January–4 Feburary, 1969), pp. 4–6.
Dadoun, R. "Qu'est-ce que le structuralisme?" *La Quinzaine Littéraire*, no. 67
     (1969), p. 15.
Damisch, Hubert. "Ceçi (donc)." *Les Lettres*, 6.
Dauenhauer, Bernard P. "On Speech and Temporality: Jacques Derrida and
     Edmund Husserl." *Philosophy Today* 18 (Fall 1974): 171–80.
Declève, H. Book Review of Derrida's *De la Grammatologie*. 9 (1970): 499–
     502.
Deese, James. "Mind and Metaphor: A Commentary." *New Literary History*
     6., no. 1 (Autumn 1974): 211–17.

De Greef, Jan. "De la Métaphore (à propos de *La Mythologie blanche*, de Derrida)." *Cahiers de Littérature et de Linguistique appliquée* (Kinshasa, Congo), nos. 3–4 (1971), pp. 45–50.

Deguy, Michel. "Husserl en seconde lecture." *Critique* 19, no. 192 (May 1963): 434–448.

Delacampagne, Christian. "Condillac et le frivole." *Le Monde,* 20 December 1973, p. 24.

————. "Derrida et Deleuze." *Le Monde,* 30 April 1976.

————. "Derrida Hors de Soi." *Critique* 30, no. 325 (June 1974): 503–14.

————. "Hegel et Gabrielle, le premier 'livre' de Jacques Derrida." *Le Monde,* 3 January 1975, p. 12.

————. "Six auteurs, une voix anonyme." *Le Monde,* 30 April 1976.

————. "Un Coup porté à la métaphysique." *Le Monde,* 14 June 1973, p. 22.

Detweiler, Robert. "The Moment of Death in Modern Fiction." *Contemporary Literature* 13, no. 3 (Summer 1972): 269–94.

Donato, Eugenio. "Structuralism: The Aftermath." *Sub-Stance,* no. 7 (Fall 1973): 9–26.

Donoghue, Denis. "Deconstructing Deconstruction." TLS, 12 June 1980, pp. 37–41.

Dufrenne, Mikel. "Pour une philosophie non théologique." In his *Le Poétique.* 2nd ed. Paris: Presses Universitaires de France, 1973, pp. 7–57.

Duval, Raymond. "Présence et Solitude: La question de l'être et le destin de l'homme." *Revue des Sciences Philosophiques et Théologiques* 57 (1973): 377–96.

Eagleton, Terry. "Marxism and Deconstruction: *Contemporary Literature,* (Fall 1981): pp. 477–88.

Eco, Umberto. "La Structure et l'absence." In *La Structure absente.* Paris: Mercure de France, 1972.

Ehrmann, Jacques. "Sur le jeu et l'origine, où il est surtout question de la dissémination de Jacques Derrida." *Sub-Stance,* no. 7 (Fall 1973), pp. 113–23.

Escarpit, Robert. *L'Ecrit et la communication.* Paris: Presses Universitaires de France, 1973, esp. pp. 17, 22, 44, 64–66.

Felman, Shoshana. "Madness and Philosophy *or* Literature's Reason." *Yale French Studies,* no. 52: *Graphesis: Perspectives in Literature and Philosophy* (1975), pp. 206–28.

Ferguson, Frances C. "Reading Heidegger: Paul De Man and Jacques Derrida." *Boundary 2,* 4, no. 2 (Winter 1976): 593–610.

Ferguson, Margaret W. "Saint Augustine's Region of Unlikeness: The Crossing of Exile and Language." *The Georgia Review* 29, no. 4 (Winter 1975): 842–64.

Finas, Lucette, Sarah Kofman, Roger Laporte, and Jean-Michel Rey. *Ecarts: Quatre essais à propos de Jacques Derrida.* Paris: Fayard 1973.

Fish, Stanley E. "With the Compliments of the Author: Reflections on Austin and Derrida." *Critical Inquiry.* (Summer 1982): 693–721.

Foucault, Michel. "Une Petite pédagogie." *Le Monde,* 14 June 1973, p. 23. Excerpt from "Mon corps, ce papier, ce feu." Appendix to *Histoire de la folie à l'âge classique.* New ed., Paris: Gallimard, 1972, pp. 583–603.

Fynsk, Christopher I. "A Decelebration of Philosophy", *Diacritics* (June 1978): 80–90.

Galay, J. L. Book Review of Derrida's *La Voix et le phénomène. Studia Philosophica* 28 (1968).

Garelli, Jacques. "de quelques erreurs statistiques." *Les Temps Modernes* 26, no. 286. (May 1970): 1929–36.

———. "L'Ecart du maintenant et l'extension de l'esprit." *Les Temps Modernes* 25, no. 281 (December 1969): 874–96.

———. "Le Flux et l'instant." *Les Temps Modernes* 26, no. 283 (February 1970): 1239–63.

Garver, Newton. Preface to Jacques Derrida's *Speech and Phenomena: And Other Essays on Husserl's Theory of Signs.* Tr. David B. Allison. Evanston: Northwestern University Press, 1973, pp. ix–xxix.

Gelley, Alexander. "Formas Force." *Diacritics* 2 No. 1 (Spring 1972): 9–13.

Genet, Jean. Letter to Jean Ristat. *Les Lettres,* 14.

Gillibert, Jean. "A propos de 'Freud et le Scène de l'écriture.'" *Les Lettres,* 8.

Giovannangeli, David. "Code et différence impure." *Littérature,* no. 12 (December 1973), pp. 93–106.

———. "La Question de la littérature." *L'Arc,* pp. 81–86.

———. "Vers un Dépassement de la phénomènologie et du structuralisme. La Reflexion sur la littérature dans la pensée de Jacques Derrida." Dissertation, Universite de Mons, 1974.

Girard, René. "Levi-Strauss, Frye, Derrida, and Shakespeare Criticism." *Diacritics* 3, no. 3 (Fall 1973): 34–38.

Goux, Jean-Joseph. "Du graphème au chromosome." *Les Lettres,* 6–7.

———. "'La Dissémination' de Jacques Derrida." *Les Lettres Francaises,* no. 1455, 11–17 October 1972, p. 15.

Granel, Gerard. "Jacques Derrida et la rature de l'origine." *Critique* 23, no. 246 (November 1967): 887–905. Rpt. in his *Traditionis traditio.* Paris: Gallimard, 1972, pp. 154–75.

Greisch, Jean. "La Crise de l'herméneutique. Reflexions métacritiques sur un débat actuel." In Jean Greisch et al., *La Crise Contemporaine: Du modernisme à la crise des herméneutiques.* Paris: Beauchesne, 1973, pp. 135–90.

Grene, Marjorie. "Life, Death, and Language: Some Thoughts on Wittgenstein and Derrida." *Partisan Review* 43 (1976): 265–79. Rpt. in her *Philosophy In and Out of Europe.* Berkeley: University of California Press, 1976, pp. 142–54.

Guibal, Francis. "Philosophie, langage, écriture." *Etudes* 5 (May 1972):. 769–81.

Hartman, Geoffrey H. "Monsieur Texte: On Jacques Derrida. His *Glas,*" *The Georgia Review* 29, no. 4 (Winter 1975): 759–97.

———. "Monsieur Texte II: Epiphany in Echoland," *The Georgia Review* 30. no. 1 (Spring 1976): 169–204.

Harvey, Irene E. "Derrida and the Concept of Metaphysics," *Research in Phenomenology,* vol. 13, 1983, pp. 113–48.

Hector, J. "Jacques Derrida: la clôture de la métaphysique." *Techniques Nouvelles,* no. 6 (June 1972).

Hefner, R. W. "The *Tel Quel* Ideology: Material Practice upon Material Practice." *Sub-Stance,* no. 8 (1974), pp. 127–38.

Henning, E. M. "Foucault and Derrida: Archaeology and Deconstruction: *Stanford French Review* (Fall 1981): 247–264.

Holland, Norman N. "Recovering 'the Purloined Letter': Reading as a Personal Transaction" in *The Reader in the Text.* Ed. Susan R. Suleiman and Inge Crosman. Princeton: Princeton University Press, 1980.

Hollier, Denis. "La Copulation labryinthique (Un détail d' interferences)," *Les Lettres,* 14–15.

Hoy, David. "Deciding Derrida—David Hoy on the work and (play) of the French Philosopher." *London Review Books* 4, no. 3 (18 February–3 March 1982), pp. 3–5.

Irigaray, Luce. "Le v(i)ol de la lettre." *Tel Quel,* no. 39 (Fall 1969), pp. 64–77.

Jabes, Edmond. "Sur la question du livre." *L'Arc,* 59–64.

Jacob, Andre. Book Review of Derrida's *L'Ecriture et la différance. Les Etudes Philosophiques* 22 (1967).

———. Book Review of Derrida's *La Voix et le phénomène. Les Etudes Philosophiques* 23 (1968).

———. Book Review of Edmund Husserl's *L'Origine de la géometrie.* Traduction et introduction de Jacques Derrida. *Les Etudes Philosophiques* 18 (1963).

———. Book Review of Jacques Derrida's *Positions and Marges. Les Etudes Philosophiques* 28 (1973): 389.

———. "De la socio-analyse à la grammatologie." Ch. 12 in his *Introduction à la philosophie du langage.* Paris: Gallimard. 1976, pp. 306–32.

Jameson, Fredric. *The Prison-House of Language: A Critical Account of Structuralism and Russian Formalism.* Princeton: Princeton University Press, 1972, esp. pp. 173–86.

Jannoud, Claude. "L'Evangile selon Derrida: sur Hegel et Genet." *Le Figaro Littéraire,* 30 November 1974.

Kanbouchner, Denis. "La Leçon de Calcul," *Nacova Corrente* 28 (1981): 87–100.

Klein, Richard. "The Blindness of Hyperboles: The Ellipses of Insight." *Diacritics* 3. no. 2 (Summer 1973): 33–44.

———. "Prolegomenon to Derrida." *Diacritics* 2, no. 4 (Winter 1972): 19–34.

———. "Kant's Sunshine," *Diacritics* 11 (June 1981): 26–41.

Krieger, Murray, ed. "Directions for Criticism: Structuralism and its Alternatives." *Contemporary Literature* 17, no. 3 (Summer 1976), passim.

Kristeva, Julia. *La Révolution du langage poetique.* L'Avant-garde à la fin du XIX siecle: Lautréamont et Mallarmé. Paris: Seuil, 1974, pp. 129–34.

Lacroix, J. "Ecriture et métaphysique selon Jacques Derrida." In *Panorama de la philosophie française contemporaine.* Paris: Presses Universitaires de France, 1968, p. 13.

———. "La Parole et l'écriture." *Le Monde,* 18 November 1967.

Lamizet, Bernard and Frederic Nef. "Entrave double: le glas et la chute (sur *Glas* de J. Derrida)." *Gramma,* no. 2 (April 1975), pp. 129–50.

Laporte, Roger. "Bief." *L'Arc,* pp. 65–70.

———. "'Les "blancs" assument l'importance' (Mallarmé)." *Les Lettres,* 5.

Lapouge, Gilles. "Six philosophes occupés à deplacer la philosophie à propos de la mimesis." *La Quinzaine Littéraire,* no. 231 (1976), p. 23.

Laruelle, Francois. "La Scéne du vomi ou comment ça se detraque dans le théorie." *Critique* 32, no. 347 (April 1976): 265–79.

———. "Le Style Di-phallique de Jacques Derrida." *Critique* 31, no. 334 (March 1975): 320–29.

———. "Le Texte quatrième." *L'Arc,* pp. 38–45.

———. *Machines textuelles: Déconstruction et libido d'écriture.* Paris: Seuil, 1976.

Leavey, John, "Derrida and Dante: Différance and the Eagle in the Sphere of Jupiter." *MLN* 91, no. 1 (January 1976): 60–68.

Levers, A. "A Theory of Writing." *The Times Literary Supplement,* 15 February 1968, p. 153.

Levesque, Claude. *L'Etrangeté du texte: Essais sur Nietzsche, Freud, Blanchot et Derrida.* Montreal: VLB, 1976.

Levinas, Emmanuel. "Tout autrement." *L'Arc,* pp. 33–37. Rpt. in his *Noms propres.* Montpellier: Fata Morgana, 1976, pp. 81–89.

Levine, Suzanne Jill. "Discourse as Bricolage." *Review,* no. 13 (Winter 1974), pp. 32–37.

———. "Writing as Translation: *Three Trapped Tigers and A Cobra.*" MLN 90. no. 2 (March 1975), pp. 265–77.

Levy, Bernard Henri. "Derrida n'est pas un gourou." *Magazine Littéraire* 88 (May 1974): 60–62.

Logan, Marie-Rose. "Graphesis . . ." *Yale French Studies,* no. 52: *Graphesis: Perspectives in Literature and Philosophy* (1975): 4–15.

Loriot, P. Book Review of Derrida's *Glas. Le Nouvel Observateur,* no. 256 (9–15 December 1974).

Lotringer, Sylvere. "Le dernier mot de Saussure." *L'Arc,* pp. 71–80.

M. A. Book Review of Derrida's *De la Grammatologie. Nice-Matin,* 12 January 1968.

Macann, Christopher. "Jacques Derrida's Theory of Writing and the Concept of Trace." *Journal of the British Society for Phenomenology* 3, no. 2 (May 1972): 197–200.

Malmberg, Bertil. "Derrida et la sémiologie: Quelques notes marginales." *Semiotica* 11. No. 2 (1974): 189–99.

de Man, Paul. "The Rhetoric of Blindness." In his *Blindness and Insight: Essays in the Rhetoric of Contemporary Criticism.* New York: Oxford University Press, 1971, pp. 102–41. A French translation by Jean Michel Rabeate and Bernard Esmein appeared in *Poétique,* No. 4 (1970), pp. 455–75, entitled "Rhetorique de la cecité."

———. Book Review of Derrida's *De la Grammatologie. Annales de la Societe J. H. Rousseau,* 1969.

Margolin, Jean-Claude. Book Review of Derrida's *La Dissémination. Les Etudes Philosophiques* 28 (1973): 389–90.

Mehlman, Jeffrey. "Orphée scripteur: Blanchot, Rilke, Derrida." *Poétique,* no. 20 (1974), pp. 458–82.

———. *A Structural Study of Autobiography: Proust, Leiris, Sartre, Levi-Strauss.* Ithaca, N.Y.: Cornell University Press, 1974.

Merlin, Frederic. "Après Mallarmé, Pour qui sonne le glas." *Les Nouvelles Littéraires,* no. 2461 (25 November 1974), p. 10.

———. "Derrida ou la philosophie éclats." *Les Nouvelles Littéraires,* no. 2415 (7 January 1974), p. 15.

Meschonnic, Henri. "L'Ecriture de Derrida." *Les Cahiers du Chemin,* no. 24 (1975), pp. 137–80.

———. Le Signe et le poème. Paris: Gallimard, 1975. Esp. pp. 401–92, *"L'Ecriture de Derrida."*

Miller, J. Hillis. "Deconstructing the Deconstructers." *Diacritics* 5, no. 2 (Summer 1975): 24–31.

———. "Geneva or Paris? The Recent Work of Georges Poulet. *"University of Toronto Quarterly* 29, no. 3 (April 1970): 212–28.

————. "Stevens; Rock and Criticism as Cure, II." *The Georgia Review* 30, no. 2 (Summer 1976): 330–48.

————. "Tradition and Difference." *Diacritics* 2, no. 4 (Winter 1972): 6–13.

————. "Williams' *Spring and All* and the Progress of Poetry." *Daedalus* 99 (Spring 1970): 405–34.

Nemo, Philippe. "L'Aventure collective d'un chercheur solitaire: Derrida et le GREPH." *Les Nouvelles Littéraires*, no. 2519 (12 February 1976).

Noguez, Dominique. Book Review of Derrida's *L'Ecriture et la différence. Nouvelle Revue Française*, no. 178 (October 1967), p. 720.

Ollier, Claude. "Ouverture." *Les Lettres*, 11–13.

————. "Pulsion." *L'Arc*, pp. 53–58.

Pachet, Pierre. "Une Entreprise troublante." *La Quinzaine Littéraire*, no. 197 (1 November 1974), pp. 19–20.

Paquet, Marcel. "Essai sur l'absolu." In *Morale et Enseignement*. Annals of the Institute of Philosophy. Brussels: Free University of Brussels, 1972, pp. 77–115.

Parenti, Claire. Book Review of Derrida's *Glas. Magazine Littérraire*, no. 96 (January 1975).

Parker, Andrew. "Taking Sides (on History): Derrida Re-Marx." *Diacritics* 11, (September 1981): 57–73. (Review of *Positions*.)

Parret, Herman. "Grammatology and Linguistics: A Note on Derrida's Interpretation of Linguistic Theories." *Poetics* 4. no. 1 (13) (March 1975): 107–27.

————. "Jacques Derrida. Een wijsbergeerte van de schriftuur." *Tijdschrift voor Filosophie* 30 (1968): 3–81. Resumé: "Une Philosophie de l'écriture," pp. 79–81.

Pavel, Toma. "Linguistique et phénomènologie du signe (Reflexions à propos de la philosophe de J. Derrida)." *Studi Italiani di Linguistica Teoretica ed Applicata* 1 (1972): 51–68.

Penel, A. "Comment échapper à la philosophie? Jacques Derrida met en question la pensée occidentale." *La Tribune de Genéve*, 15 November 1967.

Petitjean, Gerard. "Les grands prêtres de l'université française." *Le Nouvel Observateur*, no. 543 (7–13 April 1975).

Pierssens, Michel. "Introduction." *Sub-Stance*, no. 7 (Fall 1973), pp. 3–7.

Poirot-Delpech, B. "Maîtres à dé-penser." *Le Monde*, 30 April 1976.

Popkins, Richard. "Comments on Professor Derrida's Paper ('The Ends of Man')." *Philosophy and Phenomenological Research* 30, no. 1 (1969): 58–65.

Probst, Alain. "Une Critique de la métaphysique occidentale: la philosophie de Jacques Derrida." *Revue Reformée* (Société Calviniste de France) 24, no. 93 (1973): 29–43.

"A Propos de *L'ARC*, No. 54." *La Quinzaine Littéraire*, no. 175 (1973).

Rassam, J. "La Déconstruction de la métaphysique selon M. Derrida ou le retour au nominalisme le plus moyenageux." *Revue de l'Enseignement Philosophique* 25, no. 2 (1975): 1–8.

Review of Derrida's *L'Ecriture et la différance. Bulletin Critique du livre français*, nos. 260–61 (August–September 1967).

Rey, Jean-Michel. "De Saussure à Freud." *Les Lettres*, 9–10.

————. "La Scéne du texte." *Critique* 25, no. 271 (1969): 1059–1073.

Ricoeur, Paul. *La Métaphore vive*. Paris: Seuil. 1975, pp. 362–74.

Riddel, Joseph. "A Miller's Tale." *Diacritics* 5, no. 3 (Fall 1975): 56–65.

————. "From Heidegger to Derrida to Chance: Doubling and (Poetic) Language." *Boundary 2* 4, no. 2 (Winter 1976): 571–92.

————. *The Inverted Bell: Modernism and the Counterpoetics of William Carlos Williams.* Baton Rouge: Louisiana State University Press, 1974.

Ristat, Jean. "Le fil(s) perdu." *Les Lettres,* 13–14.

Robert, Jean-Dominique. "Voix et phénomène: à propos d'un ouvrage recent." *Revue Philosophique de Louvain* 66 (1968): 309–24.

Roger, Philippe. "Les Philosophes saisis par la politique, un nouvel art de l'abordage." *Les Nouvelles Littéraires.* no. 2532 (13 May 1976).

Rotry, Richard. "Philosophy as a King of Writing: An Essay on Derrida." *NLH* 10, no. 1 (Autumn 1978): 141–60.

Rosen, Stanley. Review of *Of Grammatology,* in *Philosophy and Rhetoric* 15, no. 1 (Winter 1982): 66–70.

Roudinesco, Elisabeth. "A propos du 'concept' de l'écriture. Lecture de Jacques Derrida." *Littérature et ideologies.* Colloque de Cluny II. *La Nouvelle Critique* 39b (1970): 219–30.

————. "De Derrida à Jung: une tradition." In *Un Discours au réel.* Paris: Mame, 1973.

Ryan, Michael. "Self-De(con)struction." *Diacritics* 6, no. 1 (Spring 1976): 34–41.

Said, Edward W. "*Abecedarium culturae:* structuralism, absence, writing." *Triquarterly,* no. 20 (Winter 1971), pp. 33–71. Said's comments on Derrida have been taken up in his *Beginnings: Intention and Method.* New York: Basic Books, 1975, pp. 339–43.

————. "The Problem of Textuality: Two Exemplary Positions." *Critical Inquiry* (Summer 1978): pp. 673–714.

Scarpetta, Guy. "Brecht et la Chine." *Littérature et idéologies.* Colloque de Cluny II. *La Nouvelle Critique* 39b (1970): 231–36.

Scherer, Rene. "Clôture et faille dans la phénomènologie de Husserl." *Revue de Métaphysique et de Morale* 73 (1968): 344–60.

"Scription, materialisme dialectique: Derrida-Marx." *Scription Rouge,* no. 1 (May 1972).

Singevin, Charles. "La Pensée, le langage, l'écriture et l'être." *Revue Philosophique de la France et de l'Etranger* 162, no. 2 (April–June 1972): 129–48, and no. 3 (July–Septemebr 1972): 273–88.

Smith, F. Joseph. "Jacques Derrida's Husserl Interpretation." *Philosophy Today* 9 (1967): 106–23.

Sollers, Philippe. "Transformer le statut même de la littérature." *Le Monde,* 14 June 1973, p. 23.

————. "Un Pas sur la lune." *Tel Quel,* no. 39 (Fall 1969), pp. 3–12, ET: "A Step on the Moon." *The Times Literary Supplement,* 25 September 1969, pp. 1085–87.

Spivak, Gayatri Chakravorty. Translator's Preface to Jacques Derrida's *Of Grammatology.* Baltimore: The Johns Hopkins University Press, 1976, ix–lxxxvii.

Stefan, Jude. Book Review of Derrida's *L'Archéologie du frivole. Les Cahiers du Chemin,* no. 28 (1976), pp. 157–59.

Thevenin, Paule. "Le hors-lieu." *Les Lettres,* 10–11.

Touibeau, Helene. "Le Pharmakon et les aromates." *Critique* 28, nos. 303–04 (August–September 1972):681–706.

Toyasaki, Koitchi. *Suppléments mobiles.* Tokyo: Editions Epaves, 1975.

Ulmer, Gregory L. "The Post-Age." (Review of *La Carte Postale*) *Diacritics* 11 (September 1981): 39–66.

———. "Of a Parodic Tone Recently Adopted in Criticism." *NLH* (Spring 1982): 543–559.

Valdez, Mario. "Interpretation and Translation in the Writings of Jacques Derrida." Unpublished, 20 pp.

Visscher, Luce Fontaine-De. "Des Privilèges d'une grammatologie." *Revue Philosophique de Louvain* 67 (August 1969): 461–75.

Vuarnet, Jean-Noel. "Jacques Derrida." *Littérature de notre temps.* Recueil 4. Paris: Castermann, 1970.

———. "Sans titre." *Les Lettres,* 3–4.

Vuilleumier, J. "L'Irruption du dehors dans le dedans." *La Tribune de Genève,* 1–2 October 1966.

Wahl, Francois. "L'Ecriture avant la parole?" *La Quinzaine Littéraire,* no. 4 (1966).

———. "Forcer les limites." *La Quinzaine Littéraire,* no. 32 (1967).

———. "La Philosophie entre l'avant et l'après du structuralisme." In *Qu'est-ce que le structuralisme?* ed. Francois Wahl. Paris: Seuil, 1968, pp. 299–442. Seuil reprinted this under separate cover in 1973 with the title of the article itself.

Wilden, Anthony. *System and Structure: Essays in Communication and Exchange.* London: Tavistock, 1972. pp. 395–400, 458–59.

Wood, Michael. "Deconstructing Derrida." *The New York Review of Books,* 3 March 1977, pp. 27–30.

Wood, David. "Derrida and the Paradoxes of Reflection." *Journal of the British Society for Phenomenology* 11, no. 3 (October 1980): 225–236.

———. "Style and Strategy at the Limits of Philosophy: Heidegger and Derrida." *The Monist* 63, no. 4 (October 1980): 494–511.

Wright, Edmond. "Derrida, Searle, Contexts, Games, Riddles." *NLH* (Spring 1982): 463–76.

Zaner, Richard M. "Discussion of Jacques Derrida. 'The Ends of Man.'" *Philosophy and Phenomenological Research* 32. no. 3 (March 1972): 384–89.

Other Sources

Aristotle. *Metaphysics.* Ann Arbor: The University of Michigan Press, 1960; trans. Richard Hope.

———. *Poetics.* Cambridge: Harvard University Press, 1973. The Loeb Classical Library, Ed. E. H. Warmington.

Austin, J. L. *How to Do Things With Words.* Cambridge: Harvard University Press, 1962.

Barthes, Roland. *Roland Barthes.* Paris: Editions du Seuil, 1975; trans. Richard Howard, New York: Hill and Wang, 1977.

———. *Essais Critiques.* Paris: Editions du Seuil, 1964; trans. Richard Howard, Evanston: Northwestern University Press, 1972.

———. *Elements de Sémiologie.* Paris: Editions du Seuil, 1964; trans. Annette Lavers and Colin Smith, New York: Hill and Wang, 1967.

———. *Mythologies.* Paris: Editions du Seuil, 1957; trans. Annette Lavers, New York: Hill and Wang, 1972.

———. *Le Plaisir du texte.* Editions du Seuil, 1973.

———. *Le Dégré Zéro de L'Ecriture.* Paris: Editions du Seuil, 1953; trans. Annette Lavers and Colin Smith, New York: Hill and Wang, 1967.

Benjamin, Walter. *Illuminations.* New York: Schocken Books, 1969; trans. Harry Zohn.

Foucault, Michel. *L'Archéologie du savoir.* Paris: Gallimard, 1969; trans. A. M. Sheridan Smith, London: Tavistock Publications, 1972.

——. *L'Histoire de la folie à l'âge classique.* Paris: Gallimard, 1972.

——. *L'Ordre du discours, (Lecon inaugurale au College de France).* Paris: Gallimard, 1971.

——. *Les Mots et Les Choses.* Paris: Gallimard, 1966; trans. as *The Order of Things,* New York: Vintage Books, Random House, 1973.

Freud, Sigmund. *Beyond the Pleasure Principle.* New York: W.W. Norton, 1961; trans. James Strachey.

——. *Civilization and Its Discontents.* New York: W.W. Norton, 1961; trans. James Strachey.

——. *The Interpretation of Dreams.* New York: Avon Books, 1965; trans. James Strachey.

——. *Introductory Lectures on Psychoanalysis.* Harmondsworth: Penguin Books, 1973; trans. James Strachey.

——. *Jokes and their relation to the Unconscious.* New York: W.W. Norton, 1960; trans. James Strachey.

——. *New Introductory Lectures on Psychoanalysis.* Harmondsworth: Penguin Books, 1973; trans. James Strachey.

——. *The Psychopathology of Everyday Life.* Harmondsworth: Penguin Books, 1960; trans. Alan Tyson.

——. *On the History of the Psycho-Analytic Movement.* New York: W.W. Norton, 1966; trans. Joan Riviere.

——. *Totem and Taboo.* New York: W.W. Norton, 1950; trans. James Strachey.

Genet, Jean. *Journal du voleur.* Paris: Gallimard, 1949.

——. *Miracle de la Rose.* Paris: Gallimard, 1946.

——. *Notre-Dame des-Fleurs.* Paris: L'Arbalete, 1948.

——. *Oeuvres Completes.* Paris: Gallimard, 1968, vol. 4.

——. *Oeuvres Completes.* Paris: Gallimard, 1979, vol. 5.

——. *Pompes Funebres.* Paris: Gallimard, 1953.

——. *Querelle de Brest.* Paris: Gallimard, 1953.

Hegel, G. W. F. *Encyclopedie des Sciences Philosophiques.* Paris: Gallimard, 1959; trans. Maurice de Gandillac.

——. *L'Esprit de Christianisme et son Destin.* Paris: Librairie Philosophique, J. Vrin, 1981; trans. Jacques Martin.

——. *Esthétique.* Paris: Flammarion, 1979; trans. S. Jankelevitch, 4 vols.

——. *Hegel's Logic.* Oxford: Clarendon Press, 1975; trans. William Wallace.

——. *Logique et la Métaphysique.* Paris: Gallimard, 1980; trans. D. Souche-Dagues.

——. *On Tragedy.* New York: Harper and Row, 1962; trans. J. B. Baillie et al.; ed. Anne and Henry Paolucci.

——. *Phenomenology of Spirit.* Oxford: Clarendon Press, 1977; trans. A. V. Miller.

——. *Philosophy of Mind.* Oxford: Clarendon Press, 1971; trans. William Wallace.

——. *Philosophy of Right.* London: Oxford University Press, 1967; trans. T. M. Knox.

——. *Science of Logic.* London: Humanities Press, 1976; trans. A. V. Miller.

Heidegger, Martin. *Being and Time.* New York: Harper and Row, 1962; trans. John Macquarrie and Edward Robinson.

――. *Early Greek Thinking.* New York: Harper and Row, 1975; trans. David Farrell Krell and Frank A. Capuzzi.

――. *The Essence of Reasons.* Evanston: Northwestern University Press, 1969; trans. Terrence Malick.

――. *Identity and Difference.* New York: Harper and Row, 1969; trans. Joan Stambaugh.

――. *An Introduction to Metaphysics.* New Haven: Yale University Press, 1959; trans. Ralph Manheim.

――. *Kant and the Problem of Metaphysics.* Bloomington: Indiana University Press, 1962; trans. James S. Churchill.

――. *On the Way to Language.* San Francisco: Harper and Row, 1971; trans. Peter D. Hertz.

――. *Poetry, Language, Thought.* New York: Harper and Row, 1971; trans. Albert Hofstadter.

――. *What is Called Thinking?* New York: Harper and Row, 1968; trans. J. Glenn Gray.

――. *What is Philosophy?* New Haven: College and University Press, 1956; trans. Jean T. Wilde and William Kluback.

Husserl, Edmund. *Cartesian Meditations.* The Hague: Martinus Nijhoff, 1973; trans. Dorion Cairns.

――. *The Crisis of European Sciences.* Evanston: Northwestern University Press, 1970; trans. David Carr.

――. *Experience and Judgment.* Evanston: Northwestern University Press, 1973; trans. James S. Chruchill and Karl Ameriks.

――. *Formal and Transcendental Logic.* The Hague: Martinus Nijhoff, 1978; trans. Dorian Cairns.

――. *Logical Investigations,* vols. i and ii. London: Routledge and Kegan Paul, 1970; trans. J. N. Findlay.

――. *Ideas.* New York: Collier Books, 1975; trans. W. R. Boyce Gibson.

――. *The Idea of Phenomenology.* The Hague: Martinus Nijhoff, 1973; trans. William P. Alston and George Nakhnikian.

――. *Introduction to the Logical Investigations.* The Hague, Martinus Nijhoff, 1975; trans. Philip J. Bossert and Curtis H. Peters.

――. *The Paris Lectures.* The Hague: Martinus Nijhoff 1975; trans. Peter Koestenbaum.

――. *Phenomenological Psychology.* The Hague: Martinus Nijhoff, 1977; trans. John Scanlon.

――. *Phenomenology and the Crisis of Philosophy.* New York: Harper and Row, 1965; trans. Quentin Lauer.

――. *The Phenomenology of Internal Time Consciousness.* Bloomington: Indiana University Press, 1964; trans. James S. Churchill.

――. *Philosophie de l'Arithmétique.* Paris: Presses Universitaires de France, 1972; trans. Jacques English.

Hyppolite, Jean. *Genesis and Structure of Hegel's 'Phenomenology of Spirit'.* Evanston: Northwestern University Press, 1974; trans. Samuel Cherniak and John Heckman.

Joyce, James. *Ulysses.* Harmondsworth: Penguin Books, 1960.

Kafka, Franz. *The Castle.* Harmondsworth: Penguin Books, 1930; trans. Willa and Edwin Muir.

――. *Description of a Struggle and Other Stories.* Harmondsworth: Penguin

Books, 1979; trans. Willa and Edwin Muir, Malcolm Pasley, Tania and James Stern.

———. *Letters to Felice.* Harmondsworth: Penguin Books, 1978; trans. James Stern and Elizabeth Duckworth.

———. *Metamorphosis and Other Stories.* Harmondsworth: Penguin Books, 1949; trans. Willa and Edwin Muir.

———. *The Trial.* Harmondsworth: Penguin Books, 1953; trans. Willa and Edwin Muir.

Kant, Immanuel. *Critique of Judgment.* New York: Hafner Press, 1974; trans. J. H. Bernard.

———. *Critique of Practical Reason.* Indianapolis: Bobbs-Merrill Company, Inc., 1956; trans. Lewis White Beck.

———. *Critique of Pure Reason.* New York: St. Martin's Press, 1965; trans. Norman Kemp Smith.

———. *Groundwork of the Metaphysics of Morals.* New York: Harper and Row, 1964; trans. H. J. Paton.

———. *On History.* Indianapolis: Bobbs-Merrill Company, Inc., 1975; trans. Lewis White Beck, Robert E. Anchor, and Emil L. Fackenheim.

———. *Prolegomena to Any Future Metaphysics.* Indianapolis: Bobbs-Merrill Company, Inc., 1950; trans. Lewis White Beck.

Kockelmans, Joseph J. *On Heidegger and Language.* Evanston: Northwestern University Press, 1972.

Kojève, Alexandre. *Introduction to the Reading of Hegel.* New York: Basic Books, Inc., 1969; trans. James H. Nicols, Jr.

Lacan, Jacques. *Ecrits.* New York: W.W. Norton, 1977; trans. Alan Sheridan.

———. *The Four Fundamental Concepts of Psycho-Analysis.* Harmondsworth: Penguin Books, 1977; trans. Alan Sheridan.

———. *De la Psychose paranoiaque dans ses rapports avec la personnalité.* Paris: Editions du Seuil, 1932.

Levinas, Emmanuel. *Théorie de l'intuition dans la phénomènologie de Husserl.* Paris: Vrin, 1963.

———. *De L'Existence a l'Existant.* Paris: Fontaine, 1947.

———. *Totalité et L'Infinité.* La Haye: Martinus Nijhoff, 1961.

———. *"La Trace de L'Autre," Tijdschrift voor Filosofie.* September 1963.

Lévi-Strauss. Claude. *Myth and Meaning.* Toronto: University of Toronto Press, 1978.

———. *The Savage Mind.* Chicago: University of Chicago Press, 1973; trans. George Weidenfeld.

———. *Structural Anthropology.* New York: Basic Books, 1963; trans. Claire Jacobson and Brook Grundfest Schoepf.

Nietzsche, Friedrich. *Beyond Good and Evil.* New York: Basic Books, 1966; trans. Walter Kaufmann.

———. *The Birth of Tragedy and The Geneology of Morals.* New York: Doubleday, 1956; trans. Francis Golffing.

———. *Ecce Homo.* Harmondsworth: Penguin Books, 1979; trans. R. J. Hollingdale.

———. *The Gay Science.* New York: Vintage Books, 1974; trans. Walter Kaufmann.

———. *A Nietzsche Reader.* Ed. and trans. R. J. Hollingdale. Harmondsworth: Penguin Books, 1977.

———. *Philosophy in the Tragic Age of the Greeks.* Chicago: Gateway, 1962; trans. Marianne Cowan.

——. *The Philosophy of Nietzsche,* ed. Geoffrey Clive, New York: Signet, 1965; trans. Oscar Levy.

——. *The Portable Nietzsche.* Ed. and trans. Walter Kaufman. Harmondsworth: Penguin Books, 1976.

——. *The Twilight of the Idols, The Anti-Christ.* Harmondsworth: Penguin Books, 1968, trans. R. J. Hollingdale.

——. *The Will to Power.* Ed. Walter Kaufmann. New York: Vintage Books, 1968; trans. Walter Kaufmann and R. J. Hollingdale.

O'Neill, John. *Sociology as a Skin Trade.* New York: Harper and Row, 1972.

——. *Essaying Montaigne.* London: Routledge, Kegan Paul, 1982.

Plato. *The Collected Dialogues of Plato.* Ed. Edith Hamilton and Huntington Cairns. Princeton: Princeton University Press, 1961.

Ricoeur, Paul. *Hermenuetics and the Human Sciences.* Ed. and trans. John B. Thompson. Cambridge: Cambridge University Press, 1981.

——. *Interpretation Theory.* Fort Worth: Texas Christian University Press, 1976.

——. *The Rule of Metaphor.* Toronto: University of Toronto Press, 1977; trans. Robert Czerny.

Rousseau, Jean-Jacques. *The Confessions,* Harmondsworth. Penguin Books, 1953, trans. J. M. Cohen.

——. *Discours sur les sciences et les arts, Discours sur l'origine et les fondements de l'inégalité parmi les hommes.* Paris: Garnier-Flammarion, 1971.

——. *Emile.* London: Dent, 1976; trans. Barbara Foxley.

——. *Julie ou La Nouvelle Heloise.* Paris: Flammarion, 1967.

——. *On the Origin of Language.* With J. G. Herder. New York: Frederick Ungar, 1966; trans. John H. Moran and A. Gode.

——. *Reveries of the Solitary Walker.* Harmondsworth: Penguin Books, 1979; trans. Peter France.

Saussure, Ferdinand de. *Course in General Linguistics.* New York: Fontana-Collins, 1974; trans. Wade Baskin.

Searle, John R. *Speech Acts.* Cambridge: Cambridge University Press, 1969.

Starobinski, Jean. *Jean-Jacques Rousseau—La Transparence et l'Obstacle.* Paris: Gallimard, 1971.

INDEX OF NAMES

INDEX OF SUBJECTS